GENDER, FAMILY, AND ECONOMY

OTHER RECENT VOLUMES IN THE
SAGE FOCUS EDITIONS

GENDER, FAMILY, AND ECONOMY

The Triple Overlap

Rae Lesser Blumberg
editor

SAGE Publications
International Educational and Professional Publisher
Newbury Park   London   New Delhi

For Gaia

For information address:

SAGE Publications, Inc.
2455 Teller Road
Newbury Park, California 91320

SAGE Publications Ltd.
6 Bonhill Street
London EC2A 4PU
United Kingdom

SAGE Publications India Pvt. Ltd.
M-32 Market
Greater Kailash I
New Delhi 110 048 India

Printed in the United States of America

Library of Congress Cataloging-in-Publication Data

Main entry under title:

Gender, family, and economy : the triple overlap / edited by Rae Lesser Blumberg.
　　　p.　　cm. — (Sage focus editions : v. 125)
　　Includes bibliographical references.
　　ISBN 0-8039-3755-5. — ISBN 0-8039-3756-3 (pbk.)
　　1. Sexual division of labor. 2. Sex role. 3. Work and family.
　I. Blumberg, Rae Lesser.
　HD6060.6.G46 1991
　306.3′615—dc20　　　　　　　　　　　　　　　　　90-43948

93 94 15 14 13 12 11 10 9 8 7 6 5 4 3 2

Sage Production Editor: Astrid Virding

Contents

Introduction
The "Triple Overlap" of Gender Stratification, Economy, and the Family

RAE LESSER BLUMBERG

This book brings together the work of a diverse and exciting array of social scientists who touch all three sides of an important but relatively neglected triangle. This is the intersection of gender stratification and economic variables with, and within, the family or household. The effort began with a special issue of the *Journal of Family Issues* (Vol. 9, No. 1, March 1988) that I edited. Six of the chapters, by Janet Chafetz, Marion Coleman, Randall Collins, Joan Huber, Diane Wolf, and myself, are from that issue. The remainder were written or adapted for this volume.

All the chapters provide new theory and/or data on the interrelationships among economic, gender and family (or household) variables.[1] Moreover, to varying degrees, the chapters consider this "triple overlap" at both macro and micro levels. A considerable amount of work has been done on each of the two-way relationships among the three principal variables, although the topic of intrahousehold economic relationships (Dwyer and Bruce, 1988), or "money and marriage" (Blumstein and Schwartz, 1983; Pahl, 1989), has only recently begun to receive the attention it deserves. There has been relatively little done on "triple intersection" relationships, however, and the authors of this volume seek to make a contribution in this area.

AUTHOR'S NOTE: I am grateful for all the support and advice I have gotten from Mitch Allen, Sage editor extraordinaire, and the excellent editorial help of Huma Ahmed Ghosh, Sabrina Santiago, and Suzanne L. Willis in the final rush of turning out this book. and the helpful comments and suggestions of Mary Freifeld on a draft of this chapter.

Many of the empirical findings provide support for hypotheses I have presented in recent years. Some examples will be noted, at least in passing, in my overviews of the chapters. But before presenting these summaries, let me set out some of the themes that recur in the various chapters. By noting these commonalities—and the chapters in which they appear—I hope to provide some sort of orientation for the reader. The chapter summaries give further details of the authors' arguments, including those that do not treat the common themes. By presenting both the common themes and the chapter summaries, I hope to provide the reader with enough detail to assess the last section of this Introduction. This consists of a preliminary codification—a sort of way station on the road to theory—of some of the things we have learned about the triangular relationships among economic factors, family/household and the gender stratification system in different settings.

Some Common Themes in the Chapters

First, here are three commonalities that cut across many of the chapters:

(1) Virtually all of the chapters mention intrahousehold stratification. Most confine themselves to gender stratification within the household—the differential power of men and women—but Treas, and my discussion of her chapter, below, also mention stratification by age: parents versus children.

(2) The main factor seen as affecting intrahousehold stratification is relative male versus female control of income, once ideological factors about proper male-female roles have been taken into account. (In my chapter, and in the final "theory" section of this Introduction, I mention other factors, beside ideology, that must be taken into account to get a notion of the net effect of relative male/female economic resources. I term these "macro and micro level discount factors").

(3) Specifically, with greater relative income, women are seen to have greater voice and leverage in family decisions, somewhat greater say in the overall relationship, and only a little more help from their husbands in housework.

Certain common themes are further specified by two or more authors. Here are some examples:

Two chapters (those by Huber and Chafetz) say that giving provides more intrahousehold power than receiving. But three more add that giving *surplus* provides more power than giving the basic necessities of life—that is, bare subsistence (those by Wolf, Coleman, and myself).

In other words, social class counts, because very poor people contributing basic subsistence get less leverage than people who can distribute some of the cream: surplus income and valued goods.

One chapter (Collins) tells us that class counts in another way within the household: husbands are more likely to come from the order-giver class and wives from the order-taker class, with consequences for their values and relationship.

Two chapters (Rakowski and mine) tell us that women with income and provider responsibilities for their children contribute a higher percentage of earnings than their mates. Both studies involved poor people, however, so it was subsistence, not surplus, income that the women were contributing to the household.

A number of the chapters further specify the extent to which housework is the aspect of family life most resistant to changes in the woman's economic and labor force position. Chafetz argues that fact that women remain responsible for domestic/childcare activities regardless of whatever else they do in the division of labor is what gives men their edge in economic power and gender stratification in the first place.

Three chapters then look for the conditions under which the gap between men's and women's domestic labor shrinks: Blumstein and Schwartz present data, and Coleman and I argue, that the greater the woman's relative income (i.e., the less the income gap), the less unequal the gap in housework done by husbands and wives. We all acknowledge, however, that the relationship is not very strong. Factoring in a positive ideology about male/female equality and/or male obligations to do domestic labor further narrows the gap. Coleman says that we must look at women who have long outearned their husbands and earn enough to distribute surplus to see if these wives' dominant economic power will close the gap.

Fenstermaker, West, and Zimmerman's chapter, however, implies that even here the gap will not close. This is because it is not just housework but also each partner's conception of gender roles that is being produced. Certainly this is true for Collins's order-taker wives: they give more importance than their husbands to how their house looks and how meals are served, and pay for it with increased labor.

A number of chapters mention that intrahousehold stratification is affected by external factors as well as relative male/female income.

Class, as noted, is mentioned by Collins, Coleman, and myself. Ethnicity is mentioned by both Evelyn Nakano Glenn, and Wallerstein and Smith. These authors argue that ethnicity affects both economic niche and family/household structure. Both also argue that an ethnic group's economic niche—and, consequently, family structure—can change over time. But I add (in my "Afterword" to Glenn's chapter) that within the ethnic family—at any point in time, or position in the class structure—there is still some effect caused by male versus female relative economic resources/income.

Finally, four chapters deal with the extent to which household members pool income. Three of them (those by Treas, Rakowski, and myself) argue that this is an empirical question and that family members pool income versus maintaining "separate purses" to varying degrees under different circumstances. Thus they disagree with the fourth chapter of the group, Wallerstein and Smith, which *defines* the household as an entity that pools income.

This list of common themes is far from exhaustive. Rather, it is intended as a tool to help the reader compare and contrast the various authors' differing angles of vision concerning the "triple overlap."

Plan of the Book and Overview of the Chapters

The chapters can be read in any order, but are arranged here in four sections. The first section on theory includes chapters by Huber, Collins, and Chafetz. The last part of this Introduction also fits in this section, as it presents emerging theory on the "triple overlap." The second section presents four chapters with theory and/or data on Third World peoples. My chapter combines theory with data mainly on Africa; Wolf's piece examines Java, Indonesia; Rakowski's chapter analyzes Venezuela; and Glenn's work considers three Third World "racial ethnic" groups in the United States: blacks, Mexican-Americans, and Chinese-Americans. I provide an "Afterword" to Glenn's chapter that seeks to factor in gender stratification. The third section of the book gives two contrasting conceptualizations of the household, by Treas, and Wallerstein and Smith, respectively. The final section presents three differing views of the gender division of domestic labor among American couples; these are offered by Coleman; Blumstein and Schwartz; and Fenstermaker, West, and Zimmerman.

Varieties of Theory Illuminating the "Triple Overlap"

As the broadest offering, Joan Huber presents a "Theory of Family, Economy, and Gender." The chapter spans all of human history (dealing with foraging, hoe, plow, herding, and industrial societies) and rests on three propositions. The first is micro level and applies to the family: those who produce goods tend to have more power and prestige than those who consume them. As Huber notes, "It is better to be able to give than to have to receive." The second proposition answers the macro-level question of which gender does the most productive work. Specifically, since men cannot bear or nurse a child, Huber proposes that the tasks that mesh best with childrearing tend to be assigned to women. She qualifies this, however, noting that especially where the level of living is low, women's tasks shape modes of childrearing more than vice versa. Her third proposition also holds for general stratification theory: In any society the most power and prestige accrue to those who control the distribution of valued goods *beyond* the family. Huber's historical overview of societies ranging from hunting-gathering to industrial illustrates how technological change has continually reshaped the triple overlap of gender, economy, and family. She places special emphasis on the fertility decline of the last 200 years in industrial societies:

> Industrialization first turned the cost-benefit ratio of children upside down. Then wives were drawn into the labor force, raising the opportunity cost of their time and thereby the cost of children. Now below-replacement fertility in the West has highlighted the problem of population maintenance. Parenthood may have to be made more attractive by limiting the hours of responsibility . . . But [this] would raise women's status in the family and in society in ways that were unimaginable a few decades ago. (chap. 1)

The second chapter, also from the journal special issue, is Randall Collins's heuristic "Women and Men in the Class Structure." He explains women's more complex position in the class structure in terms of a theory of organizational power position: women are more likely to be order takers than order givers. But disproportionately more than male order takers, women do "Goffmanian labor" presenting the organizational frontstage (as receptionists, waitresses, secretaries, and so forth). This affects the content of male-female gender class cultures, with women "white- *and* blue-collar working class" less cynical than male counterparts without frontstage responsibilities. It also affects marital relations in "cross-class marriages." Moreover, Collins proposes, women—both subjectively and objectively—live more in the world of status than class. They produce symbolic status through their housework, and often work for organizations producing and distributing cultural goods and status-laden objects. In addition, higher-class women focus their leisure activities on symbolic status realms, including the arts and charity. At the macro level, Collins concludes, modern capitalism depends increasingly on producing/consuming status-laden material objects and, hence, on female activities.

Janet Chafetz returns us to the realm of general theory, linking the gender division of labor to the reproduction of female disadvantage. Because women are chiefly responsible for child rearing, familial, and domestic tasks, regardless of their other work, while men focus on the more powerful arenas of the economy and the polity, women are disadvantaged from the start. Men's greater power, derived from the gender division of labor, results in a variety of other differences and inequities and further reinforces the gender division of labor. She goes on to posit sequences whereby the gender division of labor produces insidiously ranked gender ideologies, gender norms, gender socialization patterns, and gender stereotypes—all of which reverberate back to, and further reinforce, the gender division of labor. In this theory, Chafetz deliberately excludes both the *origin* of systems of gender stratification, and *change* in those systems. But she does link the macro and micro levels via her notions that men's greater economic resource power, derived from the macro-level gender division of labor, affords them a double form of micro-level leverage. Chafetz argues that this double advantage stems from the fact that the man is the main *giver* and his wife and children disproportionately the receivers. This means he gains not only economic, but also social leverage over them (e.g., via their gratitude)—and social obligations are harder to discharge.

Theory and Data from Third World Peoples About the "Triple Overlap"

My chapter presents a summary of my general theory of gender stratification, in which relative male/female control of economic resources is the main (though not sole) predictor of a wide variety of gender stratification consequences. The chapter reviews the evidence that men and women spend income under their control in different fashions, with women holding back less for themselves and spending more on child nutrition and family "basic human needs." This means that when women lose control of income, what is affected is not only their relative power position within the family, but also family well-being. Moreover, I show that planned Third World development projects that rely on female labor but don't provide women with a *return* for that labor are likely to suffer as well: to the extent they are able, women will reallocate their efforts to tasks yielding income under their *own* control. In Africa, I argue, the consequences of denying incentives to women producers (i.e., a return for their labor), can extend all the way to the region's food crises. This is because in sub-Saharan Africa women grow most locally marketed/consumed food, and have specific familial obligations that require them to have independently controlled income.

Diane Wolf's study of "Female Autonomy, the Family, and Industrialization in Java" also draws on my general theory of gender stratification, as applied to the Third World. Wolf notes that the Javanese family system's bilateral and matrilateral characteristics give women relatively good control of economic resources. Per my hypotheses, this should give women relatively high leverage within their families. Indeed, the Central Java "factory daughters" Wolf studied retain control over their own meager earnings. And, as expected, this appears to have maintained or even enhanced their status within their families. Further buttressing their family position is *how* they contribute to the home. Rather than helping out with a tiny, steady income stream aimed at day-to-day survival, they provide larger amounts on a sporadic basis: valued consumer goods and crisis aid. (This also supports my proposition that control and allocation of *surplus* provides more economic power than control and allocation of resources used for mere *subsistence*.) Wolf compares her Javanese case with East Asian "factory daughters." Following the much more patriarchal organization of East Asian families, they surrender almost all their pay to their families, and their low familial status has *not* been substantially raised by their employment.

Cathy Rakowski's chapter deals with Ciudad Guayana, Venezuela, a planned industrial city created from scratch in the 1960s by the Venezuelan Guayana Corporation, with the help of Harvard and MIT urban planners. It was designed with an overwhelmingly masculine economic base (steel and aluminum mills, construction). And to this day, she finds, a lower- or working-class woman's best economic prospect is a husband (versus the low-income informal sector or traditionally female service jobs open to her). But despite numerous planners' incentives to encourage legally married nuclear families, she finds that only 57% of working- and lower-class households consist of such "Dick and Jane" patriarchal/male breadwinner couples, almost half of which are common-law unions. Another 19% are female-headed units with dependent children (often with another relative present), and 16% are extended three-generation families.

More importantly, the planners' notion of the household as a single pooling entity supported by the male breadwinner (i.e., what I criticize in my chapter on income as the "black box" model) is called into question by Rakowski's heuristic distinction between "potential" and "real" income. "Potential" income sums what all household residents make; "real" income is what actually was contributed to the household by members and outsiders. Only 13% of the sample's "potential" and "real" monthly incomes fall within Bs. (bolivares) 500 (about $116 at the time of the study in 1980) of each other. This compares to a Venezuelan poverty line of Bs. 1,500 (just under $350) for a family of six (the average size for the working- and lower-class households sampled). Thus Rakowski finds low levels of actual income pooling (with women putting in a higher percent of income, as found in many other studies reported in my chapter). She also finds a policy issue of hidden poverty *within* households whose "potential income" seems adequate: although only 16% of sample households fall below the poverty line based on "potential income," fully one third do when the measuring stick is "real income" actually contributed (Pahl, 1989, also finds cases of hidden within-family poverty in England when husbands failed to share enough income with dependent wives and children).

Next is a composite: a reprint of Evelyn Nakano Glenn's classic 1985 article on the intersection of race, gender, and class oppression among Chinese-Americans, Mexican-Americans, and blacks is followed by an "Afterword" in which I examine the division of labor and resources by sex among these groups.

Glenn argues that racial oppression and a discriminatory labor sys-tem shaped "racial ethnic" women's work and lives in ways not taken into account in feminist analyses of female oppression. For example, women of all three groups had to struggle to hold their families together in a hostile world as well as to overcome the fact that their husbands were generally unable to earn a family wage. In particular, for black women, and Chinese-American women after the 1920s, this meant engaging in income-producing activities both within and outside the household.

She presents historical evidence on the three groups in support of her thesis that racial ethnic groups' family structure and women's labor are shaped by oppression (including discriminatory laws) and relegation to specific economic niches. For example, because 19th-century exclusion acts prevented most Chinese-American men from bringing in wives, several generations sent remittances to China, where their wives lived under their in-laws' strict control. Legal loopholes later enabled mer-chants to bring in wives, so Chinese-American women from the 1920s to the mid-1960s were likely to work as unpaid labor in a small family business. Since the mid-1960s, new immigration laws have brought a new wave of immigrants, who have been struggling to survive as dual-earner couples.

My "Afterword" then factors in an additional dimension to Glenn's analysis—gender stratification. Glenn argues that women's work to turn the family into a bulwark against racial oppression took precedence over intrafamilial conflict about gender oppression. Even so, I suggest that this did not preclude intrahousehold gender stratification—influenced by both the racial ethnic group's changing position in the larger U.S. economy over time and the group's ideology concerning the position of women.

Contrasting Conceptualizations of the Household

Judith Treas invokes the new theoretical paradigm, "transaction costs," to analyze the conditions under which households are likely to pool income via the "common pot" or use "separate purses." These, she argues, include power relations between the generations and genders, as well as transaction cost considerations about which system governs exchanges more efficiently and expeditiously.

Treas proposes that the common-pot, collectivized family leads to lower transaction costs under the following conditions: (a) threatening environments, (b) ambiguity in monitoring how well people are performing in exchanges; (c) long continuity in social relationships among members; and (d) fixed investments in specific individuals. Absent these conditions, market mechanisms, which favor separate purses and bargaining strategies, should prevail.

First, Treas looks for separate bank accounts in a random sample of 14,000 U.S. couples. She finds them more frequent among people who have experienced marital dissolution (via divorce or widowhood) i.e., among whom condition number 3—continuing social relationships—is less fulfilled. In line with Glenn and Blumberg's thoughts about black women's long history of economic autonomy, she also finds blacks generally much more likely to maintain separate accounts than whites. So, too, do employed couples where the wife works full time. She argues that a wife working for pay nullifies her condition number 2 for common-pot pooling—ambiguity in measuring how much people are contributing to an exchange—thus favoring separate accounts. (I would add that the greater economic power and autonomy provided by a working wife's paycheck also increase the likelihood of separate bank accounts.)

Second, she reanalyzes in transaction-cost terms Macfarlane's studies (1978, 1986) of individualism in England from 1250 to 1860 and finds a number of conditions that favored the separate purse, privatized family. Her case seems quite strong for individualistic relations between parents and children: Land was owned by individuals, not families, and could be sold. Heirs could be disinherited. Children often were sent off as apprentices or servants and not expected to send money home. The case for individualistic relations between husbands and wives is less compelling, however. Indeed, I suggest that a new book by Pahl (1989) undermines it.

In contrast to Macfarlane's implication that English wives had surprising independence, Pahl (1989) now presents solid evidence that *legally,* from the early middle ages (the 1200s) until 1882, when a woman married the guardianship and control of her real property (land) passed to her husband, who became absolute owner of all her other property and income. She could only make a will with his consent and since she "had no personal property, it was impossible for her to make legal contracts" (Pahl, 1989, p. 15).[2] Thus I interpret the Macfarlane/Treas data on individualistic relations between parents and children versus Pahl's new evidence that married women lost legal persona and property to their husbands as showing that within the "internal economy of the household" gender and age can vary *independently.* But *class* also must be considered (see note 2): women too poor to "wed" kept their rights to control property—and, perhaps, a separate purse.

Contrasting sharply with the approaches of Treas, Rakowski, and myself, all of whom make the degree of pooling within a household an empirical question, Immanuel Wallerstein and Joan Smith *define* the household as a unit that pools for purposes of reproduction (food, clothing, and shelter). They write that "the internal structure of households, and how power and goods are distributed internally, are not treated in this discussion" (chap. 9) and deal *only* with the pooling household.

Although they are not concerned with who earns and who spends income, they are concerned with *forms* of income: They posit a household that pools not just wages, but a total of five different kinds of income: wages, market sales (or profit), rent, transfer, and "subsistence" (or direct labor input).

They then link their monolithic pooling household with the workplace and the state via five "orienting propositions." Their first is that the pooling household and not the individual is the appropriate unit of analysis of how people fit into the labor force. Second, the household can have multiple boundaries, shifting composition, and variable time frames for pooling, and members need not be coresidents or even kin. Their third, fourth, and fifth propositions specify three types of pressures which push households to shift their boundaries: (a) The trends and cycles of the world-economy affect household structure, with households tending to expand boundaries and seek non-wage income in times of stagnation (conversely, periods of world-economy expansion accentuate the slow, long-term trend toward greater wage dependence and narrower household boundaries); (b) They argue that whereas the "obscure market forces" or world-economy affect household boundaries slowly and indirectly, state action can affect household boundaries quickly and directly;[3] and (c) They stress the role of ethnicity in socializing members into particular economic roles, as well as shaping household structure, and that the economic involvements of ethnic groups vary over time. All these points on ethnicity also emerge in Glenn's chapter on peoples of color in the United States.

The Debate About Gender, Money and Housework: Three Views

All studies agree that husbands do much less housework and child care than wives, even when the women work full time. But whether this situation is changing, and the conditions under which the gap shrinks, are hotly contested issues. In her overview, Marion Tolbert Coleman also points out the gaps in current social science research and theories about the gender division of housework and child rearing within families in the United States. She then proposes hypotheses predicting male involvement in both quantity and quality ("nice" versus "nasty") of domestic tasks. Her hypotheses draw on Blumberg and Coleman's (1989) concept of "net economic power," which takes ideological and cultural factors into account via a series of macro- and micro-level "discount factors." Coleman posits that, *ceteris paribus,* the higher a woman's "net economic power," the less disproportionate the share— and nastiness—of her double day. She also distinguishes between control over surplus and control over subsistence. Consequently, she sees "net economic power" as operating differently by *class.* Finally, she notes that our knowledge is lowest about couples wherein women have high and stabilized "net economic power"; The extent to which they share the domestic burden versus contracting it out (or reducing it via lower fertility) elicits policy, as well as social science, questions.

Philip Blumstein and Pepper Schwartz's regression analysis of the effect of male and female income on the gender division of power and housework in a large purposive sample of American couples empirically documents four critical points.

First, male and female income relates to marital *power:* increased income significantly enhances each gender's power in household decisions as well as in overall voice/leadership in the relationship. Second, the impact of male and female income on domestic tasks proved more complex and not as strong; but, in general, as income rises, hours of housework fall.

Third, men do far less housework than women, and whereas women's housework hours drop dramatically when they are employed full time, men's housework rises only slightly as we move from male sole bread-winners to husbands of wives working full time in couples rejecting the traditional patriarchal/male provider ideology. (See adaptation of Table 11.4.)

Adaptation of Table 11.4

	Husband Breadwinner Couples	All Couples	Both Spouses Employed Full Time	
			All Couples	Antiprovider Couples
Husband's hours of housework	5.28	6.57	7.33	8.40
Wife's hours of housework	32.64	21.34	13.87	12.01

SOURCE: Adapted from Blumstein and Schwartz, Table 11.4, this volume. All differences in husband's versus wife's hours are significant. "Antiprovider couples" reject the male sole provider role.

Fourth, they find an intriguing difference in how decision-making power and overall leadership power relate to male and female income (they treat each spouse's income separately, rather than use a ratio variable): (a) Vis-à-vis decision-making power, a woman's clout rises at about the same rate as a man's for every additional dollar of income she earns; (b) But for "leadership power"—overall say in the couple's relationship ("voice and vote" in the felicitous Spanish phrase for it, *voz y voto*)—women's clout rises slower than men's with increasing income. In fact, they find that it takes a wife $12,700 to get the same increase in leadership power that a man gets from an additional $10,000 (i.e., about one quarter more). Thus their data (Table 11.5) seem to provide empirical support for what Blumberg (1984) and Blumberg and Coleman (1989) term an "ideological discount rate"—that, due to pre-vailing male/female gender ideologies, a woman will get less than a full dollar's worth of economic power for every dollar she brings into the house, compared to her husband.[4]

Discussion

Ross (1987) found results quite similar to this summary of the Blumstein and Schwartz findings on housework, using a national random sample. She, too, found the ubiquitous big drop in house-work hours by wives employed full time. In addition, she found that men's share of the housework is boosted by (a) a smaller gap between husband's and wife's earnings, and (b) husband's values (but not wife's) favoring his participation in domestic tasks.

Interestingly, Ross used a *bargaining model* of male versus female income: the *subtraction score* of husband's minus wife's earnings. She argues that a husband/wife *ratio* score makes unrealistic statistical assumptions and she suggests that this accounts for the fact that the major studies linking male/female income ratios and housework have not found significant impacts (e.g., Farkas, 1976; Huber and Spitze, 1983; Coverman, 1985). Thus it is important to note that Ross, and Blumstein and Schwartz find significant income effects on housework in studies using relative income measures *other* than the husband/wife ratio. Moreover, Hood's (1983) qualitative study of 16 couples underlines the complex bargaining processes whereby the more income a woman contributed, the greater her ultimate success in getting her husband to help out around the house.

In short, these three studies (Blumstein and Schwartz; Hood; and Ross) contrast with many studies (including Fenstermaker, West, and Zimmerman, discussed below) that find that the gender division of housework is virtually cast in concrete, with few men devoting more than minimal time to such chores. Conversely, they support Blumberg and Coleman (1989) and Coleman's prediction that husband's involvement in housework and child care rises with his wife's increasing "net economic power."

The thesis of the chapter by Sarah Fenstermaker, Candace West, and Don Zimmerman is that gender is an "interactional accomplishment," and that looking at gender in this light helps us to explain gender inequality at work and at home. Basically, they argue that along with whatever other social and economic business people transact, they also invariably "do gender," and that both people and institutions are held to be "gender accountable" in their daily dealings. In other words, a person doing almost any action, task, or job will be held accountable not only for the action, but also "for her or his execution of that action *as a woman* or *a man*" (chap. 12).

They make the interesting point that people can "do gender" in single-sex groups: the women at the baby shower and the men at a fraternity initiation are "accomplishing gender" as much as those at a heterosexual wedding reception.

They also argue that in some situations, "doing gender" may be the primary work that is being done. As an example, they cite Goffman's argument that while size, strength, and age normally are distributed by sex, "selective pairing" among heterosexual couples ensures that males will be bigger, stronger, and older than their female partners, thereby buttressing gender accomplishments/displays.[5]

In the debate on whether the household division of labor is changing, the authors take the position, and focus on studies that find, that there has been little change in American men's historically low involvement in housework over the last few decades, regardless of the labor force status of the wife or the number of children (these factors drastically affect *her* housework hours but not *his*). Drawing on Fenstermaker Berk's important book, *The Gender Factory* (1985), they argue that this apparently lopsided and unfair system continues to be elected by most households because it is both housework *and* gender that are being produced. In short, her doing the laundry and his fixing the light switch not only produce clean clothes and a lit room, they also produce a reaffirmation of gender roles.

Discussion

In contrast to their view of the apparently invariant division of household labor, the evidence from Blumstein and Schwartz (this volume) and Ross (1987) indicates that male/female economic resources (as they measure them) and gender ideologies *do* affect the relative apportionment of household work. Most women have less economic power than their husbands and both still are influenced by the prevailing gender role ideology that filters down from the macro level even when both have adopted less patriarchal gender ideologies themselves.

Thus, for most women, securing their husband's help for what is still defined as the wife's primary responsibility may result in what is at best a mixed blessing: Lein's empirical work (1984) shows that when men undertake child care and domestic chores, they tend to skim off the cream (the "nicest" tasks, as discussed by Blumberg and Coleman, 1989; Coleman, this volume) and/or the absolutely nondeferrable chores. Other studies indicate that some men who do housework may perform even the simplest household tasks poorly; in fact, Fenstermaker, West, and Zimmerman cite the case of the wife who explains that her "brilliant and successful lawyer" husband "tries to be helpful" but can't sponge all the crumbs off the table (chap. 12). So wives who push their mates to do the chores risk being left with the most monotonous, "nastiest" tasks, and/or crumbs on the table. Surely this acts as a brake on the rate of change.

Nevertheless, I would argue that both prevailing notions of "doing gender" and doing housework can change when the economic/structural (and to a lesser extent, ideological) balance of power in American couples changes enough. For a further test of this hypothesis, however, we await research results from the frontier: American couples where the wife has long outearned the husband[6] *and* makes enough to allocate surplus income as well as just subsistence. I would speculate that these women also are less likely to be the junior partner with respect to age and education. And I will hypothesize that even though more of the housework may be contracted out under these circumstances, the gender balance will be more equal on what's left than has been found in other studies to date.

In summary, all the chapters make contributions to a still-implicit "megatheory" that encompasses both macro and micro, and considers historical as well as class variation in the triple overlap of gender stratification, economy, and family. Now, let us combine some of the patterns from the chapters with other generalizations that are beginning to emerge from the bivariate and trivariate literature on the economic, gender, and family/household variables. This is not yet an elaborated theory, "mega" or otherwise; rather, it is a series of empirical relationships that seem to hang together conceptually.

What We Have Learned About the "Triple Intersection" of Economy, Family, and Gender Stratification: Selected Points

Propositions About the "Internal Economy of the Household"

1. It is proposed that worldwide, there is a *continuum* of the extent to which households are unitary, "common pot" entities versus having at least partially "separate purses" for male and female, senior and junior (Blumberg 1989a, b, forthcoming).[7]

   1.1 Gender and age can vary independently within the "internal economy of the household" (my Introduction; Treas, this volume).

   1.2 There is a worldwide continuum of the extent to which women in marital unions get to keep or control independent resources (Blumberg, 1989b)—not every women generating income gets to keep or control all or even part.

   1.3 There is also a worldwide continuum of the extent to which women have provider obligations toward their families, especially their own children (Dwyer and Bruce, 1988; Blumberg, 1989a).[8]

2. The "internal economy of the household" varies greatly by geographic region, class, and ethnicity.

3. *Geographically,* the "internal economy of the household" is strongest in much of sub-Saharan Africa. Often (especially where polygyny remains

prevalent and/or marriages are unstable), men and women maintain "separate purses" for most income streams and expenditures (Guyer, 1980, 1988; Staudt, 1987; Fapohunda, 1988).[9] Conversely, the "internal economy of the household" fades to nonsignificance where women have few or no opportunities to earn own-account income, via formal or informal sector jobs or market trading. This is not too common worldwide.[10]

4. Worldwide, the central tendency of this posited "internal economy of the household" continuum is closer to the "separate purse" end than the "common pot"-single production function end.

5. The main reason number 4 is true is because of *social class*—the world majority is poor and the relationship between social class and women's economic contributions is usually, but not always (see number 6, below) *inverse* (Blumberg, 1989b):

   5.1 The farther down in the class structure or in an economic sector, the higher the proportion of women who are economically active.

   5.2 The farther down in the class structure or in an economic sector, the higher the proportion of household subsistence women contribute.[11]

   5.3 The proportion of female-headed households, where women control income by definition, is also usually inversely related to social class (Blumberg with Garcia, 1977; Buvinic, Youssef, and Von Elm, 1978).

6. The main exception to number 5—the inverse relation between social class and women's work—is by *ethnicity* (e.g., among South America's Andean Indians).[12]

7. Class also may vary between husbands and wives within households in two additional ways:

   7.1 Marriages in industrial societies often are "cross-class," especially when the dimensions of "order givers versus order takers" and presence/absence of "Goffmanian frontstage responsibilities" are considered (Collins, this volume).

   7.2 Dependent women (and children) may live in hidden poverty in households with adequate income because of inequitable distribution (Pahl, 1989 on England; Rakowski on "potential" versus "real" income, this volume).

Propositions About the "External Economy of the Household"

8. There is also a continuum of the extent to which external boundaries of the household are tight and narrow versus shifting and broad (i.e., reaching out to encompass nonresidents and/or nonkin):

   8.1 During periods of world-economy stagnation, households tend to expand their boundaries to encompass additional income earners, whereas during times of world-economy expansion, the slow trend toward narrowed boundaries and wage income is accentuated (Wallerstein and Smith, this volume).

8.2 Flexible sharing networks are most common among the poor, where resources are fluctuating and frequently scarce, especially among female-headed units in those circumstances (Stack, 1974; Brown, 1975; Blumberg with Garcia, 1977; Blumberg, 1978, my chapter, this volume; Rakowski, this volume).

9. Certain kinds of extended family structure are more favorable to women's position (e.g., the bilateral and matrilateral arrangements Wolf discusses for Java).

10. As racial ethnic groups' economic niches shift, their family structures and wives' relative earnings/power also are affected (Glenn/Blumberg, this volume).

Propositions About Women's Relative Economic Power: Earning and Spending

11. Women's economic power relative to men (defined as control of key economic resources such as income, property, and other means of production) is posited as the most important and *achievable*[13] (though certainly not the sole) independent variable affecting gender stratification at a variety of "nested" micro and macro levels ranging from the couple to the state (Blumberg, 1984).

12. A woman may not, however, "get a dollar's worth of economic power for every dollar she brings into the household" because of several caveats:

12.1 The greater the level of gender inequality at the society's macro level (i.e., the extent to which, for example, the political, economic, legal, and ideological systems disadvantage women), the greater the *negative* "discount rate" nibbling away at women's household level economic power (Blumberg, 1984).

12.2 There are also "discount factors" at the micro household level that can be either negative *or* positive, that is, factors that can add to or erode the woman's hypothetical "dollar's worth of economic power for every dollar she brings to the household" (Blumberg, 1984; Blumberg and Coleman, 1989). These include:

12.2.1 The gender role ideology of each partner (Ross, 1987; Blumstein and Schwartz, this volume). Blumstein and Schwartz's chapter provides one intriguing demonstration: among couples adhering to a patriarchal male provider ideology, the husband's relative power is synergistically strengthened by a good income but synergistically weakened if low income makes him a poor provider.

12.2.2 The woman's socialization to bargain less hard to realize economic leverage (England and Kilbourne, 1988; Chafetz, this volume). England and Kilbourne provide a fascinating example when they reinterpret Blumstein and Schwartz's findings (1983) that relative income was most strongly related to power among gay male couples (where both partners had been socialized to view money as power); intermediate among heterosexual couples; and least related among lesbian couples (where neither partner had been socialized to view money as power).

12.2.3 Each partner's relative attractiveness/local "market value" (Blumberg and Coleman, 1989). Local standards of beauty, sensuousness, and desirability as a partner may vary but there is little question that for women, in particular, ranking high on such attributes (and higher than one's spouse) often adds leverage in a relationship.

12.2.4 Each partner's relative commitment: the less committed partner has more leverage by the "principle of least interest," since the more committed partner fears that the mate will walk out (Blumberg and Coleman, 1989).

12.2.5 Personality factors, such as each partner's relative assertiveness, and, perhaps, dependency (Blumstein and Schwartz, this volume), also have a role in enhancing or undercutting the leverage one derives from bringing economic resources to the household.

12.2.6 Finally, the man's *felt* economic dependence on the woman's economic contribution, regardless of its level, also affects how much power she derives from income she brings in. One man whose wife makes as much as he may be indifferent to her income and feel no qualms about losing it. Yet another man, whose wife earns less than a fourth as much as he, may be highly dependent on her earnings to maintain what he considers his minimum acceptable standard of living (Blumberg and Coleman, 1989). His dependence should add to her power regardless of whether her income provides the margin for bare survival or provides surplus he feels he needs to maintain status.

13. "It's better to give than to receive," per Huber, but one gets less clout from allocating resources needed for bare *subsistence* than from controlling *surplus* allocation (Blumberg, 1984). (Huber would add that allocating it beyond the household gives even more power.) Withholding food from hungry children is rarely an option at the micro level, which may

be why poor women don't get more power from the often high proportion of resources they provide the household.

14. Net of the various discount factors in number 12, and the surplus versus subsistence income distinction in number 13, the greater a woman's absolute and/or relative control of economic resources—most commonly, income—the greater her efficacy and empowerment in a variety of areas:

   14.1 The greater a woman's (net) control of income, the greater her increase in self-esteem and self-confidence (Blumberg, chap. 4, this volume).

   14.2 The greater a woman's (net) control of income, the greater her leverage in fertility decisions—that is, the more these reflect her own utilities versus those of her husband, the extended family, the state, and so forth (Blumberg, chap. 4, this volume).

   14.3 The greater a woman's (net) control of income, the greater her leverage in other household economic and domestic decisions, and the greater her overall "voice and vote" (leadership) in the relationship (Blumberg, chap. 4, this volume; Blumstein and Schwartz, this volume).[14]

15. Mere work in economic activities (or even ownership of economic resources) does *not* translate into the economic leverage described in number 14 (vis-à-vis in household decisions) if the person derives no *control* of economic resources thereby (Acharya and Bennett, 1981, 1982, 1983; Blumberg, chap. 4, this volume).

16. Women who lose income lose domestic power more quickly and sharply than they gain it when income rises (Blumberg, 1989b, 1990).[15]

17. Men tend to spend income under their control differently than women who have provider responsibilities (even as "providers of last resort"), with women more focused on children's well-being and family subsistence. Specifically:

   17.1 It is *mother's*, rather than father's income or food production that tends to be more closely related to children's nutrition (Blumberg, 1989a, chap. 4, this volume).

   17.2 Women tend to contribute a higher proportion of their income to family subsistence, holding back less for personal consumption (Blumberg, chap. 4, this volume).

18. Women tend to allocate labor toward activities that put income (and/or food if they have provider obligations) under their control, and to the extent culturally feasible, away from activities that do not—even if these are (somewhat) more profitable for the household/husband (Blumberg, 1989a, 1989b, this volume).

Propositions About the Gender Division of Resources and Domestic Labor

19. The gender division of housework and childcare, including the husband's relative contribution, is affected by economic and ideological factors, namely:

   19.1 Male-female income (separate male and female income variables, as well as the gap in their earnings) relates to the gender division of housework and child care, although (a) the relationship is stronger for women, and (b) it is weaker than the income: decision-making or income: leadership power relationship (Hood, 1984; Ross, 1987; Blumstein and Schwartz, this volume).

   19.2 Gender ideology also relates to the gender division of housework and childcare, although (a) the relationship appears to be weaker than that for income (Blumstein and Schwartz, this volume), and (b) at least one study (Ross, 1987) found the link stronger for men's ideology/values.

   Net of 19.1 and 19.2:

   19.3 When women work full time, men's hours of housework are little affected, but women's drop sharply (Ross, 1987; Blumstein and Schwartz, this volume).

   19.4 Part of the reason this seemingly inequitable pattern of apportioning household labor is so little changed by women's full-time employment is the fact that *two* things are being done: housework/childcare *and* gender (Fenstermaker Berk, 1985; Fenstermaker, West, and Zimmerman, this volume).

   19.5 Another part of the reason women employed full time continue to do the lion's share of household labor is the strong tendency for the husband to pick the "nicest" chores, leaving his wife with the "nastier" ones—for example, tasks that are more monotonous, dirtier, or more quickly in need of redoing (Blumberg and Coleman, 1989; Coleman, this volume).

   19.6 Still another part of the reason women employed full time continue to shoulder most household chores is the fact that many of their husbands demonstrate that they do a less competent job (e.g., Fenstermaker, West, and Zimmerman's "crumbs on the table" example in this volume). This would be especially salient for working-class wives for whom the cleanliness and order of the house translates most directly into status production; (Collins, in Chapter 2 of this volume, describes this as "the home as a Goffmanian product").

   19.7 Still another reason for this pattern is childhood gender role socialization with respect to the division of labor (Chafetz, this volume).

19.8 Finally, also contributing to this pattern are women's socialized disinclinations to bargain hard and their emphasis on altruism and nurturing (England and Kilbourne, 1988).

In order to further tease out the conditions under which women do not do a disproportionate share of the household tasks, we must await "research from the frontier"—including an analyzable stratum of couples where the wife (a) has, for some time, earned as much as/more than the husband, (b) has an income high enough to permit allocation of surplus rather than mere subsistence income, and (c) has provider responsibilities.

20. Given those three conditions, I will venture the hypotheses that:

20.1 the ratio of his and her housework will be close, but this may be due, in good measure, to contracting out the work among those who can afford it and sluffing off more chores or lowering standards among those who cannot; and

20.2 these women will have fewer structural disadvantages vis-à-vis their spouse than traditional gender role ideology dictates for "selective pairing" (i.e., they will be less likely to be younger, less educated, and so forth).

All in all, the above propositions vary in level of empirical support from tentative hypotheses to well-backed generalizations observed worldwide (an example of the latter is the increase in self-esteem among women who earn income). In general, however, structural factors have seemed stronger than ideological ones. It is hoped that these propositions will prove useful toward further research and theory. For now, we can conclude by considering these propositions as a way station about halfway along the road to an integrated theory of the "triple overlap" of gender, economy, and family.

Notes

1. There is a long-running and complex debate concerning the extent of overlap between household and family. Sometimes the coresidential household and family groups coincide; often they do not. The family versus household topic is touched on in this introduction and dealt with in differing ways and to varying degrees in several of the chapters. I advocate no single definition or solution, however.

2. To be sure, Pahl (1989) notes that in practice, many preindustrial wives helped manage household financial affairs and tended to pay for its small daily expenditures either via an allowance from their husbands or *out of their own production for sale* (p. 33, my emphasis; women made and sold cheese, butter, and beer, and sold eggs, small

animals, and so forth). Among most landed peasants, a wife's "butter and egg money" probably was minute in comparison with her husband's resources, even if it gave her a bit more autonomy than the law allowed. Significantly, Greenfield (1966) documents that in medieval English villages, legal marriage seems to have been contracted only where property was involved ("husband" meant a propertied villager; "wed" is the gift the groom gave the bride to signify her being vested in inheritance rights to his property). In addition, the records imply not only that the propertyless in rural villages lived in common law unions, but also that many poor families had no resident male heads (Pahl, 1989, p. 165). So the case for separate purses among men and women seems stronger among the poor than among the landed classes who actually wed, thereby obliterating the woman's legal right to control her property individually.

3. I would emphasize that households do not always respond slowly to economic change: Studies finding that household composition alters dynamically in response to economic conditions include Stack, 1974 and Morgan, 1974 for the United States. But Rakowski's paper (this volume) provides partial support for their proposition that the state can affect household composition: in Ciudad Guayana, the Venezuelan Guayana Corporation in 1961 adopted a very masculine economic base and promoted laws/incentives favoring married, nuclear families headed by male sole earners. And the proportion of female-headed households did drop from 25% to 16% from the 1960s to 1980. But Rakowski also found 43% of lower- and working class households in 1980 to be non-nuclear—that is, state initiatives had only partial success.

4. England and Kilbourne (1988) propose a similar notion, arguing that women are socialized to be more altruistic in their relationships and hence tend to bargain less hard than men to seize full power advantage from their income.

5. I would add that females are socialized in a gender-stratified society to want a husband who holds most of the *structurally* important high cards. The ideal mate is not only supposed to be bigger, stronger, and older—he is also supposed to be richer, smarter, better educated, and more forceful. As a result, I suggest, the wife begins every interaction not only held accountable to extant gender norms but also with a huge structural power handicap.

6. In about one in six couples the woman now earns as much as or more than the man.

7. References in parentheses indicate where the hypothesis is discussed and/or supporting empirical materials presented. Note that many economists follow Becker (1981) in describing the "common pot" household by a single production function.

8. 1.2 and 1.3 are correlated, but not perfectly. For example, most Muslim Hausa women in northern Nigeria live in strict seclusion but engage in a variety of income-generating pursuits from within their compounds. Since, however, only their husbands have formal responsibilities as providers, these women—except during periods of intense privation—can use their income for business expansion, daughters' dowries, and so forth. (Blumberg, 1988 provides supporting references).

9. Frequently African women have strong provider obligations, especially toward their own children. Most women are economically active, predominantly in low resource farming and/or market trade, although this often is not recorded in national accounts data on the measured labor force (see Blumberg, 1989a, 1989c).

10. For example, it characterizes rural areas of the Yemen Arab Republic—where half the young men are off working in the Persian Gulf, sending remittances home to the senior male of their families, while the women act as unpaid family labor in agriculture (Howe, 1985; Carloni, 1988). It also occurs in a number of remote colonization projects in tropical lowlands, mainly in South America (Scudder, 1979; Blumberg and Colyer, 1990).

11. See, for example, Deere, 1977 on Peru; Matlon, 1979; Norman, 1982; Blumberg, 1988 on Nigeria; Mencher, 1988 on India; and Roldan, 1988 on Mexico.

12. In the dominant Spanish (Ladino) culture shared by whites and *mestizos* in most of Latin America, the traditional ideal is for women to be economic dependents, an ideology the poor cannot afford to uphold—hence, they manifest the posited inverse relationship between social class and women's economic activity. Among the rural Indians of the Andes, however, men and women tend to be economic partners, both in ideology and practice. Among them, therefore, there is little increase in women's economic dependency with increasing social class, and the proportion of female-headed households does not rise as sharply among the poorest (for Ecuador, see Alberti, 1986; Poeschel, 1988; Blumberg and Colyer, 1990).

13. Empirically, for women, economic power is the most achievable of the four major sources of power discussed by Lenski (1966): economic, political-hierarchical, force, and (slightly less importantly) ideological. Over the range of human history and human societies, we find that the power of *force* clearly is the *least* achievable for women, who are more likely to be its victims than its wielders. This is so at both the individual violence level (e.g., wifebeating) and the organized force level (police/military power), where men's one-third to one-half greater upper body strength and disproportionate control of weapons give them almost universal sway over women. With respect to *political* power, we have no data on even one society where women had a 50-50 split. Regarding the power of *ideology*, we know of a few societies/groups which proclaim women's ideological equality with men but we have no data of any where women are deemed ideologically superior. Only with respect to *economic* power does women's position run the full range from near-zero to near-total control of the local economy (e.g., the Iroquois of colonial North America); in general, however, women's predominance is more common at the micro levels of family and community, with macro levels dominated by males.

14. Note, however, that Blumstein and Schwartz found evidence of a "discount rate" for the effect of female income on leadership: it took $12,700 for a wife to get the same level of leadership in the couple that an added $10,000 brought to the husband. The relationship between income and decision-making power was stronger.

15. An example is the woman who had worked for income in Guatemala City and shared decisions with her husband there; they decided to move to land he had inherited and raise broccoli and cauliflower on contract for an agribusiness firm—that paid by check made out solely to him. Her power fell so drastically that she said that was the last decision in which she participated (Blumberg, 1989d).

References

Acharya, Meena and Lynn Bennett. 1981. *The Rural Women of Nepal: An Aggregate Analysis and Summary of Eight Village Studies,* Vol. 2, Part 9. Katmandu, Nepal: Centre for Economic Development and Administration, Tribhuvan University.

———. 1982. "Women's Status in Nepal: A Summary of Findings and Implications." Mimeograph. Washington, DC: Agency for International Development, Office of Women in Development.

———. 1983. "Women and the Subsistence Sector: Economic Participation in Household Decision-Making in Nepal." Washington, DC: World Bank.

Alberti, Amalia M. 1986. *Gender, Ethnicity and Resource Control in the Andean Highlands of Ecuador.* Doctoral dissertation, Stanford University.

Becker, Gary. 1981. *A Treatise on the Family.* Cambridge, MA: Harvard University Press.

Blumberg, Rae Lesser. 1978. "The Political Economy of the Mother-Child Family Revisited." Pp. 526-575 in *Family and Kinship in Middle America and the Caribbean,* edited by Arnaud F. Marks and Rene A. Romer. Co-publication of the Institute of

Higher Studies in Curacao, Netherlands Antilles, and the Department of Caribbean Studies of the Royal Institute of Linguistics and Anthropology at Leiden, Netherlands.

————. 1984. "A General Theory of Gender Stratification." In *Sociological Theory 1984*, edited by Randall Collins. San Francisco: Jossey-Bass.

————. 1988. *The Half-Hidden Economic Roles of Rural Nigerian Women and National Development*. Draft. Washington, DC: The World Bank. Women in Development Division.

————. 1989a. *Making the Case for the Gender Variable: Women and the Wealth and Well-Being of Nations*. Washington, DC: Agency for International Development Office of Women in Development.

————. 1989b. "Gender, Control of Household Income and Planned Development: 20 Hypotheses." Washington, DC: Paper prepared for the Agency for International Development, Office of Women in Development.

————. 1989c. "Toward a Feminist Theory of Development." Pp. 161-199 in *Feminism and Sociological Theory*, edited by Ruth A. Wallace. Newbury Park, CA: Sage.

———— (with the assistance of Maria Regina Estrada de Batres and Josefina Xuya Cuxil). 1989d. "Work, Wealth and Women in Development 'Natural Experiment' in Guatemala: The ALCOSA Agribusiness Project in 1980 and 1985." Pp. 85-106 in *Women in Development: A.I.D.'s Experience, 1973-1985. Vol. II. Ten Field Studies*, edited by Paula O. Goddard. Washington, DC: Agency for International Development, Center for Development Information and Evaluation.

————. 1990. "Gender Matters: Involving Women in Development in Latin America and the Caribbean." Paper prepared for Agency for International Development, Bureau for Latin America and the Caribbean. Washington, DC

————. forthcoming. *Women, Development, and the Wealth of Nations: Making the Case for the Gender Variable*. Boulder, CO: Westview.

Blumberg, Rae Lesser, with Maria-Pilar Garcia. 1977. "The Political Economy of the Mother-Child Family: A Cross-Societal View." In *Beyond the Nuclear Family Model*, edited by Luis Lenero-Otero. London: Sage.

Blumberg, Rae Lesser, and Marion Tolbert Coleman. 1989. "A Theory-Guided Look at the Gender Balance of Power in the American Couple." *Journal of Family Issues* 10(2):225-250.

Blumberg, Rae Lesser, and Dale Colyer. 1990. "Social Institutions, Gender, and Rural Living Conditions." In *The Role of Agriculture in Ecuador's Development*, edited by Morris D. Whitaker and Dale Colyer. Boulder, CO: Westview.

Blumstein, Philip and Pepper Schwartz. 1983. *American Couples: Money, Work, and Sex*. New York: William Morrow.

Brown, Susan. 1975. "Love Unites Them and Hunger Separates Them: Poor Women in the Dominican Republic." In *Toward an Anthropology of Women*, edited by Rayna Reiter. New York: Monthly Review Press.

Buvinic, Myra, Nadia Youssef, and Barbara Von Elm. 1978. *Women Headed Households: The Ignored Factor in Development Planning*. Washington, DC: International Center for Research on Women.

Carloni, Alice Stewart. 1988. Personal Communication.

Coverman, Shelly. 1985. "Explaining Husbands' Participation in Domestic Labor." *Sociological Quarterly* 26:81-97.

Deere, Carmen Diana. 1977. "The Social Relations of Production and Peruvian Peasant Women's Work." *Latin American Perspectives* 4:(1-2).

Dwyer, Daisy and Judith Bruce, ed. 1988. *A House Divided: Women and Income in the Third World*. Palo Alto, CA: Stanford University Press.

England, Paula and Barbara Stanek Kilbourne. May, 1988. "Markets, Marriages, and Other Mates: The Problem of Power." Paper presented at the Conference on Economy and Society, University of California, Santa Barbara.

Fapohunda, Eleanor. 1988. "The Nonpooling Household: A Challenge to Theory." In *A Home Divided: Women and Income in the Third World,* edited by Daisy Dwyer and Judith Bruce. Palo Alto, CA: Stanford University Press.

Farkas, George. 1976. "Education, Wage Rates, and the Division of Labor Between Husband and Wife." *Journal of Marriage and the Family* 38:473-483.

Fenstermaker Berk, Sarah. 1985. *The Gender Factory: The Apportionment of Work in American Households.* New York: Plenum.

Greenfield, Sidney M. 1966. *English Rustics in Black Skin.* New Haven, CT: College and University Press.

Guyer, Jane. 1980. "Household Budgets and Women's Incomes." Working Paper No. 28. Boston: African Studies Center, Boston University.

———. 1988. "Dynamic Approaches to Domestic Budgeting. Cases and Methods from Africa." In *A House Divided: Women and Income in the Third World,* edited by Daisy Dwyer and Judith Bruce. Palo Alto, CA: Stanford University Press.

Howe, Gary Nigel. 1985. *The Present and Potential Contribution of Women to Economic Development: Elements of Methodology and Analysis of the Yemen Arab Republic.* Washington, DC: Agency for International Development, Office of Women in Development.

Hood, Jane. 1983. *Becoming a Two-Job Family.* New York: Praeger.

Huber, Joan and Glenna Spitze. 1983. *Sex Stratification: Children, Housework, and Jobs.* New York: Academic Press.

Lein, Laura. 1984. *Families Without Villains.* Lexington, MA: Lexington Books.

Lenski, Gerhard E. 1966. *Power and Privilege: A Theory of Social Stratification.* New York: McGraw-Hill.

Macfarlane, Alan. 1978. *The Origins of English Individualism: The Family, Property and Social Transition.* New York: Cambridge University Press.

Macfarlane, Alan. 1986. *Marriage and Love in England: Modes of Reproduction 1300-1840.* Oxford: Basil Blackwell.

Matlon, Peter J. 1979. *Income Distribution Among Farmers in Northern Nigeria: Empirical Results and Policy Implications.* Washington, DC: Agency for International Development and Michigan State University.

Mencher, Joan. 1988. "Women's Work and Poverty: Women's Contribution to Household Maintenance in Two Regions of South India." In *A Home Divided: Women and Income in the Third World,* edited by Daisy Dwyer and Judith Bruce. Palo Alto, Ca: Stanford University Press.

Morgan, James. 1974. *Five Thousand American Families: Patterns of Economic Progress.* Ann Arbor, MI: Institute of Social Research, University of Michigan.

Norman, David W. ed. 1982. *Farming Systems in the African Savanna: Research Strategies for Development.* Boulder, CO: Westview.

Pahl, Jan. 1989. *Money and Marriage.* London: Macmillan.

Poeschel R., Ursula. 1988. *La Mujer Salasaca* (Segunda Edition). Quito: Ediciones Abya-yala.

Roldan, Martha. 1988. "Renegotiating the Marriage Contract: Intrahousehold Patterns of Money Allocation and Women's Subordination Among Domestic Outworkers in Mexico City.." In *A Home Divided: Women and Income in the Third World,* edited by Daisy Dwyer and Judith Bruce. Palo Alto, Ca: Stanford University Press.

Ross, Catherine E. 1987. "The Division of Labor at Home." *Social Forces* 65(3):816-833.

Scudder, Thayer. 1979. "Evaluatory Report on Mission to Sri Lankan Settlement Projects: A Discussion of Some Basic Issues." Washington, DC: Agency for International Development, Asia Bureau, Special Study.

Stack, Carol B. 1974. *All Our Kin: Strategies for Survival in a Black Community.* New York: Harper & Row.

Staudt, Kathleen. 1987. "Uncaptured or Unmotivated? Women and the Food Crisis in Africa." *Rural Sociology* 52(1):37-55.

Part I

Theories Illuminating the "Triple Overlap"

1

A Theory of Family, Economy, and Gender

JOAN HUBER

Until rather recently, most stratification theories were theological: God wanted things thus. In the words of a popular hymn:

The rich man in his castle,
The poor man at his gate,
God made them high and lowly,
And ordered man's estate.

In 1924 when that stanza was dropped from the hymn about all creatures great and small, God was being given less credit for stratal design than formerly. Instead, industrialization in Europe and North America during the nineteenth century had spawned grand theories about class differences in power and prestige. These came to permeate twentieth-century consciousness.

In contrast, gender differences in power and privilege were assumed to stem from inborn abilities that determined duties within the family. The most important difference was categorical: No man can bear a child. Other differences overlapped: Men tended to come in larger sizes and have heavier muscles. Many mental differences also overlapped, but the extent to which they resulted from nature or nurture was (and is) unknown.

AUTHOR'S NOTE: This chapter is a revision of "A Theory of Gender Stratification" in Laurel Richardson and Verta Taylor, eds., *Feminist Frontiers*, 3rd edition, Addison-Wesley, 1987, and is reprinted by permission of the author. Rae Lesser Blumberg's suggestions have improved it.

Industrialization reduced the functional importance of many sex differences. The importance of women's ability to breastfeed a child diminished after 1910 when techniques of sterilization enabled babies to survive on bottled milk. Neither at that time nor later did anyone remark the profoundly revolutionary effects this technological breakthrough might have on gender responsibilities. Until this century, the mother-child bond, whatever it meant for the child's spiritual or psychological well-being, involved its immediate survival. In this century for the first time in human history fathers can nourish infants from birth. However, although technological change permits new ways of behaving, it does not necessarily follow that behavior will change: Many men who have managed to accustom themselves to flying at 30,000 feet even though they lack wings have experienced difficulties in adjusting to the niceties of infant feeding.

Men's greater muscular strength also came to matter less as machines increasingly replaced human power. Today, for example, brawn gives men no real advantage in white-collar jobs, the kind where brains count. Brawn is still an advantage in such activities as shoveling heavy wet snow, but prudent men do not press it too hard. Men tend to suffer vascular problems earlier than women do.

The need to replace biological theories of sex stratification became apparent around 1970 (Huber, 1986). A new wave of the women's movement threw into relief many anomalies that had surfaced in the wake of industrialization. Sex role behaviors clearly followed no logical pattern based on biological differences. For example, even though they possessed the requisite skills, men were less likely than women to change diapers. Similarly, the hours that fully employed wives spent washing dishes and scrubbing floors stemmed from no demonstrable biological imperative. It dawned on scholars that gender stratification was a form of social stratification to which biology contributed but that biology alone could not explain.

In 1970, however, the data needed for a theory were hard to find in the relevant disciplines (Huber and Spitze, 1988). Anthropologists had long gathered data on foraging and hoe cultures, but most anthropologists, being men, had not been able to mix freely with indigenous women going about their work. In consequence, the data about women's behavior and beliefs were sketchy. Moreover, the interpretations tended to stem from the Western sex-role ideologies that male anthropologists carried in their heads as part of their intellectual equipment.

Historians had long studied the great men and great events of diplomatic history to the neglect of social history, the study of the daily lives of ordinary people. Since the historical record included few great queens and warriors, women were nearly invisible. Sociologists had analyzed women as wives and mothers in family settings or as prostitutes in the study of deviance. The literature on stratification defined women only as their husbands' dependents. A basic problem was that stratification theories, whether influenced by Durkheim, Marx, or Weber, defined social class as a market relationship. No nineteenth-century theorist had conceptualized the household division of labor as being part of the division of labor in society. In consequence, women's unpaid family work was excluded from the study of economic variables. Thus, neither European nor American grand theories of society conceptually linked family, economic patterns, and gender.

Nonetheless, the first social theories of gender stratification were the work of scholars who, influenced by Marx or Weber, tried to explain women's status in the context of received ideas about social class. They gave little heed to secular changes in fertility that had altered women's life chances. The theories influenced by Marx, almost entirely the work of women scholars, appeared first.

Marxism had been rather isolated from social science in the United States until the late 1960s when some of the under-thirties crowd rediscovered an extensive literature. A common thread was the idea that the working class had been done in by the capitalists. Early Marxist feminists, invoking the concept of patriarchal capitalism, tried to show working-class women had been done in even more. Over time, however, Marxist feminist thought divided into two streams.

One view implicitly or explicitly held that women are subordinated only in class societies; gender is simply a subset of class stratification. The other held that sex was the first and basic class division. Marx was incomplete, not wrong (Crompton, 1986). In fact, however, gender stratification seems much the same under both patriarchal socialism and patriarchal capitalism. In the people's democracies and the Western democracies alike, men do little baby tending and less housework.

In the early 1970s the Weberian tradition was subsumed within a modest but precise theory: the attainment model. Measuring effects of father's education and occupation on son's attainment dominated stratification research. When the models were extended to women in the mid-1970s, it was found that both sexes experienced similar rates of occupational mobility but, anomalously, women earned less. Later, Bose and Rossi (1983) reported that standard indicators of socioeconomic status do not tap attributes of sex-typed occupations.

In sum, social-class categories, Marxist or Weberian, ignored the economic costs of reproduction. The activities of wives and mothers were outside the system. Even in the 1950s, 1960s, and much of the

1970s no social theorist in the United States sensed the effect of a 200-year fertility decline on women's life chances. Even in the 1980s few social theorists sensed that women's entry into paid work would make men's entry into housework a new variable.

The interdependence of economic and family variables became more clear during the 1970s. New data appeared, a result of interest in the trends that had spurred a massive expansion of the women's movement. Historical demography, social history, and anthropology greatly enriched the knowledge about fertility and women's labor force participation. One research stream culminated in the life-course perspective, a mix of social psychology, demography, and history that focused on events of the industrial period. New analytic techniques and large longitudinal data sets enabled researchers to address previously unanswerable questions.

Another stream was influenced by comparative sociology—or social anthropology, which separated from sociology in those Western countries that wiped out preindustrial peoples (e.g., native Americans) or incorporated them much earlier (e.g., European peasants) (Goody, 1982, p. 2). This stream includes the work of anthropologists Friedl (1975) and Goody (1976), sociologists Lenski (1970), Blumberg (1978, 1984), and Chafetz (1984), demographers Lesthaeghe (1980) and Caldwell (1980), and economist Boserup (1970).

The theory outlined below draws heavily on this second stream. It needs to be fleshed out with much more data. Its purpose is not to lay out a tidy set of answers but rather to suggest the potential of this research strategy.

Gender stratification is a subset of social stratification. I first note the major variables of social stratification; then discuss those unique to gender. A theory of stratification must begin with what men and women do each day to secure food, clothing, and shelter, analyzing how they organize their work around the available tools. It must also consider ecological variables that affect human ability to sustain life such as climate, soil, and temperature. This approach is not new. Although often overshadowed by the abiding fascination with personal interaction as prime mover in human affairs, from its very beginnings much sociological analysis has implicitly or explicitly stressed the importance of ecology and technology. Duncan's (1964) essay on the interdependence of population, organization, ecology, and technology still stands as the best description of this perspective.

This view of subsistence technology's importance is not deterministic. A given technology only permits certain events to occur; it does not require that they occur. Nor can this approach claim to answer all the significant questions about the human condition. But it is a necessary first step. Analyses that focus primarily on thought, feeling, and belief can yield important knowledge but they are unlikely to provide much insight into the causes and effects of stratification systems that are inextricably intertwined with material reality (Harris, 1979). Humankind does not live by bread alone, but without bread no one can live at all.

The most complete analysis of the anthropological literature showing the interaction of ecology, technology, and the organization of work is in Lenski's (1966) *Power and Privilege* and his (1970) macrosociology text, indebted to Childe (1951) and Goldschmidt (1959). The approach is called evolutionary because improving tool efficiency results in a larger food supply. Such scholars as Boserup (1970), Friedl (1975), and Blumberg (1978, 1984) have shown how subsistence tools affect gender stratification in foraging and hoe cultures and in societies whose technology is partly industrial (parts of Latin America and Africa). The following theory of gender stratification—the intersection of family, economy, and gender—is indebted to their analyses and to other work that has become so much a part of my own thinking that I cannot identify the sources.

The theory focuses on foraging, hoe, plow, herding, and industrial societies. It rests on three propositions. The first one, micro level, applies to the family. Those who produce goods tend to have more power and prestige than those who consume them. It is better to be able to give than to have to receive.

The second proposition responds to a macro-level question. What determines which sex does the most productive work? Men and women can do many kinds of work, yet in all societies most tasks are allocated by sex. However, one sex cannot perform two tasks central to group survival: No man can bear or nurse a child. This suggests a second principle: The tasks that best mesh with child rearing tend to be assigned to women. Subsistence work varies in its compatibility with child rearing. Some tasks mesh so badly that women almost never do them, for example, military service. From the perspective of population replacement, men are more expendable. Preindustrial birth rates (especially in hoe and plow societies) had to be high to match the wastage of high death rates. Also, warfare meshes poorly with child rearing. But this proposition does not imply that modes of child rearing determine the work women do. Following Friedl (1975) and Blumberg (1984), it seems far more likely that women's tasks shape modes of child rearing. The lower the level of living, the more women must perform certain tasks no matter what the effects on children.

History provides grim examples. In the early years of French industrialization high rents and low wages pressured working-class wives
into paid work in household textile establishments. Infant bottle-
feeding was unsafe, but the masters wanted no nurslings around—they
decreased output. However, a surplus of country women coupled with
a high infant death rate made wet nurses available, so many babies were
sent out to nurse—only the rich could afford a live-in wet nurse. Early
in the nineteenth century, the majority of Lyonnais babies were wet-
nursed (Garden, 1975) and nearly all Parisian babies were (Sussman,
1982, p. 183) even though the death rates for wet-nursed babies were
much higher than for mother-nursed babies. The custom ceased when
textile production in small establishments became unprofitable.

The third proposition also holds for general stratification theory. In
any society the most power and prestige accrue to those who control the
distribution of valued goods beyond the family. In foraging societies,
for example, hunters have more power than gatherers. They can distribute a large kill to the entire group. The gatherers, in contrast, can glean
enough food only for the nuclear family.

Together, these principles compose a theory that can explain how
ecological conditions and tool use interacted with childbearing and
suckling to shape gender stratification in five of the most important of
the ten basic types that Lenski (1970) analyzed.

The oldest type was based on hunting and gathering. Throughout
most of our species' history, the entire human population lived in such
societies. This period of relative technological uniformity ended only
within the last 10,000 to 12,000 years (Lenski and Lenski, 1982, p. 87).
Hoe cultures first appeared in the Middle East over 9,000 years ago.
Plow societies appeared about 5,000 years ago, with herding societies
somewhere in between. The most modern type is based on industrial
technology.

In foraging societies the tools consisted of spears, bows and arrows,
digging sticks, and baskets. Such tools yielded a meager food supply
hence these groups were small, averaging fewer than 50 in number. The
level of equality was high; slim pickings flattened the distribution of
power and privilege. Men hunted large animals; women and children
gathered roots, plants, seeds, nuts, berries, insects, and small animals.
Although gathering is usually much more reliable than hunting, a
woman could typically gather enough roots, nuts, berries, and the like
to feed only her immediate family. In contrast, the hunters could distribute a large animal to the entire group. Men therefore tended to have
more power and prestige than women did. Their dominance was greatest when hunting was the main source of food, as in Eskimo societies.

Men and women were more equal when they both contributed to subsistence tasks (Friedl, 1975, p. 32). Polygyny was permitted in most of these societies, but it was rare. Surplus food was too scarce to enable a hunter to supply more than one set of affinal relatives. Divorce was fairly common since it had little effect on the subsistence of either spouse or the children. Premarital sexual relations were usually permitted.

Why did women rarely hunt? They could master the necessary skills. However, the functional requirements of pursuing large game a long distance conflict with those for child rearing. A hunt typically requires an uncertain number of days away from camp. To offset the wastage of a high death rate, women were pregnant or breastfeeding during most of their productive years. Children were breastfed to age four to increase their survival rate. A woman could not carry a nursling on a hunt nor could she readily return to camp to feed it. Thus, the need for population replacement excluded women from the task that yielded the most power and prestige.

What induced a shift to plant cultivation as the basis for subsistence? Lenski and Lenski (1982, p. 135) suggest a new answer. Until the 1960s, it was thought that the benefits of a more advanced technology were obvious to early peoples. During the 1960s and 1970s, many theories stressed gradually increasing population pressure as the factor pushing foragers to increase their food supply via cultivation. But in the last decade new evidence suggests that between 22,000 and 7,000 years ago the number of large animals declined and human diet shifted. In North America, for example, 32 genera of large mammals became extinct, including horses, giant bison, oxen, elephants, camels, and giant rodents. The pattern was similar in Northern Europe, where the woolly mammoth, woolly rhinoceros, steppe bison, and giant elk vanished. People in these areas increasingly relied on fish, crabs, birds, snails, nuts, and wild grains and legumes. The shift may have resulted from striking advances in weapons technology that began 20,000 years ago. The increase in kills of large animals led, in turn, to an increasing human population, which had a feedback effect on the big game kills. In consequence (and perhaps combined with a climate change), large mammals' reproductive rates could no longer match kill rates. According to this new (and still controversial) theory, one species after another was killed off, resulting in food shortages that induced peoples to domesticate whatever plants and animals they could. Despite the extra work, plant cultivation was attractive because it yielded so much more food per unit of land.[1]

Regardless of whether or not population pressure or killing off large animals was more determinative, it is known that simple hoe cultures appeared in the area touched by Eurasia and Africa before 9,000 years ago and probably at still earlier dates in sub-Saharan Africa and the Nile Valley. The major tool, a wooden digging stick, did not dig deeply enough to raise soil nutrients nor eradicate weeds. Consequently, groups had to move every few years to find fertile soil. Subsistence was supplemented by hunting, herding, or gathering in various combinations. Nonetheless, the digging stick produced enough surplus that these groups averaged about 95 persons (Lenski and Lenski, 1982, p. 91). The only such societies that remain today are in Pacific and New World islands.

Advanced hoe cultures appeared about 6,000 years ago when the invention of metallurgy permitted the making of metal tools and weapons, which, in turn, increased the size of the surplus and the size of the societies. They appeared in North and South America (the Mayas, Aztecs, and Incas), Africa, Asia, and Europe. Today almost all remaining ones are in sub-Saharan Africa (Robertson, 1984), where, for the most part, tropical soils are so thin, acidic, and easily leached as to make plow cultivation counterproductive (Blumberg, 1987).

Thus the introduction of the hoe, especially with a metal tip, marked the beginnings of modern social stratification. The hoe enabled people to settle for several years and thus to accumulate more goods. Dwellings became more substantial, settlements grew larger and more dense, and the creation of a stable economic surplus made occupational specialization common which, in turn, increased the level of social inequality. Kinship systems, which represented social security, became extremely complex. Since the use of metal made weapons more effective, for the first time in human history waging war became a profitable alternative to technological innovation as a means of increasing a surplus.

For our purposes the most important aspect of hoe technology is that, under certain structural conditions, women's proportionately high share in food production can translate into higher levels of power and prestige (Blumberg, 1984, p. 29). Tending a garden meshes readily with pregnancy and lactation. Yet there is no simple division of labor with men producing one kind of food and women another and no universal pattern of women producing one type of craft object and men another, except that routine domestic cooking tended to be women's work and metallurgy, men's. Men monopolized land clearing in most simple hoe cultures. In advanced hoe cultures they monopolized waging war (Friedl, 1975, pp. 53-60), which advantaged them over women in the right to distribute valued goods beyond the family.

One would expect women's substantial contribution to food production to improve their status relative to men. Indeed, the data show that the incidence of matrilineality (tracing descent in the mother's line) and matrilocality (newlyweds move in with the wife's family) is greatest in hoe cultures, although such practices occur only in a minority of them. Both practices improve women's status. A bride in her husband's extended kin household suffers depressed status, isolated from her own family and with little access to economic resources and control over even fewer.

Women's contribution to food production also affects the divorce rate. In hoe cultures it tends to be high, higher on average than in the United States today. High divorce rates are more common when dissolving a marriage interferes with the subsistence of neither of the spouses nor their children.

Women's ability to feed their children also permits what we have elsewhere called *populist polygyny* (Huber and Spitze, 1988), as in sub-Saharan Africa. In this type of polygyny nearly everyone marries. The sex ratio problem is solved by women marrying at young ages and men marrying when they are older. A postpartum taboo on sexual relations decreases child mortality by ensuring longer birth intervals. As an appropriation of female labor and sexual gratification by those who by virtue of age, sex, and descent, form the ruling group, it serves male gerontocratic control (Lesthaeghe, 1980, p. 531). However, the need for women's productive work ensures them a measure of freedom of movement.

Herding societies occur where low rainfall, a short season, or mountains preclude growing crops as in Central Asia or the American high plains. The roles, norms, and ideologies of such societies have acquired importance because the Jewish, Christian, and Muslim religions originally developed in herding cultures; their beliefs and rules affect communities all over the world. The need for water and grazing rights made war an important means of acquiring a surplus and enabled elites to control economy and polity. Since warfare and herding both involve absence from home over long periods, they are incompatible with pregnancy and nursing. Women therefore lack access to major tools of food production. These circumstances make it possible to practice elite polygyny—only rich men have plural wives (Huber and Spitze, 1988). In contrast to the freedom of movement enjoyed by sub-Saharan African women, the wives of elite polygynists tend to be secluded if the group is sedentary. Nomad wives have more freedom (Boulding, 1976).

Plow societies are of special importance because they immediately preceded the industrial societies that developed in Europe and Asia. The laws, customs, and beliefs that have governed men's and women's behavior in all of the industrialized societies were therefore directly inherited from those of the plow kingdoms and empires of Eurasia.

The earliest plows were made of wood. After the invention of techniques to smelt iron, which was commonly available, the plow was equipped with an iron blade, making it much more efficient. The effect on the food supply was fantastic. The plow could dig much deeper than the hoe, bringing plant nutrients to the surface and eradicating weeds. It stimulated the domestication of draft animals. In turn, confining oxen in stalls to prevent their wandering away encouraged the collection of manure to fertilize fields, further increasing food production. Eurasian stratification patterns assumed the pyramidal form that characterized feudal societies: a tiny political and economic elite, artisans and craftworkers of lesser rank, and swarms of peasants, serfs, or slaves. The plow's effect on the status of ordinary people was devastating. The presence of a food surplus in the countryside coupled with the availability of iron weapons tempted elites to extract as much as possible from impoverished peasants. The flatter and richer the land, the worse off were the common people, probably much worse off than were their hunting and gathering ancestors (Lenski and Lenski, 1982, p. 206).

For two reasons the plow had an enormous effect on patterns of gender stratification. First, wherever it has been introduced, men tended to monopolize its use. Larger fields much further from home make it hard to arrange work to suit a nursing baby (Blumberg, 1978, p. 50). Women therefore supplied a much lower proportion of food in plow than in hoe cultures (Giele and Smock, 1977). However, the effect of the plow on women's status went well beyond what was implied by women's reduced participation in food production. The basic reason was that the use of the plow required a particular kind of inheritance pattern which, in turn, affected marriage and sexual behavior. Land ownership became the basis for social stratification. The plow makes land the chief form of wealth because its use permits land to be used indefinitely, which increases its value. By contrast, hoe peoples had to move when soil fertility was exhausted.

However, unlike gold and silver trinkets, cowrie beads, or money, land is an inheritance of limited partibility. At a given level of technology, a piece of land can support only a given number of persons. The number of legal heirs must therefore be controlled. The dominant form of marriage must be monogamy because polygyny permits the uncontrolled proliferation of legal heirs. Divorce must become difficult or impossible because serial monogamy regulates the number of legal heirs less efficiently than does lifetime marriage. Women's premarital and marital sexual behavior must be governed by law and custom lest a man's property go to another man's child. Wealthy Eurasian men can in effect practice polygyny by keeping mistresses or concubines whose children have few or no inheritance rights. The concern with women's sexual purity derives from their status as transmitters of male property (Goody, 1976, pp. 15, 97). Engels's insight about the effect of private property on women's status still rings true. Severe constraints governed women's behavior in Asian plow kingdoms. For example, there was footbinding in China except in the irrigated rice areas where women were needed in the fields, and *suttee* (widow-burning) was practiced by certain propertied castes in India. Clitoridectomy occurs in Muslim countries of mixed plow and herding culture and certain African hoe cultures as well. The discussion of each one follows the account in Huber and Spitze (1983).

The Chinese custom of footbinding arose about a thousand years ago, during a period marked by increased control of women's behavior. An emperor was said to have admired a dancer's feet. Loosely bound in linen cloths, they resembled those of a ballerina (Levy, 1966). The rationale for the custom was that the resulting hobbled gait so tightened the muscles in the genital region that sleeping with a woman with bound feet was like sleeping with a virgin. Western physicians report that no evidence supports such a belief. Whatever the rationale, women with bound feet certainly did little running around.

The mother applied the bindings when the little girl was three to five years old, depending on how small a foot was desired. The richer the girl's family, the less work she would have to do, and the smaller the foot could be. Rich women were so crippled that they could not walk at all. The pain resulted primarily from bending the four smaller toes underneath the foot, then successively tightening the bindings until the broken toes atrophied.

The custom was widespread (Gamble, 1943), especially in the colder and drier regions of the north where wheat was the main crop. In the south where rice, a much more labor-intensive crop was the main staple, the entire family was needed to work in the paddies. Early in the industrial period, opposition to the custom increased. Footbinding was outlawed in 1911.

The Hindu custom of *suttee* requires a widow to be burned alive on her husband's funeral pyre. Some widows climbed up willingly; others had to be tied down. The rationalization was that a widow, by sinning in a previous life, caused her husband to die first. Her death also gave the husband's male relatives undisputed influence over the children and precluded her lifetime rights in the estate. The incidence of *suttee* was low compared to that of footbinding since only women of certain propertied castes were at risk.

Clitoridectomy, apparently widespread in Egypt, Yemen, Ethiopia, Somalia, the Sudan, Kenya, and Muslim West Africa (Hosken, 1979; El Saadawi, 1982), shows the importance of protecting a daughter's reputation for chastity (Paige, 1982). It is often called female circumcision, but this is a euphemism because it is like slicing off the glans penis or the entire penis. The operation (extremely painful) was—and still is—practiced on prepubertal girls; its purpose is to prevent sexual pleasure so that women will find it easier to remain chaste. A popular belief held that women, by nature, are so lascivious that chastity is inordinately difficult for them.

The operation takes three forms. In traditional circumcision the clitoral prepuce and tip of the clitoris are removed. In excision, the entire clitoris is removed. Infibulation involves removal of the clitoris, the labia minora, and part of the labia majora. The two sides of the vulva are partially sliced or scraped raw and then sewn together, obliterating the entrance to the vagina except for a tiny posterior opening to allow urine, and, later, menstrual blood, to drain. Primary fatalities result from hemorrhage, shock, and septicemia. Long-term problems include urinary disturbance due to chronic infection and difficulties in coitus and childbirth.

So far as I know, European women during the plow era suffered no restraints comparable to footbinding and suttee. But if not, why not? Recent work of anthropologist Jack Goody (1983) suggests that their greater freedom may have been an unplanned outcome of efforts by the Roman Catholic Church to increase its land (but see Herlihy, 1985, who argues that the Church was trying to distribute women, concentrated in rich households, more equitably). The Church tried to influence inheritance patterns by controlling marriage and the legitimation of children. After 325 A.D., the Church established measures to reduce a person's supply of close relatives to persuade the pious to bequeath their property to the Church. It encouraged celibacy, prohibited close cousin marriage and adoption (both widespread in Biblical and Roman times), condemned polygyny and divorce, and discouraged remarriage. It stressed mutual consent as a requirement for valid marriage, which decreased the incidence of child marriage and reduced chances that a marriage would serve family interests. European women could also avoid marriage altogether by entering the cloister, which tended to increase their control over property. Such measures arguably gave

European women more freedom than South or East Asian women for more than a millenium before the Industrial Revolution. Such freedom should have made European women more able than Asian women to adapt to new circumstances and seize new opportunities. It would be ironic were historians one day to find that the spirit of capitalism in Europe was spurred not so much by the Protestant ethic as by a Catholic ethic that incidentally permitted women a modest measure of control over property.

Industrialization ended the plow era in Europe during the nineteenth century. The primary event was the invention of machines that made cheap cotton cloth. Rapid acceleration in the development of machines that replaced human labor stimulated a train of events that sharply altered the work men and women did. Over time, changes in behavior led to changes in beliefs.

Men's work behavior changed first. The factory system transformed erstwhile peasants, serfs, and slaves into urban wage workers, giving rise to a series of men's movements that voiced the claims of ordinary men for a fair share of a rapidly increasing surplus. These movements represented men's response to the changes that industrialization had wrought in the conditions of their lives. However, historians do not refer to these struggles as the men's movement. Instead, they write about socialist and labor movements that swept nineteenth-century Europe, labels that tend to obscure the fact that women played little part in them. A mass movement that would represent women's occupational claims would appear only after women had entered the labor market in large numbers. This could not occur until after three trends spawned by industrialization had irrevocably altered the conditions of women's lives: the first two, a decrease in mortality and the attainment of widespread literacy preceded the third, a decrease in fertility. The stage is set for a massive increase in the formal labor force participation of married women only if the first three trends are well underway. I briefly explain this process below.

Mortality, primarily of infants, declined in response to improved nutrition, reduced exposure to disease, and (in the twentieth century) to medical measures (Collins, 1982). The mortality decline reduced the average number of births per woman needed to ensure population replacement. Then, after 1910, the invention of sterilization techniques permitted safe bottle feeding; for the first time in history, artificially-fed babies had about the same survival probabilities as babies nursed by their mothers. Population replacement now poses fewer constraints on women's work.

Education was compulsory in most Western countries by 1880. As Caldwell (1980) notes, it restructures family relations by redirecting generational wealth flows and thereby profoundly affects fertility. In preindustrial societies family wealth flowed from children to parents. Mass education redirects these flows by first reducing the child's potential for employment outside the home. Second, it increases the cost of children far beyond the fees that must be paid. Schools place indirect demands on families. The child's appearance must enable him or her to participate equally with other children. Third, schooling speeds cultural change by propagating the values not of local families but of the Western middle classes. The main message of schooling is not spelled out in textbooks; it is assumed. Schools destroy the corporate identity of the family for those members previously the most submissive: children and women (Caldwell, 1980, p. 241). Schooling causes parents to lose control over their children's labor (Lesthaeghe, 1980).

The fertility decline was triggered by the mortality decline, the spread of mass education, and rapid economic growth. The costs of children rose, and their benefits tended to decline. A rapid increase in real income—it doubled in the West between 1860 and 1910—fuels individual aspirations and opens up new opportunities, creating an impression of lowered economic vulnerability. In turn, this allows individuals to be more independent. The net outcome is an alteration in preference maps. Since the new maps require legitimation, periods of economic growth also generate various emancipation movements (Lesthaeghe, 1983, p. 430).

During the demographic transition, fertility declined from more than seven to fewer than three children (United Nations, 1973, p. 63). The methods used required self-discipline and courage: abstinence, withdrawal, or abortion, which had been a major means of fertility control in all industrializing societies until women learned other ways (Mohr, 1978). The decline occurred despite the massive opposition of church and state. When people are motivated to reduce their fertility, they find ways of doing so. From early in the industrial period, women had worked for pay, but the typical worker was either young and unmarried or poor. Young women who expect to be briefly employed are unlikely to be aware of discrimination. Moreover, young women and poor women lack political clout. What matters politically is the participation of educated women who expect to remain in the work force. Such women entered the labor force in ever larger numbers after 1950 in response to strong demand for female labor (Blau and Ferber, 1986) and their rates of participation are still rising (Mott, 1982). Although most women work in heavily feminized occupations (Rytina and Bianchi, 1984), the wage gap is beginning to close. A generation ago most highly educated men were employed; many of their female counterparts were housewives. This pattern is reversing. The higher a woman's level of education, the more likely is she to be employed. From now to the end of the century, young women's wage rates are expected to rise about 15% faster than young men's (Smith and Ward, 1984).

In sum, changes in the work people do has altered the stratification and family systems of plow societies. Declines in mortality and fertility and changes in lactation customs have reduced the time that women spend pregnant or nursing. Increases in educational levels and employment rates enable women to provide sizable shares of family income. These trends have increased the centrality of individual goal attainment in the Western ideational system (Lesthaeghe, 1983, p. 429). Now women, along with men, have been swept into the occupational streams of the industrial revolution. But not quite into the mainstream. Still in question is the extent to which women will hold a fair share of top positions. This will hinge on responsibility for housework and childcare early in a woman's career, a time when most single parents or couples lack resources to command full-time quality care for the daily needs of their children—or themselves. Young executives who care for daily family physical needs cannot compete effectively with those who benefit from that care. Ambitious women can avoid much conflict by remaining childless but that is just the point; ambitious men need not make that choice. Women cannot become men's social equals until the most talented women can aspire as realistically as their male counterparts to contribute in proportion to their talents.

Thus, the triple overlap of family, economy, and gender, reshaped by continuing technological change, continues to affect women's status. Industrialization first turned the cost-benefit ratio of children upside down. Then wives were drawn into the labor force, raising the opportunity cost of their time and thereby the cost of children. Now below-replacement fertility in the West has highlighted the problem of population maintenance. Parenthood may have to be made more attractive by limiting the hours of responsibility, as has happened for medical practice in this century (Keyfitz, 1986, p. 152). Such measures would be expensive. But they would raise women's status in the family and in society in ways that were unimaginable a few decades ago.

Note

1. Still, in Australia, although many large species also died out at this time, cultivation never began. Accordingly, the extent to which the animal deaths were due to human agency or climate change is unclear.

References

Blau, Francine and Marianne Ferber. 1986. *The Economics of Women, Men, and Work.* Englewood Cliffs: Prentice-Hall.

Blumberg, Rae Lesser. 1978. *Stratification: Socioeconomic and Sexual Inequality.* Dubuque: William C. Brown.

———. 1984. "A General Theory of Gender Stratification." In *Sociological Theory* edited by R. Collins. San Francisco: Jossey-Bass.

———. 1987. Personal communication.

Boulding, Elise. 1976. *The Underside of History.* Boulder, CO: Westview.

Bose, Christine and Peter Rossi. 1983. "Gender and Jobs: Prestige Standings of Occupations and Gender." *American Journal of Sociology* 48:316-330.

Boserup, Ester. 1970. *Woman's Role in Economic Development.* London: George Allen & Unwin.

Caldwell, John. 1980. "Mass Education as a Determinant of Fertility Decline Timing." *Population and Development Review* 6:225-256.

Chafetz, Janet Saltzman. 1984. *Sex and Advantage.* Totowa, NJ: Rowman & Allenheld.

Childe, Gordon. 1951. *Man Makes Himself.* New York: Mentor.

Collins, James. 1982. "The Contribution of Modern Medicine to Mortality Decline." *Demography* 19:409-427.

Crompton, Rosemary. 1986. "Women and the 'Service Class.' " In *Gender Stratification* edited by R. Crompton and M. Mann. Oxford: Polity.

Duncan, O. D. 1964. "Social Organization and the Ecosystem." In *Handbook of Modern Sociology* edited by R.E.L. Faris. Chicago: Rand McNally.

El Saadawi, Nawal. 1982. *The Hidden Face of Eve.* Boston: Beacon.

Friedl, Ernestine. 1975. *Women and Men: An Anthropologist's View.* New York: Holt, Rinehart and Winston.

Gamble, Sidney. 1943. "The Disappearance of Footbinding in Tinghsien." *American Journal of Sociology* 49:181-183.

Garden, Maurice. 1975. *Lyon et le Lyonnais au XVIIIe Siècle.* Paris: Flammarion.

Giele, Janet Zollinger and Audrey Chapman Smock. 1977. *Women: Roles and Status in Eight Countries.* New York: John Wiley.

Goldschmidt, Walter. 1959. *Man's Way.* New York: Holt, Rinehart and Winston.

Goody, Jack. 1976. *Production and Reproduction.* Cambridge: Cambridge University Press.

———. 1982. *Cooking, Cuisine, and Class.* Cambridge: Cambridge University Press.

———. 1983. *The Development of Family and Marriage in Europe.* Cambridge: Cambridge University Press.

Harris, Marvin. 1979. *Cultural Materialism.* New York: Random House.

Herlihy, David. 1985. *Medieval Households.* Cambridge, MA: Harvard University Press.

Hosken, Fran. 1979. *The Hosken Report.* Lexington, MA: Women's Network News.

Huber, Joan. 1986. "Trends in Gender Stratification, 1970-1985." *Sociological Forum* 1:476-495.

Huber, Joan and Glenna Spitze. 1983. *Sex Stratification*. New York: Academic Press.

———. 1988. "Family Sociology." In *The Revised Handbook of Sociology* edited by Neil Smelser. Newbury Park, CA: Sage.

Keyfitz, Nathan. 1986. "The Family That Does Not Reproduce Itself." Pp. 139-154 in *Below-Replacement Fertility in Industrial Societies,* edited by Kingsley Davis, Michael Bernstam, and Rita Ricardo-Campbell. Supplement to *Population and Development Review,* 12.

Lenski, Gerhard. 1966. *Power and Privilege.* New York: McGraw-Hill.

———. 1970. *Human Societies.* New York: McGraw-Hill.

Lenski, Gerhard and Jean Lenski. 1982. *Human Societies* (4th ed.). New York: McGraw-Hill.

Lesthaeghe, Ron. 1980. "On the Social Control of Reproduction." *Population and Development Review* 6:527-548.

———. 1983. "A Century of Demographic and Cultural Change in Western Europe." *Population and Development Review* 9:411-435.

Levy, Howard. 1966. *Chinese Footbinding.* New York: Walton Rawls.

Mohr, James. 1978. *Abortion in America.* New York: Oxford University Press.

Mott, Frank, ed. 1982. *The Employment Revolution.* Cambridge: MIT Press.

Paige, Karen. 1982. "Patterns of Excision and Excision Rationale in Egypt." University of California at Davis. Mimeograph.

Robertson, Claire C. 1984. *Sharing the Same Bowl: A History of Women and Class in Accra, Ghana.* Bloomington: Indiana University Press.

Rytina, Nancy and Suzanne Bianchi. 1984. "Occupational Reclassification and Changes in Distribution by Gender." *Monthly Labor Review* 107:11-17.

Smith, James P. and Michael Ward. 1984. *Women's Wages and Work in the Twentieth Century.* Santa Monica: Rand Corporation.

Sussman, George, 1982. *Selling Mothers' Milk: The Wet-Nursing Business in France 1715-1914.* Urbana: University of Illinois Press.

United Nations. 1973. *The Determinants and Consequences of Population Trends. Population Studies 50.* New York: United Nations Department of Economic and Social Affairs.

2

Women and Men in the Class Structure

RANDALL COLLINS

Everyone, both male and female, has some sort of relationship to the systems of economy, family, and gender. But males and females are not related to these systems in the same way. Consider the question: What is the social class position of women? If we take class narrowly to mean one's position in relation to the means of economic production, we come immediately to certain problems. For the once-large (but now diminishing) group of women who are full-time housewives, this approach can lead us to place women in the realm of consumption rather than production and thus to assimilate them to the class position of their husbands. If we reconceptualize housework as itself a form of economic production, we raise the possibility of women having their own class position independent of their husbands; but this leaves the problem of explaining why women so seldom see their class position in this light. Similarly, in dual-income families it has been conventional to conceptually subordinate the class position of women's jobs to those of their husbands. Rejecting this we can, in principle, conceive of mixed-class marriages (in fact, a very large proportion of dual-income families); but again we must ask why this apparent objective situation does not correspond to people's subjective experience. The older sociology that reduced women to the class position of their husbands seems conceptually wrong, yet it is closer to people's real-life consciousness than the revisionist positions.

I suggest a solution in the form of a two-dimensional theory of stratification. There are two dimensions of social hierarchy: class and status. I use a conflict theory of the class dimension as organizational power position (*order givers* versus *order takers*); and I stress that status is itself not merely given by the cultural order but is produced by the *material means of cultural production.*

Women's stratification position in these dimensions is generally much more complex than that of men. When women have paid employment, their jobs frequently are in an anomalous, seemingly middle-class sector; but by the criterion of order giving and order taking, most of these women are actually "white-collar working class." The class dimension, though, is usually papered over by a strong admixture of status display—what I call "Goffmanian labor"—within the job itself. At home, the relations of husbands and housewives (as well as of parents and children) can be analyzed again using the class criterion of order givers and order takers; below we shall see that the "domestic class position" of women is heavily overlaid by work in the area of status production (more than economic reproduction) for the family. More generally, when we consider the organization of cultural production in relation to the economic and occupational structure of the entire society, we find that women frequently are involved in the production and consumption of culture, whereas men are more concentrated in the realm of material production and its power relations. It is because men and women are located across the grid of class structure in these different ways that they experience life in gender-distinctive patterns.

Women's Jobs

The classic position that assimilates the class position of women to that of their fathers and husbands implies that women will share their respective life-styles, that is, male class cultures. But is this empirically so?

We can give no definitive answer as most studies of class cultures have focused on men. But what evidence there is suggests a distinctive cultural style for such typically female jobs as secretaries (Kanter, 1977). One can, of course, argue that married couples, even if they have two incomes, are dominated by the male class culture as males usually have larger incomes; this is all the more true if the male is the only breadwinner (Lockwood, 1986). But this seems unsatisfactory as it assumes life-style is merely a function of income level; although this is one factor, occupational experience itself is a crucial influence on attitudes and behaviors (Kohn, 1971, 1977; Collins, 1975, pp. 56-81; Kohn and Schooler, 1983). Dual-income families, then, may well be in a clash of class cultures, deriving from male and female jobs. The result may be a compromise or a blend of cultures as well as latent or even overt class-cultural antagonism.[1]

Unmarried or divorced women who do not live with their fathers (a group that makes up at least 11% of the female population: Statistical Abstract of the United States, 1984, Table 58) also are likely to acquire a cultural outlook from their own circumstances. In all cases, it is foolish to assume males are directly affected by class conditions where they work, but women are affected only indirectly via their male relatives.

Female White-Collar Working Class

It has frequently been noted that women are more middle class than men. Many blue-collar, male, manual workers are married to women who hold white-collar jobs: secretaries, office clerks, bookkeepers, sales clerks, nurses, and schoolteachers. (These occupations make up 48% of the female labor force: Statistical Abstract, 1984, Tables 692-693.) Hence working-class males (whose wives are more likely to work than wives of middle-class males) are particularly likely to cross the class lines in the social contacts within their own homes (Halle, 1984).

But this picture of mixed-class marriages is incorrect. The fallacy is to assume that white-collar work cannot be working class. If we use the Dahrendorfian criterion of organizational power levels, however, the crucial dividing line is between persons who give orders and those who take orders in an organization. There is considerable evidence from a variety of sources that this distinction is correlated with a wide range of behavior and attitudes (Collins, 1975, pp. 62-75, 298-299).[2] By this criterion, the most typical female occupations today are *white-collar working class*. Secretaries, clerks, and retail sales positions are order takers, not order givers. Many of them are also manual workers, operators of machines (telephones, photocopiers, typewriters, word processors) within an office setting. Nurses, who conventionally are classified as professionals, nevertheless tend to be clerical workers within a medical setting, and assistants who perform manual work for physicians (although they may sometimes have some order-giver power vis-à-vis patients). Of the most common female occupations, only schoolteachers (5.3% of the female labor force) would be considered genuinely middle class by the criterion of order giving and order taking.

Most of the alleged class inconsistency within working-class males' marriages, then, disappears when we see that most of their wives are of the white-collar working class. (Many others, of course, are blue-collar working-class women: factory workers, janitors and cleaners, food service workers—altogether 33% of the female labor force: Statistical Abstract, 1984, No. 693). On the other hand, this approach introduces an opposite kind of inconsistency into many middle-class males' marriages: Now we see many middle- or even upper-middle-class males are married downward to white-collar working-class women (especially secretaries and other office workers).

This reclassification seems not quite satisfactory from the point of view of cultural consciousness. The *white-collar working class* seems to have a social image and outlook that is somewhat distinctive from the *blue-collar working class*. Halle (1984) reports that male oil refinery workers frequently get into disputes over life-style issues with their wives who are office workers. The men keep up a rough, obscene vocabulary and carousing behavior that is criticized by their wives, who push them toward "respectability" and cultural uplift.

Order Givers and Order Takers

Nevertheless, we do not need a separate theory to explain how occupations create the class cultures of women, distinct from the processes that explain male class cultures. The same variables operate; the main difference is that women are distributed differently in the class structure and, especially, that they tend to experience particular combinations of occupational variables more than men. Although we lack systematic comparative studies of males and male occupational situations and resulting cultural traits, I suggest the following principles of class cultures apply to both:

1.1 The more one gives orders, the more one identifies with the organizational ideals in whose name one justifies the orders, and the more one identifies with one's formal position.

1.2 The more one takes orders, the more one is alienated from organizational ideals, withdraws into informal relationships, is externally conforming to organizational demands, and is concerned with extrinsic rewards (modified from Collins, 1975, pp. 73-74).

These principles summarize research carried out primarily on men. But they are consistent with the picture of women secretaries' attitudes (Kanter, 1977). She describes secretaries as powerless and hence oriented toward personal relationships and outside interests as compared to the workaholic absorption into jobs characteristic of managers pursuing successful careers in the organizational power hierarchy. Kanter shows that it is the job itself rather than gender that makes the difference in attitudes, since males occupying positions of blocked power similarly are alienated from the official sphere and withdraw into the private domain.

Goffmanian Labor

But it would appear that the female white-collar working class is not as alienated from official ideals as is the male blue-collar working class. The latter is cynically critical of their superiors and their pretensions (Halle, 1984), whereas the white-collar working-class women are more concerned about being respectable. I believe this can be explained by a Goffmanian twist to the order-giver/order-taker principles stated above. Many white-collar working-class women are in frontstage jobs. Secretaries frequently are the first persons that outsiders meet in an organization; a high-ranking secretary typically has the job of controlling access to her boss and arranging communications for (usually) him. In other words, they are the first line of Goffmanian organizational self-presentation (Goffman, 1959). Within the organizational structure, women tend to be the specialists in initial impression-management and in backstage access to the order givers. Sales clerks perform this organizational public presentation for retail stores; nurses do it in a medical setting.[3]

The female white-collar working class thus tends to include a great deal of "Goffmanian labor." We might amend principle 1.1 with this:

1.11 The more one works at presenting an organizational frontstage impression, the more one identifies with organizational ideals.

Goffmanian labor results in a tendency to self-indoctrination, self-idealization, and formal manners. The nature of this Goffmanian work prevents the cynicism that is characteristic of the male working class. The latter typically are workers in the ungarnished backstage, and they encounter Goffmanian frontstage mainly when it is used against them by order givers, their own hierarchical superiors. The interest of backstage workers is in puncturing idealizations, since these are used against them in the operation of organizational power; hence the cynicism typical of the male working class and their ritual defamations such as obscene language.

Male blue-collar workers and female white-collar working class thus share cultural traits on the power dimensions (they are both order takers, as in 1.2), but they differ typically on the Goffmanian staging dimension (1.11). This is a class-anchored source of differences in gender cultures.[4]

Housework: Labor Force Reproduction or Status Production?

Housework can be regarded from the Marxian viewpoint as unpaid labor that reproduces the capitalist labor force (Sokoloff, 1980). Wives provide services of cooking, cleaning, and clothing as well as psychological support for male workers; as mothers, women physically and emotionally care for the next generation of workers. The consequences that can be drawn from this argument, however, are not straightforward. One argument is that capitalism depends on the unpaid labor of women. Although they are not involved in market relations and the direct extraction of surplus value, they provide a necessary input without which the costs to capitalists would be much higher. No one, however, has gone so far as to draw the conclusion that the withdrawal of housework services—a housewives' strike—would bring the downfall of capitalism. This seems unrealistic.

The principal inference is political: Women, as housewives, are members of the working class and presumably have an anticapitalist interest. There are two reasons why this conclusion need not follow. One is that women perform the bulk of the housework in socialist societies (Goldberg, 1972) as well as in many precapitalist agrarian societies. The male-dominated organization of household work, sometimes subsumed under the concept of patriarchy, clearly antedates capitalism and can apparently survive beyond it.

Moreover, even within the Marxian framework, one may argue that the household reproduction of labor divides women from men. The male, as worker in a capitalist enterprise, sells his labor power, to which the capitalist adds capital inputs of raw materials and tools, to produce goods and profits. The worker in turn brings home his pay, which enables him to play the role of capitalist *within his own household*. His pay constitutes that with which to buy raw materials of household production: uncooked food, clothes and household furnishings that require cleaning, and implements for housework. The housewife, providing nothing but her labor power, transforms these inputs of household capital into consumable goods: edible food, usable clothing and bedding, a livable home. Thus there are two distinct class struggles: male workers versus capitalists in the external economy and housewives versus husband-capitalists in the domestic economy. Women, as housewives, would have to fight a second revolution, even in a socialist setting. Note, though, that women in this model have a consistent class position, whereas men have a *mixed* class position: workers in one sphere, capitalists in the other. Men, then, might be expected to be politically more conservative or at least cross-pressured.[5]

Surplus Domestic Labor

The strictly economic interpretation of housework is inadequate. There is evidence that much of the household labor is in excess of what is necessary to reproduce the labor force. American full-time housewives report an average of 38-55 hours of housework per week (the higher figure if they have children: Davidson and Gordon, 1979, p. 42). British housewives report even longer hours: 77 hours per week (Oakley, 1974). One might be suspicious of what is being implied here about necessary labor. The latter figure for the British housewives is 11 hours per day, every day of the week. One British housewife reported 105 hours per week, that is, 15 hours a day, leaving little time except for sleep! Housewives who are employed outside the home, however, reduce their housework to about 26 hours a week (Davidson and Gordon, 1979, p. 42). Since the hours their husbands help with housework does not increase substantially when their wives are employed (Berk, 1985, p. 64; Davidson and Gordon, 1979, pp. 43-44), we can infer the 26 hours that employed housewives put in is an approximation to the economically necessary time. The remainder—of 55, 77, or even 105 hours per week—is *surplus domestic labor.* I will discuss its meaning presently.

Another piece of evidence comes from historical trends. The amount of time American housewives spent in housework did not decline during the twentieth century, but actually increased (Vanek, 1974; Cowan, 1983). In the 1920s, American housewives did about 52 hours per week; in the 1960s, the figure rose to 55 hours. The introduction of household appliances (washing machines to replace hand laundering; automatic dryers to replace hanging clothes on lines; dishwashers; vacuum cleaners, and so forth) did not reduce labor time; instead it seems to have raised standards, so that more time was spent on clothes, food, and cleanliness. Again we see surplus domestic labor being generated as more time and resources become available.

A third piece of evidence concerns class differences. Working-class, full-time housewives appear to spend more time on housework than their middle- and upper-middle class counterparts (Rainwater, Coleman, and Handel, 1962; Komarovsky, 1962; Lopata, 1971). This is not merely a matter of higher classes putting off their housework on hired help, since there is only one domestic service worker per 88 American households (Statistical Abstract, 1987, No. 55 and No. 657). Rather, it appears that working-class housewives have often been obsessed with cleanliness of their homes and with the housework role generally. This was apparent in studies made during the 1940s and 1950s (Rainwater, Coleman, and Handel, 1962; Komarovsky, 1962), the period in which the familistic ideal was at its highest. The move to the suburbs at that time was primarily a working-class phenomenon (Berger, 1960; Gans, 1967). Economic growth had reached the level when, for the first time in history, many working-class families could leave urban tenements and acquire single-family dwellings in the country-style settings that had previously been a mark of the middle class (and before that, of the upper class with their country estates).[6] In many ways, of course, working-class suburban life generally continued the traits of working culture (Berger, 1960; Gans, 1967; Rubin, 1976). However, suburban residence represented a claim for middle-class status style at least in the realm of consumption—the very possession of a single-family dwelling (Halle, 1984).

From the point of view of upper-middle class observers, including most of the literary elite, this culture appeared only as a dilution of inward-oriented, cultivated aesthetic and moral values of their own class tradition and the ascendancy of gross materialism and conformity. Commentators like Riesman (1950) and Whyte (1956) assumed it was a change in middle-class culture, deteriorated by suburban mentality, and missed the extent to which what they witnessed was the appearance of working-class culture in ostensibly middle-class settings. Working-class culture in general emphasizes group conformity, localism, and a reified attitude toward cultural objects (Collins, 1975, pp. 75-77). I suggest that this "consumerism," moreover, is not so much material-istic and self-centered, as a striving to live up to the dominant status ideals of the higher social classes. There is a characteristic irony here: The differences in class cultures remain precisely in the structure of this emulation. The working-class outlook fixes on externals, reifies status symbols and takes them literally, as if they were Durkheimian sacred objects worshipped with primitive faith. The upper-middle class, with its more abstract and reflexive consciousness, is concerned largely with the aesthetic dimensions of consumption (Bourdieu, 1984). The higher classes, moreover, observing the cultural style of the classes below them, engage in reflexive role distancing that reestablishes their supe-riority to those who have a less sophisticated view of cultural symbols.

It is the working-class housewife, above all, who operates most literally in this realm of symbolic status emulation—that is, who tends to identify status with the appearance of the household itself. For this reason, working-class housewives tend to spend much more time in housework than their middle-class counterparts. There are several complexities here. One is the attitude of women toward paid employment. For upper-middle class women, a career has recently become an ideal of feminist liberation. For working-class/lower-middle-class women, however, their family tradition has usually meant that women generally worked out of dire necessity, and the standard of middle-class status appeared to be *not* to be employed but to be a full-time housewife. Although working-class women are more likely to be employed than their middle-class counterparts, to some extent this split apparently still exists in the greater antifeminism and attachment to "traditional" familism found among working-class women.[7] As is usual, the working class pursues the status ideals of an earlier epoch that come within their means only generations later; but, by this time, the higher social class has moved on to a new (and often contradictory) status ideal.

The other major source of class differences in housework comes from the fact that nonemployed women of middle, upper-middle, and, above all, upper classes do most of their work in the realm of status production outside the home. The higher the social class, the more likely wives are to belong to clubs and organizations (Lopata, 1971). Here, again, we see the greater cosmopolitanism of the upper classes. The localism of the working class is manifested in the status realm as well as in working-class housewives' focus on housework itself.

Realms of Status Production

My general argument, then, is that housewives' activities are primarily in the realm of status production (see also Papanek, 1979, 1985). An equivalent expression would be "Goffmanian status presentation in the private sphere." In our society, it is largely women who perform the Weberian task of transforming class into status group membership. This status production is done in a number of realms.

Household Status Presentation

This is the home as a Goffmanian product, which includes the cleanliness of the house, the style and orderliness of its furnishings, and the presentation of food. Not surprisingly, there are class differences in the styles in which this is done (Laumann and House, 1970; Bourdieu, 1984). The working-class emphasis is on orderliness and (when possible) material opulence, and its aesthetics are blatant colors and artistic sentimentality. These are straightforward claims for status attention, whereas cosmopolitan upper-middle classes value more subtly symbolic presentations.[8]

Another class difference is that in the working class, women are more exclusively in charge of status display. Working-class males are less likely to concern themselves with how the housework is done and with entertaining guests "respectably," preferring the crude and hearty informalities of male carousing as a form of relaxation. This conflict between female "respectability" and male informality or even cynicism is one of the chronic sources of disputes in working-class families (Halle, 1984). In upper-middle class families, on the other hand, males are themselves highly cosmopolitan and oriented toward entertaining their business and professional acquaintances (Kanter, 1977). For this reason, upper-middle-class males take more of an interest in the aesthetic display of the home. Such "female" realms as cooking may even become male realms on formal occasions, when high-status males become involved in cooking or at least in the choice and presentation of dishes.

Cooking is the most ceremonial form of household work (Douglas, 1982). The presentation of food to outside guests is a Goffmanian ritual par excellence. Any meal eaten collectively has the characteristic of a ritual: It assembles a group, focuses attention on a common activity, and ceremonially marks the boundary between members and nonmembers. The formalities and customs of a meal, though often taken for granted, nevertheless have a symbolic significance as signs of "proper" group behavior. This includes the placement of dishes and silverware on the table, the custom of beginning and ending eating together, as well as more explicit formalities that are sometimes found (perhaps only on special occasions), such as saying grace, carving the meat, offering toasts, or presenting a birthday cake. Frequently, ritual praises of the food and compliments to the cook are expected and given.

If rituals create a sense of group solidarity and personal identity, this is particularly so for the person who is in charge of the ritual. This is one reason, I suggest, why housewives tend to identify with their role; and it explains why cooking is their favorite form of housework (Davidson and Gordon, 1979, p. 42).[9]

On the other hand, the value of meals as ritual occasions makes them a possible source of conflict. Numerous family disputes break out, usually between mother (sometimes also father) and children, over the issue of getting children to come to the table on time, to eat their food, and generally to "behave themselves properly." These disputes cannot be understood as merely utilitarian matters. There is usually no reason of efficiency why family members have to eat their food at exactly the same time, and the nutritional value of children eating all their food is probably overrated. Instead, these are ceremonial issues: Eating together is a sign of solidarity; not eating is a rejection of ritual participation and hence is an affront to the person in charge of the ritual. Housewives thus are engaged in making their children into full ritual members by requiring them to participate in these meal-time rituals (not always with success, of course).

We see here another aspect of the housewife position. There is a stratification within the home between parents and children. The role of mother is a position of power over children (although also involving labor services for their benefit). The mother is in the order-giving class vis-à-vis her children, especially regarding ceremonial aspects of the home and of status presentation vis-à-vis outsiders. The latter includes making sure children present a neat, cleaned-up, and even stylish physical appearance as well as proper moral demeanor to the outside world. As predicted by the principle that giving orders leads to identifying with one's official role (Collins, 1975, p. 73-74), housewives with children are less alienated from their role and more likely to identify with it than housewives without children (Lopata, Miller, and Barnewolt, 1984-1985).[10] This makes yet another complication in the class position of women: The same individual may be order taker in her white-collar working-class employment, and order giver as well as ritual leader within the home in relation to her children, and sometimes even in relation to her husband. And even if she does not dominate the domestic ritual sphere without opposition from her children (or husband), she takes part in a domestic "class conflict" as representative of the ritually official class.

Female Work in the Nonhousehold Status-Production Sector

Women's paid employment is also heavily concentrated within the status-production sector. Let us look analytically at the nature of this sector in relation to class structure (see Figure 2.1). Class positions directly generate certain attitudes and habits. These are *indigenously produced class cultures,* ways of thinking and behaving that are developed by experiences as order givers and order takers and by being members of cosmopolitan or localistic occupational networks. More elaborate forms of culture are produced by specialized organizations

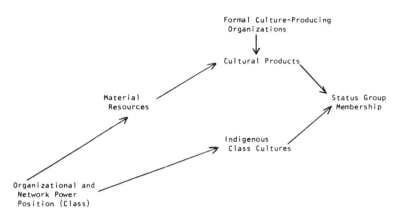

Figure 2.1. Class, Culture, and Status Production

(Collins, 1979, pp. 60-71). This *formally produced culture* requires a material input, specialized labor, and sometimes long periods of training on the part of consumers. Culture-producing organizations include all those involved in producing styles, art objects, musical and dramatic entertainments, and literature as well as general training in tastes such as those provided by schools and museums.[11]

Class positions provides individuals with some of the resources for access into the cultural production sector: above all, the money with which to consume these products, but also access to these markets through networks of personal and organizational connection. In addition, indigenous class cultures predispose individuals to consume particular kinds of formally produced culture. Formally produced culture is stratifying, but it does not merely reflect the class hierarchy, for several reasons.

1. Culture is materially produced; hence money (or similar material resources) is necessary if individuals are to acquire particular kinds of formal culture. But cultural tastes build up over extended periods of time. It is this *time lag in the production of cultural tastes* that decouples culture from immediately expressing class position. This is the reason why long-standing elites typically look down on the "nouveau riche" who don't know the tasteful ways of spending money. The "high arts" and "sophisticated tastes" are not marked by an intrinsic quality, but they are not arbitrary. They are those styles that are produced by the specialized professionals of the formal culture-producing sector. Members of the higher classes can build up their sophisticated tastes and pay attention to subtleties and esoteric references to previous high-cultural

developments because they have had long years of training as consumers of art, entertainment, and everyday styles, often by years of education devoted to acquiring those tastes, and still further, by the indirect transmission of such tastes by personal association with family members and sociable acquaintances who have undergone years of previous cultural training.

2. The larger the specialized institutions within the culture-producing sector, the more this sector develops its own internal organizational structure. A specialized class of persons make their occupations as culture-producers: artists, teachers, actors, designers, publishers, and all the ancillary personnel connected with them. People who work in this sector have an especially easy access to consuming formal culture and to acquiring the most "sophisticated" tastes—that is, those that are historically latest, built upon the longest accumulation of organizational development within the culture-producing sector. This enables them to short-circuit the loop between class and culture. Their class position may be more modest than their cultural level, because they work where the culture is produced, and so to speak, pilfer it for themselves in the process of purveying it to others. This explains why the audiences for the "high arts" (classical music, "serious" drama, museum-going, and so forth) are disproportionately composed of educators and other professionals in these cultural fields (DiMaggio and Useem, 1978).

The historical trend in modern societies has been for individuals to place more and more emphasis upon status production. Once the basic physical necessities and creature comforts became widely available, most people invested their surplus money and time in cultural goods. These goods cover a wide range. At one end are physical objects of everyday life, permeated with status symbolism (such as clothing styles, home furnishings, and cuisine); at the other end are activities like experiencing literature and art. But the crucial distinction is not physical versus nonphysical; there is always a material input into the allegedly etherealized "high arts," and the cultural aspect of everyday physical objects is the style of their appearance. As indicated above, the working class tends to reify their status symbols, to take material objects as directly embodying their status value. Members of the cosmopolitan higher classes emphasize the immaterial qualities, the nature of the tastes themselves and the aesthetic qualities for which the material object is a vehicle. It is only an ideology of the higher classes that identifies "culture" entirely with the immaterial side and that fails to recognize the symbolic aspect of the "materialism" of popular culture.

Women are disproportionately involved in this culture-production sector. As housewives, their role has increasingly shifted from the production of domestic necessities to the consumption of cultural objects for the home: that is, they convert money and time into appropriating products from the culture-producing sector. As we have seen, this takes place in different ways in different social classes. Women's paid employment also tends to be concentrated in the culture-production sector itself. This takes place in several ways.

1. Some women are directly involved in the most professional and self-consciously aesthetic levels of culture-production: as artists, writers, actresses, and performers. The great desirability of such occupations explains why they attract so many career aspirants, so much so that competition for paying jobs is always high. Hence only a few top artistic professionals may command great prestige and high incomes; the average economic return may be very low or even negative (Becker, 1982). We have no systematic studies of how many individuals have ever trained themselves in acting or music, have written unpublished literature, have painted, sculpted, or otherwise attempted to enter a "creative" field. I would guess that a considerable proportion of the wives of upper-middle-class men, women who are not employed in some salaried occupation, pursue careers as artists of various sorts. Frequently, the expenditure (e.g., for art supplies) is greater than the professional income; but this material expense is balanced by the subjective status of working in the core sector of cultural production itself.

2. The largest paid employment of women in the professions is in teaching. This too is largely cultural production, in the sense that the main payoffs of education are cultural sensibilities and "cultural capital" in general (DiMaggio and Mohr, 1985). It is true that the mass bureaucratized educational system has resulted in an empty formalization of schooling, where grades and degrees have become a purely external credential (Collins, 1979), and the "inner" cultural meaning of education has diminished for most students. Nevertheless, the social identity of teachers still carries some of the subjective prestige of participating in the culture-production sector, and it motivates teachers themselves to consume the aesthetic rather than the reified material aspects of culture.

3. Aesthetic values are embodied in styles of physical objects, and these are sold in a series of markets specialized by their proximity to the core culture-production sector (see Douglas, 1979). At the most aesthetic end are contemporary art galleries; at a level closer to "everyday consumption" we find antiques and artistic furnishings as well as

clothing permeated with high prestige (i.e., professionally esoteric) style. Women are also prominent in this sector. Again systematic data are lacking, but it appears that women who own businesses are heavily concentrated in little stores which sell art and antiques and in boutiques for stylish clothing.[12] It also seems that the customers of these stores are largely women. A considerable sector of the economy consists of women selling formal-culture-permeated goods to women consumers.

4. Another sector concentrates on producing women's physical demeanor. A considerable proportion of female manual working class works in this area, the so-called "pink-collar" sector of beauticians and hairdressers. This section would include contemporary forms of body-image production such as aerobics and other exercise classes. Again, this is a sphere of cultural production and consumption but related to women's bodies. There is a component of erotic attractiveness in this: Women to some extent are making themselves physically attractive in the sexual market in relation to men. But feminine styles are somewhat autonomous of erotic impression management. There are professional networks and trendsetters within the world of "beauty" who generate their own innovations and competitions. The status dynamic of female appearance may well consist largely of women observing and commenting on each other's hairstyles, cosmetics, and clothes, with very little input from male consumers of these female presentations at all. One might say the realm of culture status production differentiates into branches, each of which can escalate its own competition as long as material resources keep flowing in.

We should note that in virtually all of the sectors of formal culture-production and distribution there are also male professionals. Even though women may numerically predominate, men tend to occupy the top positions: as leading artists and directors, as antique appraisers and connoisseurs, and as famous hairstylists. As yet, we have no good explanation from sociological theory as to how and why males dominate even in female culture sectors. A comparative and historical analysis here would be useful in isolating causal conditions.

Volunteer Activities of Middle- and Upper-Class Wives

Finally, we should touch on the cultural activities of wives that do not fall into either the realm of housework or of paid employment. A major difference between wives of working-class men and those of men higher in the class hierarchy is the shorter hours spent in housework by the latter and their greater participation in voluntary organizations such as clubs, civic organizations, and charities. Although many of these often are described as "social clubs," their activities are not merely leisure entertainment. These organizations' official self-definitions usually stress their civic or charitable purposes. Upper-class wives, in particular, spend a great deal of time on boards of charitable organizations in fund-raising (Ostrander, 1984).

The fact that these organizations bring together persons of similar class ranking tends to make them emblems of class status. "Social climbing" typically consists in maneuvering to be invited to charity balls and luncheons with members of the upper class. But participation in charities can also be a more direct form of status production rather than merely a reflection of class. Charities are themselves organizations within the cultural status-production sector. Charity is a ritual activity in the sense described by Mauss (1967). Gifts that are not reciprocated on the material level bring a status return to the giver. Since poorer people cannot recompense the gifts of the wealthy, the latter reap a return in prestige. Charity participation, then, is perhaps the "purest" form of the conversion of wealth into status. There are no physical embodiments at all (such as the objets d'art that exist in the aesthetic side of cultural production). Charity itself cannot be reified into material symbols taken literally as ends in themselves; charity always draws attention to the attitude of the giver rather than the object given. The highest form of the production of status, then, is precisely the nonwork activity that is today most closely identified with the upper class.

Although men tend to dominate the highest positions in charitable organizations, as they dominate elite positions in other formal culture-production sectors, for most families of the higher classes, it is the wives who specialize in this charity-participation role. There is a family division of labor along Weberian lines. Men tend to specialize in the class sector; their wives specialize in converting these male-generated resources of money and leisure time into status. Women do this through their surplus domestic labor as housewives; in the upper-middle class, frequently as aspiring (if unrecognized) artistic culture-producers; often they hold middle-class positions as teachers, or as owners of small businesses retailing culture-laden objects; they are consumers (and sometimes producers) of specifically feminine self-presentations; and (especially in the upper class) they are core participants in the rituals of public altruism.

Conclusion

We can see that the position of women in the stratification system is complex. Insofar as women are employed, their most typical positions are in the "white-collar working class"; they also work in a wider range of positions, from elite down to manual levels, within the formal culture-production sector itself. All these jobs carry a cultural component that orients them more toward the status hierarchy and its upward emulation, rather than toward the class conflicts of order givers versus order takers. The "white-collar working class" of secretaries and clerks does have a number of the attitudes typical of working-class order takers: a privatized rather than official organizational orientation and a tendency to localism rather than cosmopolitanism. But their activities as secretaries frequently have a Goffmanian frontstage quality that tones down class alienation more than in the male working class. Many women, of course, are in unambiguously manual working-class jobs, especially as factory workers and as cleaning service workers. A big sector of female manual service workers, though, are waitresses—a job that has an important Goffmanian frontstage component. Some of these jobs, cocktail waitresses in particular, have roles that emphasize a female erotic image, and hence crosscut the order-taking class role with their sexual marketplace role, another Goffmanian sphere with many complexities of its own.

I have barely touched on this final aspect of male/female stratification: the relations among males and females in the aspect that most explicitly brings them into contact, the erotic sphere. There is no opportunity to go into this topic here at the necessary length. Suffice it to say that, in addition to the class and status differences noted above, males and females are further differentiated socially by their typical styles of operating upon the sexual marketplace. These styles have varied historically, including the group-controlled alliance politics of kinship-structured tribes, the "Victorian" marriage market, and modern individually-negotiated, short-term sexual relations (Collins, 1975, p. 225-54). Generally, males and females have different motivations and styles of negotiating sexual relationships and emphasize different standards of sexual morality. The greater conservatism of women about the symbolic aspects of sexual communication adds a division of male "macho" and sexual carousing versus female "respectability" to the other features that distinguish male and female cultures. As Halle (1984) found in his study of working-class men, these differences in emphasis on respectability play a frequent role in male versus female conflict within the family.

Altogether, the differences between male and female cultures are likely to be greatest in those families where manual working-class males are married to white-collar working-class females. At the highest class level, strong differences may again appear with organization-dominating, upper-class men inhabiting quite different life spheres than their wives, who specialize in culture-production activities. Probably male/female cultural differences are minimized for upper-middle-class men who themselves work in the culture-production sector; their own class positions are already involved in culture-laden activities that match those of their wives whether the latter are employed or not.

If we remove the culture-production sector, however, and concentrate on the fundamental organizations of power and property within our society, one basic pattern stands out: The higher reaches of the core *class* structure are overwhelmingly inhabited by males. It is the culture-production sector, above all, which connects women into the higher reaches of the stratification system. It is the production and consumption of symbols of status that give women virtually all of their autonomous success. Women live subjectively—and objectively as well—much more in the realm of status than in the realm of class.

This might make it seem that women are living mainly in a realm of illusion, a cultural fluff floating over the hard material basis of our society. But the capitalist economy of the twentieth century has increasingly derived its dynamism from the permeation of status symbolism into the material objects of everyday consumption. The promotion of new products is done largely by connecting ordinary objects of physical consumption with recent symbols from the culture-production sector. Since there is continuous competition and innovation among culture producers, this gives a dynamic to the material economy, creating symbolically new products and creating demand for them via status consumption. The activities of women, both in the production and consumption of status culture, may well constitute the feature which keeps modern capitalism alive.[13]

Notes

1. It is also possible that, despite independent inputs from male and female jobs, the home culture is the same for both, because husbands and wives really are anchored in the class structure in the same way: for example, they could both be working class or upper-middle class.

2. Wright (1979), in effect, uses this same distinction, although he interprets it in neo-Marxian terms. Kanter's (1977) criterion of class, open or blocked opportunities to move into organizational power positions, is an equivalent distinction; so is Kohn's (1977)

and Kohn and Schooler's (1983) criterion of autonomous versus supervised jobs. All these sources present evidence that power divisions correlate with important cultural or material differences among occupational members.

3. Not all white-collar female workers have these kinds of Goffmanian duties, however. Research is needed on the actual distribution of secretaries with staging responsibilities and those (such as clerical-pool typists) who are more strictly office machine operators. Similar information is needed for medical settings. We could then test for the differences in class culture hypothesized for "Goffmanian labor."

4. I would expect female blue-collar working class (insofar as they are at the low end of the Goffmanian dimension [1.11], similar to blue-collar males) to have a similarly unidealized, cynical culture. Although working-class women have not been explicitly studied from this angle, the image of the tough-talking "fish wife" fits the expected pattern. However, the Goffmanian dimension also exists in the blue-collar female working class. Waitresses, who are order takers, nevertheless have a degree of Goffmanian frontstaging as part of their jobs, which may move them more toward the "official" and "idealizing" kinds of attitudes. There is an additional complexity in some of these jobs, such as cocktail waitresses in fancy bars, which adds an erotic self-presentation to the rest of her frontstaging duties. But erotic staging between males and females is rife with distrust over potential exploitation; hence this variety of frontstage behavior may result in identifying with the backstage self and alienation from the frontstage. This is another issue in need of research.

5. One might attempt the technical exercise of calculating whether housewives' domestic labor is exploited by their husbands, that is, produces a profit for males in their roles as domestic capitalists. On the face of it, the household seems a stable system, without the tendencies of cyclical growth, unrealized surplus value, falling profit, and crisis schematized in the Marxian model of the economy. However, a version of this dynamic may have existed in some unilineal tribal societies. Lévi-Strauss (1949/1969; Collins, 1981) argued that some families are profit-making "capitalists," so to speak, in tribal marriage markets, because of their investments in risky "long chains" of indirect marriage exchanges. These families become a tribal upper class because of the political power entailed in having many families allied with them through the exchange of women; these families also accumulate material wealth (much of it produced by the activities of women), since marital alliances also bring with them repeated obligations of material gifts. In this system, women may be analyzed as both the medium of exchange (in both political and economic spheres) and the principal labor power. Male lineage heads are decidedly in the role of kinship capitalists. Lévi-Strauss argued that the polarizing tendencies in these particular dynamic marriage markets brought a "kinship revolution" that created an aristocracy and brought tribal society to an end.

6. "Working class" here should probably be taken in the broad sense, to include white-collar working class, both male and female; much of what is called "lower-middle class" underwent the same process of suburbanization and "family-ization" as the manual working class.

7. This familistic lifestyle, however, is of relatively recent historical origin. Domestic servants were the largest category of nonfarm employment as late as 1900 in England (Laslett, 1977, p. 35) and included men as well as women. At least in England, the typical life-cycle pattern of most families included a period of service in another household before the possibility might open up of marriage and setting up one's own household. Much of the movement for democratization, from the time of the French Revolution onwards, was couched in terms, not of the demands of factory workers, but of the desire of household servants to escape from the demeaning status of personal service in a patriarchal household. (See Tocqueville, "How Democracy Affects the Relations of Masters and Servants," 1856/1966.) The growth of the capitalist market economy was

liberating for domestic workers because it opened up employment outside the households of their class superiors. Generally speaking, it liberated virtually all males from domestic service. For women, the change was more complex. In the long run, the middle-class household became defined as one in which a woman did not have to work as a servant elsewhere but presided over her own domestic establishment and did her own housework. This middle-class housewife, in turn, became a status ideal for the working-class women. Even if she did housework, she had made an historical shift from being an order taker to an autonomous worker in the household.

8. This follows from the principle of class culture 2.2: cosmopolitanism leads to abstraction and reflectiveness (Collins, 1975, pp. 75-76).

9. Next favorite is shopping. Their least favorites are washing, cleaning house, doing dishes, and ironing: these are Goffmanian backstage work, which result in frontstage presentations, but ones in which the workers do not get to participate in the frontstage portion of the ritual. It is invisible work, whereas cooking generally culminates with the housewife calling family or guests to the table and presiding there to receive compliments on the results of her stage—(or rather table)—setting. An alternative explanation why cooking is the favorite form of household labor is that it is unalienated labor in the Marxian sense. It is craft work, capable of considerable variety chosen by the worker, who controls her own instruments of production; and its products are for direct consumption. But even here we must depart from a strictly Marxian format, since it is not physical consumption of food that is most satisfying, and especially not merely consuming it oneself, but group consumption in a ritual setting producing solidarity within the family. Moreover, I would hypothesize that the most satisfying form of cooking is for outside guests. Here the cook is producing for a market, but it is a symbolic market of status within the community. Conversely, I would hypothesize that the less ceremonial and collective eating is within a family, the more the cook feels cooking is merely a burden.

10. A related pattern is reported by Schooler et al. (1984): The dimensions of autonomy and complexity of work, which Kohn had demonstrated to influence the mentalities deriving from paid employment, can be applied to housework and have similar effects on the psychological functioning of housewives. In other words, a general theory of class cultures can be applied to situations both within homes and outside of them.

11. Bourdieu (1984) tends to subsume both kinds of culture, indigenously and formally produced, into a general category of "cultural capital," although most of his research focuses on the latter kind. This makes it difficult for his analysis to separate the autonomous aspects of the culture-producing system from the operations of class reproduction.

12. The main distinctiveness of a boutique's products, that enables it to find a market niche not already filled by large chain and department stores, is the emphasis on ultracurrent styles and tastes nearer to the core of the culture-production sector.

13. Here we may find, from the point of view of neo-Weberian economics, an answer to the question posed in note 5, whether there is a dynamic within the "domestic capitalism" of the family. As a strictly Marxian system, the answer appears to be no: Surplus value is not realized, there is no falling rate of profit nor economic crisis in the household. But we have seen a number of elements of dynamism in the material aspects of the status realm. The amount of "surplus domestic labor"—that is, inputs into the production of status-symbolizing objects—has risen as more material resources have become available and as greater material productivity has liberated more time for status-producing activities. The dynamic mechanism involves the greater material resources of the higher classes for creation and consumption of status-giving objects and their emulation by lower classes as their standard of living also rises. Furthermore, one can argue that capitalism would collapse without new products and new markets (see my argument "Weber and Schumpeter: Toward a General Sociology of Capitalism," in

Collins, 1986). The consumption of cultural objects in the household (both in finished form and as raw materials transformed by housewives' labor) may thus be the feature which makes capitalism itself dynamic and on which its continued expansion rests.

References

Becker, Howard S. 1982. *Art Worlds*. Berkeley: University of California Press.

Berger, Bennett. 1960. *Working-Class Suburb*. Berkeley: University of California Press.

Berk, Sarah Fenstermaker. 1985. *The Gender Factory: The Apportionment of Work in American Households*. New York: Plenum.

Bourdieu, Pierre. (1979) 1984. *Distinction. A Social Critique of the Judgement of Taste*. Cambridge, MA: Harvard University Press.

Collins, Randall. 1975. *Conflict Sociology: Toward an Explanatory Science*. New York: Academic Press.

———. 1979. *The Credential Society: An Historical Sociology of Education and Stratification*. New York: Academic Press.

———. 1981. "Lévi-Strauss' Structural History." Pp. 109-132 in *Sociology Since Mid-century: Essays in Theory Cumulation." New York: Academic Press*.

———. 1986. *Weberian Sociological Theory*. New York: Cambridge University Press.

Cowan, Ruth Schwartz. 1983. *More Work for Mother. The Ironies of Household Technology from the Open Hearth to the Microwave*. New York: Basic Books.

Davidson, Laurie and Laura Kramer Gordon. 1979. *The Sociology of Gender*. Chicago: Rand McNally.

DiMaggio, Paul and John Mohr. 1985. "Cultural Capital, Educational Attainment, and Marital Selection." *American Journal of Sociology* 90:1231-1261.

DiMaggio, Paul, and Michael Useem. 1978. "Cultural Democracy in a Period of Cultural Expansion: The Social Composition of Arts Audiences in the United States." *Social Problems* 26:180-197.

Douglas, Mary. 1979. *The World of Goods: Toward an Anthropology of Consumption*. London: Allen Lane.

Douglas, Mary. (ed.). 1982. *Food in the Social Order*. New York: Russell Sage.

Gans, Herbert J. 1967. *The Levittowners*. New York: Random House.

Goffman, Erving. 1959. *The Presentation of Self in Everyday Life*. New York: Doubleday.

Goldberg, Marilyn Power. 1972. "Women in the Soviet Economy." *Review of Radical Political Economies* 4:1-15.

Halle, David. 1984. *America's Working Man: Work, Home, and Politics Among Blue-Collar Property Owners*. Chicago: University of Chicago Press.

Kanter, Rosabeth M. 1977. *Men and Women of the Corporation*. New York: Basic Books.

Kohn, Melvin L. 1971. "Bureaucratic Man: a Portrait and an Interpretation." *American Sociological Review* 36:461-474.

Kohn, Melvin L. 1977. *Class and Conformity*. Chicago: University of Chicago Press.

Kohn, Melvin L. and Carmi L. Schooler. 1983. *Work and Personality*. Norwood, NJ: Ablex.

Komarovsky, Mirra. 1962. *Blue-Collar Marriage*. New York: Random House.

Laslett, Peter. 1977. *Family Life and Illicit Love in Earlier Generations*. Cambridge: Cambridge University Press.

Laumann, Edward O. and James S. House. 1970. "Living Room Styles and Social Attributes: The Patterning of Material Artifacts in a Modern Urban Community." In *The Logic of Social Hierarchies,* edited by Edward O. Laumann, Paul M. Siegel, and Robert W. Hodge. Chicago: Markham.

Lévi-Strauss, Claude. (1949) 1969. *The Elementary Structures of Kinship.* Boston: Beacon.

Locksley, Ann. 1982. "Social Class and Marital Attitudes and Behavior." *Journal of Marriage and the Family* 44:427-440.

Lockwood, David. 1986. "Class, Gender, and Status." In *Gender and Stratification,* edited by Rosemary Crompton and Michael Mann. Cambridge: Polity.

Lopata, Helena Z. 1971. *Occupation: Housewife.* New York: Oxford University Press.

Lopata, Helena Z., Cheryl Allyn Miller, and Debra Barnewolt. 1984-1985. *City Women: Work, Jobs, Occupations, Careers,* 2 Vols. New York: Praeger.

Mauss, Marcel. (1925) 1967. *The Gift.* New York: Norton.

Oakley, Ann. 1974. *The Sociology of Housework.* New York: Pantheon.

Ostrander, Susan A. 1984. *Women of the Upper Class.* Philadelphia: Temple University Press.

Papanek, Hanna. 1979. "Family Status Production: The 'Work' and 'Non-Work' of Women." *Signs* 4(4):775-781.

————. 1985. "Class and Gender in Education—Employment Linkages." *Comparative Education Review* 29(3):317-346.

Rainwater, Lee, R. P. Coleman, and G. Handel. 1962. *Workingman's Wife.* New York: Macfadden.

Riesman, David. 1950. *The Lonely Crowd.* New Haven: Yale University Press.

Rubin, Lillian. 1976. *World of Pain: Life in the Working-Class Family.* New York: Basic Books.

Schooler, Carmi, Joanne Miller, Karen A. Miller, and Carol N. Richtand. 1984. "Work for the Household: Its Nature and Consequences for Husbands and Wives." *American Journal of Sociology* 90:97-124.

Sokoloff, Natalie J. 1980. *Between Money and Love: The Dialectics of Women's Home and Market Work.* New York: Praeger.

Tocqueville, Alexis de. (1856) 1966. "How Democracy Affects the Relations of Masters and Servants." In *Class Status and Power,* 2nd edition, edited by Reinhard Bandix and S. M. Lipset. New York: Free Press.

Vanek, Joann. 1974. "Time Spent in Housework." *Scientific American* 231 (November):116-120.

Whyte, William H. 1956. *The Organization Man.* New York: Doubleday.

Write, Erik Olin. 1979. *Class Structure and Income Determination.* New York: Academic Press.

3

The Gender Division of Labor and the Reproduction of Female Disadvantage
Toward an Integrated Theory

JANET SALTZMAN CHAFETZ

In recent years a variety of theories dealing with gender differences and inequality has been developed in the social and behavioral sciences, primarily by feminist scholars. Regardless of perspective or theoretical emphasis, virtually all have recognized that the family and the economy constitute the central arenas wherein gender stratification is produced and sustained. The diverse theories reflect a substantial array of more general orientations, which often are viewed as conflicting, competing, or incompatible. Theories as different as Marxian, Freudian, symbolic interactionist, exchange, role, ethnomethodology, cognitive development, and learning have all spawned versions and contributed to eclectic theories that address the topic of gender inequality—its causes, maintenance mechanisms, and/or processes of change (see Chafetz, 1988, for a more complete review). There is substantial convergence implicit in many concerning some of the general mechanisms that undergird gender stratification.

The *gender-based division of labor,* by which women are chiefly responsible for child rearing, familial, and domestic tasks regardless of their other work, and men's main responsibilities are to nondomestic tasks in the economy, polity, and other social and cultural institutions, is seen as the root of gender-based power differences. Stated otherwise, the division of labor assigns to women priority for the family and to men priority to economic or other extradomestic roles regardless of

AUTHOR'S NOTE: I would like to thank Helen Rose Ebaugh, A. Gary Dworkin, and Rae Blumberg for their helpful comments on an earlier draft of this chapter.

their other commitments. Because the economy and polity (rather than the family) constitute the central institutions of modern societies, this division of labor, priorities, and responsibilities produces power inequities between the genders. In turn, the greater power that accrues to men results in a variety of other differences and inequities as well as reinforces the gender division of labor.

In this chapter I will develop this assertion into a general theory of how systems of gender stratification are maintained and reproduced. In the process I will integrate insights from a variety of contemporary feminist theories in the social and behavioral sciences, with a special emphasis on sociological theories. I view these different theories not as conflicting but rather as providing one or a few pieces of a puzzle that, when put together, can give us a far more complete picture of gender inequality than that afforded by any one perspective.

The questions that can be posed about systems of gender stratification are several. In this chapter my main goal is to delineate the general mechanisms that perpetuate systems of female disadvantage. Such a theory presupposes gender inequality and does not attempt to address the origins of such systems (see Chafetz, 1984, and 1988, chap. 2, for such discussions). Origin and maintenance mechanisms are not necessarily the same, and understanding one does not, logically, permit generalization to the other. Analysis of the basic mechanisms that sustain gender stratification constitutes an important step in developing viable strategies for change. By identifying the main supports for a system, one hopefully can develop a clearer set of priorities concerning the most fundamental targets of change. However, a theory of maintenance is not a theory of social change; it does not inform us about how change can, could, or does occur.

Most theories that deal with the reproduction of gender systems focus their attention on one of two types of mechanisms. On the one hand, there are theories that stress that during childhood most people become engendered in ways that are defined as socially normative. The result is that in adulthood, their differentially gendered personalities and self-concepts lead men and women to make different *choices*, which in turn result in the perpetuation of the gender labor division and inequality. On the other hand, there are theories that argue that existing structures of gender labor division and inequality *constrain* women's options and relegate them to work roles and behaviors that reinforce superior male power and privilege regardless of the choices women may wish to make. Frequently, a theory of one type recognizes the relevance of the other approach. What is lacking is a *systematic* integration of the two, which also constitutes a goal of this chapter.

Existing theories concerning gender inequality often focus attention on either micro- or macro-level processes, only rarely attempting to systematically articulate the relationships between levels (for some exceptions see Holter, 1970; Blumberg, 1984). By *micro level,* I mean those processes that occur in face-to-face interaction and, in the area of gender, especially those that occur within families. I define *macro level* as a residual category, composed of structures and processes that exist in units that encompass families or other small, primary groups. This level includes units that range from organizations to communities to total societies and also includes broadly accepted social definitions such as ideologies, stereotypes, and social norms. Clearly, families within a given community or society constitute a social institution, deeply intertwined with the macro structures of a society and characterized by common features. The line between micro and macro levels is thus fuzzy at best. Regardless of conceptual imprecision, the point is that there needs to be more systematic attention focused on integrating the processes that occur at the various levels if we are to further our understanding of how systems of gender inequality perpetuate themselves. This constitutes yet one more goal of this chapter.

In summary, I propose in this chapter to delineate the main components, and the relationships between them, of a theory explaining how gender stratification systems maintain and reproduce themselves. I will focus on processes of both constraint and choice and integrate ideas from a variety of theoretical perspectives concerning all levels of social life.

Conceptual Definitions

This chapter focuses on how systems of gender stratification are perpetuated. *Gender stratification* (or its synonyms sex/gender inequality; patriarchy; male dominance; sexism; female disadvantage) "refers to the extent to which societal members are unequal in their access to the scarce values of their society" on the basis of their membership in a gender category (Chafetz, 1984, pp. 4-5). These values include such things as power, material goods, the services of others, prestige-conferring roles, discretionary time, food and medical care, personal autonomy, educational and training opportunities, and safety from physical coercion or assault. The degree of gender stratification in a society refers to the extent to which females are systematically disadvantaged in their access to these values relative to males in their own society who are otherwise their social equals (in social class, race and ethnicity, age, religion, and so forth). Within complex societies, the level of gender inequality may, and probably often does, vary by class or other social stratification variables (Blumberg, 1984). However, in this chapter such variation will not be addressed. Gender stratification serves as a given, not as a variable of the theory, with the exception of one of its components, power.

As mentioned previously, undergirding all systems of gender stratification is a *gender-based division of labor,* by which women are chiefly responsible for different tasks than are men. There is little, if any, disagreement among anthropologists that the earliest form of the division of labor in society, and the most widespread cross-culturally, has been by gender (and age). In most respects, the precise nature of women's and men's work varies cross-culturally, especially across societies that differ in their technological level and primary mode of subsistence. However, there are a few important uniformities. Primary responsibility for the care of infants and young children is everywhere vested in women. The degree to which men participate in this work varies from essentially not at all to a substantial level, but they apparently never constitute the primary, not to mention, exclusive, child care-givers of a society (Sanday, 1981). Women also are chiefly responsible in almost all societies for familial food preparation and usually for other tasks related to the maintenance of the family and domicile, while men's contribution to such work is variable. Men, on the other hand, are virtually always the warriors. They also uniformly participate in the extrafamilial work of the society, in the economy, polity, religious, educational, and other sociocultural institutions (which may not exist as separate institutions in simple societies). Such work may be monopolized by men or shared with women, but the fact of male participation is uniform. Given both the uniformities and differences in the gender division of labor cross-culturally, the following general statement can be made. Societies vary on a continuum from almost complete task segregation, which has women solely responsible for family-centered labor and men for extra-domestic work, to societies where both genders perform work in both spheres, although women are more responsible for family tasks than are men.

The fact that men and women do *different* work is not tantamount to saying that their work is *unequal* in value. In the next section of this chapter I will discuss how the gender division of labor comes to be associated with the unequal ranking and rewarding of tasks and therefore of the genders associated with various tasks. A key variable in this process is power. Two conceptually different but related aspects of power are germane to this theory, which I term *resource* and *definitional.*

Resource power refers to the ability of a person or group to extract compliance, even in the face of resistance, by real or threatened bribery or coercion. Such power is a function of the extent to which the wielder controls resources (including the ability to affect the other's physical safety) that are valuable and otherwise inaccessible, or insufficiently accessible, to the complier. *Definitional power,* which is rooted in resource power, refers to the ability of a person or group to impose values, norms, standards of judgment, and situational definitions on others. By definition, in gender-stratified societies, men possess superior power over women, and indeed there is widespread agreement that in virtually all societies this has been the case. However, the degree of such inequality has been highly variable cross-culturally. Both forms of power can be exercised at the macro levels of social life and at the micro levels of interpersonal interaction.

In stable systems of inequality people often are unaware of power because it is typically legitimated as *authority.* This concept refers to consensus among both super and subordinates concerning the duty of some to comply with the demands and requests of others. Such consensus arises out of a secular or religious ideology (belief system) that justifies the rights, obligations, and rewards of different societal members with reference to some broad principle (e.g., God or nature). A *gender ideology* is one that legitimates male power and justifies male advantage by "explaining" why and how males and females are different and should therefore have different—and typically unequal—rights, obligations, restrictions, and rewards.

Men and women may not differ simply in the labor they perform and the amount of power or authority they are able to exercise. In most societies the genders appear, or are at least thought, to systematically differ in basic personality, cognitive skills and style, motivation, specific task competencies, or any number of other types of personal traits. To the extent that men and women are, on the average, dissimilar in such traits, there exist *gender differences.* Such differences may, however, exist more in the perceptions of societal members than in the reality of men's and women's behaviors and are therefore *gender stereotypes.* Regardless of the extent to which gender differences are real or stereotypical, the contents of socially expected gender differences are expressed in gender norms. *Gender norms* delineate the specific behaviors and personal attributes deemed socially desirable for members of each sex. To the extent that there is general consensus on such norms, lack of conformity is defined as deviance and is stigmatized and sanctioned by other societal members, including social peers and inferiors as well as superiors. In specifying the particulars that constitute masculinity and femininity in a given culture and era, gender norms, like the gender division of labor, pertain conceptually to difference, not inequality. Logically, males and females may be expected to differ in myriad ways—and may in fact do so—without this explaining why male attributes are valued more highly than are female ones. I will argue that power and ideology are crucial mechanisms that translate gender norms and differentiation into female disadvantage.

The Gender Division of Labor and Male Resource Power

My theory of how systems of gender inequality are maintained and reproduced begins with two assumptions: (a) There exists a division of labor by gender, and (b) men have more power than women at the macro level. The first assumption reflects the empirical uniformity mentioned earlier. The second is true by definition. Any system of stratification may be defined as one in which the superior group possesses power over the subordinate, whatever the bases and manifestations of that power may be in particular instances. The issues for this section concern how the gender division of labor continually produces superior male resource power and how this in turn serves to reproduce the division of labor.

Any division of labor requires cooperation and interdependence among people, each of whom is performing only some of that which is necessary to sustain life. Implicit in this assertion is an exchange perspective, by which people specializing in one kind of work swap goods or services (or the equivalent in money) with people performing a different kind of work. Social exchange theorists (e.g., Homans, 1961; Blau, 1964) argue that for relationships to continue over time in a stable fashion, partners must provide for one another approximately equal values. If one partner has access to superior resources needed or desired by the other, something must be offered in return to balance the exchange for stability to be maintained in the relationship. Given unequal resources, the most valuable "something" that can be offered to achieve balance is deference to, or compliance with, the requests of the provider of superior resources (Blau, 1964; Parker and Parker, 1979). To the extent, then, that the gender division of labor results in superior male access to valued resources, females will acquire access primarily by complying with the requests and demands of, or by deferring to, men— which is to say, by granting power or authority to men.

At least since the inception of settled agrarian communities (and certainly in industrial societies) the gender division of labor has placed primary (and often exclusive) access to surplus- or money-generating work in male hands. In turn, surplus commodities (and especially money) are generalized resources that can be exchanged for any number of other valued resources. Women have labored at unpaid subsistence and maintenance tasks primarily within and for the household, and/or have been employed in gender segregated jobs that pay substantially less than men's jobs. For Marxist-feminists such as Sacks (1974), Eisenstein (1979), and especially Vogel (1983) and Hartmann (1984), women's economic dependence on men is the primary basis of patriarchy or male dominance. Other structural theorists as well have asserted this position at least implicitly (e.g., Holter, 1970; Lipman-Blumen, 1976; Blumberg, 1984; Chafetz, 1984).

Recently, Curtis (1986) provided a more subtle analysis of exchange relationships between spouses. He argued that social exchange must be distinguished from a very different kind of exchange: economic. Economic exchange is based on an enforceable agreement between the parties and relies upon trust in impersonal systems of enforcement. It specifies in detail what is to be traded for what, and it does so at the actual time of the transaction. By contrast, social exchange, which consists of gifts and favors, is more implicit; it is not rooted in explicit agreement. It relies "entirely on the debtor's good will at some time in the future" (pp. 175-176). This type of exchange is rooted in trust of the individual. Social exchange sets up a diffuse debt for the recipient that can be called in at any later point. The result is that a person who has accumulated social debts acquires interpersonal power. Social, not economic, exchange is the primary basis of family relations and hence family power structures. Curtis argued that "the smoothest way to convert patriarchal authority into power is to store up debts for the future with lots of gifts to wife and children" (p. 177; see also Bell and Newby, 1976, p. 162). Men can do this because their extrafamilial roles provide them income, social connections, and skills in the use of authority and power, traditionally superior to those of their wives. The dependence that results from social exchange far surpasses that which results from contractual inequality: "The amount of debt incurred in noneconomic exchange, though unspecified, can be infinite in effect" (Curtis, 1986, p. 179). It is not at all clear when such debt has been discharged. By focusing on social exchange, Curtis did not ignore the fundamental importance of gender inequities in economic resources. Rather, he argued that within families, economic exchange becomes social, which has more far-reaching consequences for enhancing male power than would simple, economic exchange. In this way, his approach incorporates that of the many theorists who stress female economic dependence as the root of superior male power.

To the extent that women are economically dependent on their husbands, men accrue superior power at the micro level. This dependence is a function of the gender division of labor. The process which links these phenomena is circular and self-reinforcing. At the micro level, men can use their power to avoid labor they do not wish to perform, namely, most domestic and many forms of child rearing work. As will become apparent later, normally they do not have to exercise power to avoid this work, which is normatively assigned to women. But men's potential exists to avoid most such work regardless of their wives' wishes. Male micro power therefore contributes to maintaining female responsibility for family and domestic tasks regardless of other work women might do. Where women are also active in nondomestic work roles, they therefore face a double workday not faced by married men. In turn, the double day reduces women's ability to compete with men for better-paid jobs thereby reinforcing men's resource and power advantages (Curtis, 1986, p. 180; see also Sacks, 1974 and Hartmann, 1984). Moreover, if they choose, male power at the micro level can be used to keep wives out of the paid labor force altogether or restricted to part-time jobs, thereby also reinforcing their resource and power advantages. Given the burdens of a double workday, women may choose to abandon their labor-force job (the choice of abandoning the domestic not usually being available), which, too, serves to reinforce male micro power. It should be noted that where women do earn money, their husbands' micro power is undermined, but usually not totally eliminated. This results from several factors, not the least of which is the fact that women rarely match or exceed their husbands in the provision of economic resources. Moreover, as Blumberg (1984) argued, male macro power functions to discount the value of economic resources for women as a basis for micro power.

Superior male power at the macro level exists by definition in a gender-stratified society. Such power allows men, as employers, union officials, lawmakers, and other societal gatekeepers, to segregate women into low-paid jobs, restrict their opportunities to acquire skills and credentials needed for better jobs, or even bar them from paid employment altogether. As just explicated, this reinforces male micro power. Absent from the paid labor force, or segregated into low-paying jobs, women as a collectivity tend to lack the resources necessary to challenge male power at the macro level as well. In short, male power at the macro level sustains a gender division of labor that supports male micro power, which, in turn, further reinforces that division of labor and therefore male macro power. The general process linking the gender division of labor to male power is depicted in Figure 3.1.

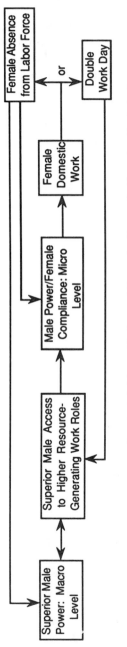

Figure 3.1. Relationship Between the Gender Division of Labor and Resource Power (in Complex Societies)

Definitional Power and the Gender Division of Labor

Religious and secular ideologies, social values, and norms (namely, social definitions) are produced and legitimated primarily by those who occupy elite positions in dominant social institutions. In gender-stratified societies, most elite positions are filled by males, and therefore men comprise the producers and legitimators of societal conceptions of the real, the worthwhile, the proper, true, and good. I am not arguing that men actively conspire in producing such definitions. Rather, because elite members are overwhelmingly male, gender ideology and norms are developed from men's experiences, that is, from a masculine perspective, and are therefore androcentric in content. This is the general position of most Marxist-feminist theories (Sacks, 1974; Eisenstein, 1979; Vogel, 1983; Hartmann, 1984; Bennholdt-Thomsen, 1984) but also of symbolic interactionist theorist Ferguson (1980) and labeling theorist Schur (1984).

Presumably, elite members do not produce ideologies and norms that serve to systematically disadvantage themselves or challenge their own dominance. Quite the contrary, dominant social definitions typically function to preserve, enhance, and legitimate the advantages that accrue to elite members. Of course, social definitions do not arise anew each generation; they are historically rooted. However, historically elite members have also been male. Gender ideologies in gender-stratified societies therefore usually define gender differences as real and immutable—by nature or God's will—and maleness and presumed masculine attributes as superior to femaleness and femininity (Chafetz, 1984, chap. 2). Indeed, some ethnomethdologists suggest that it is ideology that creates the very idea that two (and only two) immutable genders exist, into only one of which all people fit (Kessler and McKenna, 1978). Gender norms in such societies will assign to females behaviors and attributes that are of low social esteem and, more importantly, those that function to reinforce the gender division of labor and male dominance. Conversely, masculine norms will stress traits that are defined as socially valued and those associated with dominance—at least over women—and male segregated work roles. Moreover, the very assignment of a trait or behavior to masculinity enhances its social value, while the converse is true of femininity, given a gender ideology that defines femaleness as inferior to maleness. Within these broad parameters, there is substantial cross-cultural variation in the specific content of gender ideologies and norms.

The existence of a gender ideology and gender norms help to create the third type of social definition discussed earlier: stereotyped expectations concerning the traits and competencies of members of each gender. In turn, such stereotypes reinforce employers' and other societal gatekeepers' tendency to assign work roles according to gender thereby supporting the gender division of labor. Finally, the stereotypes produced in this fashion function to reinforce the gender ideology and norms that are instrumental in their very production. They do this because stereotypes prompt selective perception that screens out disconfirming evidence and concentrates attention on supporting evidence. Women are therefore "seen" as that which they are supposed to be, according to the stereotype. The effects of gender stereotyping and selective perception are mainly confined to women, for whom gender is a master status. Men are more likely to be treated as individuals rather than as representatives of a gender (Schur, 1984, pp. 28-29; see also Kanter, 1977). The general relationships just postulated are depicted in Figure 3.2.

A major component of the social definitional system in contemporary gender-stratified societies defines women, but not men, as first and foremost parents and spouses, whose family obligations take priority over all else. "Therefore, even when engaged in commodity production, the kinds of work they are involved in are established on the basis . . . of an image [stereotype] of women defined in terms of the housewife" (Bennholdt-Thomsen, 1984, p. 254; see also Coser and Rokoff, 1982). The labor force jobs considered appropriate for women often entail nurturance and serve social needs, both of which are devalued and poorly paid. Masculinity is defined in terms of the dominant cultural values of competitiveness, rationality, and domination (Hartmann, 1984, pp. 186-187). Because the economy and polity, not the family, constitute the central institutions of industrial societies, social definitions gear women to grant priority to a peripheral institution while they orient men to the central ones. In more general terms, gender norms discourage an autonomous self-definition for a woman (Ferguson, 1980, p. 155), and, instead, encourage her to define herself by her husband's or male boss's achievements (see also Kanter's discussion of the private secretary, 1977). They are therefore expected to acquiesce and defer to men and to subordinate their needs to those of both their children and men (Haavind, 1984). Male power at both the micro and macro levels is thereby enhanced to the extent that women behave normatively.

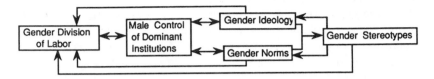

Figure 3.2. Relationship Between the Gender Division of Labor and Macro-Social Definitions

Micro-Definitional Power

I have argued that macro resource power permits male elites to develop and impose upon women social definitions advantageous to their own gender. In turn, gender ideologies, norms, and stereotypes reinforce the gender division of labor and male power at both the micro and macro levels. A number of theorists have suggested that superior resources also permit males to exercise micro definitional power, that is, the power to control and shape conversations and interactions with women and to define situations for women in ways that bolster male power.

From an ethnomethodological perspective, couples produce and sustain the reality of the world and their relationship through conversation (Fishman, 1982). Fishman argued that men exercise their superior power by making women "work" at conversation, with the result that "the definition of what is appropriate and inappropriate conversation becomes the man's choice. What part of the world the interactants orient to, construct, and maintain the reality of, is his choice, not hers" (p. 178; see also Sattel, 1976; Ferguson, 1980). Moreover, interaction work appears natural for women because it is socially required of them. Women who manage to successfully control interactions are negatively sanctioned by others, who label them with pejorative terms (Fishman, 1982, p. 179). By appearing natural, the fact that women actually work in an unreciprocated fashion at supporting men conversationally is obscured, and the maintenance of male-female power relations is hidden as well (p. 180). In a similar manner, West and Zimmerman (1977) argued that men use interruption to display domination over women and to control their behavior, while Mayo and Henley (1981) analyzed the manner in which nonverbal communication between men and women encodes and communicates covert power messages. They, too, stressed that women's traditional stance of adapting to the needs and styles of men functions to reinforce that very power differential (see also Ferguson, 1980). Working from a Weberian perspective, Bell and Newby argued that women are systematically encouraged to define male interpretations as correct interpretations, the result being powerful support for a system of wifely deference. Moreover, for isolated housewives, this process will be especially potent because a husband's interpretations of his wife's situation are often the only ones available to her (pp. 158-159).

In summary, male macro power results in social definitions (gender ideologies, norms, and stereotypes) that support the gender division of labor and reinforce their power and privilege. Women are confronted by social definitions that devalue them as people and encourage behaviors and traits that disadvantage them in terms of their ability to compete with men for resources and power (see especially Schur, 1984). Moreover, at the micro level, men also exercise definitional power, which serves to further reinforce their dominance at that level, while simultaneously obscuring gender inequities. I might add that these definitional processes are typically subtle and relatively unconscious to members of both genders. To this point in the chapter, my emphasis has been upon the *constraints* women face that serve to maintain and reproduce gender stratification. In the next section the central issue focuses upon the more voluntaristic argument that women come to *choose* that which they would probably be constrained to do anyway.

Gender Differentiation and the Division of Labor

If women make choices that function to reproduce their disadvantaged status in a gender-stratified society, their choices must logically be different from the choices made by men. Therefore, gender differentiation of some magnitude must exist. In turn, gender differentiation contributes to the creation and reinforcement of gender stereotypes. Furthermore, to the extent that gender differentiation exists and women choose the labor they perform, the resultant inequities tend to be both legitimated and obscured. They are therefore unlikely to be challenged. Finally, if women choose to do that which men want them to do, superior male power remains a potential; it need not actually be used. Ironically, by not having to use their power, male superiority may be reinforced. This results from two factors. First, individual men may appear to have more power resources than they actually can command. In the absence of a need to employ power, the extent of their real ability to do so remains unknown and may be exaggerated. Second, every exercise of power expends some power resources, which may therefore be less available for subsequent use. In this section processes from three very different theoretical traditions will be discussed that contribute to the production of real differences (on the average) between men and women: gender differentiation as a result of (a) the gender division of labor, (b) socialization, and (c) the structure of infant and early childhood nurturance.

Two approaches that exist in the feminist theoretical literature are often thought to be contradictory or mutually exclusive. One, best represented by the work of Kanter (1977; see also Barron and Norris, 1976; Chafetz, 1984; Schur, 1984, pp. 38-42), argues that the kinds of roles in which adults find themselves produce characteristic behaviors and attitudes. To the extent that men and women perform different work, and fill roles offering differential advancement opportunities, power, and social support, gender differentiation is the result. In turn, the future choices made by women reflect the attributes produced by past roles. Therefore, the power of men to determine role allocation is the power to produce in members of both genders the very attributes that are stereotyped as gender-specific and used as the basis upon which to justify the gender division of labor.

The other approach, which I call *socialization,* argues that from the moment of birth onward, males and females are encouraged and rewarded by parents, peers, schools, the media, and other social influences to learn and conform to the gender norms modeled for them and punished for deviance from them. During childhood, people develop a self-concept, a major component of which is their gender identity. In turn, that gender identity typically incorporates substantial conformity to gender norms (Lever, 1976; Constantinople, 1979; Cahill, 1983). Therefore, by adulthood, men and women are really different in myriad ways that affect their preference for, and selection of specific social roles and work tasks, within and outside the family. Moreover, when interacting with one another, males and females throughout their lives actively seek confirmation of their gender identity by "doing gender," that is, by behaviorally and linguistically conforming to gender norms (Goffman, 1977; Constantinople, 1979; Cahill, 1983; West and Zimmerman, 1987). Because the learning of gender occurs at such an early age and is integrally bound up with the development of a self-concept, theorists in this tradition often suggest that the components of it are quite resistant to change (Holter, 1970, p. 20; Constantinople, 1979). From this perspective, the gender division of labor results from men and women making different choices. In turn, those choices are rooted in different stable traits of personalities, priorities, and competencies that arise from childhood gender socialization. Finally, because same-sex modeling is a basic component of gender socialization, the gender division of labor itself reinforces traditional gender socialization.

I do not think that these two processes, one of which stressed adult role-playing, the other childhood socialization, are as incompatible as they appear. Rebecca, Hefner and Oleshansky (1976; see also Katz, 1979) pointed out that members of both genders learn during childhood socialization the behaviors and attributes normatively appropriate to the other gender as well as those pertaining to their own. However, in seeking confirmation of their gendered identity in interactions with others, people, typically, behaviorally repress those that are deviant for their own gender. This means that the potential behavior repertoire of adults is much broader than the actual behavior of most people most of the time. The socialization process functions to encourage the internalization of gender normative attitudes, behaviors, and self-concepts. However, these are not set in stone. Contextual or situational exigencies produce actual behavior, selected from the repertoire of potential behaviors. Therefore, within broad limits emanating from socialization, which set the outer boundaries of behavior possible for a given individual, it is the actual roles and situations in which men and women find themselves that produce their behaviors and attitudes. In gender-stratified societies, role allocation (that is, the division of labor) and socialization are both likely to reflect gender norms and therefore are likely to be mutually reinforcing of one another in the production of gender differentiation.

A very different approach to the genesis of gender differentiation is to be found in the work of the neo-Freudian feminist theorists, of whom Chodorow (1978) is the chief sociological representative. From this perspective, children don't actively learn to be gendered from ongoing social reinforcement, modeling, punishment, in the manner stressed by the socialization theories. Rather, the fact that boys and girls both have a woman as their primary nurturer during infancy and early childhood automatically results in deeply-rooted, unconscious differences in their personality structures. Because both girls and boys have a woman as their primary love object in infancy, the pre-oedipal and oedipal stage processes by which they establish their independence, heterosexuality, and gender identities will automatically be very different. According to Chodorow (1978), the result for females is that they remain throughout life "preoccupied with issues of symbiosis and primary love without sense of the other person's separateness" (p. 115). It is this preoccupation that ultimately leads women (but not men) to reproduce mothering and prefer the domestic and maternal roles. They spend their lives substantially more preoccupied with relational issues than do males, for whom denial of connectedness is equivalent to denial of femininity. In turn, boys are psychically prepared for participation in "nonrelational spheres" of life such as economic and other public roles. In this way the gender division of labor is reproduced, along with the system of inequality that it undergirds (p. 173).

Chodorow's theory would appear to preclude both of the two previous approaches discussed in this section by making them all but irrelevant. Just as I argued that rather than viewing childhood socialization as casting engendered personalities in steel, so I argue with reference to feminist neo-Freudian theory. I reject the idea that the gender differences produced in the fashion postulated by Chodorow are all-pervasive in their effects and all but immutable (short of individual-level therapeutic intervention, at any rate). If women's mothering in fact functioned in the extreme manner suggested by this theory, not only would change be all but impossible, but substantial variation in the degree of gender differentiation and stratification, both of which have been observed empirically, would be inexplicable (see Chafetz, 1984). Rather, I think a weakened contention may be warranted. On the average, because young children receive almost all of their nurturing from women, females will have a somewhat greater interest in and capacity for relationships than men, and males will be more oriented toward separation and instrumentality than women. As with the socialization argument, this sets the outer boundaries of personality but does not directly cause specific choices made by adults. The gender differences produced in this fashion are typically strengthened in childhood by gender socialization and later by the gender division of labor. What I am suggesting is that in gender-stratified societies the three very different types of dynamics usually work together over the course of the life span to continually reproduce gender differentiation. The relative importance of each is a matter to be decided by systematic empirical testing. This integrated approach is depicted in Figure 3.3.

Conclusion

Figure 3.4 summarizes the main elements of my theory of how systems of gender stratification are sustained and reproduced. It subsumes Figures 3.2 and 3.3. Figure 3.1 is a detailed depiction of the linkages between the gender division of labor and superior male power. The central components of the summary chart are precisely these two variables, which in gender-stratified societies continuously bolster one

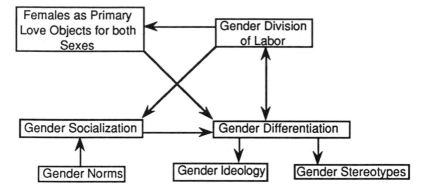

Figure 3.3. Relationship Between the Gender Division of Labor and Gender Differentiation

another. Men can use their power, individually at the micro level and collectively at the macro, to allocate work roles and to create social and interpersonal definitions that justify their superior position, their behavior, and their treatment of females. In this way, they individually and collectively coerce women into behaviors and roles that perpetuate their subordinate status. Yet except for occasional times of women's movement activism, most women do not feel coerced, and most members of both genders do not consciously perceive the system as fundamentally inequitable. Indeed, women are likely to feel that they have chosen the lives they lead as freely as have men. This results from the various processes that contribute to the production of gender differentiation, by which both males and females come to want to behave in gender normative ways.

I am not *blaming the victim* or arguing that women choose their subordinate status. Indeed, my theory suggests that in the absence of gender differentiation and gender-normative choices, women would nonetheless be constrained to perform the work that more powerful men delegate to them. I am arguing that, to the extent women perceive that they choose the roles they play, the system of gender stratification is substantially bolstered because of its apparent legitimacy. Most women do not feel that their domestic and child-rearing responsibilities, and therefore (too frequently today) a heavy double workday, result from male power. Rather, they define them as their natural, God-given, or desired labors. Under such circumstances, male power is only potential: It need not be employed. Likewise, most employed women probably perceive their segregation into clerical, secretarial, teaching, nursing

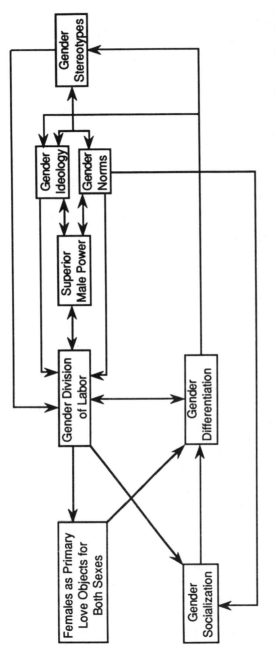

Figure 3.4. Summary of the Main Elements in the Process of the Reproduction of Female Disadvantage in Gender Stratified Societies

and a few other occupations as a function of their own occupational preference. Again, male gatekeepers need not discriminate against women if women choose those jobs that would have been delegated to them.

When, as in the past 20 years, a women's movement alerts some women to the coercive aspects of the process, system legitimacy may be called into question. Nonetheless, the system itself continues to function largely unchanged for the great majority. For instance, after 20 years of legislation and feminist activism, full-time employed women still average only $0.63 for every $1.00 earned by men, largely because most women still work in traditionally female-dominated occupations (Fox and Hesse-Biber, 1984). Moreover, employed wives continue to be responsible for the overwhelming bulk of domestic and child rearing work, with little contribution from their husbands (Huber and Spitze, 1983). Major change in the proportion of women employed outside the home has apparently done little to change the power and status of women as an aggregate category compared to men.

Systems of gender stratification are highly resistant to substantial change toward greater equality. The elements that support such systems are many and varied in their particulars. I have tried to present only the most general types of support mechanisms and to demonstrate the ways they function to continuously bolster and reproduce one another. Such mechanisms exist at all levels, from the intrapsychic to the highest macro social level. They include structural, interactional, and definitional phenomena. They function in all institutional arenas but most centrally in the family and in the economy. Understanding them clearly requires not only multidisciplinary perspectives but the integration of a wide array of very different theoretical traditions. I hope this chapter represents only the beginning of more systematic, integrative efforts.

The focus of this chapter has been on mechanisms that maintain and reproduce gender stratification. Despite my earlier assertion that little aggregate change has occurred recently in the relative power and status of men and women, I believe that many aspects of the gender system are in the process of change in advanced industrial societies such as the United States, especially for younger cohorts. The precise variables (e.g., social definitional, division of labor, power, socialization), levels (micro and/or macro), and extent of such change, as well as the theoretical explanation of why and how such change occurs, are topics that must be deferred to another time.

References

Barron, R. D. and G. M. Norris. 1976. "Sexual Divisions and the Dual Labour Market." Pp. 47-69 in *Dependence and Exploitation in Work and Marriage,* edited by Diana Leonard Barker and Sheila Allen. London: Longman.

Bell, Colin and Howard Newby. 1976. "Husbands and Wives: The Dynamics of the Deferential Dialectic." Pp. 152-168 in *Dependence and Exploitation in Work and Marriage,* edited by Diana Leonard Barker and Sheila Allen. London: Longman.

Bennholdt-Thomsen, Veronika. 1984. "Towards a Theory of the Sexual Division of Labor." Pp. 252-270 in *Households and the World Economy,* edited by Joan Smith, Immanuel Wallerstein, and Hans Dieter Evers. Beverly Hills, CA: Sage.

Blau, Peter M. 1964. *Exchange and Power in Social Life.* New York: John Wiley.

Blumberg, Rae Lesser. 1984. "A General Theory of Gender Stratification." Pp. 23-101 in *Sociological Theory,* edited by Randall Collins. San Francisco: Jossey-Bass.

Cahill, Spencer. 1983."Reexamining the Acquisition of Sex Roles: A Symbolic Interactionist Approach." *Sex Roles* 9(March):1-15.

Chafetz, Janet Saltzman. 1984. *Sex and Advantage: A Comparative, Macro-Structural Theory of Sex Stratification.* Totowa, NJ: Rowman and Allanheld.

———. 1988. *Feminist Sociology: An Overview of Contemporary Theories.* Itasca, IL: F. E. Peacock.

Chodorow, Nancy. 1978. *The Reproduction of Mothering: Psychoanalysis and the Sociology of Gender.* Berkeley, CA: University of California Press.

Constantinople, Anne. 1979. "Sex-Role Acquisition: In Search of the Elephant." *Sex Roles* 5(June):121-133.

Coser, Rose Laub and Gerald Rokoff. 1982. "Women in the Occupational World: Social Disruption and Conflict." Pp. 39-53 in *Women and Work,* edited by R. Kahn-Hut, A Kaplan Daniels, and R. Colvard. New York: Oxford University Press. First published 1971 in *Social Problems* 18(Spring):535-554.

Curtis, Richard. 1986. "Household and Family in Theory on Inequality." *American Sociological Review* 51(April):168-183.

Eisenstein, Zillah. 1979. "Developing a Theory of Capitalist Patriarchy and Socialist Feminism," and "Some Notes on the Relations of Capitalist Patriarchy." Pp. 5-55 in *Capitalist Patriarchy and the Case for Socialist Feminism,* edited by Zillah Eisenstein. New York: Monthly Review Press.

Ferguson, Kathy. 1980. *Self, Society, and Womankind.* Westport, CN: Greenwood.

Fishman, Pamela. 1982. "Interaction: The Work Women Do." Pp. 170-180 in *Women and Work: Problems and Perspectives* edited by R. Kahn-Hut, A. K. Daniels, and R. Colvard. New York: Oxford University Press.

Fox, Mary Frank and Sharlene Hesse-Biber. 1984. *Women at Work.* Palo Alto, CA: Mayfield.

Goffman, Irving. 1977. "The Arrangement Between the Sexes." *Theory and Society* 4(3):301-331.

Haavind, Hanne. 1984. "Love and Power in Marriage." Pp. 136-167 in *Patriarchy in a Welfare Society,* edited by Harriet Holter. Oslo: Universitetsforlaget.

Hartmann, Heidi. 1984."The Unhappy Marriage of Marxism and Feminism: Towards a More Progressive Union." Pp. 172-189 in *Feminist Frameworks: Alternative Theoretical Accounts of the Relations Between Women and Men,* edited by Alison Jaggar and Paula Rothenberg. New York: McGraw-Hill.

Holter, Harriet. 1970. *Sex Roles and Social Structure.* Oslo: Universitetsforlaget.

Homans, George C. 1961. *Social Behavior: Its Elementary Forms.* New York: Harcourt Brace Jovanovich.

Huber, Joan and Glenna Spitze. 1983. *Sex Stratification: Children, Housework, and Jobs.* New York: Academic Press.

Kanter, Rosabeth Moss. 1977. *Men and Women of the Corporation.* New York: Basic Books.

Katz, Phyllis. 1979. "The Development of Female Identity." *Sex Roles* 5(June):155-178.

Kessler, Suzanne and Wendy McKenna. 1978. *Gender: An Ethnomethodological Approach.* New York: John Wiley.

Lever, Janet. 1976. "Sex Differences in the Games Children Play." *Social Problems* 23-4(April):478-487.

Lipman-Blumen, Jean. 1976. "Toward a Homosocial Theory of Sex Roles: An Explanation of the Sex Segregation of Social Institutions." *Signs* 1(Spring):15-31.

Mayo, Clara and Nancy Henley. 1981. "Nonverbal Behavior: Barrier or Agent for Sex Role Change?" Pp. 3-13 in *Gender and Nonverbal Behavior,* edited by Clara Mayo and Nancy Henley. New York: Springer-Verlag.

Parker, Seymour and Hilda Parker. 1979. "The Myth of Male Superiority: Rise and Demise." *American Anthropologist* 81(2):289-309.

Rebecca, Meda, Robert Hefner, and Barbara Oleshansky. 1976. "A Model of Sex-Role Transcendence." Pp. 90-97 in *Beyond Sex-Role Stereotypes: Readings Toward a Psychology of Androgyny,* edited by Alexandra Kaplan and Joan Bean. Boston: Little, Brown.

Sacks, Karen. 1974. "Engels Revisited: Women, the Organization of Production, and Private Property." Pp. 207-222 in *Women, Culture, and Society,* edited by Michelle Zimbalist Rosaldo and Louise Lamphere. Stanford, CA: Stanford University Press.

Sanday, Peggy Reeves. 1981. *Female Power and Male Dominance: On the Origins of Sexual Inequality.* Cambridge: Cambridge University Press.

Sattel, Jack. 1976. "The Inexpressive Male: Tragedy or Sexual Politics." *Journal of Social Problems* 23-24(April):469-477.

Schur, Edwin. 1984. *Labeling Women Deviant: Gender, Stigma, and Social Control.* New York: Random House.

Vogel, Lise. 1983. *Marxism and the Oppression of Women: Toward a Unitary Theory.* New Brunswick, NJ: Rutgers University Press.

West, Candace and Don Zimmerman. 1977. "Women's Place in Everyday Talk: Reflections on Parent-Child Interaction." *Social Problems* 24(June):521-529.

———. 1987. "Doing Gender." *Gender & Society* 1(June):125-151.

Part II

Theories and Data from Third World Peoples

4

Income Under Female Versus Male Control
Hypotheses from a Theory of Gender Stratification and Data from the Third World

RAE LESSER BLUMBERG

The relationships among control of income, marital power, and gender stratification in the capitalist societies of the "First World" raise questions that provide food for academic thought. In contrast, in much of the Third World, especially sub-Saharan Africa, the consequences of their interconnections involving food are not metaphorical but *literal*. Relative male/female control of income and marital power, I propose, affects outcomes that run the gamut from how much food is available to the children in a family to how much food is grown in a country. In much of Africa, in fact, the implications of husbands' versus wives' control of resources may extend all the way to the region's recent food crises.

But the neoclassical economists whose paradigm dominates "mainstream" development policy fail to consider what husband versus wife may control or do *within* the household. In general, their view of the household follows Gary Becker's influential "New Home Economics" model (see, for example, Becker, 1981). This treats the household as a monolithic and unitary entity, for which a single production function is description enough. Accordingly, they see no need to peer inside this "black box" of the household because, according to their paradigm, it doesn't matter who works and who brings in the income. Somehow—

AUTHOR'S NOTE: The helpful comments of Bennett Berger and Mary Freifeld are gratefully acknowledged.

and it doesn't matter if this ideal-type family is a perfect dictatorship or a perfect democracy—resources, work, and information get redistributed in some fashion.

In the views of most sociologists, of course, what goes on within the family does matter, and the phenomenon that the economists would hold constant (i.e., the contents of the "black box") is precisely that which must be studied. In fact, U.S. sociologists have been debating about gender, relative resources, and marital power since Blood and Wolfe (1960). Since then, the marital/family power literature has revolved around each spouse's resources, whether and how many hours the wife works, which spouse is interviewed, and the appropriate measures of household decision making that are used as operationalizations of power (see Safilios-Rothschild, 1970; Gillespie, 1971; Cromwell and Olson, 1975; McDonald, 1980; Blumstein and Schwartz, 1983; Huber and Spitze, 1983; Blumberg and Coleman, 1989; and, for a contrasting view, Kranichfeld, 1987).

Yet, to reiterate, it is the views of the economists that dominate the "mainstream" approach to Third World development. In this article I suggest that serious negative consequences can result from the fact that their paradigm is blind to the possibility that the family has an "internal economy" differentiated primarily along the axes of gender and age. As a first consequence, development planning using the "household as black box model" often undercuts the economic position of women. Based on my gender stratification theory and Third World data, I argue that this can lead to a "ripple effect" of further negative effects extending from the well-being of the women's families, to the well-being of particular development projects, to the well-being of entire regions.

The article is organized as follows: The first part presents hypotheses culled from my general theory of gender stratification (Blumberg, 1984); these also informed our recent paper on marital power in the United States (Blumberg and Coleman, 1989). These hypotheses emphasize the importance of relative male/female control of income and other resources as a major, although not sole, determinant of a wide array of dependent variables ranging from control of one's body to degree of marital power.

Then, in the second part I attempt to make a case that at the micro level of the family, it matters *who* earns, controls, and spends the money. Drawing on recent studies, I show that men and women in much of the Third World have distinct expenditure patterns. Specifically, Third World data are presented to address three issues relating to how women versus men *allocate resources* under their control vis-à-vis family: (a) the proportion of income under their control that they devote to family well-being versus personal expenditures; (b) their propensity to devote resources they control to family (especially children's) nutrition; and (c) women's involvement in exchange/risk-sharing networks with extended kin.

In the third section I examine three micro-level *consequences for women* of having income under their control: (a) effects on the extent of women's say in fertility practices; (b) effects on women's input into household decisions of various types; and (c) effects on women's self-esteem.

In the fourth section I attempt to link micro and macro and give examples from Africa on what happens to agricultural output when planned development projects (which assume the "black box" model of the monolithic household) increase women's labor but reduce their independently controlled returns from that labor.[1] The ultimate impact, I suggest, may include worsening the region's grim food crisis.

The fifth and concluding section reconsiders the U.S. family/marital power debate in the light of the Third World data and hypotheses from my theory presented herein.

Hypotheses from a General Theory of Gender Stratification

Biology is a constant, but gender stratification is a variable. In other words, in all times and places, (a) females (so far) are the ones who give birth to all the babies and lactate, and (b) males have some one-third to one-half more upper body strength. Yet the extent of gender inequality varies from era to era (including phases of individuals' life course), place to place, class to class, and society to society. To be sure, biology plays a role in gender stratification. But none of the main theories of *social* stratification argue that all human societies are ruled by the most aggressive, largest, and physically strongest males. Why then should this be the case for *gender* stratification?

At the same time, although my gender stratification theory stresses economic factors, it is *not* monocausal. I have conducted field work in over a dozen countries around the world. One cannot observe the rich diversity of gender role ideologies, cultural practices, socialization patterns, legal systems, and ways of being among different Third World peoples whose economic development levels are similar and assert that gender stratification is fully explained by economic variables alone. The following summarizes aspects of my theory relevant to the present paper (see Blumberg, 1984, for these hypotheses' rationales and the remainder of the theory).

Selected Hypotheses from a Gender Stratification Theory

1. Relative male/female economic power is the most important of the major independent "power variables"[2] affecting overall gender stratification.

a. Women's relative economic power is conceptualized in terms of degrees of *control* of key economic resources: income, property, and other means of production. In other words, neither mere work in economic activities nor even ownership of economic resources is enough if the person doesn't control them.

b. Furthermore, the degree of control over *surplus* allocation is more important for relative male/female economic power than is the degree of control over resources needed for bare subsistence (i.e., withholding food from hungry children is rarely an option at the micro level).

2. Relative male/female economic power varies—and not always in the same direction—at a variety of "nested" levels ranging through the micro-macro continuum. These levels extend from the male/female dyad, to the household, the community, the class, the ethnic group, the state, and even our world capitalist economy.

3. The macro levels influence the micro levels more than vice versa once they emerge historically. (For example, Khomeini's decrees in Iran drastically restricted women's occupational options, dress, and legal rights. They diminished women's position within the family as well as the larger society.)

4. Furthermore, the more macro levels of the "pyramid of political economy" in stratified societies are highly male-dominated, although the degree varies.

5. Therefore, the extent to which the more macro levels are male-dominated and repressive of females affects how much actual leverage a woman can wield for any given amount of economic resources she controls at the micro level:

a. In other words, the macro levels act as a kind of "discount rate" on the exercise of women's relative economic power at the micro levels.

b. Such discount rates are most often *negative:* Greater relative male control of the macro levels means that economic, political, legal, religious, and ideological factors (including their internalization in gender socialization patterns) act to *nibble away at* the amount of economic power a woman actually can realize from any given amount of micro-level economic resources.[3]

6. The greater women's relative economic power, the greater their control over their own lives.

a. The greater a woman's relative economic power, the greater the likelihood that her *fertility* pattern will reflect her own perceived utilities and preferences (rather than those of her mate, family, state, and so forth).

b. The greater her relative economic power, the greater her control over a variety of other "life options," including marriage, divorce, sexuality, overall household authority, and various types of household decisions.

7. Women's relative economic power rises and falls in different trajectories with different consequences. In general, it falls more rapidly than it rises.

a. On the up side, when a woman's relative economic leverage increases (net of the various macro- and micro-level "discount factors" mentioned above), her self-confidence and sense of self also increase (Kusterer, Estrada de Batres, and Cuxil, 1981; Crandon with Shepard, 1985; Blumberg, 1985, 1989b). Her input into household decision making (domestic, economic, and fertility issues) also tends to grow, albeit slowly and not always smoothly or uniformly. In such times of transition, violence may result if men use their greater power of force to keep women from consolidating a rising economic position (Roldan, 1982, 1988).

b. On the down side, however, a decline in her base of independently controlled resources often portends a quite rapid decrease in her relative power position in household decisions (Blumberg, 1985; 1989a, 1989b, forthcoming-a, forthcoming-b).

In short, there is a whole *chain* of consequences that emerges from a change in the micro-level gender balance of economic power between male and female. One of the most important consequences affects family well-being. As indicated in the following section, a number of studies show that women tend to spend income that flows through their hands differently than men, holding back less for personal use and devoting more to children's nutrition and family welfare.

Differences in Micro-Level Spending of Income Under Male/Female Control

Is Women's Spending More Altruistic?

Do women contribute more of what they earn to family sustenance? Why?

Higher proportionate female contributions in 20 villages in South India. Mencher's purposive-sample study of desperately poor landless farm laborers indicates that: (a) Women's earnings are essential for family survival, and (b):

> Although the amounts contributed by males are sometimes greater than the female contributions in *absolute* terms, the *proportion* of male contributions to male earnings is always much lower than that of females. (Mencher, 1988, p. 113, emphasis added).

Table 4.1 Male/Female Earnings Versus Contributions, Kerala and Tamil Nadu Villages

	Wife Earn.	Cont.	C/E	Husband Earn.	Cont.	C/E	Earned W/H	Contrib. W/H
Kerala								
Cannanore-1	1,138	962	0.85	1,954	1,249	0.64	0.58	0.77
Palghat-1	—	854	—	—	645	—	—	1.31
Palghat-2	1,065	990	0.93	2,039	1,406	0.69	0.52	0.70
Malappuram-1	435	421	0.97	1,219	1,020	0.84	0.36	0.41
Trichur-1	—	467	—	—	377	—	—	1.24
Trichur-2	786	688	0.88	1,787	1,294	0.72	0.44	0.53
Alleppey-1	752	691	0.92	748	569	0.76	1.01	1.21
Alleppey-2	530	438	0.83	743	541	0.73	0.71	0.81
Trivandrum-1	1,027	938	0.91	2,214	943	0.43	0.46	0.99
Trivandrum-2	1,420	1,209	0.85	2,235	1,141	0.51	0.64	1.06
Mean			0.89			0.66	0.59	0.90
Median			0.90			0.70	0.55	0.90
Tamil Nadu								
Chingleput-1	—	301	—	—	155	—	—	1.94
Chingleput-2	—	265	—	—	216	—	—	1.23
South Arcot-1	699	693	0.99	1,449	1,226	0.85	0.48	0.57
South Arcot-2	587	566	0.96	935	667	0.71	0.63	0.85
Thanjavur-1	—	468	—	—	490	—	—	0.96
Thanjavur-2	759	756	1.00	1,247	901	0.72	0.61	0.84
Tirunelveli-1	1,173	1,099	0.94	1,653	1,478	0.91	0.71	0.74
Madurai-1	564	556	0.99	1,240	938	0.76	0.45	0.59
Kanya Kumari-1	—	369	—	—	365	—	—	1.01
Kanya Kumari-2	599	570	0.95	1,297	808	0.62	0.46	0.71
Mean			0.97			0.76	0.56	0.94
Median			0.98			0.74	0.55	0.84

SOURCE: Adapted from Mencher, Joan. 1988. "Women's Work and Poverty: Women's Contribution to Household Maintenance in Two Regions of South India," Table 2, p. 108. In *A Home Divided: Women and Income in the Third World,* edited by Daisy Hilse Dwyer and Judith Bruce. Palo Alto, CA: Stanford University Press.
NOTE: Amounts given in Rupees when 1 Rupee = U.S. $.11.

As Table 4.1 shows, women *earned* a median of 55% of male income. But they *contributed* a median of 90% of what they earned in Kerala and 98% in Tamil Nadu versus male median contributions of 70% and 74%. Work-related transport and lunch costs accounted for most instances where women contributed less than about 95% of their earnings to family sustenance. Men, however, also held back a portion of income for such leisure and "status production" activities as "sitting in teashops, eating food and drinking toddy or *arrack* with friends, and having a clean white shirt for special occasions" (Mencher, 1988, p. 100).

Problems arise because during the period when women earn least, men still keep money for personal expenses. Mencher examined a subsample of six villages (three each in Kerala and Tamil Nadu). She found that in the month when wives earn *least,* men in five of the six villages actually contributed a *lower* percentage of earnings than they did in the month when wives earn most. (Men contributed 76% of earnings in both months in the sixth village.) For example, in South Arcot-2, Tamil Nadu, men contributed 85% of earnings in January when both spouses earn the most; in April, when wives earn the least and there is not enough money to feed the family adequately, husbands contributed only 71% of income.

Conversely, in hard times even activist union women will accept below the minimum wage "if there is nothing else available, especially if they have had to stay at home for a few days listening to the cries of hungry children" (Mencher, 1988, p. 100).

Men also held back more income in a Mexico City study. Roldan (1982, 1988) studied 140 Mexico City women doing garment/textile industry piece-work in their own homes. Among 53 households studied in depth, spouses pooled income in 33 households, generally the poorest. As wives renegotiated power relationships based on their new, albeit small earnings, how much husbands kept for themselves became the main source of (verbal and physical) fights.[4] This was because wives claimed to put 100% of earnings in the common fund, whereas husbands kept back 25% or more as a personal allowance. Moreover, nearly half the men withheld income information in what wives resentfully viewed as a control technique to keep them dependent. Still, 77% of men kept final say on how much they retained.

Alternate female spending patterns. Is it invariable that women devote their earnings, unselfishly, to their families' subsistence? Carloni (1984) provides two examples that when women have no structural obligations to aid in family sustenance, they may *not* have a more "altruistic" spending pattern. First, among the Berber of the Atlas mountain village studied by Maher (1981) in Morocco, wives do not have an independent income and the responsibility for family maintenance is the husband's. The woman often spends cash gifts on gold or silver jewelry. Similarly, among the Serahuli, one of the ethnic groups studied by Dey (1981) in the Gambia, wives expect their husbands to buy both sauce and staple ingredients for the stews, while they spend their money on gold jewelry and clothes for themselves and their children. Among other groups, the women step into the breach only when male efforts fall short. This is the case among the Kusasi of northeast Ghana, studied by Whitehead (1981). Even though men are viewed as the primary farmers and staple food providers, an ideology of "maternal altruism" dictates that a "strong" woman devote her own income (e.g., from beer brewing and grain trading) to feeding her children during the hungry season.

What explains women's higher proportionate contribution to family? Is it Engel's Law, "maternal altruism," or "maternal self-interest" that is behind women's motivation to devote more of their income to the family's, especially children's, "basic human needs"? Formulated in 1857 by Ernst Engel, the German economist, Engel's Law asserts that the lower the income, the higher the proportion of it spent on life's basic necessities (Houthakker, 1957). Women's earnings in virtually all the Third World studies cited in this paper average far lower than their husbands, and almost all the groups studied were at the bare survival level. Therefore, because of the women's greater poverty, one must consider that their expenditure patterns were more influenced by Engel's Law than in the case of their men. Here, the data from Mencher are quite relevant. In all 20 villages, women contributed a higher proportion of earnings than men (see Table 4.1). This was true even in the sole case where men and women had *equal* income (Alleppey-1, one of the 10 Kerala villages): Women devoted 92% versus 76% for men to household survival.

In addition, it may be difficult to separate "maternal altruism" from "maternal self-interest" in certain cases. There are instances where children genuinely *are* the best investment open to women with low access to earning an income and high likelihood of being widowed or divorced: Cain, Khanam, and Nahar (1979) found precisely this for Bangladesh. Be that as it may, there is evidence from a wide array of cultures and circumstances that women not only hold back less for personal expenditures, but they also target more of the resources and income under their control to family provisioning, especially children's nutrition.

Is There a Female Focus on Food?

Cameroon: Female income/food strategies in relation to male income and the crop cycle. Guyer (1980, 1988a, 1988b) argues compellingly that in Africa, it is misleading to rely on the Western concept of the unitary, isolated household; *both* men and women's income flows and expenditures must be taken into account, individually and in interaction. As part of her Cameroon research in two villages of the patrilineal Beti people, she studied the daily income and expenditure budgets of a subsample of 26 women during July and November. Women raise most family staple foods, and July is their peak harvest month. Men's cocoa, the main cash crop, is harvested in November. Women earn only about one-third as much *cash* as men, although if their in-kind contributions are measured, their food crops produce about half of "full income."

How do the genders spend their money? Women, *on top of their food production,* spend fully 74% of their *cash* income on "supplements to the family food supply in the form of meat, salt and oil, and household needs such as kerosene and soap" (Guyer, 1988b, p. 165). From Guyer's data, it can be calculated that men spend only 22% of their income on food. Overall, males supply 33% of cash expenditures for food/household supplies, while females contribute 67%. So when the men's cocoa money comes in November, women don't rely on men's voluntary and perhaps less dependable transfers; instead, they seek to capture a share by their own activities: distilling/selling alcohol; trading in wine, beer, and cigarettes; preparing/selling cooked foods; and working in the cocoa harvest (p. 168). Women's strategy seems to work: Their "own earnings" more than doubled in November (to 3,603 CFA francs from 1,518 in July, per Guyer, 1988b, p. 168; 1,000 CFA then equalled U.S. $5.00), while transfers from men went *down* as a proportion of female income (to 36% in November versus 45% in July, per Guyer, 1988a, p. 13). Moreover, "women use their higher November incomes largely to enrich the diet" (Guyer, 1988b, p. 168).

South India: Mothers' gardens or income means better-nourished children. Kumar (1978) studied nutrition in a stratified random sample of 120 households in three rural villages in Kerala, in south India. A subsample was drawn of 48 impoverished landless/near-landless households (72% had less than one-tenth acre) with children ages 3-36 months. This subsample was intensively followed for an entire crop cycle. Kumar's regressions on the subsample showed that resources under the *mother's* control—her home garden and, if she did agricultural day labor for wages, *her* earnings (versus those of her husband)—

proved most important in accounting for the level of child nutrition. In fact, "increasing [paternal] wage income has no incremental benefit on child nutrition" (Kumar, 1978, p. 45).

Ghana: Child nutrition and parental trading income. Life is hard in the northern Ghana farming village where Tripp (1981) studied factors associated with good nutrition in a sample of 187 children. Cultivation is so precarious due to uncertain rainfall and declining soil fertility that a preharvest hungry season and periodic food shortages characterize the area. Among these Nankane-speaking people, it was *trading* income in general and *mother's* trading income in particular that proved most important for child nutrition:

> Of all the variables tested, the trading activity of the *mother* is the one most significantly associated ($p < 0.001$) with the nutritional status of the child. In no case does a woman's trading generate profits that are equivalent to those of male long-distance traders, but the *relatively small amount of money that a female trader ?arns is translated more directly to the nutrition of her children. The woman has complete control over her earnings,* and [her trading furnishes her] with a small steady income that she can use to buy food to augment that provided by the farming activities of her and her husband. (Tripp, 1981, pp. 19-20, emphasis added)

Belize: A rise in male income doesn't help child nutrition as much as a drop in female income may hurt it. Stavrakis and Marshall (1978) studied the impact of the introduction of cash-cropped sugarcane on women's economic roles and family nutrition in a Belize village. Sugarcane generated quite a bit of income locally, which accrued overwhelmingly *to* the men. However:

> Money flowed out of the system as fast as it came in, spent on drink, trucks, travel and purchased female companionship. By and large, it did not benefit the women at home tending the children and animals. (Stavrakis and Marshall, p. 158)

To the contrary, women suffered economically as production of corn and other foods declined. Women had depended on corn for food, exchange with kin (see below), and food for their pigs, their main independent source of income. They fed the pigs the 25% to 40% of the corn yield that was spoiled or blighted. So as corn yields declined, so did pig production and female economy autonomy.

Meanwhile, higher male income did *not* help child nutrition, according to a study of 59 people in 8 households surveyed in both 1973 and 1974:

First, in all the families the smallest children ate the least well, and no children in the sample ate very well. . . . Second, there was no drastic improvement from 1973 to 1974 [i.e., despite the sugarcane boom]. . . . The children of the rich did not fare better nutritionally than the children of the poor, indicating a link between the status, autonomy, and well-being of the woman to the child's nutritional condition. (Stavrakis and Marshall, p. 165)

As a final note, while consumption of local fruits from women's gardens declined 34% between 1973 and 1974, consumption of purchased soft drinks and frozen Koolaid increased by 255% (Stavrakis and Marshall, p. 161).

Female Investments in Extended Kin Exchange/Sharing Networks

In the United States, it has become a truism that women are the "kinkeepers" (see, e.g., Kranichfeld, 1987). But for many poor Third World women, keeping ties to extended kin provides more tangible benefits than solidarity. Among African patrilineal peoples, for example, one of the reasons women need their *own* income is so they can maintain their obligations/exchanges with natal extended kin. To illustrate, Guyer found that transfers from people other than a woman's husband (mostly her kin) accounted for 34.4% of her transfer income and 15% of her total cash income.[5] Such largess must be reciprocated. Thus when a woman's independently controlled income drops, so may her ability to maintain kin ties, to her family's as well as her own detriment. Here are two examples:

Belize. First, Stavrakis and Marshall's study found that an exchange network among female kin redistributed corn for past favors and provided food and aid to women whose husbands had had a bad crop year. This provided a valuable insurance function for both genders as well as serving as a main basis for female power (Stavrakis and Marshall, 1978, p. 161). Thus the drop in both corn production and women's independent income from pig sales dealt a double blow to "kin insurance."

Upper Volta (Burkina Faso). Second, Conti (1979) found that women who were hurt economically when a resettlement project caused at least a 50% drop in their own-account commercial activities were much less able to continue in extended family exchange networks. Their plight came about because the project did not give women personal plots; instead, they were expected to work on the project's cotton. But the cotton was so labor-intensive it required 15-hour workdays during the agricultural season; yet the profits went to their husbands. Bereft of economic independence and time, the women mounted numerous protests.

The importance of poor women's kin-based "sharing networks" for keeping their households above the "survival line" has been documented empirically for the United States by Lombardi (1973) and Stack (1974). Other studies offer anecdotal evidence of the same phenomenon elsewhere (e.g., S. Brown, 1975 for the Dominican Republic). This is an aspect of the relationship between male/female control of economic resources and family well-being that merits further research.

Meanwhile, women's ability to exchange resources and services with kin might be hypothesized as especially important under certain circumstances: (a) in Africa, in particular, where both men and women retain reciprocal obligations to their natal kin; (b) wherever marriages are polygynous, unstable, and/or marriage rates are low (a woman's extended family exchange network may then prove a more reliable source of aid than a husband); and (c) in general, where women participate in a sharing/exchange network: The poorer she is, the more important the insurance/risk spreading function served by her network.

All in all, kin exchange networks are important in many parts of the world, sometimes for one sex, sometimes for both. This is another reason why the model of the "household as black box" may obscure more than it reveals. Individual members *within* that household may be differentially involved not only in the household's "internal economy" but also in an "external economy" with kin.

In sum, the above discussions of differential male/female spending patterns and women's use of kin sharing/exchange networks as both insurance and resource lead to a clear conclusion: Wherever women have any structural obligation as providers, income (or food crops) under their control seem to translate more fully and more directly to family sustenance and child nutrition.

What Women Gain in Micro-Level Power and Self-Esteem from Control of Income

At the micro level, as the proportion of income under female control rises, what benefits accrue directly to the woman herself? Evidence is presented for three benefits: more say in fertility, more say in household decisions, and enhanced self-esteem.

The Fertility Payoff of Female Control of Income

Third World women do not always want the two-child family beloved of family planners. Indeed, where a woman sees children as unsubstitutable sources of labor, future crisis aid, old-age security, and so forth, she may want many more. But regardless of her fertility preferences, she may be more likely to realize them when she controls enough income to influence marital power. For example, a study by Weller (1968) in Puerto Rico found that when women entered the labor market, their household decision-making power rose, and initiating contraception was one of the first ways in which they exercised their greater control.

Fertility findings from Mexico City. Roldan's study (1982, 1988) provides added support. The women's new status as earners did not translate to more power in all aspects of their marriages. But the higher women's contribution to the total household "pool," the more leverage they had over *fertility* decisions (see Table 4.2).

Development, female income, and fertility in Guatemala. In 1985, I followed up a 1980 study by Kusterer, Estrada de Batres, and Xuya Cuxil (1981) in four research sites in Guatemala (Blumberg, 1985, 1989b). Three were villages where poor, mainly Indian, farmers grew broccoli, cauliflower, and snow peas on contract for ALCOSA, a wholly-owned subsidiary of Hanover Brands, a U.S. multinational company. The fourth site was ALCOSA's processing plant, where the vegetables were frozen and packed for export to the United States. My research grew out of a discovery that I could rearray the 1980 results in an ascending sequence akin to a *natural experiment* on what happens when women's involvement in a development project's activities and benefits ranges from low to high.

In brief, in 1980 the success of the project followed the same trajectory: In Patzicia, the first village, women did not work in the fields due to cultural constraints, and the project was floundering for lack of labor. Women in the second village, Chimachoy, had been pulled into three days a week in the fields, reducing their independent earnings from selling in the market; but the company paid by a check made out to the husband. In Santiago Sacatepequez, the third village, women had a long horticultural tradition. Moreover, a cooperative ran the project (in the other two villages, farmers dealt directly with the company). Women spent three days a week in the fields and three selling in the market. Both men and women could deliver produce and be paid in cash. Yields and quality were far higher than in the other two sites. In the firm's processing plant, an overwhelmingly female, Ladina work force earned the rarely-paid minimum wage. Long shifts (12-16 hours during the 8-9 month "high season") resulted in earnings 150% to 300% above the average for women. They earned as much, in fact, as a male blue-collar worker or farmer in their town. Productivity and their

Table 4.2 Women's Pooling Contribution by Input into Fertility Decisions

	Use of Contraceptives	Have More Children
1. Women in pooling subgroup contributing > 40% of total; husbands also provide ($N = 11$)		
wife's decision	50%	50%
joint decision	40%	40%
2. Women in pooling subgroup contributing < 40% of total; husbands are main providers ($N = 19$)		
wife's decision	40%	20%
joint decision	53%	68%

SOURCE: Compiled from Roldan, Martha. 1982. "Intrahousehold Patterns of Money Allocation and Women's Subordination: A Case Study of Domestic Outworkers in Mexico City." Unpublished paper circulated at the Population Council seminar on Women, Income, and Policy, New York, March; and Roldan, Martha. 1988. "Renegotiating the Marital Contract: Intrahousehold Patterns of Money Allocation and Women's Subordination: A Case Study of Domestic Outworkers in Mexico City." In *A Home Divided: Women and Income in the Third World,* edited by Daisy Hilse Dwyer and Judith Bruce. Palo Alto, CA: Stanford University Press.
NOTE: Missing percentages inferred to be husbands' decisions.

satisfaction with their income and its impact on their lives were exceptionally high. Kusterer and colleagues also found the first signs of women taking control of their fertility.

Between 1980 and 1985, Guatemala's economy plummeted. And the military government's "dirty war" against a guerrilla insurgency, which peaked in 1980-1981, left some 30,000-100,000 dead (mostly Indians). When I arrived in Patzicia, the first village, I found women working in the fields as I had predicted: Economics had overcome tradition. The second village, tragically, had been virtually wiped out. And in the third, in 1984 the co-op adopted the policy of paying by check only to the (male) "official member," so women's power had plunged. But at the processing plant, women continued to earn the minimum wage for long shifts. The income gave them control over their lives and fertility; 100% claimed satisfaction with their jobs and pay.

By 1985, the fertility effect was unmistakable. Among 15 "1980 veterans" in the processing plant (median age = 32.5 years), only 13 babies had been born between 1980-1985. The 15 women have an average of 2.2 children each and have taken control of their fertility. When discussing future fertility, a number cited the high costs of children to them, given their work schedules. And 7 of the 15 say they will not have any more children (at median age = 37, mean = 2.3 children). In contrast, 20 women from the first village, Patzicia (the only one with a substantial Ladina population), averaged 5.2 children at median age 33.5. These women did not receive direct benefits even if they worked in the fields (the check was made out solely to the husband). When asked about future fertility, a frequent response was: "Well, I don't want any more but my husband does so I'll have to continue."

Women's Independent Income and Household Decision-Making Power

In the United States, this would be the crux of most of the marital power literature. In this section, three cases from the Third World "gender and development" literature are presented. All indicate the relationship is positive.

Nepal: Women's subsistence production versus cash earnings and effects on decision-making power. Acharya and Bennett (1981, 1982, 1983) provide a rich, massively documented study of 279 households in eight villages in Nepal. Four are Tibeto-Burman and four are Indo-Aryan (Hindu). The former have traditions of female long-distance and local entrepreneurial activity and low preoccupation with female sexual purity. The latter restrict women geographically, economically, and sexually. Acharya and Bennett conceptualize four activity spheres in which males versus females contribute, in differing degrees, to their family's living standard. Sphere I = domestic/household maintenance; Sphere II = family farm enterprise (subsistence production); Sphere III = local market economy (home production for local sale; locally generated wages/trade income); and Sphere IV = wider market economy beyond village (accessed by short-term migration for employment or trading requiring at least an overnight absence from village). Overall, women accounted for 86% of person days in Sphere I, 57% in II, 38% in III, and 25% in IV. There is little variance in Tibeto-Burman and Hindu women's involvement in Spheres I and II, but Tibeto-Burman women are much more involved in Spheres III and IV (a mean of 54% are active in III and 39% in IV compared to means of 29% and 9% for Hindu women's participation in III and IV, respectively). Moreover, only 31% of income in the eight villages was generated through market intervention: These remain subsistence households consuming over 86% of what they produce.

Nevertheless, when it comes to input into household decision making, it is the extent to which a woman derived income from the *market* economy—Spheres III and IV—that proved more important. In fact, their regressions show that only a woman's Sphere IV involvement had a significant *positive* impact on her decision-making power over the household's most important resource allocation decisions (e.g., to buy or sell land or large animals). At the same time, her greater involvement in Sphere I had a significant *negative* effect on her input into those major resource decisions (Acharya and Bennett, 1983, p. 39). In fact, taking into account three categories of decisions (domestic and farm management decisions as well as major resource allocation decisions), they found that

> women's involvement in market activities [Spheres III and IV] gives them much greater power within the household in terms of their input in all aspects of household decision making. At the same time, confining women's work to the domestic [Sphere I] and the subsistence [II] sectors reduces their power vis-à-vis men in the household. (Acharya and Bennett, 1982, p. ix)

Finally, those women earning income spent it primarily on items for daily household consumption or children's support, hardly a surprise by this point.

Women's differential resource control and decision making in two Kenyan villages. Even though women had been the chief cultivators in their home villages, the Kenyan Mwea resettlement scheme, Hanger and Moris (1973) found, failed to provide them enough land to grow their own food crops. Instead, the project necessitated their working long hours in their husband's irrigated rice fields. But management paid cash earnings from rice, the only project crop, solely to the husband. Just as in Stavrakis and Marshall's (1978) Belize study, although *household* income rose, nutritional levels fell as women became very dependent on their husbands for household expenditures. Many women deserted their husbands; many others processed rice for black market sale or brewed beer (thereby increasing male drunkenness) but earned little. Meanwhile, in comparison with an off-project village (Nembure), where women farmed their own plots, traded the surplus on their own account, and supplied much of the family food, Mwea women had distinctly lower power in family decision making (see Table 4.3).

Guatemala: effects of falling versus rising income. First, the "down side": In my 1985 research, several co-op staff in Santiago Sacatepequez underlined to me how rapidly women's autonomy and household decision-making power had plunged after the co-op switched payment systems in 1984 (Blumberg, 1985, 1989b). Instead of paying cash to whichever spouse came to collect, it changed to payment by a check made out solely to the husband-legal member. A purposive sample of 17 women concurred. Since then, they felt, wives' position had eroded. For example, wives had less say in planting decisions—how much land would be devoted to broccoli and cauliflower for sale to the

Table 4.3 Women's Participation in Household Decision-Making

	Percentage of Decisions Made by Wife	
	Mwea	Nembure
I. General Decisions		
Family budget planning	20	40
Spending of money	15	35
Schooling of children	10	20
II. Household Decisions		
What to eat	98	100
Taking of maize to the mill	80	90
Purchase of firewood	20	90
What food to buy	64	80
Household replacements	60	70

SOURCE: Adapted from Hanger, Jane and Jon Moris, 1973. "Women and the Household Economy" p. 228, Table 5. In *Mwea: An Irrigated Rice Settlement in Kenya,* edited by Robert Chambers and Jon Moris. Munich: Weltforum Verlag.

co-op versus how much would be planted in other horticultural crops (radishes, cabbage, and so forth) women traditionally had sold in the Guatemala City market. Consequently, with almost all land going to the crops bought by the co-op, women ended up with less produce to sell to generate an income for themselves. Several women complained that their husbands wouldn't tell them the amount of the co-op check. Husbands also were described as reluctant to let wives take time off from farming to go to home economics meetings co-op staff tried to arrange. And staff felt that even though *husbands* had more money, they were more likely to spend it on land, transport, and items other than nutritious food. Again, akin to the Belize study, they saw no improvement in nutrition from men's better position.

Second, the "up side": Kusterer, Estrada de Batres, and Xuya Cuxil (1981) had found the converse. The new high earnings of the women processing plant workers had empowered them in their domestic relationships and decision making. Moreover, not one woman reported giving her pay to her husband. My 1985 processing plant findings provided further corroboration that the women's substantial earnings brought them leverage at home. And out of my purposive sample of 30, only two newlyweds reported sharing *any* of their income with their husbands (they pooled part of it into a common fund).

Women's Independent Income and Self-Esteem

Many studies of "women and development" projects report that women's self-esteem grows when they begin earning independent income. Here space dictates that only findings from studies reviewed above are presented. But self-esteem, we are learning, can have important consequences for women. For example, it is a main variable explaining women's persistence in science careers (Freifeld, 1987).

According to Roldan, all of the 53 women in her Mexico City in-depth subsample gained in self-esteem. This was born from the enhanced sense of control over their own lives they gained from their income: Now *they* had the autonomy to budget among food versus children's clothing versus medicine, and so forth. Although they were merely allocating between subsistence expenditures (their husbands retained more, or complete say over "big ticket" *surplus* expenditures), they felt good. Per Sra. S, one of the 20 slightly less poor and more subordinate women who did not pool into a common fund (instead, their husbands gave them a "housekeeping allowance"; their own pay went for what he, but not she, defined as "extras"):

> Of course [working for pay] is important, because if you earn your own money, you yourself distribute it, and you do not have to beg for it. You buy food, or a dress for your daughter, the socks for your son. He used to tell me, "You just wait, because I do not have enough this month; I will buy it next month." But he would never do it, neither today nor tomorrow. Now if I want to buy it, I buy it. If he gives me the money, fine. If not, I buy it myself. *And one feels fine [se siente bonita]* and useful with one's own money. (Roldan, 1988, p. 245, emphasis added)

Both Kusterer, Estrada de Batres, and Xuya Cuxil (1981) and I (Blumberg, 1985, 1989b) recorded similar findings about the well-paid Guatemalan women processing plant workers (who retained ultimate control over their earnings in both the 1980 and 1985 studies). Specifically, they increased in independence, self-reliance, self-respect, the perceived respect of their families, and self-esteem. Kusterer calls this change in self-image perhaps "the most important and most positive [finding] of all" (Kusterer, Estrada de Batres, & Xuya Cuxil, 1981, p. 81). Last, I found just as positive a change in sense of self-reliance/self-worth among a subsample of 10 women "microentrepreneurs" whose businesses really took off thanks to short-term credit from a Dominican Republic project (Blumberg, 1985, 1989c). They, too, controlled their own income.

Connecting Micro and Macro: How Lack of Returns for Labor for Women Farmers Can Affect the African Food Crisis

We already have seen the important micro-level consequences of women's independent control of income: The Third World studies cited above provide support for the gender stratification theory's hypotheses about females' greater relative control of income enhancing their control over fertility and, to a certain extent, other types of household decisions as well. We also have seen that, as posited, the consequences to a woman's micro-level power are faster and more direct when her relative control of income *drops* than when it rises.

But in the macro context of Africa, development experts rarely consider women as autonomous economic actors who generally *require* income under their control to fulfill responsibilities toward family provisioning and kin. When development planners—especially in Africa—ignore the "internal economy" of the household at the micro level, women's possibilities and incentives for food production may be reduced. That's serious; women tend to be the primary cultivators of food crops in most of sub-Saharan Africa. Indeed, the Economic Commission for Africa credits women farmers with from 60% to 80% of all labor in agriculture (United Nations, 1978, p. 5). Nevertheless, women are rarely *seen* as farmers by development officials. They are still overwhelmingly shut out of agricultural extension, training, credit, fertilizer, and other assistance. Aggregated to the macro level, this neglect of female farmers (and their incentives) may contribute to outcomes ranging from failed development projects to famine.

Female Farmers, Income Incentives, and the African Food Crisis

The argument can be summarized in brief in the following six points:

1. Women in much of Africa raise the bulk (up to 80%) of locally produced/marketed food crops but rarely obtain direct benefits from agricultural development projects.[6]
2. In Africa, especially, men and women not only tend to have some separate income, but also separate obligations for spending it. Women's duties often include providing much of the family food. Accordingly, the sexes tend to maintain "separate purses" for at least part of their resources—especially where polygyny and/or marital instability are high (see Staudt, 1987, for a fine overview).
3. Women's control of income has direct implications for family welfare: As we have seen, where women have resources under their independent

control, they tend, more than men, to devote them to feeding the family
and to children's well-being.

4. Given so many African women's needs for resources to provision their
   family, they will tend to allocate their labor *toward* activities that put
   income and/or food under their direct control, and—to the extent culturally possible—*away* from activities that don't. This seems to hold true
   even if the latter activities are substantially more profitable to the house-
   hold/husband (see Jones, 1983, below).

5. Therefore, if development projects fail to provide (sufficient) economic
   returns, especially income incentives, for the women's labor, both the
   project's and the women's goals are likely to suffer (see below). In other
   words, the impact of new macro-level "structural adjustment" policies that
   try to "get the prices right" to provide incentives for agricultural producers
   (see World Bank, 1981)[7] will be reduced if *women* producers don't get
   enough of the resulting income to provide incentive.

6. In effect, then, the combination of a gender-differentiated "internal economy" of the household, female predominance in food crops grown for
   local consumption or market, and insufficient incentives for women producers may be an important but unheralded factor in Africa's recent food
   crises.

When Development Projects Need
Female Labor But Decrease Their Income

Space constraints limit this section to four projects from Africa. But
the annals of the "gender and development" (also known as "women in
development") literature document this phenomenon around the world.
Since Boserup (1970) first noted the "double whammy" whereby both
planned and unplanned development were likely to increase poor
Third World women's workload while undermining their economic
autonomy, researchers have provided considerable empirical documentation of just such negative effects on *women*. Recently, however,
attempts are being made to compile empirical documentation of the
negative effects on the *projects* themselves when women are bypassed
and undercut (see, e.g., Carloni, 1987). The rationale, of course, is
that this is a tack more likely to result in policy changes that will "make
them stop doing it."

Cameroon: Women's return to labor affects how much rice they grow.
In the Cameroon SEMRY I irrigated rice project, Jones's (1983) sophisticated econometric analysis provides the best documented case of a
development project suffering because women were not given sufficient
compensation for their labor. Jones's data stem from a random sample
of 102 Massa women from three villages. They provide support for
the following: (a) The project's long-term prospects are doubtful since

it has not been able to get farmers to grow enough rice; (b) There is a clear relationship between women's incentives and their rice output; and (c) Women who grew rice on their own account—or were especially well compensated by their husbands—cultivated approximately twice as much rice acreage as women whose husbands provided lower compensation.

1. SEMRY's problem with uncultivated fields: The SEMRY I project in Cameroon involves about 5,400 hectares of pump-irrigated rice fields. Although yields and prices have both been good,

> every year many fields go uncultivated for lack of farmer interest. . . . In the 1981 rainy season . . . only 3,228 hectares were cultivated, despite [a 45%] increase in the producer price in 1980. (Jones, 1983, p. 30)

Unless SEMRY can get farmers to cultivate those unused fields, its prospects are grim: At present hectarage, its "revenues are not sufficient to cover both operating costs and amortization" (Jones, 1983, p. 31). To understand why SEMRY can't find takers for its idle irrigated fields, we must see who works versus who benefits.

2. Women with more incentive raise more rice: Irrigated rice cultivation on SEMRY fields is a *joint conjugal* activity. But *the husband gets all the income*—and then compensates his wife as he sees fit for her work on his rice fields. "In return for [her] sweat,

> a woman receives about 7,700 CFA in cash and about 9,200 CFA worth of paddy from her husband after the harvest, or about 16,900 CFA in total. This is less than a quarter of the net returns from rice production—about 70,000 CFA. Valued at the market wage rates . . . a woman's labor contribution is worth about 31,200 CFA, so her husband makes a profit of about 14,300 CFA from her labor. (Jones, 1983, p. 51)

And "husbands are quite aware that their wives' continued participation depends on their own generosity [i.e., their wages]" (p. 51); wives' rice labor—especially transplanting—is done "at the expense of [women's] sorghum production and other income-generating activities" (p. 4). Specifically, sorghum, which is the mainstay of the diet (100% of households surveyed cultivated it), is grown on an *individual* basis by both men and women. In other words, even though a married woman uses her sorghum primarily for subsistence, it is her *own* sorghum. Not surprisingly, then, Jones's first regression analysis establishes a very strong "relationship between the amount of compensation women receive from their husbands and the number of days they worked on their husbands' rice fields" (p. 52; $R^2 = .70$).

Moreover, Jones establishes empirically that the average 16,900 CFA that husbands gave to wives as "wages" is about one-third more than the "opportunity costs" of women's labor—that is, what they could have earned if they had engaged in their own income-generating activities. But even this one-third "premium" was insufficient to induce the average wife to raise more rice: She devoted some labor to growing rice for her husband, but spent the rest of her time on less profitable activities under her *own* control.

It must be emphasized that transplanting rice competes directly with women's planting and weeding sorghum on their own fields. In fact, Jones's regressions show that women must make literally a one-to-one tradeoff between the number of days they work on rice versus sorghum cultivation during the peak transplanting season (Days Rice = 28.57 − 1.04 Days Sorghum; R^2 = .77; F = 230.93). Yet rice gives the better return. So, not surprisingly, independent women (mostly widows) who grew rice on their *own* account spent 24.7 days transplanting it. This is half again as many days as married women transplanting their husband's rice (they transplanted for only 16.4 days; the difference is significant). As a result, the married women transplanted only .31 hectare per adult worker versus the .47 hectare (half again as much) transplanted by independent women's households.

Furthermore, since both independent and married women obtained yields of about 4,300 kilos/hectare, it was *quantity* of rice land planted, not quality of cultivation, that differentiated the two groups.

3. Specifically, women with more incentives cultivate twice as much rice land: One subgroup of married women *did* cultivate as much land as independent women—and these were wives who received a significantly *higher rate of compensation* from their husbands. In one of the three villages, Jones compared independent women with two groups of married women: those whose households grew more than .75 "piquet" (1 piquet = .5 hectare) per household worker and those whose households grew less. The independent women averaged .94 piquet per household worker. And the 13 households in the .75+ piquet category averaged an almost identical .95. This was *twice as much* rice land as that cultivated in the 18 households below .75 piquet, which averaged only .47 piquet per household worker. The secret? Married "women who cultivated .75 piquet or more per household worker were compensated at the mean rate of 363 CFA/day, while the group of women who cultivated less than .75 piquet per household worker received only 302 CFA/day from their husbands" (p. 133). The difference is significant.

In sum, although wives were compensated above opportunity costs, lack of sufficient incentive explains why so few "take on the cultivation of an additional rice field" (p. 83). And this, in turn, surely is a major reason why SEMRY can't get farmers to cultivate its unused fields. The next three African examples are shorter but tell the same basic story.

Kenya. In an area where Kenyan women traditionally grew pyrethrum (used in insecticide), sold the dried flowers, and kept the income, a project organized a co-op to exploit this crop. But it enrolled (and paid) men almost exclusively. The discouraged women reduced their output (Apthorpe, 1971).

The Gambia. An irrigated rice project was developed by male Taiwanese technicians. Men were targeted, despite the fact that women traditionally not only cultivated swamp rice but also controlled its disposition and cash returns. But men needed women's labor. So they blocked women from owning or cultivating irrigated rice land on their own account. The results? Rice production decreased under the project as women held back their labor (Dey, 1981, 1982).

The Turkana of Kenya. Traditionally, Turkana males were herders; Turkana females were cultivators, and produce from their rain-fed sorghum plots long had been under female control. An irrigation project was launched. It paid all cash earnings to the (male) head of household, but nevertheless counted on women providing unpaid family labor for their husband's irrigated crops. Instead, women neglected the irrigated project crops in favor of their own rain-fed sorghum plots located away from the project area. Those few women who had their own irrigated plots, however, allocated relatively less time to off-project cultivation. Output on the project's one-acre irrigated plots proved so far below projections that women had to work on off-project activities for their family to survive. (Two other consequences also bear mentioning. First, a nutrition study found that children in project tenant households had the worst nutrition of all groups studied, including people in famine relief camps receiving food rations. Second, to fill their provider role, women sold surplus sorghum, did petty trading, and brewed beer from their sorghum. Accordingly, as in the Kenyan Mwea project above, another outcome of concentrating all project income in male hands has been an increase in beer drinking [Broch-Due, 1983]).

Women: The Missing Variable in Analyses of the African Food Crisis

The list of variables found in analyses of African food crisis and famine reads almost like the biblical 10 plagues: War. Drought. Ecological degradation. Unfavorable insertion into the capitalist world economy. Bad government macroeconomic policies (including (a) inefficient "parastatals" and government marketing boards that don't pay farmers enough to stimulate output; (b) distorted, urban-biased factor prices that may make it cheaper to import wheat from the United States than get farmers to grow local food staples; (c) misguided exchange rate policies; and (d) a long list of other "macroeconomic mortal sins"). Lack of breakthrough research on African food crops. Inadequate extension. Insufficient use of agricultural inputs (e.g., fertilizer, chemicals). Inadequate management of development projects. Corruption. Insufficient funding from the international donor agencies. Indeed, this list could be doubled without depleting the factors found in the growing literature on the African food crisis.

But with few exceptions, when the *African farmer* is discussed, the personal pronoun used is *he*. That women are the main producers of African food crops[8]—and *especially* their need for incentives—are almost never mentioned (see Staudt, 1987, for a first-rate discussion of this blindness).

As background on Africa's food situation, here is Hyden's summary:

> According to a recent African survey (ECA, cited in Hyden, 1986, pp. 8-9) for the whole of [the 1970s], when Africa's population was expanding at an average annual rate of around 2.8%, total food production in Africa was rising by no more than 1.5%. Food self-sufficiency ratios dropped from 98% in the 1960s to approximately 86% in 1980. This means that, on average, each African had about 12% less homegrown food in 1980 than 20 years earlier. With food production stagnating and demand, particularly for cereals, keeping pace with population growth, the volume of food imports between 1970 and 1980 increased by an average annual rate of 8.4%. In 1980, imports of food grains alone reached 20.4 million tons, costing African countries over $5 billion (not including heavy ocean freight costs). Food aid to Africa in 1980 was 1.5 million tons. (ECA, cited in Hyden, 1986, p. 11)

All this was before the drought that brought Africa's second major famine since the early 1970s to the world's television screens in 1984-1985. Since then the crisis has continued, although generally at less than famine levels. Yet most of even the newest "mainstream" analyses largely ignore women (e.g., Mellor, Delgado, and Blackie, 1987).

In conclusion, all of the evidence presented above indicates that the consequences of this omission are indeed serious at both micro and macro levels.

Bringing It All Back Home: Male/Female Income and the U.S. Marital Power Debate

Although the above has yet to have much of an impact on the African food crisis debate,[9] it might expand the U.S. debate on marital/family power[10] in two ways. First, it is germane that studies of varying methodologies and degrees of quantification, but from quite disparate cultures (e.g., Guatemala, Kenya, Nepal), indicate a relationship between relative male/female control of economic resources (especially cash income) and the woman's say in family decisions. Moreover, this link seems stronger and more direct when the woman's economic power drops relative to the man's than when it rises. In short, the above studies seem to bolster the "relative resources" approach to marital/familial power in the United States and also provide support for my theory. Because I have a theoretical axe to grind in favor of a positive link between women's relative economic power and family/marital leverage, these cross-cultural examples cannot be considered convincing "convergent validation." They are, however, suggestive that such a link exists.

Second, the Third World findings about women's differential contribution and spending patterns pose an intriguing challenge: Can they be extended to the United States? Is food, in the literal sense, more associated with the "bacon" brought home by a woman rather than by a man? In other words, would U.S. studies find that at every level of income, (a) women hold back a smaller percent of income for personal expenditures and (b) spend more on family and children's well-being and "basic human needs"? Naturally, in the United States the much higher levels of living and the much lower levels of fertility must be taken into account. For example, a U.S. mother's expenditures might be devoted to a general greater persistence on behalf of her children's welfare rather than strictly on calories.

In sum, further exploring the question of gender-disaggregated income and expenditure streams might provide rich new food for academic thought for U.S. social scientists studying family, marital power, and gender stratification.

Notes

1. Boserup's pathbreaking 1970 book was the first to assert and document that development—both planned projects and unplanned macro trends of the world economy—resulted in precisely this combination of more toil and an eroded resource base for

many Third World women. A voluminous literature has emerged since then on gender (or women) and development (see, e.g., Tinker and Bo Bramsen, 1976; Blumberg, 1979, 1989a; Black and Cottrell, 1981; Tiano, 1987).

2. The main "power variables" include economic, force/coercion, political position, and, to a lesser extent, ideology (see Lenski, 1966). Their relative importance in societal stratification and specific instances of major social change are the subject of endless debate. But for gender stratification, the greater relative importance of economic power stands out empirically as well as theoretically. Empirically, economic power has been the most achievable for women (see Blumberg, 1978). We know of pre-state societies where women control more than half of major economic resources (e.g., the horticulturist Iroquois of colonial North America, described in J. Brown, 1975). Moreover, we know of a number of hunting-gathering societies with a roughly equal male/female division of economic resources (e.g., the Mbuti—Turnbull, 1961, 1981; the !Kung—Lee, 1968, 1969; Draper, 1975; and the now-controversial Tasaday—Fernandez and Lynch, 1972; Nance, 1975). In contrast, women are more likely to be victims rather than wielders of the power of force. Nor do we know of a single human society where women have achieved even a 50-50 share of political control. Finally, although there are a few societies whose ideology considers women equal, we know of none where they are held superior.

3. Macro-level discount rates can occasionally be positive (e.g., when women are given the vote from above, or when a Kemal Ataturk rams through greater powers and privileges for women, or when a state's laws award a widow a share of her husband's estate even though she had been economically dependent throughout her marriage.) In addition, there are also *micro-level* discount factors that can be either positive or negative and also affect the "net" male/female balance of power. These include each partner's commitment to the relationship, relative attractiveness, and so forth (see Blumberg and Coleman, 1985, 1989b for further elaboration).

4. Doña B describes the effect of her new earnings (she provides over 40% of the household pool). Before he gave her a daily allowance and shouted if she spent too much on the children or didn't give him the food he wanted. "Now I tell him, 'with the small salary you earn you go and spend it on drinking with your friends. Look at me, I am also earning, and I do not buy anything for me, but *all I get I put into the house.*' It is not fair. Once or twice he slapped me in the face [for shouting]. . . . I felt I was right. . . . I am helping him, so . . . I have the right to expect him to change" (Roldan, 1982, p. 15, emphasis added).

5. The other 65.6% of transfer income came from her husband. In all, transfer income came to 43.5% of her total cash income, with her own earnings accounting for the rest (Guyer, 1988b, Tables 1 and 2).

6. Since Boserup (1970), a large literature now supports these assertions. And as part of a team studying the impact of U.S. foreign assistance on three Nigerian universities in 1986 (Gamble, Blumberg, Johnson, and Raun, 1988), I saw that even in eastern Nigeria, a classic "female farming" area, all university, governmental, and international farming extension, research, and assistance was directed to men. Yet aid focused on crops grown (e.g., cassava) and operations (fertilizing) done largely by women.

7. "Structural adjustment" policies are being strongly urged on debt-ridden and food-short African countries by the World Bank and the International monetary Fund. These policies call for macro-economic policies that promote exports and reduce government intervention in markets. In this regard, countries are urged to reorient factor prices to reduce the urban bias that has led to insufficient incentives for agricultural producers— that is, "structural adjustment" stresses "getting the prices right."

8. There is, of course, considerable variation in the extent to which African women are the main producers of food crops grown for local consumption/marketing. There are even a few areas where women do very little field work (as among the Muslim Hausa of

Northern Nigeria, where women are secluded during daylight hours), and others where men are the primary farmers (as among the Yoruba of Western Nigeria). As an overview, however, it is accurate to say that African women farmers produce far more of the locally grown food than their male counterparts.

9. An unfolding exception involves the World Bank's Agricultural Development Projects in Nigeria. A recent convergence of factors is creating a major shift to pay more attention to female farmers. We are hopeful our research will prevent women's *returns* being ignored, but it's still too soon to tell (Blumberg, 1988).

10. One of the confusions in the U.S. literature is between marital versus family power (McDonald, 1980; Blumberg and Coleman, 1985, 1989; Kranichfeld, 1987). McDonald has concluded that most of the U.S. studies on family power actually measure marital power. The Third World studies also share the same ambiguity.

References

Acharya, Meena and Lynn Bennett. 1981. *The Rural Women of Nepal: An Aggregate Analysis and Summary of Eight Village Studies,* Vol. 2, Part 9. Katmandu, Nepal: Centre for Economic Development and Admin: tration, Tribhuvan University.

———. 1982. "Women's Status in Nepal: A Summary of Findings and Implications." Mimeograph. Washington, DC: Agency for International Development, Office of Women in Development.

———. 1983. "Women and the Subsistence Sector: Economic Participation in Household Decision-Making in Nepal." Washington, DC: World Bank.

Apthorpe, Raymond, 1971. "Some Evaluation Problems for Cooperative Studies, with Special Reference to Primary Cooperatives in Highland Kenya." In *Two Blades of Grass: Rural Cooperatives in Agricultural Modernization,* edited by Peter Worsely. Manchester: Manchester University Press.

Becker, Gary. 1981. *A Treatise on the Family.* Cambridge, MA: Harvard University Press.

Black, Naomi and Ann Baker Cottrell, eds. 1981. *Women and World Change: Equity Issues in Development.* Beverly Hills, CA: Sage.

Blood, Robert O. and Donald M. Wolfe. 1960. *Husbands and Wives.* New York: Free Press.

Blumberg, Rae Lesser. 1978. *Stratification: Socioeconomic and Sexual Inequality* Dubuque, IA: William C. Brown.

———. 1979. "Rural Women in Development: Veil of Invisibility, World of Work." *International Journal of Intercultural Relations* 3:447-472.

———. 1981. "Rural Women in Development." Pp. 32-56 in *Women and World Change: Equity Issues in Development,* edited by Naomi Black and Ann Baker Cottrell. Beverly Hills, CA: Sage.

———. 1984. "A General Theory of Gender Stratification." Pp. 23-101 in *Sociological Theory 1984,* edited by Randall Collins. San Francisco: Jossey-Bass.

———. 1985. "A Walk on the 'WID' Side: Summary of Field Research on 'Women in Development' in the Dominican Republic and Guatemala." Draft, Agency for International Development. Paper presented at the International Conference on "Gender and Farming Systems," Gainesville, FL, April, 1986.

———. 1988. "Gender Stratification, Economic Development, and the African Food Crisis: Paradigm and Praxis in Nigeria." In *Social Structures and Human Lives: 1986 American Sociological Association Presidential Volume in Honor of Matilda White Riley,* edited by Matilda White Riley, Beth B. Hess, and Bettina Huber. Newbury Park, CA: Sage.

——. 1989a. *Making the Case for the Gender Variable: Women and the Wealth and Well-Being of Nations.* Washington, DC: Office of Women in Development. Agency for International Development. Technical Reports in Gender and Development, No.1.

——. 1989b. "Work, Wealth, and a Women in Development 'Natural Experiment' in Guatemala: The ALCOSA Agribusiness Project in 1980 and 1985." In *Women in Development: A.I.D.'s Experience, 1973-1985. Vol. II. Ten Field Studies,* edited by Paula O. Goddard. Washington, DC: Agency for International Development.

——. 1989c. "Entrepreneurship, Credit and Gender in the Informal Sector of the Dominican Republic: the ADEMI Story." In *Women in Development: 1973-1985. Vol. II. Ten Field Studies,* edited by Paula O. Goddard. Washington, DC: Agency for International Development.

——. forthcoming-a. *Women, Development and the Wealth of Nations: Making the Case for the Gender Variable.* Boulder, CO: Westview.

——. forthcoming-b. *Women and the Wealth of Nations: Theory and Research on Gender and Global Development.* New York: Praeger.

—— and Coleman. 1985. "Who's on Top? A Theoretical Look at the Gender Balance of Power in the American Couple." Paper presented at the annual meeting of the American Sociological Association, Washington, DC, August.

—— and Coleman. 1989. "A Theoretical Look at the Gender Balance of Power in the American Couple." *Journal of Family Issues,* 10(2):225-250.

Blumstein, Philip and Pepper Schwartz. 1983. *American Couples.* New York: William Morrow.

Boserup, Ester. 1970. *Woman's Role in Economic Development.* New York: St. Martins.

Broch-Due, Vigdis. 1983. "Women at the Backstage of Development: The Negative Impact on Project Realization by Neglecting the Crucial Roles of Turkana Women as Producers and Providers." Rome: Food and Agricultural Organization.

Brown, Judith. 1975. "Iroquois Women: An Ethnohistoric Note." In *Toward an Anthropology of Women,* edited by Rayna R. Reiter. New York: Monthly Review Press.

Brown, Susan E. 1975. "Love Unites Them and Hunger Separates Them: Poor Women in the Dominican Republic." In *Toward an Anthropology of Women,* edited by Rayna R. Reiter. New York: Monthly Review Press.

Cain, Mead, Syeda Rokeya Khanam, and Shamsun Nahar. 1979. "Class, Patriarchy and Women's Work in Bangladesh." *Population and Development Review* 5(3):405-438.

Carloni, Alice Stewart. 1984. "The Impact of Maternal Employment and Income on Nutritional Status in Rural Areas of Developing Countries: What is Known, What is Not Known, and Where the Gaps Are." Rome: United Nations, ACC, Subcommittee on Nutrition.

——. 1987. *Women in Development: A.I.D.'s Experience, 1973-1985. Vol. 1. Synthesis Paper.* Washington, DC: Agency for International Development.

Conti, Anna. 1979. "Capitalist Organization of Production Through Non-Capitalist Relations: Women's Role in a Pilot Resettlement in Upper Volta." *Review of African Political Economy* 15/16:75-91.

Crandon, Libbet with Bonnie Shepard. 1985. *Women, Enterprise, and Development.* Chestnut Hill, MA: Pathfinder Fund.

Cromwell, Ronald E. and David H. Olson. 1975. *Power in Families.* New York: John Wiley.

Dey, Jennie. 1981. "Gambian Women: Unequal Partners in Rice Development Projects?" In *African Women in the Development Process,* edited by Nicci Nelson. London: Frank Cass.

——. 1982. "Development Planning in the Gambia: The Gap Between Planners' and Farmers' Perceptions, Expectations and Objectives." *World Development* 10(5):377-396.

Draper, Patricia. 1975. "!Kung Women: Contrasts in Sexual Egalitarianism in Foraging and Sedentary Contexts." In *Toward an Anthropology of Women*, edited by Rayna R. Reiter. New York: Monthly Review Press.

Dwyer, Daisy Hilse and Judith Bruce. eds. 1988. *A Home Divided: Women and Income in the Third World*. Palo Alto, CA: Stanford University Press.

Economic Commission for Africa. 1983. *ECA and Africa's Development 1983-2008: A Preliminary Perspective Study*. Addis Ababa: Economic Commission for Africa (April).

Fernandez, C. A., II, and Frank Lynch, 1972. "The Tasaday: Cave-Dwelling Food Gatherers of South Cotabato, Mindanao." *Philippine Sociological Review* 20:279-330.

Freifeld, Mary. 1987. Personal communication about ongoing research. San Diego, CA.

Gamble, William K., Rae Lesser Blumberg, Vernon C. Johnson and Ned S. Raun. 1988. *Three Nigerian Universities and Their Role in Agricultural Development*. Washington, DC: Agency for International Development. Project Impact Evaluation Report No. 66.

Gillespie, Dair. 1971. "Who Has the Power? The Marital Struggle." *Journal of Marriage and the Family* 32:445-458.

Guyer, Jane. 1980. "Household Budgets and Women's Incomes." Working Paper No. 28. Boston:African Studies Center, Boston University.

——. 1988a. "Synchronising Seasonalities: From Seasonal Income to Daily Diet in a Partially Commercialised Rural Economy (Southern Cameroon)." In *Causes and Implications of Seasonal Variability in Household Food Security*, edited by David Salin.

Guyer, Jane. 1988b. "Dynamic Approaches to Domestic Budgeting: Cases and Methods from Africa." In *A Home Divided: Women and Income in the Third World*. edited by Daisy Dwyer and Judith Bruce. Palo Alto, CA: Stanford University Press.

Hanger, Jane and Jon Moris. 1973."Women and the Household Economy." In *Mwea: An Irrigated Rice Settlement in Kenya*, edited by Robert Chambers and Jon Moris. Munich: Weltforum Verlag.

Houthakker, H. S. 1957. "An International Comparison of Household Expenditure Patterns, Commemorating the Centenary of Engel's Law." *Econometrica* 25:532-551.

Huber, Joan and Glenna Spitze. 1983. *Sex Stratification: Children, Housework and Jobs*. New York: Academic Press.

Hyden, Goren. 1986. "The Invisible Economy of Smallholder Agriculture in Africa." In *Understanding Africa's Rural Households and Farming Systems*, edited by Joyce Lewinger Moock. Boulder, CO: Westview.

Jones, Christine. 1983."The Impact of the SEMRY I Irrigated Rice Production Project on the Organization of Production and Consumption at the Intrahousehold Level." Washington, DC: Report prepared for the Agency for International Development, Bureau for Program and Policy Coordination.

Kranichfeld, Marion L. 1987. "Rethinking Family Power." *Journal of Family Issues* 8(1):42-56.

Kumar, Shubh K. 1978. "Role of the Household Economy in Child Nutrition at Low Incomes: A Case Study in Kerala." Occasional Paper No. 95. Ithaca: Department of Agricultural Economics, Cornell University.

Kusterer, Ken, Maria Estrada de Batres, and Josefina Xuya Cuxil. 1981. *The Social Impact of Agribusiness: A Case Study of ALCOSA in Guatemala*. AID Evaluation Special Study No. 4. Washington, DC: Agency for International Development, Bureau for Program and Policy Coordination.

Lee, Richard B. 1968. "What Hunters Do for a Living, or How to Make Out on Scarce Resources." In *Man the Hunter*, edited by Richard B. Lee and Irven DeVore. Chicago: Aldine.

———. 1969. "!Kung Bushmen Subsistence: An Input-Output Analysis." In *Environment and Cultural Behavior*, edited by Andrew P. Vayda. Garden City, NY: Natural History Press.

Lenski, Gerhard E. 1966. *Power and Privilege: A Theory of Social Stratification.* New York: McGraw-Hill.

Lombardi, John R. 1973. "Exchange and Survival." Paper presented at the meetings of the American Anthropological Association, New Orleans, November.

Maher, Vanessa. 1981. "Work, Consumption and Authority Within the Household: A Moroccan Case." In *Of Marriage and the Market*, edited by Kate Young, Carol Wolkowitz, and Roslyn McCullagh. London: CSE Books.

McDonald, Gerald W. 1980. "Family Power: The Assessment of a Decade of Theory and Research, 1970-1979." *Journal of Marriage and the Family* 42:841-854.

Mellor, John W., Christopher L. Delgado, and Malcolm J. Blackie, eds. 1987. Accelerating Food Production in Sub-Saharan Africa. Baltimore: Johns Hopkins.

Mencher, Joan. 1988. "Women's Work and Poverty: Women's Contribution to Household Maintenance in South India." In *A Home Divided: Women and Income in the Third World.* edited by Daisy Dwyer and Judith Bruce. Palo Alto, CA: Stanford University Press.

Nance, John. 1975. *The Gentle Tasaday.* New York: Harcourt Brace Jovanovich.

Rogers, Beatrice. 1983. "The Internal Dynamics of Households: A Critical Factor in Development Policy." Nutrition and Development No. 83-2. Washington, DC: Bureau for Program and Policy Coordination, Agency for International Development.

———. 1984. "Intrahousehold Allocation of Resources and Roles: An Annotated Bibliography of the Methodological and Empirical Literature." Nutrition and Development No. 83-3. Washington, DC: Bureau for Program and Policy Coordination, Agency for International Development.

Roldan, Martha. 1982. "Intrahousehold Patterns of Money Allocation and Women's Subordination: A Case Study of Domestic Outworkers in Mexico City." Unpublished paper circulated at the Population Council seminar on Women, Income, and Policy, New York, March.

Roldan, Martha. 1988. "Renegotiating the Marital Contract: Intrahousehold Patterns of Money Allocation and Women's Subordination Among Domestic Outworkers in Mexico City." In *A Home Divided: Women and Income in the Third World.* edited by Daisy Dwyer and Judith Bruce. Palo Alto, CA: Stanford University Press.

Safilios-Rothschild, Constantina. 1970. "The Study of Family Power Structure: A Review, 1960-1969." *Journal of Marriage and the Family* 31:290-301.

Stack, Carol. 1974. *All Our Kin: Strategies for Survival in a Black Community.* New York: Harper & Row.

Staudt, Kathleen. 1987. "Uncaptured or Unmotivated? Women and the Food Crisis in Africa." *Rural Sociology* 52(1):37-55.

Stavrakis, Olga and Marion Louise Marshall. 1978. "Women, Agriculture and Development in the Maya Lowlands: Profit or Progress?" Paper presented at the International Conference on Women and Food, Tucson.

Tiano, Susan. 1987. "Gender, Work, and World Capitalism: Third World Women's Role in Development." Pp. 216-243 in *Analyzing Gender: A Handbook of Social Science Research,* edited by Beth B. Hess and Myra Marx Ferree. Newbury Park, CA: Sage.

Tinker, Irene and Michele Bo Bramsen, eds. 1976. *Women and World Development.* Washington, DC: Overseas Development Council/American Association for the Advancement of Science.

Tripp, Robert B. 1981. "Farmers and Traders: Some Economic Determinants of Nutritional Status in Northern Ghana." *Journal of Tropical Pediatrics* 27:15-22.

Turnbull, Colin. 1961. *The Forest People.* New York: Simon & Schuster.

———. 1981. "Mbuti Womanhood." In *Woman the Gatherer*, edited by Frances Dahlberg. New Haven: Yale University Press.

United Nations. 1978. *Effective Mobilization of Women in Development.* Report of the Secretary General. UN A/33/238. New York: United Nations.

Weller, Robert H. 1968. "The Employment of Wives, Dominance and Fertility." *Journal of Marriage and the Family* 30:437-442.

Whitehead, Ann. 1981. "I'm Hungry, Mum: The Politics of Domestic Budgeting." In *Of Marriage and the Market,* edited by Kate Young, Carol Wolkowitz, and Roslyn McCullagh. London: CSE Books.

World Bank. 1981. *Accelerated Development in Sub-Saharan Africa: An Agenda for Action.* Washington, DC: World Bank.

5

Female Autonomy, the Family, and Industrialization in Java

DIANE L. WOLF

It is generally argued that industrialization has an adverse effect on the position of women due to their exclusion from industrial employment and the resultant erosion of their status[1] (Boserup, 1970; Saffioti, 1978). This chapter addresses a case study to the question of gender stratification and industrialization by analyzing the relationship between factory daughters and their families in Java, Indonesia. Using data gathered in rural Central Java, I juxtapose the East Asian experience with this Southeast Asian case to illuminate the crucial role family systems play in mediating the type, extent, and direction of change industrialization can have upon individuals, gender, and family relationships. My data portray a more ambiguous relationship between industrialization and women's position, suggesting that at the micro level, industrialization may even enhance the status of female workers.

Blumberg's theory of gender stratification guides this inquiry into the relationships between gender, labor, industrialization, and family change. Blumberg (1984, p. 47) defines women's economic power as the degree of control women exert over the means of production, the allocation of surplus or of surplus value, and distinguishes between at least two different spheres in which women's economic power can be

AUTHOR'S NOTE: Field research was supported by a Title XII grant administered through the Program in International Agriculture, Cornell University (1981-1983) and the Graduate School Research Fund, University of Washington (1986). The Lembaga Pengatahun Ilmu Indonesia (LIPI) and the Population Studies Center, Gadjah Mada University, Yogyakarta, sponsored my research. I am grateful to Rae Lesser Blumberg, Judith Howard, Charles Hirschman, Daniel Lev, and Christine Di Stefano for comments and advice.

analyzed: the micro level (i.e., married couple, household) and the macro level (i.e., community, ideology, religion, state, economy). While the macro and micro levels of women's position are interrelated, they can be distinguished analytically. Industrialization induces change at both the macro and micro levels, which affect gender stratification and women's status. Macro-level change occurs slowly but wields considerable influence over women's status, whereas micro-level change is fairly rapid. The extent to which women fully realize power will ultimately depend upon macro-level change. Predicting the overall effects of Indonesian industrialization upon the status of all Javanese women would entail combining and weighing micro- and macro-level factors—including family, community, state, economy, religion, ideology, and the legal system—which is beyond the scope of this chapter. I will limit the inquiry here to the micro level, specifically, the effects of increased income on the status of female factory workers within the family.[2]

At the micro level, the kinship system mediates between women's productive activities and their control over the fruits of their labor; it shapes the parameters of women's power. Blumberg evaluates three crucial features of the kinship system as they affect the power of women: rules of inheritance, residence, and descent. Women's status would be highest in a matrilineal, matrilocal system (Chafetz, 1980, p. 112) and lowest in a patrilineal, patrilocal system, such as the Chinese family.

The Javanese Family System and Women's Status

In Java, inheritance is bilateral, although females may receive less than their brothers (Geertz, 1961). Wet-rice cultivation systems such as those found in Indonesia, the Philippines, and Thailand are associated with bilateral inheritance and high female social status (Goldschmidt and Kunkel, 1971, p. 1,069; Blumberg, 1984).[3] Descent is also bilateral. Residence is usually matrilocal initially and then neolocal once the couple can afford to set up their own home. However, rules of residence are not rigid and, in some cases, the couple may initially live with the groom's parents if they are much better off than the bride's parents. Geertz (1961, p. 78) argues that there is a strong network between kinswomen in Java that affects household organization and decision making and offers mutual aid and loyalty in times of distress. These bilateral and matrilocal characteristics found in the Javanese family rank high on Blumberg's scale of female power.[4] Cross-cultural family researchers have noted the flexibility of family systems in Southeast

Asia, including the Javanese family (Goldschmidt and Kunkel, 1971; Todd, 1985). This characteristic can work to women's benefit but does not automatically do so.

In most Third World countries, colonial rule radically disrupted the division of labor and the system of production, leading to changes in the value of traditional female economic activities that were detrimental to women's status (Boserup, 1970; Tinker, 1976). Java is one of the few historical exceptions in which women maintained their precolonial high position during colonialism (Chafetz, 1980). The Dutch imposed export crop production upon the traditional Javanese household economy, maintaining the high economic contribution of women in productive activities such as wet-rice cultivation and in sugar factories (Stoler, 1977).

Field research was conducted in Central Java. In general, Central Java is Islamic but not very strict. While women are not secluded and retain considerable economic autonomy (i.e., they work for pay and trade in the market on their own account) men try to assure the sexual propriety of their wives, daughters, and sisters. Research has also shown that the high status of Javanese women is conditioned by their class standing in an increasingly stratified agrarian economy (Stoler, 1977; Sajogyo, 1983). There are significant differences in control over economic resources such as land that shape women's income-seeking options and strategies. Village studies show that the majority of households and therefore the majority of rural women do not control sufficient amounts of land to meet subsistence needs (White, 1976; Hart, 1986; Wolf, 1986). While poorer women may control the returns from their labor thereby maintaining "high economic power," it is important to recognize that there may be little income to control.[5]

Until now, research on the economic power of Javanese women has focused upon rural, agriculturally based settings (Geertz, 1961; Jay, 1969). Javanese women are ubiquitous as traders in the market (Dewey, 1962), and they exert some control over agricultural production as owner-cultivators (Stoler, 1977). Recent large-scale industrialization in Java draws heavily upon female labor as in most Southeast Asian settings, but the relationship between industrialization and women's position has received relatively little scholarly attention.

Existing research is at the micro level but suggests that the effects of industrialization upon Javanese women's status and power at a macro level would be negative due to women's loss of control over the means and processes of production (Mather, 1985; Wolf, 1986). Javanese women fare worse within the social relationships of production in industrial capitalism than they do in agriculture. This fits with the general assertion that industrialization leads to a decline in female status in agricultural or horticultural societies in which women had high status (Boserup, 1970).

Industrialization, the Family, and Female Status

It is of interest, therefore, to ascertain if the preindustrial levels of status and power of Javanese women are being maintained as they leave agricultural cultivation and enter large, modern, manufacturing firms. Blumberg (1988, p. 28) argues that women's relative control over economic resources is the "single most important—although far from only—factor affecting women's overall equality." Economic resources in this case pertain to earnings. I evaluate female power in the family by examining the level of control factory daughters exert over their income. Using Blumberg's model, high female economic power is generally expected within the Javanese kinship system. Increased income earning opportunities from industrial employment should therefore enhance women's high status in the family.

Analysis of possible changes in female status leads implicitly to an exploration of the stability of the family system in light of economic structural change. While standard family sociological theory predicts that industrial capitalism will eventually erode the strength of kinship ties and patriarchal family organization, giving way to more egalitarian family relationships (Goode, 1963), gender subordination within the family has changed little in East Asian countries that have undergone substantial industrialization. In Hong Kong and Taiwan, the predominantly female factory workers remain embedded in patriarchal family relationships, despite their recent and substantial income-earning capacities (Salaff, 1981; Kung, 1983; Greenhalgh, 1985). Industrial capitalism has not brought with it concurrent autonomy for women workers but rather, preindustrial norms of filial piety and female subordination are perpetuated—and even intensified (Greenhalgh, 1985)—within a new system of production.

The question addressed here provides a window onto the Javanese family and its reaction to industrialization. Because the preindustrial Javanese family system was relatively egalitarian and accorded women economic autonomy, standard family sociological theory would predict that an even higher degree of autonomy will result from such structural change.

Research Site

The research site is a rural district *(kecematan)* in Central Java with a population of 83,500 located approximately 16 miles south of Semarang, a large port city. There is easy access in the site to the highway that connects Semarang to several cities in Central Java. In the early 1970s, provincial and district-level government officials began to encourage foreign and domestic urban investment in this area. Factories began to locate in this rural subdistrict in 1972 and still continue to do so. The area may eventually develop into a periurban site, but it is still rural, with the majority of the population engaged in agricultural production.[6] The factories[7] are located in two villages and many are, in fact, sitting in the middle of rice fields.

This burst of industrial activity can be partially attributed to the new international division of labor. This phenomenon, also termed "industrial redeployment," is typified by the movement of capital, technology, and the production process to Asia and Latin America, where the cheap labor of young "nimble-fingered" females produces cheaper commodities for the global market. Studies of Free Trade Zones in Latin America and Southeast Asia have found that workers are single females between the ages of 15 to 25 (UNIDO, 1980; Elson and Pearson, 1981). In this rural site, three-fourths of the 6,000-person industrial work force was female, most of whom were young and single. This site, however, was not a Free Trade Zone.[8] Most contemporary research on women and industrialization focuses on migrants because they constitute the bulk of the manufacturing work force in Free Trade Zones and/or in urban areas (Salaff, 1981; Nash and Fernandez-Kelly, 1983). In this study, local residents living at home constituted 90% of the work force. Both the rural location and the familial context added an important dimension rarely found in other Third World locales, allowing an in-depth analysis of the relationship between worker-daughters and their families.

Research Design and Analysis

I lived in an agricultural village, Nuwun (a pseudonym), located several miles from the factories, with easy access to public transportation, so that I could compare commuting factory workers and their peers who remained in the village and were engaged in domestic or agricultural activities.[9] I found that factory workers came from poorer households,[10] at a later stage of the family life cycle, meaning that there were few young children and a low dependency ratio.[11] In land-poor families, more members must seek wage labor to ensure the perpetuation of the household (de Janvry and Deere, 1978). Therefore, from a household economy perspective, I expected that workers would remit substantial proportions of their wages to the family as factory daughters have done in Western Europe (Tilly and Scott, 1978), North America (Dublin, 1979; Hareven, 1982), Hong Kong (Salaff, 1981), Taiwan (Arrigo, 1980; Huang, 1984; Kung, 1983), Malaysia (Ong, 1987), and elsewhere (Fernandez-Kelly, 1982).

Design of Income-Expenditures Survey

From an initial one-month daily survey of income and expenditures conducted among 14 workers in Nuwun, I found that although they contributed 28% of their wages to the family, in cash or in kind, they overspent their wages by 40% (Wolf, 1984). During subsequent interviews, workers and families confirmed that workers borrowed small amounts of money from parents and friends, usually for transportation and lunch.

I then designed a more extensive survey, including questions about access to other income (other economic activities, money borrowed, loans repaid, and so forth), debts, and savings.[12] To determine if the relationship between daughters and family economy was related to residence, I expanded the survey to include three different groups of workers: commuters, migrants, and residents. Commuters lived with their parents in the agricultural village, Nuwun, and were the sole focus of the first income survey. Migrants were boarders in an industrialized village, Pamit, and residents walked to work. Single, rather than married women are the focus of this paper due to the very different contribution daughters can make potentially to the family's welfare.

Worker's Income and Expenditures

The average salary earned by commuters, migrants, and residents was 15,600 rupiahs ($24.00) per month for a 48-hour work week.[13] However, owing to debts, savings, and loans, workers often had access to more cash than wages alone, averaging 18,850 rupiahs ($29.00) per month.

In Table 5.1 the proportion of wages spent on selected expenditures illustrates several striking patterns. Commuters spent more than 40% of their salaries on two basics that only partially reproduced the ability

Table 5.1 Selected Expenditures as Proportion of Salary of Worker
Residence Status

	Commuters	Migrants	Residents
Clothing[a]	14%	11%	16%
Food[b]	20	29	20
Transportation	25	9	10
Household goods	0.1	2	0.6
Toiletries	3	5	9
To family	2.5	6.3	17.7
Haircuts, jewelry, entertainment	6.1	2.6	10
Savings	26	40	30
Average monthly salary (Rps.)	15,383	16,211	15,324

NOTES: a. Clothing includes clothes bought outright and debts paid for clothing.
b. Food includes lunch, snacks, and food bought for the household. In general, commuters and residents bought little food for their households: most of their expenditures on food were for lunch and snacks.

to work daily—transportation and lunch. The 20% spent on clothing included both necessary goods and less necessary items that might be considered luxury spending, such as long pants or expensive umbrellas. The juxtaposition of unexpectedly small amounts contributed to families with that spent on luxury goods is most striking; workers contributed little directly to their family's subsistence.

Migrants tended to lead the most frugal lives of all three categories of workers, perhaps because they were more on their own financially. Although they spent less than other workers on themselves (clothing, haircuts, jewelry, and movies), they spent more on such daily needs as food and toiletries. Migrants brought back food supplies from visits home (i.e., cooking oil, sacks of rice, cassava), so the amount they spend on food does not represent all food consumption.[14] Those who returned home during the month of the survey gave more to parents than did commuters.

The consumption patterns of residents suggests that they spent more on luxury goods and leisure than other workers. Although a higher proportion of their money was given to their families, residents also received a substantial amount of money from their families, resulting in a small net flow to the family. Clothing—both necessary and luxury—consumed approximately 15% of salaries of all three groups.

General expenditure patterns in all three groups of workers show that they are controlling most, if not all, of their wages. In other words, after deducting basic fixed costs (lunch and/or transportation), residents and commuters could conceivably turn over 55% to 80% of their wages to their families. Instead, they spent much of their wages as they pleased, with the exception of savings that will be discussed shortly.

A more detailed view of the contribution of workers' wages to the family economy is presented in Table 5.2. The net contribution was calculated by subtracting the amount of money the worker received from her family from the total value of money or goods she gave to the family.[15] With the exclusion of two outliers, the net contribution to the family economy was extraordinarily small: 3.6%, 5.5%, and 13.6% for commuters, migrants, and residents, respectively.[16] These small contributions indicate a high degree of female control over income, particularly in light of their families' poverty.

A total of 30% of the commuters gave nothing or actually took money from their families; the remaining 70% contributed small amounts. As seen in Table 5.2, 50% gave 1,000 rupiahs ($1.50) or less and 20% gave 1,001 rupiahs ($1.50) or more. The average amount contributed by commuters to their families that month was less than $.50 from a $24.00 wage. Their small contribution to the family economy in this survey corroborates findings from my first survey. Partiyem, a single commuting worker who lived with her family, said: "I rarely give money to my parents, it's used for transport only, and then I still have to ask my parents for money."

I compared the amount remitted to the family from workers in Nuwun in the two different surveys. In the second survey, workers consistently gave a lower percentage of their wages to their families. This suggests that workers adjust their contributions to the family economy, particularly if the household is experiencing strain, such as the period right before the harvest when cash and food supplies are low. However, this also means that workers do not remit a steady flow to their families upon which the family can depend. Rather, transfers of cash and goods have more the quality of a gift than an obligatory, expected contribution.

More than half of the migrants gave nothing to the families of origin during the month surveyed, but those who contributed gave more than the commuters, averaging 900 rupiahs ($1.50). Many migrants said they did not want to return home unless they could bring money to their families. When asked about money given to parents, Siti, a migrant worker in the textile factory, answered,

> If I go home, I sometimes give money to my younger siblings, which is a good feeling because the money is from my work; but what can I do if I don't have money.

Table 5.2 Net Contribution to the Family Economy

	Commuters N = 10	Migrants N = 15	Residents[a] N = 7
Average net contribution[b]	300 Rps.[c]	900 Rps.	−400 Rps. (2,011 Rps.)[d]
Net contribution as proportion of salary	−9% (3.6)[d]	5.5%	−8.6% (13.6%)[d]
RANGE OF NET CONTRIBUTION TO FAMILY ECONOMY			
Negative[e]	10%	6.7%	28.6%
Zero	20	46.7	0
1-1000 Rps.	50	13	0
1001-3,000 Rps.	20	13	28.6
+3,000 Rps.	0	19	42.8
	100	98.4	100

NOTE: Net contribution for commuters and residents was calculated as the following: money to family plus goods and food bought for family minus money from family. For migrants, it was calculated as money to family minus money from family. Many migrants brought rice and other foodstuffs from home, but it was not possible to calculate this for the month of the survey.
a. Residents were daughters living at home in an industrialized village, walking to work.
b. The average wage was 15,600 Rps. or $24.00 per month.
c. At the time of the research, 650 Rps. = $1.00.
d. Excluding one outlier.
e. Ranging from −15,000 Rps. to −4,000 Rps.

Ambarwati, another migrant worker, said,

It's already been three months that I haven't returned home even though my mother already ordered me to come home. I'll go home later when I have money; if I go home and don't bring anything, I'll feel ashamed.

Alfiah's parents live nearby, but, nevertheless she boards near the factories. She stated,

My mother sells food from our house. For my food, usually she sends things home with me, like rice. I never have enough money; there's always a shortage and I ask my mother for money.

With the exception of one resident, who received 15,000 rupiahs ($23.00) from her family, the average net contribution of residents' wages to their families was higher than that of commuters. Suyatmini worked in the textile factory and lived with her mother and older brother in an industrialized village:

Ah . . . my wage is very low. I only use it for my own needs and sometimes also I give some to my mother. Basically, the money is only enough for my own needs.[17]

By contrast, in Taiwan, parents feel entitled to most, if not all, of a daughter's wages, and a daughter feels obligated to remit a high proportion of her income to them. The financial contract between parents and daughters is implicit, understood, and accepted with little discussion (Kung, 1983, p. 116). Researchers have found that workers remit 50% to 100% of their wages to the family, which often subsidizes a younger brother's education (Diamond, 1979; Arrigo, 1980; Salaff, 1981; Kung, 1983; Thornton, Chang, and Sun, 1984; Greenhalgh, 1985).

Compare the above responses from Javanese factory workers with those from their Taiwanese counterparts: A young Taiwanese who works in a textile firm, who lives at home, and who turns over her entire wage to her mother, said, "After all, our parents raised us. If we don't give them money, who else should it go to?" (Kung, 1984, p. 112). Another worker said:

For women like myself, when we take money home it's because we feel we ought to; it's the right thing to do and not because our parents demand it. On what we make, there isn't much left over after expenses (meals), but whatever remains, whether a lot or a little, should be taken home. (Kung, 1983, p. 117)

Parental Responses

When asked if their daughters' wages contributed to the family economy, most Javanese parents felt that their daughters contributed in one of two ways: either directly—with cash and goods—or, more commonly, indirectly—by taking care of her cash needs. Others were not so sure, and a few were forthright about their feelings that their daughters were concerned solely with their own pleasures. There was clearly a range of contributions, subsidizations, and parental discontent.

Comments, such as the following, illustrate the variation of responses to the question of whether their daughter contributed to the family economy:

Yes, a little, for example she often leaves money underneath the tablecloth for daily (food) shopping. But if she doesn't leave it, I don't ask for it. I've never looked for money in her room.

Or, "If she's asked, yes, she gives us money. But if we don't ask, she doesn't. Sometimes we ask, but she says she doesn't have any." Another parent was pleased that her daughter, formerly a servant to another family in the village, was a factory worker because she could "buy anything . . . I'm happy she can work, and I don't want to ask her to contribute to the family."

Although factory wages may not necessarily contribute directly to the family economy, parents generally felt that factory wages played a role they couldn't:

> At home we can't fulfill her needs, so it's better she's working in the factory. We're happy she's working because we can't buy her anything; we can only feed her.

Another ambivalent parent said:

> At home, what kind of work can she find? Anyway, we can't fulfill her needs. If it was only food she needed, we could. But I can't buy other things. Anyway, girls need a lot things. She has three kinds of face powder, shoes, and sandals. But a girl working in a factory isn't right [literally, *adalah kotor*—it's dirty/garbage] and shames us. But at home, we don't have money for her needs.

Not all parents responded positively. A disgruntled father said, "She spends her salary as she pleases, for shopping; she doesn't even tell me what she earns." Another worker's mother agreed: "Everyday she just has fun from morning till evening. Her money is spent just for play. She never helped us; in fact, she often asks us for transportation money." Or, "No, she doesn't contribute to the family. Her money is spent just for her own pleasure" *(untuk senang-2 sendiri)*.

All of these parental responses, regardless of their content, indicate that daughters controlled their own wage. Again, this contrasts sharply with the high remittances from Taiwanese or Hong Kong factory daughters to parents who then give working daughters a small allowance (Salaff, 1981; Kung, 1983). The behavior exhibited by Javanese factory daughters would be unacceptable and the source of shame and perhaps scandal within a Chinese familial context.

Chinese parents expect financial returns from a daughter in return for bringing her into the world and bringing her up. The high remittances of young women are repaying parents. Kung (1983) reports that many Taiwanese mothers she interviewed said: "The minimum a daughter should give is 50% to 80% of her earnings, and a daughter who turns over all her wages would be considered the most filial" (p. 116). Javanese parents also expect economic returns from their daughters, but they expect less than Chinese parents, and expectations are expressed less directly. Two examples are representative of parental responses to my question, "Should a working daughter give her wage to her parents?" and also illustrate these cultural differences.

Case 1: No, don't! Use your money for yourself or save it. You can also give some to parents, but just enough for their needs (secukupnya saja). Good parents shouldn't want much money from their children.

Case 2: Parents shouldn't be like that. If they're given money, yes, they should accept it, but if they're not given money, never mind. My daughter works and I'm happy. I rarely ask for money, but she knows when I need it. Sometimes, she brings home a blouse for me.

There is yet another link between wages and the family economy besides food, clothing, or cash remittances that made parents tolerant of such low remittances. Approximately one third of the wages of most workers went to savings. And savings, unlike weekly wages, were more accessible to familial control.

Savings

Table 5.1 demonstrates that workers saved approximately 30% of their wages. Most workers surveyed participated in a rotating savings association (arisan). Every payday, members of the arisan met and contributed a certain amount of cash to a pool. One or two members' names were drawn from a bottle to receive the cash. It was a fixed lottery: each person received the cash once before someone received it twice. Depending upon the size of the group, a worker might receive the arisan once to several times a year. It was a safe way to save money without the dangers of loss or corruption and, in addition, served as a social function. It is an antihousehold strategy to accumulate capital as it keeps cash out of circulation. Otherwise, workers found it impossible to save since parents and siblings asked for small amounts of money.

Due to such low wages, one commuting worker said, "If you don't participate in an arisan, there's nothing left over to show for your week." During the month of the survey, 8 out of 39 workers received an arisan, averaging 39,000 rupiahs ($60.00) and ranging from 5,000 to 100,000 rupiahs.

One third of all the single factory workers sampled did not participate in the *arisan*. Only those from families in which there was a slight
margin of economic safety could afford to save money. Poorer families
have a greater daily need for cash, which leaves less or no money for
savings.

Workers used their savings first to pay off debts incurred (usually for
clothing) and to buy consumer goods for the family; parents were quick
to point out the much appreciated consumer goods their daughters had
bought—cupboards, radios, beds, clocks, and dishes. Some of these
were high status luxury goods—radios, tape recorders, clocks, and
pressure lamps. While daughters did not usually consult with parents
about what to buy with their savings, they used most of it to buy
consumer goods for family or reinvested it in a form families could use
if necessary.

A substantial proportion of the *arisan* was spent on gold jewelry or
livestock, both of which are considered savings in a peasant economy
and can be resold quickly for cash. The gold or livestock belonged to
the daughter and most workers said these possessions would go with
them when married and they moved elsewhere. However, these savings
were made available to the family in times of need—debts, emergen-
cies, and life-cycle events (circumcision, ritual feast) including the
daughter's own wedding. For example, one worker sold her 10 ducks
at a loss at the end of the fasting month (Ramadan), a consumption-
oriented time of year, when her family needed cash. Several workers
gave part or all of their gold savings to family members who needed
cash, but the loan was not always repaid. When I returned in 1986, I
found that crop failure had forced many families to rely upon a factory
daughter's savings to stay afloat. While parents did not control a daughter's savings in the way that Taiwanese parents control a daughter's
income, it was accessible to them and their requests were not refused.

One commuting worker, Suniwati, rarely gave her parents cash from
her wages, but, as her mother explained:

> She saved money and bought plates, glasses, clothing, and ducks which we
> sold at Lebaran. She had earrings of two and one half grams but then sold
> them to buy a goat. The goat didn't have kids so we sold it.

Siti, a commuting worker, lived with her mother. They were one of
the poorest families in the village. They owned a small amount of land
that provided only four months of rice needs. They needed cash to buy
rice for the remaining eight months of the year. Siti's mother worked
for a *penebas*—a middleman who bought harvests still on the ground—

and traveled from harvest to harvest, often far from home. Siti and her mother lived in a tiny two-room house made of bamboo, one wall of which separated them from the neighboring family. There was no furniture in the house—not even a chair—and all interviews were conducted outside. After receiving an *arisan* of 100,000 rupiahs ($154.00), Siti had the inner walls of the house rebuilt with wood and bought a set of living room furniture. The *arisan* allowed her to buy goods for family use that she and her mother could not have otherwise afforded.

In addition, once a year, at Idul Fitri (the end of the fasting month of Ramadan), factory workers received an annual bonus. This is a very consumption-oriented time of year, when people buy new clothes, fix up their homes, and cook special food for guests. The average bonus of workers in Nuwun in 1982 was 22,000 rupiahs ($33.85), ranging from 8,000 to 35,000 rupiahs. Most workers bought gold jewelry and new clothes for themselves and family members, and some bought new furniture. The cash bonus at Lebaran was expected to be spent for the family's needs.

Therefore, while daughters control petty amounts of cash from their weekly wages, spending it for their own benefit, they are more family oriented with larger sums of capital. Although factory workers decided what to purchase with their savings, they relinquished control over savings (cash, gold, livestock) if a family member was in need. Parental access to savings made a daughter's frivolous and self-centered consumption behavior with her wages more acceptable. Indeed, without the long-term benefit of savings, parents might have expressed more discontent with a daughter's daily economic behavior.

Discussion and Conclusions

The Status of Javanese Women

How has industrialization affected the autonomy of the female worker within the Javanese family? While many preindustrial gender and familial relationships are maintained, industrialization has engendered certain changes that fortify and increase female economic power in the family.[18] Javanese factory daughters combine adherence to traditional filial norms with control over more income.

While autonomy exists in some realms, patriarchal control was exerted over issues of female propriety and freedom. Javanese factory workers still operate according to certain ascribed traditional, submissive, and dependent female roles within the family. First, large sums of money—that acquired from bonuses or through savings—are relinquished to familial control if needed. Daughters are passive and accepting of such demands. Second, factory workers in Nuwun still obeyed their fathers *(harus ikut Bapak)* in decisions ranging from working in a sex-segregated factory (garments), migrating to a city, or renting a room in the village next to the factories. When a father was not present, young women obeyed the decision of older brothers who stepped in when a sister's honor or sexual reputation was at stake. Migrant workers in the industrialized village either left home with a father's permission or ran away without it. Finally, despite the high economic power of factory workers, a contradictory situation prevails: These women remain financially dependent upon their families for free food, lodging, and other necessities because wages paid to female workers are below subsistence level.[19] These low wages are justified by factories with traditional Javanese norms that consider women's income as secondary and therefore unnecessary (Mather, 1985).

At the same time, industrialization has brought with it specific changes that strengthen female autonomy and economic power within the family. Factory work brings young women more cash than seasonal agricultural employment and trade or the low wages of domestic service. Perhaps because of the new life-cycle state of these young women—single young adulthood—these earnings are subject to fewer regular familial economic obligations, and workers can freely exert more control over higher earnings. These changes in cash and control can be seen in their new consumerism and in their appearance—factory workers dress differently, often wearing make-up and daring to sport long pants or nail polish. They perceive that their status is higher due to factory employment and exert increasingly assertive behavior—refusing to help out on the family's rice field or stating that they would choose their own spouse.

Daughters living at home who do not work in factories usually contribute their labor to the family economy and, more sporadically, cash from returns to their labor. Factory daughters, however, contribute only cash, but they contribute it to families operating in a cash- and employment-scarce society. Their importance to the family economy as a steady source of capital accumulation will increase over time, particularly in light of broader changes occurring in the political economy of rural Java. For example, recent government budget cuts have eliminated projects that provided village males with nonagricultural employment. One test of this hypothesized increased power at the family level will be an analysis of their control over marriage.[20]

To summarize, if a family can release a daughter for factory employment and can forego the returns from her labor, there are eventual benefits for both the worker and her family. Worker-daughters are less of a financial burden on families. Their savings provide surplus income that is not used for subsistence needs. Families gain tangible "status goods" that are displayed in the house and, at the same time, have access to insurance for crises and cash needs. Daughters, on the other hand, choose what to purchase and for whom. They gain prestige as donors of thoughtful gifts to family members (a blouse, a bar of soap, a radio), and gifts are symbols of independence. They also gain prestige as providers of emergency aid. These contributions bring them higher status than would remitting a steady but tiny flow of cash to the family economy.[21]

Comparative Perspectives

In Taiwan and Hong Kong, the changes in women workers' lives are of a different magnitude than those of Javanese workers. Kung notes that in previous times, a father was given the wage his daughter earned. One change is that women workers receive their wages directly, creating the fiction that daughters choose how they dispose of their income (Kung, 1983, p. 116). Second, researchers found that while the percentage of workers remitting most of their wages to their families has decreased over time, "the magnitude of that decline was fairly small" (Thornton, Chang, and Sun, 1984, p. 484). More working women among younger cohorts had significantly more spending money of their own than the older cohorts. However, this does not imply financial independence or autonomy, for the strong familial and patriarchal controls are still perpetuated.

The comparison of Javanese and Chinese families and factory daughters showed that in both cases, industrialization did not result in substantial changes in preindustrial female economic power within the family. The values and organization of the preindustrial Chinese family system appear to remain intact after industrialization, with few indications as of yet that patriarchal relationships will give way to egalitarianism. The Javanese family system is maintained during early industrialization, but the implications for women's autonomy in Java are antithetical to the Chinese case: Chinese factory daughters maintain their subordinate status while Javanese factory workers maintain or perhaps increase their economic power within the household.[22]

This comparison underscores the importance of understanding family systems in evaluating social change, particularly with regard to women's status. The type, degree, and direction of change differ in these cases because these two family systems operate within distinct and incongruent boundaries. An analysis of the Java data without considering the family system would lead to the faulty interpretation that industrialization created *modern,* individualistic behavior when in fact the behavior of factory workers is completely recognizable within Javanese cultural boundaries. If Taiwanese factory workers began to retain most of their income, indeed such an argument would be valid.

The Larger Context of Women and Industrialization

A current and complex debate among those studying gender and socioeconomic change concerns whether the process of industrial development inevitably contributes to the relative marginalization of women (Scott, 1986). This study has demonstrated that during early industrialization, Javanese women enhance their high status within the family. Lest we conclude simplemindedly, it is important to recognize that despite economic power, low wages force factory workers to remain financially dependent upon their families. The challenge ensues—both theoretically and empirically—to investigate these micro-level processes, analyze their relationships to macro-level structures, and weigh the contradictions therein.

Notes

1. See Mason (1985) for a succinct discussion of the complexity of defining and measuring female status.

2. My focus is limited to unmarried working daughters between the ages of 15 to 24; generalizations about wives or women of other generations are not made.

3. Goldschmidt and Kunkel suggest that the bilateral inheritance systems and the "permissive, egalitarian" family structures found in certain Southeast Asian countries are associated with a particular ecological situation—large frontier areas that were recently brought into wet-rice cultivation (Goldschmidt and Kunkel, 1971, p. 1,069). See Moore (1973) for a fuller discussion of ecology, female economic activities, and family structure in Southeast Asia.

4. It must be understood, however, that while the status and economic power of Javanese women is high in relation to East Asian and South Asian women, this does not imply that patriarchal controls over women are absent in Java (Mather, 1985).

5. White and Hastuti's (1980) study of household decision making in West Java demonstrated mixed responses with regard to female autonomy in decisions. Wives controlled food-related decisions, but other domestic decisions (clothing, purchase of household utensils, education) were usually joint decisions. The dynamic of the joint decision ranged from wife dominant to husband dominant. One explanation may be that West Java is ethnically Sundanese and more Islamic in belief and practice than other parts

of Java, contributing to less female power in family relationships. Women in West Java, however, do have property rights, work outside the home in agriculture and trade, and control the returns from their labor. Thus far, conclusions about patterns of decision making in Java are impeded by a lack of systematic research.

6. Only a small minority of Javanese rural households own or control enough land to meet household subsistence needs. However, in this area, the majority of households still engage in some form of agricultural production—as owner-operators, sharecroppers/renters, or wage laborers—as one of several economic activities.

7. There were nine large-scale factories and three medium-sized factories when I conducted my research in 1981-1983, with three large-scale firms under construction. When I returned in 1986, all 15 factories were in production and more were still being built. The largest factories are textiles, followed by garments and food processing (bread, cookies, bottling), furniture, and buses. The two largest firms are foreign-owned (textiles and spinning), and the four largest (textiles, spinning, garments, and glassware) are export-oriented. Most are typically female-intensive industries except glassware and buses.

8. The latter tend to be dominated by multinational corporations and exclusively export-oriented. In this site, the firms were both nationally and foreign owned. Most firms were domestically oriented in their markets even if they also exported. Thus, unlike studies on industrialization in Southeast Asian Free Trade Zones, this site had stronger ties with domestic (national) capital and the domestic market.

9. De Janvry and Deere's model (1978) provided a framework for the analysis of the integration of peasants into a capitalist economy. In my research the model was applied to analyze class differentiation, household employment strategies, the determinants of factory employment, and the relationship between factory wages and the reproduction of the household. This framework integrates key variables for analysis at the micro level— that is, age, gender hierarchies, class differentiation, life-cycle stage, and labor allocation—with macro-level structural change.

10. A household was defined as a coresidential group sharing the kitchen and food. In the two agricultural villages studied, almost all of the 250 households consisted of nuclear or extended families. I use *family* and *household* interchangeably, although no assumptions are made about family structure.

11. I compared 39 village females (and their households) who worked in factories with 90 village females who had never worked in a factory. Factory workers came from poorer households at a later stage of the life cycle (as indicated by the consumer-worker and dependency ratios) such that parents could forego the daily returns to an adult member's labor. Households with a land and labor shortage could not afford to release a daughter for factory employment. Results from a logistic regression model demonstrated that the most significant factors affecting the probability of a female seeking factory employment were children ever born ($p < .01$); followed by class status ($p < .05$); and two life-cycle measures, the consumer-worker ratio ($p < .10$) and the presence of other able-bodied females ($p < .10$) in the household (Wolf, 1986).

12. Literate workers kept daily records on the provided forms and were visited every three days; illiterate workers were interviewed every 48 hours.

13. Wages in Indonesian manufacturing are reported to be among the lowest in their world (Frobel, Heinrichs, and Kreye, 1980, p. 35). The minimum wage in 1982 was 625 rupiahs daily ($0.96) for eight hours work, but due to the low educational level of workers in this rural site, most factories paid *below* the minimum wage.

14. Rent was not included in the table because boarders paid rent in two to three annual installments. None of these migrants paid rent during the time surveyed. However, the average monthly rent was 1,180 rupiahs ($1.82) or 7.3% of their average monthly salary.

15. Typically, workers bought food for the family or goods such as cooking oil and spices or kerosene. Occasionally, they purchased a durable good such as a tray or a small tablecloth. They reported whatever they spent on such goods bought expressly for household consumption.

16. If I had attempted to value a worker's household consumption—food or goods produced by the household, excluding the market value of rent—it is likely that the net contribution would be negative in all cases. Such an effort was beyond the limits of this research project.

17. "Pokoknya, uang itu cukup untuk keperluan saya sendiri."

18. Any analysis comparing women's position in preindustrial and industrial settings must proceed with caution. Until very recently, young women in this age group (18 to 24) already would have been married and have had children due to arranged marriages at an early age. An increase in self-selection of both spouse and age at marriage creates an unprecedented life-cycle state of single late adolescence and early adulthood still at home.

19. The union estimated that to subsist, a worker in Central Java would need approximately 40% more than what these women earn. Male workers earn more but do not necessarily have a higher skill level than their female counterparts. Of the five male workers I surveyed, four earned subsistence level wages or slightly less (Wolf, 1986).

20. When I returned to Java in 1986, I studied the marriage patterns of workers and nonfactory workers and am currently preparing this material for publication.

21. Blumberg (1984) proposes that control of surplus enhances one's position more than control of resources used for (bare) subsistence.

22. See Heyzer (1986) for similar findings among Malaysian migrant factory workers in Singapore.

References

Arrigo, Linda Gail. 1980. "The Industrial Work Force of Young Women in Taiwan." *Bulletin of Concerned Asian Scholars* 12(2):25-38.

Blumberg, Rae Lesser. 1984. "A General Theory of Gender Stratification." Pp. 23-101 in *Sociological Theory* edited by Randall Collins. San Francisco: Jossey-Bass.

———. 1988. "Income Under Female Versus Male Control: Differential Spending Patterns and the Consequences When Women Lose Control of Returns to Labor." Unpublished report prepared for the World Bank. Washington, DC.

Boserup, Ester. 1970. *Woman's Role in Economic Development*. New York: St. Martin's.

Chafetz, Janet S. 1980. "Toward a Macrolevel Theory of Sexual Stratification and Gender Differentiation." Pp. 103-125 in *Current Perspectives in Social Theory I,* edited by S. McNall and G. Howe. Greenwich, CT: JAI.

Dewey, Alice. 1962. *Peasant Marketing in Java*. NY: Free Press.

Diamond, Norma. 1979. "Women and Industry in Taiwan." *Modern China* 5:317-340.

Dublin, Thomas. 1979. *Women at Work*. NY: Columbia University Press.

Elson, Diane and Ruth Pearson. 1981. "Nimble Fingers Make Cheap Workers: An Analysis of Women's Employment in Third World Export Manufacturing." *Feminist Review* 4:87-107.

Fernandez-Kelly, Maria Patricia. 1982. *For We Are Sold, I and My People: Women and Industry in Mexico's Frontier*. Albany: SUNY Press.

Frobel, Folker, Jurgan Heinrichs, and Otto Kreye. 1980. *The New International Division of Labour*. Cambridge: Cambridge University Press.

Geertz, Hildred. 1961. *The Javanese Family*. NY: Free Press of Glencoe.

Goldschmidt, Walter and Evelyn Kunkel. 1971. "The Structure of the Peasant Family." *American Anthropologist* 3(5):1058-1076.

Goode, William. 1963. *World Revolution and Family Patterns.* NY: Free Press.

Greenhalgh, Susan. 1985. "Sexual Stratification: The Other Side of 'Growth with Equity' in East Asia." *Population and Development Review* 11(2):265-314.

Hareven, Tamara K. 1982. *Family Time and Industrial Time.* NY: Cambridge University Press.

Hart, Gillian. 1986. *Power, Labor and Livelihood: Processes of Change in Rural Java.* Berkeley: University of California Press.

Heyzer, Noeleen. 1986. *Working Women in Southeast Asia: Development, Subordination and Emancipation.* Philadelphia: Open University Press.

Huang, Nora Chiang. 1984. "The Migration of Rural Women to Taipei." Pp. 247-268 in *Women in the Cities of Asia: Migration and Urban Adaptation,* edited by James T. Fawcett, Siew-Ean Khoo, and Peter C. Smith. Boulder, CO: Westview.

de Janvry, Alain and Carmen Diana Deere. 1978. "A Theoretical Framework for the Empirical Analysis of Peasants." Working Paper no. 60. Giannini Foundation Paper, University of California, Berkeley.

Jay, Robert. 1969. *Javanese Villagers.* Cambridge: MIT Press.

Kung, Lydia, 1983. *Factory Women in Taiwan.* Ann Arbor: University of Michigan Press.
———. 1984. "Taiwan Garment Workers." Pp. 109-122 in *Lives: Chinese Working Women,* edited by Mary Sheridan and Janet Salaff. Bloomington: Indiana University Press.

Mason, Karen Oppenheim. 1985. *The Status of Women: A Review of its Relationships to Fertility and Mortality.* Research Monograph. New York: Rockefeller Foundation.

Mather, Celia. 1985. " 'Rather Than Make Trouble, It's Better Just to Leave': Behind the Lack of Industrial Strife in the Tangerang Region of West Java." Pp. 153-182 in *Women, Work, and Ideology in the Third World,* edited by Haleh Afshar. NY: Tavistock.

Moore, Mick. 1973. "Cross-Cultural Surveys of Peasant Family Structures: Some Comments." *American Anthropologist* 75(3):911-915.

Nash, June and Maria Patricia Fernandez-Kelly, eds. 1983. *Women, Men, and the International Division of Labor.* Albany: SUNY Press.

Ong, Aihwa. 1987. *Spirits of Resistance and Capitalist Discipline: Factory Women in Malaysia.* Albany: SUNY Press.

Saffioti, Heleith. 1978. *Women in Class Society.* NY: Monthly Review Press.

Sajogyo, Pudjiwati. 1983. *Peranan wanita dalam Perkembangan Masyarakat Desa (The Role of Women in Developing Village Society).* Jakarta: CV. Rajawali.

Salaff, Janet W. 1981. *Working Daughters of Hong Kong.* NY: Cambridge University Press.

Scott, Alison MacEwen. 1986. "Women and Industrialization: Examining the 'Female Marginalisation' Thesis." *Journal of Development Studies* 22(3):649-680.

Stoler, Ann. 1977. "Class Structure and Female Autonomy in Rural Java." Pp. 74-89 in *Women and National Development,* edited by Wellesley Editorial Committee. Chicago: University of Chicago Press.

Thornton, Arland, Ming-Cheng Chang, and Te-Hsiung Sun. 1984. "Social and Economic Change, Intergenerational Relationships, and Family Formation in Taiwan." *Demography* 21(4):475-499.

Tilly, Louise A. and Joan W. Scott. 1978. *Women, Work and Family.* NY: Holt, Rinehart and Winston.

Tinker, Irene. 1976. "The Adverse Impact of Development on Women." Pp. 22-34 in *Women and World Development,* edited by Irene Tinker and Michele Bo Bramsen. Washington, DC: Overseas Development Council.

Todd, Emmanuel. 1985. *The Explanation of Ideology: Family Structures and Social Systems.* NY: Basil Blackwell.

UNIDO. 1980. "Women in the Redeployment of Manufacturing Industry to Developing Countries." Working Paper on Structural Change, No. 18, New York.

White, Benjamin N. F. 1976. "Production and Reproduction in a Javanese Village." Doctoral dissertation, Columbia University.

White, Benjamin and Endang Hastuti. 1980. "Different and Unequal: Male and Female Influence in Household and Community Affairs in Two West Javanese Villages." Working Paper, Center for Rural Sociological Research, Bogor Agricultural University, Indonesia.

Wolf, Diane L. 1984. "Making the Bread and Bringing It Home: Female Factory Workers and the Family Economy in Rural Java." Pp. 215-234 in *Women in the Urban and Industrial Workforce,* edited by Gavin Jones. (Development Studies Centre Monograph No. 33.) Canberra: Australian National University.

——. 1986. *Factory Daughters, Their Families, and Rural Industrialization in Central Java.* Doctoral dissertation, Cornell University, Ithaca, NY.

6

Gender, Family, and Economy in a Planned, Industrial City
The Working- and Lower-Class Households of Ciudad Guayana

CATHY A. RAKOWSKI

The ideology of the household as a private, cohesive unit synonymous with the patriarchal nuclear family is pervasive in contemporary Western cultures, even where a significant proportion of the population has living arrangements that don't conform to expectations. As Blumberg (this volume) points out, mainstream development policy (which is based on Western neoclassical economics) not coincidentally tends to "treat the household as a monolithic and unitary entity"—a "black box" where income is pooled and "resources, work, and information get distributed in some fashion."

When the patriarchal ideology already firmly rooted in the less developed countries of Latin America joins forces with development policy, the result is the increasing "underdevelopment of women" relative to men and often an absolute decline in their well-being and those of their children. Typically, women's access to the tools and knowledge of development is severely restricted in favor of men and male authority is promoted in the name of a "modern family." Women are expected to confine themselves primarily to domestic tasks. In the event they must do something else, they often find themselves left with subsistence activities or self-generated employment in the small-scale "informal sector" of the economy. Under appropriate conditions, planners' expectations could become self-fulfilling prophecies as women find their choices constrained by the options permitted them (Boserup, 1970; AWID, 1985; Carloni, 1987).

149

This chapter examines the relationship between family structure, women's roles, and state-coordinated planned development through a study of the working and lower class households of Ciudad Guayana, Venezuela. Venezuela is a country of approximately 18 million people located on the Caribbean coast of South America. Over one fifth of the population resides in the capital of Caracas. Since oil production began in earnest in the 1920s, the country has become increasingly dependent on petroleum revenues. With the establishment of a stable democracy in 1958, petroleum revenues have been used to finance state-coordinated planning and investment in resource development, industrialization, and social services with a long-range goal of diversifying the national economy. Since 1960, the state has been implementing an ambitious regional development program in the Guayana, a frontier zone low in population. This program is based on the construction of major hydroelectric facilities, a complex of state-run heavy industries (largely steel and aluminum plants), and a new city—Ciudad Guayana—founded in 1961 to provide the urban infrastructure for industrial workers and their families and to serve as a growth pole for the surrounding region.

I argue that planned development in this setting has promoted a patriarchal nuclear family model that has contributed to an exaggeration of women's domestic roles, occupational segregation by sex and, consequently, female dependence on men. Specifically, planners assigned men to roles as workers and family heads and women to a supportive role as housewives responsible for the reproduction of male labor power. To reinforce these roles, development planning established financial incentives and a discriminatory structure of opportunities and benefits. These efforts built on certain features of Venezuelan culture which supported a patriarchal nuclear family: stipulations of the Venezuelan Civil Code (which includes family law) and other legislation (such as "protective" labor legislation), a tradition of *machismo* (male dominance), and an idealization of self-sacrificing motherhood which is a part of popular culture. But other features of Venezuelan culture hindered planned goals for family life. These include an acceptance among the working and lower classes of consensual unions as an alternative to legal marriage, a long history of childbirth outside of marriage (52% of all births each year), "irresponsible paternity" (abandonment of children and mothers), and a highly mobile population which forms and re-forms households through migration (Montero, 1983; Rakowski, 1985).

The discussion is organized into five sections. First, a brief background section reviews the concept of family as applied to Venezuela.

Second follows a description of the study setting. Third is an explanation of the assumptions regarding gender, household, and family that planners integrated into development plans and an outline of the specific policies and programs directed at promoting the patriarchal nuclear family. The fourth section presents data from the study and the fifth and final section summarizes conclusions regarding the impact of development planning on gender, family, and economy.

Background

Venezuela has strong family and gender ideologies. The former legitimates and specifies the gender division of labor in the family; the latter legitimates male authority and unequal rights and responsibilities at both the micro (family) and macro (institutional) levels (see Chafetz, this volume). These ideologies have their roots in the Spanish occupation of the colonial era. However, the specific family/gender rights, obligations, and restrictions incorporated into development planning evolved in the last century when they were consecrated in Venezuela's legislation. Family, as defined by Venezuelan law, traditionally has supposed a stable bond between a man and a woman. The former has been seen as the authority figure upon whom falls the protection, support, and education of the children. The latter was (until 1982 when the Civil Code was reformed), by law, charged with upholding and "assisting" the father by caring for the children and the home and obeying the husband. This family had its origins in Roman law and the concept of *paterfamilias* and is the basis of property relations and inheritance as well as other legislation and regulations (Montero, 1983). Common usage and tradition treat family and household as the same and assign authority to men and a supportive role to women.

Among the discriminatory practices which have had (and continue to have) the greatest impact on women are the following. Prior to the reform of the Civil Code women were considered legal minors under the tutelage of the husband. He set the conjugal domicile and managed community property; the wife could not enter into contracts without his permission and he could deny her right to employment. The husband had final authority and rights over children, even following divorce. Uxoricide (the murder of a woman to protect family honor) was condoned by light sentences and infidelity was defined differently for men and women, which allowed men the freedom to engage in extramarital liaisons without fear of divorce. Some of the common problems associated with the pre-1982 Civil Code include no legal obligation of fathers to recognize or support children born out of wedlock; married fathers could not recognize these children without permission from the legal wife. Children were classified as "legitimate," "recognized," "illegitimate," and "adulterous" and the law placed restrictions on the rights of inheritance of nonlegitimate children. The pre-1982 Civil Code also made possible the abandonment of women and children by men who, establishing a new legal domicile, then divorced the wife for "abandonment" or disposed of community property prior to a divorce, leaving wives penniless. (If the situation for legally married women was difficult, even more dismal was that of women in consensual unions who had no legal rights whatsoever. Yet consensual unions have been the norm in rural areas and represent one fourth to one third of all unions in urban areas, especially among low-income populations). Although since 1982 these practices have become "illegal," they still receive widespread cultural acceptance; behaviors often reflect old expectations, not the new law.[1]

According to Montero (1983), among low-income groups "father" is often a series of men who cohabit temporarily with the mother. The patriarchal family consecrated in law and supported by the Catholic church is more typical of the middle and upper classes although men of these classes also frequently maintain "little houses" *(casas chicas)* where mistresses and their children reside.

The Study Setting

As a planned city, Ciudad Guayana was to provide basic urban infrastructure for heavy industry (mainly large-scale steel and aluminum manufacturing) and the laborers and their families who would migrate in response to job opportunities. Planners estimated the program would create 100,000 jobs between 1965 and 1980 and, given their concentration in heavy industry and construction, would demand a primarily male labor force.

The process of development was speeded up and coordinated by the creation of the Corporación Venezolana de Guayana (CVG), a development agency responsible for planning, directing, and coordinating all industrial, urban, and social development in the region. Although the CVG employed a variety of professionals (including social workers, anthropologists, demographers, sociologists, and so forth), most decision making was controlled by the majority professions of economists and engineers. Approximately 10% of all state investment was allocated to the program during its first 25 years (Rakowski, 1989).

Despite the enormous sums of money made available for the Guayana Development Program, the magnitude of the task and the impossibility of financing all aspects of development led to selective investment decisions which favored the industrial program and the construction of the new city. Planners recognized the need for supportive and complementary activities such as transportation, business services, intermediate and small industry, commercial and distribution systems for foodstuffs and consumer goods, and personal services to maintain the growing male labor force. Some planners were also concerned with creating employment for women, especially household heads. But no provisions were made for state investment in supportive activities or industrial jobs for women. This presented opportunities for entrepreneurs with little capital, using less sophisticated tools, to engage in small-scale, unregulated activities known as the "informal sector." It also created a demand for female labor in personal services as workers or as "spouses." As a result, Ciudad Guayana, Venezuela's planned industrial miracle, shows a significant proportion of its labor force (19%-24% from 1975-1982) in the informal sector and a low labor force participation rate for women (26% of the labor force in 1980) (Rakowski, 1984b, 1989).

In 1980, as part of the research for my dissertation (Rakowski, 1984a), I conducted a study of a sample of 208 households selected from 28 census tracts corresponding to what the CVG has designated as Strata 5 and 6. These show the lowest average income levels in the city and correspond to zones classified as "unplanned"—meaning squatter settlements not officially sanctioned by the CVG. (Some public housing has been constructed in several zones.) Officially, CVG planners refer to the population of Stratum 5 as the "working class" and of Stratum 6 as the "lower class" or "marginals." The population of Stratum 5 shows a high proportion working in construction or industry while Stratum 6, with the lowest income levels, shows a high proportion in the informal sector.

Those studied comprise a representative sample of the working and lower classes, which make up approximately 65% of the city's population. The sample included 329 adult men, 313 adult women, 332 children age 7 to 14, and 284 children under 7 years of age; 93% of the adults were migrants. Data from the study were supplemented when possible with those produced by the CVG yearly household surveys and occasional fertility and migration surveys. Planning documents, financial reports, other studies, and reports of CVG staff were used to ascertain background data on development planning, implementation, and impact.

Planned Development, Gender Ideology, and Family

For the most part, planners in Ciudad Guayana have paid little overt attention to women except as reproducers. Their views have taken what Papanek (1981) calls the "curious 'as if' stance" of development planners in general—"as if women were like men, as if all women were alike, as if women did not exist at all" outside the household. The original development plans, drawn up in 1963, set the tone for the next 20 years. "Man"[2] was considered a "condition for the success of development," who needed preparation to improve his "quality" and to encourage acceptance of an "attitude" appropriate and adequate to a "society of the type desired for Guayana." The development program was considered dependent not only on natural resources and technology but on "able hands and minds eager to work" with a "spirit of sacrifice and constructive attitudes" (CVG, 1963, pp. 39-47; 1964, pp. 29-44; 1968; 1980). Analyses of planning documents indicates clearly that planners believed they could structure urban life in such a way that the population would adopt new patterns of behavior and life-styles typical of a "modern" city, avoiding the social problems which characterized Venezuela's other urban areas (García and Blumberg, 1977; Garcia, 1982).

Planners expected the patriarchal nuclear family to be the medium for promoting these "proper attitudes," that is, the creation of the Protestant ethic in Guayana. A stable family situation was supposed to contribute to a man's greater sense of responsibility for his work and for his family's "social and economic welfare" (CVG-Sidor, 1973, p. 16). Therefore, in direct support of the industrial program, planners deliberately sought to promote a nuclear family household composed of husband-worker-head and mother-housewife and their mutual children (see Wallerstein and Smith, this volume). A number of policies and programs were instituted to reinforce this patriarchal family (Rakowski, 1984a, 1985, 1989).

1. Excluding a brief period during the oil boom of the mid-1970s, women were deliberately excluded from industrial and construction employment except as secretaries, social workers, cleaning women, and other traditional "feminine" activities.

2. Planners prepared and promulgated campaigns directed at women reinforcing the notions that domestic tasks are "women's work" and the productivity of male labor is in part the product of the psychological well-being associated with a comfortable home environment.

3. The CVG created educational, social, and cultural programs for working- and lower-class communities. These emphasized the "development of women" or "the integration of women in development" as homemakers and volunteers in community development. Classes were offered in sewing, cooking, child care, and handicrafts and women were encouraged to organize in groups for community volunteer work.

4. The industries added social service programs to counsel workers on their home lives and design educational, medical, and cultural programs for family members, especially homemaking classes for wives and daughters. The steel mill's social service program, founded in 1966, is a good example. One of the program's key objectives was to "make available to the wives, mothers, daughters and sisters (of workers) training in new tasks, techniques, and arts related to the administration of the household . . . with the goal of achieving a better understanding of the situations affecting the personality of the worker" and achieving greater "efficiency in woman's function as manager of the home . . ." thus helping to "consolidate the social stability of the worker" (CVG-Sidor, 1973, pp. 18-19).

5. State industries and the CVG offered financial incentives to their employees and workers to legalize consensual unions and legally recognize children born outside of marriage. These included marriage bonuses and holidays, bonuses for the birth of a child, tuition and book grants for children, and so forth.

6. Public housing and credit programs for construction of self-help housing, important incentives to attract and stabilize a trained labor force, included rules that favored the acquisition of housing and credit by male workers with spouses. (Single parents were excluded until the early 1980s.) In part, these rules were modeled after the Civil Code and in part they reflected real patterns of industrial employment which were overwhelmingly masculine.

7. State-supported training programs discriminated against women who wanted to participate in nontraditional technical training. Although such programs were opened to women in the late 1970s, placement of women in appropriate jobs was often difficult.

Study Results

How do planners' assumptions regarding family life and appropriate roles for men and women relate to the real patterns detected for working- and lower-class households? Study results are organized around issues of migration, household structure, the division of labor, and income pooling.

Migration

Since planners assumed projects would create a demand for male labor, they also assumed only male migrants would be attracted by expanding job opportunities. Female migration would be restricted primarily to family migration—women accompanying or following men. As early as 1965, some researchers suspected single females were also migrating (MacDonald, 1969) and noted that female-headed households were still common. The index of masculinity between 1965-1987 indicates female migration kept pace with male migration for most of the period. The index of masculinity varied between 99 and 103 (CVG household survey data; Martinez and Holmes, 1980; Rakowski, 1984a).

Migration surveys were introduced by the CVG in the mid-1970s. But analyses have been plagued by conceptual and coding difficulties. For instance, surveys code data on migrants age 10 and older at the time of the survey, obscuring information for the time of migration. Additionally, coding incorporates gender and family stereotypes. When household members migrate together or join earlier migrants, only the head's reason for migrating is noted and all others are classified as accompanying family members. The study of working- and lower-class households attempted to overcome these limitations by asking information on all migrants, including those who migrated in groups, and coded information by characteristics of migrants at the time of migration.

Initially, results appeared to support CVG analyses; but, in reality, data present a more complex view of the dynamics of migration. If family migration is defined as the migration of family members together, following other members, or for a joint reason, then the working- and lower-class households show greater diversity than the concept of family migration permits. Almost half the men migrated alone. Women are more likely to migrate with someone else, but only for slightly over one third is this someone else a spouse (including both legal marriages and consensual unions). A striking feature of female migration is the proportion of single women who migrate with children—but not to join a spouse (22%). Most of these are younger women with small children. This finding is supported by a study of net migration carried out by CVG staff (Martinez and Holmes, 1980) that suggested that female and child migrants show greater permanence in Ciudad Guayana while male migration is more likely to be temporary, with rapid turnover of a significant proportion of the male migrants and their replacement by new migrants.

Even when family members migrate together or join other members who migrated earlier, members may have diverse reasons for

Table 6.1 Conditions of Migration

	Men (%)	Women (%)
Migrated alone	47.8	13.7
With or to join spouse	27.6	35.8
With children only[a]	1.0	22.1
With someone else	23.6	28.4
	100.2	100

NOTE: a. But not to join a spouse.

migrating.[3] As expected by the CVG planners, working- and lower-class men indicate they migrate for work-related reasons (60%) or to accompany or join someone else (28%). In apparent support of planners' assumptions, the majority of the working- and lower-class women (65.9%) did indicate they migrated to accompany or join someone else. But only half these came with or joined a spouse. The rest most commonly accompanied or joined a parent, an adult child, a sibling, or a friend. While only 15% of the women declare migrating for work-related reasons, many sought and found work within the first year.

In-depth interviews with a subsample of the migrants suggested that gender roles and appraisals of opportunity are reflected in respondents' answers regarding reasons for migrating. Women and men perceive themselves and their choices differently. Job opportunities for men in Ciudad Guayana were advertised nationally and men, whose masculine identity is more likely to hinge on occupation, see themselves as clearly responding to job opportunities. Women, however, are more likely to see themselves as family-oriented and dependent in a culture which does not stress female employment. Thus, even when women intended to work, they chose Ciudad Guayana as their destination because they could count on the assistance of family members or friends already in the city. In interviews, they emphasize this factor over work in the decision to migrate.

Some planners' assumptions did not hold up for the working- and lower-class households. This is the case for conjugal status. Of those working- and lower-class persons who migrate at age 15 or over, only 21% of the men and 24% of the women are married and 23% of the men and 24% of the women are in consensual unions. Together this is still less than half of all men and women who migrate as adults. Additionally, a small proportion of female migrants with spouses left the spouse to migrate; a larger proportion of males with spouses left families in the place of origin and migrated alone.

But single and separated migrants don't stay single for long. Within the first year of arrival, most migrants over age 18 form a relationship whether or not they have a spouse in the place of origin. Some relationships are long-term but many are temporary arrangements. Two factors probably play a role in the rapid formation of couples. First, Ciudad Guayana is relatively inhospitable to both men and women. No provisions were made to meet the personal care needs of either; in particular, men turn to women to meet these needs. Second, the structure of employment opportunities and the social programs that favor access by males with partners encourage women to depend on men both financially and socially—even if only temporarily.

Household Structure

Planners promoted the patriarchal nuclear family and hoped to decrease the proportion of households headed by women and the proportion of illegitimate and abandoned children that characterize other Venezuelan and Latin American cities. Were their campaigns and programs at least partially successful in spite of the high rate of turnover among male migrants?

In the 1960s, women were heads in about 25% of the households in Bolivar State where Ciudad Guayana is located. The proportion of female heads has declined. In 1980, the CVG surveys showed 16% of all households headed by women in the city; the working- and lower-class study found 19%. This compares with 20% of all households in Venezuela. About half of the female-headed households in the sample consisted of older women with grown children who declared her the head out of respect; the other half were younger women, most of whom had been abandoned with dependent children.

A study carried out by Pazos, Castellano, and Rojas (1975) found that the proportion of illegitimate births in Ciudad Guayana (35%) was substantially below the 52% at the national level. This might give the impression that campaigns have had the hoped-for effect. However, the study of working- and lower-class households found that many women return to the place of origin to give birth. Their children are not registered in Guayana, possibly affecting the illegitimacy rate.

The study also found cases of couples in consensual unions who shared several children, only some of whom had been recognized by the father. Respondents indicated the father recognized children born while he worked at an industry which offered incentives, but did not recognize children born prior to or after this employment. This indicates the impact of incentives may only be short-term and not change attitudes or long-term behavior.

The proportion of couples in legal marriages has been increasing in Venezuela since the 1960s. But Ciudad Guayana shows a much higher proportion of its couples in consensual unions than most urban areas in Venezuela—a trend which contradicts the expected impact of urbanization[4] and the changes promoted by planning. In 1971, 20.5% of the couples in Ciudad Guayana were in consensual unions, but by 1980, 30% of all couples in Ciudad Guayana and 46% of the working- and lower-class couples were in consensual unions.[5] This represents 26% of both men and women in the sample. These figures are not surprising in light of the migratory trends discussed.

The working- and lower-class households are large; they show an average of six members compared to three members for middle-class households (CVG data). About three fourths of the households surveyed had between 3 and 8 members and the range was from 1 through 15. Only 57% of these households conform to planners' expectations for a nuclear unit of husband-wife-children. An additional 19% are single mothers with dependent children (and often with a grandparent or other relative present) and 16% are extended families of three generations (some with additional persons in the household). Only a few households were comprised of single or unrelated persons.

Movement in and out of households is common. Adult children frequently live with parents and households take in "visiting" members or send members to "visit" elsewhere. Over one fourth of the households include a single adult male over age 18 and 18% include a single adult female (a difference related to the greater demand for male labor). About 89% of the households include children under 18 and half include children under age 4. Despite programs designed to strengthen family ties and, especially, to reinforce paternal responsibility, 29% of the children age 7 to 14 and 16% of those age 0 to 6 have a parent absent, usually the father. Less than half the children in the sample live in a patriarchal nuclear family in which the male parent is breadwinner and the female parent is a housewife; 17% of those who do live with a stepfather.

The study found that respondents frequently listed as members of a household persons who lived elsewhere temporarily. About 30% of the households had members outside, most frequently due to work-related reasons, but some for studies or military service. Monies commonly flowed back and forth between households and these members.

Child sharing is also common. Parents "lend" children to relatives who live alone or are childless. The movement of persons in and out of the household on a temporary or long-term basis belies the notion of the household as a closed "black box." Flows of money and goods between households confirm the fluidity of rights and responsibilities among members and suggest that the concept of household may need to expand to include something more than a common residence (the standard census and survey definition) or "sharing a common pot." Other authors have suggested that flows of goods and monies should be used to define household limits, assuming income pooling and maintenance are important functions of "households" (Friedman, 1984).

Income Pooling

An important assumption of patriarchal family ideology is that household members pool their income (see Wallerstein and Smith, this volume, for a discussion of pooling within and across residential units and for an alternative concept of household). Standard census and survey techniques define household or family income as the sum of all individual incomes in the household. Planners in Venezuela (like planners elsewhere) also assume that employment of one household member will benefit other members through pooling. Venezuelan labor laws and labor union contracts favor the employment of household heads since a third common assumption is that the head is the person who supports the household. Of course, in the case of couples, a fourth assumption is that the husband is the head.[6] Do these assumptions hold up under scrutiny?

For the study of working- and lower-class households, income was coded in two ways. First, the sum of all individual incomes was coded as "potential income." Since respondents were asked detailed information on how much, if any, income in kind or cash was contributed by each household member or by someone outside the household, this was coded as "real income."[7] When comparing the two incomes, the study found that only 13% of the households showed real and potential incomes which were within 500 bolivares (Bs.) of each other (Bs. 4.3 = U.S. $1 in 1980). This indicates low levels of pooling. For some households, real income was as low as 25%-30% of the potential. These findings challenge assumptions regarding the functioning of families—traditional nuclear or other forms—and the role of female and child dependence in promoting worker responsibility for support.

A substantial proportion of individual income does not wind up in the household pool; standard survey methods can grossly overestimate income available for household maintenance. For instance, real income figures indicate one third of the working- and lower-class households had incomes below the official poverty level of Bs. 1,500

Table 6.2 Comparison of Potential and Real Monthly Incomes

Income in Bolivares	Percentage Real Household Income[a]	Percentage Potential Household Income[b]
None	1.0	5.5
150-550	2.4	1.6
551-1,000	8.3	2.7
1,001-1,500	21.5	6.6
1,501-2,000	26.8	9.3
2,001-2,500	17.6	10.9
2,501-3,000	6.8	9.8
3,001-3,500	9.7	9.8
3,501-4,000	2.4	8.7
4,001-4,500	1.5	10.9
4,501-5,000	0.5	7.1
5,001-5,500	—	5.5
5,501-6,000	0.5	3.8
6,001-7,000	1.0	2.7
7,001-9,000	—	3.3
9,001-15,000	—	1.1
15,001-21,000	—	0.7
	100	100

NOTE: In 15.8% of the cases, potential income was *lower* than real income due to the importance of contributions and gifts received from nonhousehold members.
$N = 208$
Bs. 4.30 = U.S. $1 (1980)
a. Reported by respondent as real contributions to income pool.
b. Sum of all individually earned incomes.

for a household of six. Potential income figures would suggest only 16.4% below the poverty level. Real income figures show only 3.5% of households with "comfortable" income levels of over Bs. 4,000 compared with 35.1% of households if we use potential income.

Do male heads support the households studied as planners assume? Most respondents named as head a husband or grandparent explaining "he supports us." In the majority of the cases with male heads, this person had the highest individual income in the household, but the sum of contributions by other members often exceeded his contribution. Yet the contributions of nonheads was referred to as "help" *(una ayuda)* beyond the "main" support of the head. Some respondents explained that the head's contribution was allocated to basic purchases and other contributions went for "extras." In the case of female heads, only half actually have employment (the younger women with dependent children) and they earn less than half what male heads earn. While they usually contribute the greatest share of their households' incomes, they often receive assistance from other persons both in and outside the household. (See Wallerstein and Smith, this volume, for a discussion of transfers and other sources of income.)

Whether or not a working- or lower-class wife has independent income depends on several factors. Older women in consensual unions are most likely to have independent income from employment (especially the informal sector) or as gifts from adult children and extended family members both in and outside the household (the latter is also true for older female heads). Husband's employment status and income levels also play a role for both married women and those in consensual unions. Only 18% of the wives whose husbands earn over Bs. 3,500 have employment compared with about one fourth of those whose husbands earn between Bs. 1,350-3,500, and about half of those whose husbands earn less than Bs. 1,350. Similarly, wives of men who work in the public or private sector are less likely to have employment than wives of the self-employed (24.8% versus 34.4%).

Does women's independent income contribute to potentially greater power in decision making? The study suggests that for most women their incomes are so low relative to those of men that they don't increase women's status or power in the household and women interviewed "acknowledge" men's "rights" to authority (see Blumberg, 1984; Chafetz, this volume). At the same time, women rate highly the small measure of independence that deciding how to spend even a tiny income gives them.

How do incomes compare by gender among couples? For the working- and lower-classes, 98% of the wives earn less than Bs. 2,250 while 49% of the husbands earn more (73% earn more than Bs. 1,800). Female economic dependence is an important feature of life in Ciudad Guayana. A women's best income opportunity is her husband, not her own labor.

This is further supported by data on housewives who had prior employment (about 64% of all housewives). Almost half of these (45.5%) had worked as domestic servants or in other personal services, including prostitution; 15.2% worked as low-skilled office workers and 17% as salesclerks—relatively low-paying jobs. Being a housewife represents an improvement in status to which working- and lower-class women aspire (Harkess, 1973).

What about the children? Patriarchal family ideology and development policy argue that the male-worker-head should receive hiring preference because he should and does maintain both women and children. Study data were coded separately for children ages 0 to 6 and 7 to 14.

Table 6.3 Primary Source of Children's Support

Primary Source	Age 0-6 (%)	Age 7-14 (%)
Father/stepfather		
in home	67.6	54.8
absent	1.8	2.4
Both parents equally	10.6	14.8
Mother alone	3.8	7.5
Other persons	16.2	20.5
	100	100

A father or stepfather (including those few absent who pay child support) is sole or primary support in 69.4% of the cases of children age 0 to 6 but only 57.2% of those age 7 to 14.[8] So a significant proportion of children require assistance from additional persons, in some cases the mother but in others grandparents, uncles, aunts, and so forth.

That brings us to the question of women's contribution to household income. Studies in other cultures (some cited in Blumberg, this volume) indicate that women contribute more of their income to the household—especially for food, clothing, and education for children—while men retain more for personal use. The same is true for these working- and lower-class households.

Over half the women contributed all or almost all their income to the household compared with less than 10% of the men. Men are most likely to contribute between 40% to 85% of their incomes, retaining 15% to 60% for personal use.[9] Behind these figures are several trends. First, married men contribute a higher proportion than those in consensual unions. Unattached males "visiting" the household during a temporary work contract do not contribute. Women with sporadic, part-time work and young, single daughters of men with high incomes are least likely to contribute to household income (but they also earn the lowest incomes). Finally, women as a group earn about half what men earn, so they have fewer funds to allocate to their various expenditures. In fact, women contribute more than 75% of the household income in only 18% of the households with both male and female income earners; men contribute more than 75% of household income in 47% of these households. Women may be more "generous" with their incomes, but they have less to give so men still end up as the more important contributors.

Table 6.4 Proportion of Individual Income Contributed to Household[a]

Percentage of Individual Income Contributed	Men (%)	Women (%)
less than 1	1.3	18.4
2-25	5.0	5.6
26-40	15.1	8.4
41-60	32.1	5.6
61-85	33.3	7.1
86-97	4.4	4.2
over 97	8.8	50.7
	100	100

NOTE: a. Includes only households with at least one man and one woman who earn income.

The Division of Labor

Planners promoted the housewife role for women and created a structure of opportunities designed to reinforce male authority. Has this had an impact on women's labor force participation compared with men's?

Women's labor force participation in Ciudad Guayana increased between 1971 (19% of the labor force) and 1980 (26%), consistent with trends at the national level, especially during the petroleum boom of 1974-1979. But female participation in Guayana is "depressed" when compared with the national average (29%), the regional average (30%), and other urban areas like Caracas (34%). In great part, the lower participation rate in Ciudad Guayana can be explained by the relatively unattractive jobs and income levels open to women and the availability of a large population of single male migrants earning high incomes in industry and construction. As indicated in the section on income pooling, a working- and lower-class woman's best income opportunity is a husband.

Ciudad Guayana shows greater occupational segregation by sex than other urban areas or the country as a whole. In this new industrial city over 35% of the male workers are in the manufacturing sector, compared with about 13% of the women. Most women in manufacturing are office workers and cleaning women. Women, in general, comprised only 3.8% of the artisans and operatives in Ciudad Guayana in 1980, compared with 15.8% at the national level and 25.8% in the capital of Caracas. No woman in the working- and lower-class sample was an operative. (Between 1983-1986, women were 5.9% of the artisans and operatives in Ciudad Guayana.)

In general, women in Ciudad Guayana are 72% of the clerical and office workers (compared with 55.2% at the national level). They are more likely than their counterparts in other cities to be cleaning women, secretaries and office workers, salesclerks and informal vendors, nurses, and teachers (CVG data; Rakowski, 1985).

The women of the working- and lower-class households reflect this trend. They make up 63.3% of workers in the public sector, but only 15.6% of those in private enterprise. A greater proportion of employed women than of employed men work in the informal sector in family businesses or as self-employed (57.2% versus 21.9%). And the most common occupations among these women are cleaning women (25% of employed women), informal vendor (25%), office worker/secretary (8.7%), informal cook (8.7%), and teacher (5.4%). Working- and lower-class men, on the other hand, are most likely to be operatives in heavy industry or construction (60.5%), informal vendors (8.2%), or drivers of taxis, buses, and trucks (8.3%). Although men predominate in both the formal and informal sectors, women comprise a higher proportion of the informal sector than of the formal sector (33% versus 22%), indicating pressures to depend on self-employment or to opt for part-time, sporadic work.

Men and women of the informal sector were asked why they chose self-employment and if it offered any advantage. Men gave a variety of answers including "there are no jobs," "I like being my own boss," and "if I work longer or harder, I get more money." Women typically responded that this kind of work allowed them to attend to home and children (98% of them operated a business in the home), often adding "my husband won't let me work outside." (Some women expressed pride at this explanation.) In other urban areas of Venezuela, women are more likely to operate an informal business outside the home (Rakowski, 1983).

Women of the working- and lower-class say they take jobs out of financial need or to pass the time until they "fall in love." Some older housewives start a small, sporadic business to earn "a little money of my own" and not have to "always ask permission" to buy some small item they want. But seldom were comments made about "careers" and when they were it was usually a mother speaking of wanting her daughter to have an independent income (e.g., as a teacher, nurse, secretary). In addition to husband's reluctance and the type of low-status employment open to women, costs of transportation, child care, and the work load of the double day would hardly be compensated by low incomes.

How great a burden is housework? Would employment compete with domestic tasks? Or are tasks distributed among several household members, relieving the burden on any one member? The study looked at the allocation of responsibilities for domestic tasks and found that in at least half the households, several people share domestic tasks. Female heads of households and wives of male heads receive collaboration from other women and from older children, especially daughters. Yet the majority of women *perceive* domestic tasks to be an obstacle to employment, a perception reinforced by the husbands during interviews.

Husbands do not collaborate with housework. Only a few men participate and these limit themselves to child care (6.7% of the working- and lower-class men) and shopping (10%)—the latter also being a mechanism for controlling the household budget and restricting the wife's trips away from home. Sons help with child care and run errands. But the greatest assistance comes from grandmothers, sisters, daughters, and friends in the household. Other adult women and girls are most likely to share child care, cleaning, and laundry, while female heads and wives of male heads retain cooking responsibilities. Data indicate that, theoretically, wives' housework burdens could be transferred to others in the event of employment.

Conclusions

In the interest of a "modern" city and the success of the industrial program, Ciudad Guayana's planners attempted to reinforce the patriarchal nuclear family which is the norm if not the reality in Venezuela. They did so through programs, financial incentives, and the structure of opportunities and benefits emerging from planned development. Efforts were legitimated by traditional gender and family ideology and legislation even though patterns of family life and household organization among the lower-income population deviated markedly from the patriarchal nuclear model. Did planners' assumptions about the family become self-fulfilling prophecies? Were structural pressures and incentives successful in achieving greater conformity to the norm of the patriarchal nuclear family?

The study of working- and lower-class households—the population targeted for many programs—indicates that the impact of incentives, programs, opportunities, and benefits varies and that aspects of household organization and family life also reflect not only pressures created by planned development, but also traditional patterns of organization as well as high rates of migration. These variables interact in complex and sometimes contradictory ways.

Some working- and lower-class family patterns through 1980 show change in the direction promoted by development planning. Such patterns include lower labor force participation rates for legally married women, women in nuclear households, or women whose partners work in industry and at the highest income levels; the high proportion of women in home-based self-employment; female economic dependence and women's deference to male authority; the rapid formation of couples by single migrants; and the declining proportion of female headed households.

But other patterns do not conform to planners' expectations or respond to policies designed to encourage patriarchal nuclear households. These patterns include the large proportion of nonnuclear households (43%); the high proportion of consensual unions in Ciudad Guayana; continued abandonment of women and children by fathers; the large proportion of children relying on support of family members other than the father; low rates of income pooling for nonmarried couples and nonnuclear households; the continued importance of networking and the retention of important amounts of income by men for discretionary use.

Although the specific factors associated with patterns are numerous and the relationships are complex, five are particularly important. First, female labor force participation increases initially because the rapid expansion of jobs is greater than the male labor supply and later when male unemployment rises or men leave at the end of the boom (e.g., in 1979), requiring greater financial inputs by women to the household. Second, female labor force participation continues to be disadvantaged by the demand for male labor in the major industries. The concentration of females in the informal sector and "feminine" occupations is directly related to the opportunities created by selective investment in industrial and urban development. This is reinforced by discriminatory training and hiring practices, gender ideology, and women's responsibility for domestic tasks. An important consequence is a lower income-earning potential for women. Third, male migration responds to the demand for male labor while female migration is more likely to respond to the presence of friends or family, the availability of single males with high incomes, and the range of services available in the city for women and their children. This reflects and reinforces traditional gender roles and relations. Fourth, the high proportion of consensual unions is related to the migratory status of adults, especially the temporary status of many men. Being in a consensual union is then associated with lower rates of income pooling and support of children, subsequent abandonment, and female labor force participation (though constrained by the factors mentioned above). And fifth, female economic dependence and the greater share of household income supplied by men is related to women's lower income-earning potential despite their tendency to share a greater proportion of their income.

In conclusion, direct planned activities and the structure of opportunities and benefits in Ciudad Guayana have interacted with traditional family patterns and gender ideology to create a family structure in that city which diverges in important ways from other urban areas *and* from planners' expectations. Has the period through 1982 been a transitional phase, especially in light of the 1982 reform of the Civil Code which granted equal rights to women? Recent inquiries indicate both continuity and important changes.

Interviews conducted in 1984 and 1988 reveal that many lower- and middle-level planners are aware of the importance of including gender issues in planning and evaluating the impact of proposed policies on family patterns and employment opportunities. But most of the upper-level managers who make final decisions do not assign priority to gender issues, especially since the economic recession initiated in 1980. Gender issues receive only nominal attention in regional and urban plans and the CVG continues to sponsor programs for women which focus primarily on handicrafts, domestic skills, and health.

Despite the lack of attention to gender in planning, labor force growth reflects important changes documented by biannual studies of employment. Between 1981 and 1985, in a period when male unemployment rates hovered around 14%, the male labor force increased by only 9%. Female unemployment varied between 7% and 11%, yet both the female labor force and self-employment increased by 34%. Some of this growth is attributed to homemakers and daughters previously inactive who have entered the labor force full or part time due to unemployment of or desertion by the male family breadwinner. But this does not account for all of the increase, since the number of housewives also increased by 14%. There appears to be a generalized trend toward increasing employment for women; by 1985 they comprised more than 30% of the labor force. This trend is true of other urban areas but is more pronounced in Ciudad Guayana.

In-depth analyses have not been released, so it is difficult to predict what long-range consequences may result from the experience of employment for increasing numbers of women. But over time, both men and women in Ciudad Guayana have been exposed to the cyclical nature of male employment and to national campaigns to eliminate job discrimination; this may encourage women to maintain employment even when males in the household find new jobs. As the city enters a new boom period (in evidence in 1988), shortages of male labor and reforms in the labor law and training practices may facilitate improved employment and income opportunities for women.

New Developments

On the other hand, the latest data available show that recent changes in employment across industry sectors reflect continued segregation by sex and help explain high male unemployment during the recession. Construction employment declined by 63% between 1978 and 1985 (90% of construction workers were male). Manufacturing, another male-dominated activity, increased by only 7.2% between 1981 and 1985. But employment in two sectors where women are concentrated— commerce (including restaurants and hotels) and services—show increases of 16.6% and 34.4% respectively in the same period. So women's recent employment experience is also a low-wage, low-prestige experience. This factor may discourage long-term participation for women with employed partners.

Although no studies are available regarding possible changes in the dynamics of family relations and decision making, some visible changes taking place in Ciudad Guayana (and elsewhere in Venezuela) suggest a potential for impact on family dynamics. For instance, radio stations and newspapers now allocate time and space to feminist groups. This provides an opportunity to discuss gender issues, especially topics such as spousal abuse, rights and responsibilities during divorce proceedings, availability of free counseling and legal services, and the meaning of changes in the Civil Code, among others. More importantly, women's groups of all types are multiplying and interacting with municipal and state officials and with planners at the CVG. For instance, women in several working- and lower-class neighborhoods have formed their own women's groups sometimes with the assistance of local feminists or community action consultants working for a national program called "Women's Circles."[10] These women's groups defend neighbor women who are threatened with eviction, subjected to spousal abuse, unemployed, or have problems in dealing with local authorities. Some also operate consumer cooperatives, child care networks, or informal job referral services, and cooperate with school programs and participate in medical campaigns (e.g., for vaccinations). In interviews conducted in 1984 and 1988, local officials pointed out that neighborhood associations (legally designated as the organizations with which officials must work prior to any community intervention) are primarily staffed by women. As a result, women have been learning more about the planning process and many have become adept at managing the bureaucracy, making their needs known, and achieving demands. These experiences suggest that while the structure of employment and income opportunities may still discriminate against women, 25 years of living in Ciudad Guayana and dealing with its structure of opportunities and benefits—and an equal number of years dealing with male migration, abandonment, and cyclical unemployment—may contribute to change in family dynamics. Women have increased their importance to the labor force, to family survival, and to the community. This reduces pressures for female dependence and male authority (although the wage and employment structure and *machismo* still promote dependence). At least this experience has provided women with mechanisms for increasing their control over their lives both inside and outside the household. This, plus legal reforms, may lead to genuine long-term improvements in the lives of working- and lower-class women and their families in Ciudad Guayana.[11]

Notes

1. The reform of the Civil Code did not automatically imply reform of other legislation, regulations in effect in government offices, or customs. Many discriminatory practices remain in effect. For instance, under the new Civil Code parents share authority over children (the *patria potestad*). However, the office of passports will not issue a child's passport to a mother without the father's permission; fathers are not required to have the mother's permission. Lawyers reported a booming business post-1982 as couples drew up documents where the wife ceded to the husband powers of attorney to dispose of community property without her consent (the reform granted women shared rights of control).

2. The generic term "man" is used here by CVG staff to mean, literally, men, since in other sections of the same document women are referred to separately.

3. In some cases, husbands came for work reasons and wives chose to accompany them because of opportunities for housing or schooling for the children.

4. The city grew from a population of about 5,000 in 1950 to 350,000 in 1980 and 500,000 in 1990.

5. For instance, in the capital city of Caracas, approximately 21% of all couples are in consensual unions. In the industrial city of Valencia, 13% are in consensual unions.

6. Until about 1983, interviewers and coders were instructed to check to see if a woman named head of household had a spouse. If so, the spouse should be coded as head of household. Only unattached women could be heads.

7. The questionnaires included mechanisms for cross-checking data on income, work, and household contributions. I found that potential income could be underestimated for some men who withheld accurate income information from spouses. For instance, in the case of workers at the steel mill, I had access to job and salary data which allowed

me to cross-check the information given by (mainly) female respondents for spouses. I found that not all salary data coincided with those established by the mill for a given job.

8. Data reflect the likelihood of abandonment as well as the need for additional income as household size grows. Older children are more likely than younger children to have been abandoned by fathers and they are also more likely to live in larger households.

9. Male contributions may, in some cases, be overestimated because of the tendency of some men to conceal correct income from spouses.

10. Women's Circles started out as "rap" groups for poor women, then moved on to networking for community action.

11. The recently created Ministry of the Family initiated a nationwide campaign in 1988 to teach families to be more egalitarian as defined by the 1982 Civil Code. This follows campaigns to combat, among other issues, family violence and irresponsible paternity.

References

AWID. Association for Women in Development. 1985. *Women Creating Wealth: Transforming Economic Development.* Washington: AWID.

Boserup, Ester. 1970. *Woman's Role in Economic Development.* New York: St. Martins.

Blumberg, Rae Lesser. 1984. "A General Theory of Gender Stratification." In *Sociological Theory,* edited by Randall Collins. San Francisco: Jossey-Bass.

Carloni, Alice Stewart. 1987. *Women in Development: AID's Experience. 1973-1985.* Vol. 1 Synthesis Paper. Washington: Agency for International Development.

CVG. Corporación Venezolana de Guayana. 1963. *Informe Anual.* Caracas: CVG.

——. 1964. *Informe Anual.* Caracas: CVG.

——. 1968. *Informe Anual.* Caracas: CVG.

——. 1978. *La Estrategia Económica de la Nación y el Programa de Desarrollo de la Región Guayana Hacia el Año 2000.* Caracas: CVG.

——. 1980. *Region Guayana. Plan Regional 1981-1985. Síntesis.* Caracas: CVG.

CVG-Sidor. 1973. "El Trabajo Social en Sidor." Paper presented at the First Venezuelan Congress on Social Work. Caracas.

Friedman, Kathie. 1984. "Households as Income-Pooling Units." In *Households and the World Economy,* edited by Joan Smith, Immanuel Wallerstein, and Hans-Dieter Evers. Beverly Hills: Sage.

García, María Pilar. 1982. "La Marginalidad Planificada." Paper presented at the X World Congress of Sociology. Mexico City.

—— and Rae Lesser Blumberg. 1977. "The Unplanned Ecology of a Planned Industrial City: The Case of Ciudad Guayana, Venezuela." In *Urbanization in the Americas: From the Beginning to the Present,* edited by Richard F. Schaedel and Nora Scott Kinzer. The Hague: Mouton.

Harkess, Shirley J. 1973."The Pursuit of an Ideal: Migration, Social Class, and Women's Roles in Bogotá, Colombia." In *Female and Male in Latin America,* edited by Ann Pescatello. Pittsburgh: University of Pittsburgh Press.

MacDonald, John Stuart. 1969. "Migration and the Population of Ciudad Guayana." In *Planning Urban Growth and Regional Development,* edited by Lloyd Rodwin. Cambridge: MIT Press.

Martinez. Migdalia and David Holmes. 1980. *Análisis Demográfico de la Región Guayana entre 1961 y 1978 y Proyecciones para el VI Plan de la Nación.* Caracas: CVG.

Montero, Maritza. 1983. "La estructura familiar venezolana y la transformación de estereotipos y roles sexuales." Paper presented at the national meeting of the Feminist Front, Socialist Party, Programming Committee. Caracas.

Papanek, Hanna. 1981. "The Differential Impact of Programs and Policies on Women in Development." In *Women and Technological Change in Developing Countries,* edited by Roslyn Dauber and Melinda L. Cain. Boulder, CO: Westview.

Pazos, Henry, Pedro Luís Castellano and Fabrio Arias Rojas. 1975. *Macrodiagnóstico y Proyección Epidemiológica de Ciudad Bolivar y Ciudad Guayana para los Próximos Cinco Años.* Caracas: CVG.

Rakowski, Cathy A. 1983. "Hacia una política de apoyo a la mujer del sector informal urbano." Document SIU 7 presented to Cordiplán and the International Labour Office as part of the project PNUD/OIT/VEN/82/003. Caracas: Cordiplán.

————. 1984a. "The Division of Labor by Sector and by Sex in a Developing Economy: The Case of Ciudad Guayana, Venezuela." Dissertation. Department of Sociology, University of Texas at Austin.

————. 1984b. "El comportamiento de la mano de obra masculina y femenina en Ciudad Guayana con enfoque especial en el más reciente período de boom (1975-79) y post-boom (1980-82)." Report prepared for the Division of Planning, Corporación Venezolana de Guayana, Ciudad Guayana: CVG.

————. 1985. "The Planning Process and the Division of Labor in a New Industrial City: The Case of Ciudad Guayana, Venezuela." In *Capital and Labour in the Urbanized World,* edited by John Walton. London: Sage.

————. 1989. "Evaluating Development: Theory, Ideology, and Planning in Ciudad Guayana, Venezuela." *International Journal of Contemporary Sociology* 26(1,2): 71-91.

7

Racial Ethnic Women's Labor
The Intersection of Race, Gender, and Class Oppression

EVELYN NAKANO GLENN

The failure of the feminist movement to address the concerns of black, Hispanic, and Asian-American women is currently engendering widespread discussion in white women's organizations. Paralleling this discussion is a growing interest among racial ethnic women[1] in articulating aspects of their experiences that have been ignored in feminist analyses of women's oppression (e.g., oral histories by Sterling, 1979; Elessar, MacKenzie, and Tixier y Vigil, 1980; Kim, 1983, and social and historical studies by Dill, 1979; Mirande and Enriquez, 1979, Davis, 1981; Hooks, 1981; Jones, 1984).[2]

As an initial corrective, racial ethnic scholars have begun research on racial ethnic women in relation to employment, the family, and the

AUTHOR'S NOTE: This paper grew out of studying with members of the Inter-University Group Researching the Intersection of Race and Gender: Bonnie Dill, Cheryl Gilkes, Elizabeth Higginbotham, and Ruth Zambrana. I am also grateful to members of the Women and Work Study Group for their contributions to my thinking: Carole Turbin, Natalie Sokoloff, Susan Lehrer, Amy Kesselman, Amy Srebnick, Myra Ferree, Nadine Felton, Roz Feldberg, Peggy Crull, Carol Brown, and Chris Bose. Finally, I thank Nancy Breen, Gary Dymski, Betsy Jameson, Bill James, and Laurie Nisonoff for their careful critiques even though I was unable to incorporate all their suggestions. An early version was presented at the Meetings of the American Association for the Advancement of Science, Washington, DC, January 1982. This is a substantially revised version of a paper published in the proceedings volume and is reprinted by permission of Westview Press from *Social Power and Influence of Women,* Liesa Stamm and Carol D. Ryff (eds.) Westview Press, 1984, Boulder, Colorado. Copyright © 1984 by the American Association for the Advancement of Science. This version originally appeared in the *Review of Radical Political Economics,* 1985, 17(3):86-108 (which holds the copyright); and is reprinted by permission of the Union for Radical Political Economics.

ethnic community, both historically and contemporarily (e.g., Acosta-Belen, 1979; Mora and Del Castillo, 1980; Melville, 1980; Rodgers-Rose, 1980; Tsuchida, 1982). The most interesting of these studies describe the social world and day-to-day struggles of racial ethnic women, making visible what has up to now been invisible in the social sciences and humanities. These concrete data constitute the first step toward understanding the effects of race and gender oppression in the lives of racial ethnic women.

A necessary next step is the development of theoretical and conceptual frameworks for analyzing the interaction of race and gender stratification. Separate models exist for analyzing race, ethnic, or gender stratification. Although the "double" (race, gender) and "triple" (race, gender, class) oppression of racial ethnic women are widely acknowledged, no satisfactory theory has been developed to analyze what happens when these systems of oppression intersect. A starting point for developing such a theory would appear to lie in those models which view race and gender stratification as part of a larger system of institutionalized inequality. During the 1970s two models which view race and gender divisions as embedded in and helping to maintain an overall system of class exploitation came to the fore: the *patriarchy* model developed by Marxist-feminists to explain the subordination of women (e.g., Weinbaum and Bridges, 1979; Sokoloff, 1980; Brown, 1981; and Hartmann, 1981a) and the *internal colonialism* model developed by activists and scholars to explain the historic subordination of blacks, Hispanics, Asian-Americans, and other people of color in the United States (e.g., Clark, 1965; Carmichael and Hamilton, 1967; Moore, 1970; Barrera, Muñoz, and Ornelas, 1972; and Blauner, 1972).

At the center of the Marxist-feminist analysis is the concept of patriarchy, which may be defined as a hierarchical system of power which enables men as a class to have authority and power over women (Hartmann, 1976; Sokoloff, 1980). In this model the main mechanism by which control is achieved and maintained by men is the *sexual division of labor,* which places men in positions of authority over women and permits them to reap disproportionate benefits. Similarly, at the center of the internal colonialism model is a system of power relations by which subordinate minorities are kept politically and economically weak so they can be more easily exploited as workers. The main mechanism by which economic dependency is maintained is a *colonial labor system,* characterized by a segmented labor market, discriminatory barriers, and separate wage scales. This system ensures that people of color are relegated to the worst jobs (i.e., insecure, low-paying, dangerous, dirty, and dead-end).

Neither model explicitly recognizes the specific situation of racial ethnic women. The patriarchy model ignores differences among women based on race. When race is discussed, it is treated as a parallel system of stratification: an analogy is often made between "women" and "minorities," an analogy that involves comparison of the subordinate status of white women and minority men. Minority women are left in limbo. Similarly, the internal colonialism model ignores gender by treating members of colonized minorities as undifferentiated with respect to gender. Analyses of racial ethnic labor have generally focused only on male workers. Yet, these studies also assume that the detrimental impacts of the labor system on men is synonymous with the impacts on the group as a whole, men and women alike.

Despite the focus on only one axis of stratification, the patriarchy and internal colonialism models have some important commonalities. Each focuses on explaining the persistence of inequality and sees gender/race stratification as dynamically related to the organization of the economy. Thus, each implies a historical perspective, one that traces changes in the relations between dominant and subordinate groups in relation to the development of capitalism. Each emphasizes institutional arrangements that ensure control by the dominant group over the labor of the subordinate group. There thus seems to be some common ground for developing a more integrated framework by combining insights from the two perspectives.

This paper is a preliminary effort to identify aspects of the two models that might contribute to an integrated framework. I will start by briefly reviewing the Marxist-feminist analysis of women's subordination. I will then review racial ethnic women's experience as members of colonized minorities in the United States. In light of this experience, I will examine the paid and unpaid work of Chinese, Mexican-American, and black women from the mid-nineteenth century to the present, showing how they diverge from those presumed to be typical of white women. In the concluding section, suggestions are made for revision of Marxist-feminist theory to be more inclusive of the race-gender interaction.

Marxist-Feminist Analysis

The Marxist-feminist perspective views women's subordination as a product of two interacting systems: patriarchy and capitalism. While generally adhering to the Marxist analysis of class exploitation. Marxist-feminists diverge by giving equal importance to patriarchy, which, they argue, existed prior to capitalism, though interacting with it as capitalism developed. According to this analysis, the main mechanism by which patriarchy was established and is maintained today is the sexual division of labor. The assignment of certain tasks (usually the more onerous and/or less valued) to women, and others (usually the more highly valued) to men, is considered more or less universal.

Under capitalism the sexual division of labor takes a particular form due to the separation of production of goods, and then services, from the household. As production was industrialized the household became increasingly privatized, and its functions reduced to consumption, which includes shopping and negotiating for services (Weinbaum and Bridges, 1979), and biological and social reproduction, including child care, cleaning, preparing food, and providing emotional support for the breadwinner. As capital took over production, households became increasingly dependent on the market for goods and therefore, on wages to purchase goods and services needed for survival. During the nineteenth century—in part because men could be more intensively exploited as wage laborers, while women could benefit capital as full-time consumers and reproducers—a specialization developed, whereby women were assigned almost exclusive responsibility for household consumption and reproduction and men were allocated responsibility for publicly organized production. This division became prescribed in the mid-nineteenth century with the development of the cult of domesticity, which idealized the woman as the center of home and hearth (Welter, 1966). This division of labor contributed to the subordination of women by making them economically dependent on a male wage earner. Simultaneously, the domestic code controlled women's behavior by threatening those who deviated from it with the loss of their feminine identity.

The ideal of separate spheres was, of course, unattainable for many women whose fathers or husbands were unable to earn a family wage and who therefore had to engage in income producing activities to support themselves and their families (Lerner, 1969; Easton, 1976). Yet the conception of women as consumers and reproducers affected them too, depressing their position in the labor market. Women were defined as secondary workers, a status maintained by a sexual division in the labor market (i.e., occupational segregation). Jobs allocated to women were typically at the bottom of the authority hierarchy, low in wages, dead-end and frequently insecure. The secondary position of women in the labor force meant that women had little leverage to shift the burden of household work onto husbands, so they continued to be responsible for the domestic sphere. Moreover, because of low wages and insecure jobs, even when employed, women remained dependent on the additional wages of the male earner (Hartmann, 1976; Kessler-Harris, 1982).

This analysis has much to offer: it permits us to view women's subordination as part of a larger framework of economic exploitation. It also draws connections between women's domestic work and their work in the labor force, and shows how subordination in one sphere reinforces subordination in the other. It is intended as a general analysis that encompasses all women. Yet, it is built on class- and race-bounded experiences. To what extent do the concepts developed in the Marxist-feminist model apply to the experience of racial ethnic women? To what extent does the private-public split and women's association with the domestic sphere exist for racial ethnic women? To what extent has economic dependence on men been an important basis for racial ethnic women's subordination? To what extent do struggles over allocation of household labor create gender conflict in racial ethnic households?

In order to begin addressing these questions we need to examine the impacts of race stratification on racial ethnic women's work, both paid and unpaid. For this, I draw on both earlier and more recent research on the labor histories of "colonized minorities." Because histories of the various peoples in different regions of the country vary and because of the limited size and scope of this paper, I will limit my examination to three case studies for which there is comparable information from the mid-nineteenth century to the present: Mexican-Americans in the Southwest, Chinese in California, and blacks in the South.

Colonized Minorities in Industrializing America

The United States started out as a colonial economy which offered raw resources and land to European and American capitalists. In order to develop the economic infrastructure and extract resources, capitalists needed labor, which was always in short supply. The presence of racial ethnic groups in this country is tied to this demand for labor. Most were brought to this country for the express purpose of providing cheap and malleable labor (Cheng and Bonacich, 1984).

Although European immigrants were also welcomed as a source of low-wage labor, they were incorporated into the urban economies of the north. Racial ethnics were recruited primarily to fill labor needs in economically backward regions: the West, Southwest, and South (Blauner, 1972). In the late nineteenth and early twentieth century, Chinese men constituted from a quarter to a third of the work force (reclaiming agricultural lands, building railroads, and working in mines), and 90% of the domestic and laundry workers in California (Saxton, 1971). During this same period, native Chicanos and Mexican immigrants (Mexicanos) were employed as miners, railroad hands, and agricultural laborers in the western states (Barrera, 1979). In the years following emancipation blacks were concentrated in agriculture, as well as in heavy labor in construction and domestic service in the South (Cheng and Bonacich, 1984). All three groups helped build the agricultural and industrial base on which subsequent industrial development rested, but were excluded from the industrial jobs that resulted.

Racial ethnic labor was cheaper for infrastructure building in two senses: racial ethnics were paid less (including lower benefits) and provided a reserve army to be drawn in when the economy expanded or labor was needed for a short-term project, and pushed out when the economy contracted or the particular project ended. Their cheapness was ensured by institutional barriers that undercut their ability to compete in the labor market. The labor market itself was stratified into separate tiers for whites and racial ethnics. The better paying, more skilled, cleaner, and secure jobs in highly capitalized industries were reserved for white workers, leaving the low paying, insecure, dangerous, seasonal, and dead-end jobs in competitive industries for people of color. A dual wage system was also characteristic of the colonial labor system; wages for racial ethnics were always lower than for whites in comparable jobs (Barrera, 1979). White workers benefited because better jobs were reserved for them. The dual labor system also buffered them from the effects of periodic depressions, since racial ethnics took the brunt of layoffs and unemployment.

Further, racial ethnics were prevented from competing for better work and improved conditions by legal and administrative restrictions. Restrictions on their rights and freedoms began right at the time of entry or incorporation into the United States. While the exact form of entry for the three groups differed, in all cases an element of subordination was involved. The most striking instance of forced entry was that of blacks, who were captured, torn from their homelands, transported against their will, and sold into slavery. This institution so structured their lives that even after emancipation former slaves were held in debt bondage by the southern sharecropping system (Painter, 1976). Equally involuntary was the incorporation of Mexicans residing in territories taken over by United States military conquest. Anglo settlers invaded what is now California, Texas, Arizona, New Mexico, and Colorado. When the United States seized the land, native Mexicans living in those areas were reduced to agricultural peons or wage laborers (Barrera,

1979). An intermediate case between forced and free entry was that of the Chinese. Their immigration was the result of the economic and political chaos engendered, at least in part, by western colonial intrusion into China (Lyman, 1974). Many Chinese men entered the United States as contract laborers so they could support destitute kin in their villages. Under the credit ticket system they signed away seven years of labor in exchange for their passage (Ling, 1912).

These unfree conditions of entry imposed special liabilities on racial ethnics. Blacks were not citizens and counted in the census as only three-fifths of a person, Mexicans were defined as second-class citizens, and Chinese were aliens, ineligible for citizenship. All three groups were placed in separate legal categories, denied basic rights and protections, and barred from political participation. Thus, they could be coerced, intimidated, and restricted to the least desirable jobs, where they were especially vulnerable to exploitation.

The process of incorporation and entry into the labor system in turn had profound effects on the culture and family systems of racial ethnics. Native languages, religion, and other ways of life were constrained, destroyed, or transformed and kin ties and family authority undermined. As Blauner (1972, p. 66) notes:

> The labor system through which people of color became Americans tended to destroy or weaken their cultures and communal ties. Regrouping and new institutional forms developed, but in situations with extremely limited possibilities.

We are most familiar with assaults on family ties of blacks under slavery due to sale of individuals regardless of kin ties, slave master control over marriage and reproduction, and the brutal conditions of life. Scholars and policy analysts in the past argued that slavery permanently weakened kin ties and undermined the conjugal household, thereby creating a legacy of family pathology (Frazier, 1939; Moynihan, 1965). More recently, revisionist historians have argued that slaves resisted assaults on family integrity and managed to maintain conjugal and kin ties to a greater extent than previously believed (Blassingame, 1972; Fogel and Engerman, 1974; and Gutman, 1976). Gutman (1975) found that a large proportion of slave marriages were of long standing and many couples legalized their marriages when given the opportunity to do so after emancipation. Black families showed great strength in the face of assaults on kin networks, though their survival required great struggle and exacted great costs.

Less well known are the assaults on the culture and family lives of Chicanos and Chinese-Americans. In both groups households were broken apart by the demand for male labor. Many Mexican-American men were employed in the mining camps and on railroad gangs which required them to live apart from wives and children (Barrera, 1979). This was also true for male migrant agricultural workers until the 1880s when the family labor system became the preferred mode (Camarillo, 1979). In the case of the Chinese, only prime age males were recruited as workers, and wives and children had to be left behind (Coolidge, 1909). The Chinese Exclusion Act of 1882 not only prohibited further entry of Chinese laborers, it also barred resident laborers from bringing in wives and children (Wu, 1972; Lyman, 1974). This policy was aimed at preventing the Chinese from settling permanently, once their labor was no longer needed.

Given these conditions, what was the work of racial ethnic women in the nineteenth and early twentieth centuries?

Racial Ethnic Women's Work in Industrializing America

The specific conditions of life experienced by the three groups of women differed. However, the women shared some common circumstances due to their similar positions in the colonial labor system and the similar difficulties the system created for their families. All three groups of women had to engage in constant struggle for both immediate survival and the long-term continuation of the family and community. Because men of their groups were generally unable to earn a family wage, women had to engage in subsistence and income producing activities both in and out of the household. In addition they had to work hard to keep their families together in the face of outside forces that threatened their integrity.

Chinese-American Women

Perhaps the least is known about Chinese-American women in the nineteenth and early twentieth centuries. This may be due to the fact that very few working class Chinese women actually resided in the United States then. For most of the period from 1860 to 1920 the ratio of men to women ranged from 13 to 20 males for every female. As late as 1930 there were only 9,742 females aged 10 or over in a population that included 53,650 males of the same age (Glenn, 1983). It is estimated that over half of the men had left wives behind in China

(Coolidge, 1909). Although most of these wives never came to the United States, their lives must be considered as part of the experience of analytic racial ethnics, for they raised subsequent generations of sojourners who went to America, often with false papers. Little research has been done on what women did in their home villages or how they survived. The available evidence, based partly on some family history interviews I conducted and partly on other sources (Kingston, 1977; Hirata, 1979), suggests the following: the wife often resided with the husbands' parents or other kin, who received remittances from the husband, acted on his behalf and oversaw the household. Wives took care of children, performed household work under the direction of the mother-in-law, and helped in subsistence farming. Her sexual chastity was carefully guarded, as was her overall behavior. She might never see her husband again or, if lucky, see him once or twice over the course of 20 or 30 years during his rare visits home.

In the late nineteenth century, aside from wives of merchants who were still allowed entry into the United States, the only notable group of Chinese women were prostitutes (Hirata, 1979; Goldman, 1981). The imbalanced sex ratio created a demand for sexual services. Except for a few years when some women were able to immigrate on their own as free entrepreneurs, Chinese prostitutes were either indentured servants or outright slaves controlled by Chinese tongs or business associations. They had been sold by their parents or kidnapped and involuntarily transported. The controllers of the trade reaped huge profits from buying and selling women and hiring out their services. Women who ran away were hunted down and returned to their captors, usually with the collusion of the police and courts. Unable to speak English and without allies, the women could not defend themselves.

Initially the Chinese were dispersed throughout the West in mining towns, railroad camps, and agricultural fields. They were subjected to special penalties, such as a foreign miner's tax in California that rendered it difficult for them to make a living. Finally, during the economic depression of the 1870s, the Chinese were forcibly driven out of many areas (Nee and Nee, 1972). They congregated in urban Chinatowns, so that by the 1880s the Chinese were a largely urban population. In place of households, the men formed clan and regional associations for mutual welfare and protection (Lyman, 1977). By the early 1900s some Chinese men were able, with minimal capital, to establish laundries, restaurants, and stores, thereby qualifying as merchants eligible to bring over wives (Lyman, 1968). These small businesses were a form of self-exploitation; they were profitable only because all members of the family contributed their labor and worked long hours. Living quarters were often in back of the shop or adjacent to it, so that work and family life were completely integrated. Work in the family enterprise went on simultaneously with household mainte-nance and child care. First up and last to bed, women had even less leisure than the rest of the family. Long work hours in crowded and rundown conditions took its toll on the whole family. Chinatowns had abnormally high rates of tuberculosis and other diseases (Lee, Lim, and Wong, 1969).

It is unclear what proportion of women laboring in family laun-dries and shops were counted as gainfully employed in the census. They were undoubtedly severely undercounted. In any case some sizable proportion of women were employed as independent wage workers. As employees, Chinese women were concentrated in ethnic enterprises because of color bars in white-owned businesses. Nearly half of all gainfully employed women in 1930 worked in jobs that were typical of Chinese enterprise. Out of a work force of 1559, garment operatives and seamstresses accounted for 11.7%, sales and trade for 10.6%, laundry operatives for 7.3%, waitresses for 8.2%, and clerical workers for 11.2%. The only major form of employment outside the ethnic community was private household service, which accounted for 11.7% of Chinese women (U.S. Census 1933; for broad occupational distribu-tions, see Table 7.1).

Mexican-American Women

The information on the work of Chicanas in the late nineteenth century is also sparse. Barrera (1979) suggests that prior to the 1870s Chicano families followed the traditional division of labor, with women responsible for household work and child care. Thus, Mexican-Ameri-can women worked largely in the home. Under the conditions of life among working class and agricultural families this work was extensive and arduous (Jensen, 1981). In rural areas the household work included tending gardens and caring for domestic animals. Many Chicano men were employed in extracting industries which required them to live in work camps and company towns in unsettled territories. If a wife remained behind with the children in the home village, she had to engage in subsistence farming and raise children on her own. If she joined her husband in camp, she had to carry on domestic chores and child rearing under frontier conditions, forced to buy necessities in company stores that quickly used up meager wages. Even in the city the barrios often had no running water, and unsanitary conditions added to women's burdens of nursing the sick (Garcia, 1980).

Table 7.1 Occupational Distribution of Employed Black, Chinese-American, Mexican-American, and White Women, 10 Years of Age and Over, 1930

Occupation	Percentage Black	Percentage Chinese	Percentage Mexican	Percentage White
Professional	3.4	11.3	3.0	16.5
Trade	0.8	15.3	9.0	10.7
Public Service	0.1	0.0	0.1	0.2
Clerical	0.6	11.2	2.6	22.4
Manufacturing	5.5	20.4	19.3	20.0
Transportation	0.1	1.1	0.5	3.1
Agriculture	26.9	1.5	21.2	4.5
Service (excluding servants and laundresses)	35.4	27.6	13.5	20.1
Servants/Laundresses	27.2	11.7	30.8	2.5
TOTAL	100.0	100.1	100.0	100.0

SOURCE: U.S. Bureau of the Census, *Fifteenth Census of the United States: 1930, Population, Volume 5, General Report on Occupations, Chapter 3, Color and Nativity of Gainful Workers.* *(Washington, DC: Government Printing Office, 1933), Tables 2, 4, and 6.*

By the 1880s Mexican-American women were increasingly being brought into the labor force. In cities such as Los Angeles, Santa Barbara, and El Paso, Chicanas were employed as servants, cooks, and laundresses (Camarillo, 1979; Garcia, 1980). An economic depression in the 1880s forced more women to seek outside wage work, not only in private households, but also as washer-women in commercial laundries, and as cooks, dishwashers, maids, and waitresses in hotels and other public establishments. In this same period women entered the agricultural labor market. Prior to that time prime-age male workers were preferred for seasonal and migratory field work. In the 1880s whole families began to be used, a pattern that accelerated during World War I (Camarillo, 1979, p. 91). By the 1920s family labor was common throughout the Southwest. Describing the situation in Colorado, Taylor (1929) noted that landowners felt that families, despite their lower productivity per unit, were preferable because they were a more stable work force that could be counted on to return year after year.

These trends are reflected in occupational patterns of Chicana women. Between 1880 and 1930, they tended to be employed in two main types of situations. A large part of the Chicana work force, 20% officially, were employed as farm laborers (Barrera, 1979). Many of these were employed as part of the piece rate system in which entire families worked and moved with the crops (Taylor, 1937; Fisher, 1953;

McWilliams, 1971). Under this system women had to bear and raise children, cook and keep house, while also working long hours in the field or packing house. Infants accompanied their parents to the fields, and children started working from an early age. Living conditions in migrant camps were extremely harsh. Adults rarely lived past 55 and infant and child mortality was high. Children had no regular schooling because of constant movement and the need for their labor. Schools were geared to fit agricultural schedules and provided minimal training (Taylor, 1929). Once into the migrant pattern it was almost impossible for families or individuals to break out.

The second type of employment for Chicanas, primarily those in cities and towns, was in unskilled and semi-skilled "female" jobs. The distribution of jobs varied in different areas of the Southwest, but the most common occupations in all areas were service positions (household servants, waitresses, maids, cooks, and laundry operatives), which accounted for 44.3% of all employed Chicanas in 1930, and operatives in garment factories and food processing plants, which together employed 19.3% in 1930 (Table 7.1). The latter industries also employed Anglo women, but Chicanas were given the worst jobs and the lowest pay. They were victims of both occupational stratification and a dual wage system. Their plight was revealed in testimony by employers before the Texas Industrial Welfare System in El Paso in 1919. For example, F. B. Fletcher, a laundry owner representing the owners of the four largest laundries in El Paso testified that almost all the unskilled labor was performed by Mexican women, while the skilled positions as markers, sorters, checkers, supervisors, and office assistants went to Anglo women. Further, Mexican women were paid an average of $6.00 a week while Anglo women received $16.55. Fletcher argued that:

This difference indicates that in this industry, the minimum wage can be fairly fixed for Mexican female help and for the American entirely different and distinct. (Garcia, 1981, p. 91)

Only by combining their wages with those of husbands and older children could Mexican-American women survive.

Whether engaged in subsistence farming, seasonal migratory labor, agricultural packing, laundry work, domestic service, or garment manufacturing, Chicanas had to raise their children under colonized conditions. As part of the continued legal and illegal takeover of land by Anglos in Texas and Colorado from 1848 to 1900, the Chicanos became a conquered people (McLemore, 1973, 1980). Defined and treated as inferior, their language and culture became badges of second-class status. Through their daily reproductive activities and work women played a critical role not only maintaining the family, but also in sustaining Mexican-American ways of life.

Black Women

Perhaps more than any other group of women, black women were from the start exempted from the myth of female disability. To be sure, they were exploited on the basis of their gender as breeders and raisers of slaves for plantation owners (Genovese, 1974). Their gender also made them liable to a special form of oppression, sexual assault. Nevertheless, their gender did not spare them from hard physical labor in the field (Jones, 1984). Hooks (1981) claims plantation owners often preferred women for the hardest field work because they were the more reliable workers. In addition black women did the heavy housework and child care for white women; in that role they were subject to abuse and even physical beatings at the hands of their mistresses. As Angela Davis (1971) notes, under conditions of plantation slavery, staying alive, raising children, and maintaining some semblance of community were forms of resistance.

After emancipation, life for rural blacks remained harsh under the sharecropping system; blacks found themselves held in debt bondage. Hooks (1981) suggests that landowners preferred sharecropping to hiring labor because black women were unwilling to be employed in the fields once slavery was abolished. With sharecropping women's labor could be exploited intensively, since women had to work hard alongside the men in order to pay off the ever-mounting debt to the owner. One observer of black farmers noted that these women:

> do double duty, a man's share in the field, and a woman's part at home. They do any kind of field work, even ploughing, and at home the cooking, washing, milling and gardening. (Lerner, 1973)

Although there were some independent black farmers, it became increasingly difficult for them to make a living. Jim Crow laws deprived blacks of legal rights and protections, while national farm policies favored large landowners. Independent black farmers were increasingly impoverished and finally driven off the land (Painter, 1976).

Aside from farming, the next largest group of black women were employed as laundresses and domestic servants. Black women constituted an exclusive servant caste in the South, since whites refused to enter a field associated with blacks from slave times (Katzman, 1978).

As servants, black women often worked a 14- to 16-hour day and were on-call around the clock (Brown, 1938). They were allowed little time off to carry out their own domestic responsibilities, despite the fact that the majority of black domestics had children of their own. A married domestic might see her children once every two weeks, while devoting night and day to the care of her mistress's children. Her own children were left in the care of husband or older siblings (Katzman, 1978). Low wages were endemic. They had to be supplemented by children taking in laundry or doing odd jobs. Many black women testified that they could only survive through the tradition of the service pan—the term for leftover food that was left at the disposal of the colored cook (Lerner, 1973, p. 18).

Manufacturing and white-collar jobs were closed to black women, though some of the dirtiest jobs in industry were offered to them. They were particularly conspicuous in southern tobacco factories and to some extent in cotton mills and flour manufacturing. In the cotton mills black women were employed as common laborers in the yards, as waste gatherers and as scrubbers of machinery. The actual manufacturing jobs were reserved for white women (Foner and Lewis, 1981). Regarding black women in the tobacco industry, Emma Shields noted in a pamphlet she prepared for the Women's Bureau in 1922:

> Conditions of employment throughout the tobacco industry are deplorably wretched, and yet conditions for Negro women workers are very much worse than those for white women workers. . . . Negro women are employed exclusively in the rehandling of tobacco, preparatory to its actual manufacture. Operations in the manufacture of cigars and cigarettes are performed exclusively by white women workers. Negro women workers are absolutely barred from any opportunity for employment in the manufacturing operations. . . . It is not unusual to find the white women workers occupying the new modern sanitary parts of the factory, and the Negro women workers in the old sections which management has decided to be beyond any hope of improvement. (Quoted in Lerner, 1969)

World War I saw increasing migration of blacks to the urban North and, simultaneously, the entrance of blacks into factory employment there. As late as 1910, 90.5% of all black women were farm laborers and servants, but between 1910 and 1920, 48,000 black women entered factory work (Lerner, 1969). Most were employed in steam laundries, the rest in unmechanized jobs in industry as sweepers, cleaners, and ragpickers (Foner and Lewis, 1981).

During the entire period from 1870 to 1930 black women, regardless of rural or urban residence, were notable for their high rates of labor force participation, particularly among married women. In 1900, 26.0% of married black women were in the labor force compared to 3.8% of married white women (Pleck, 1980). They thus had to contend with the double day long before this became an issue for a majority of white women. Moreover, although their wages were consistently lower than those of white women, their earnings constituted a larger share of total family income, due to the marginal and low wage employment of black men (Byington, 1974). Finally, they had to perform their double duty in the face of poor and crowded living conditions, an educational system that provided inferior schooling for their children, uncertain income, and other trials.

Racial Ethnic Women's Work in the Contemporary Period

All three groups are predominately urban today, a process that began in the late nineteenth century for the Chinese, during World War I for blacks and after World War II for Chicanos. All also have experienced dramatic changes in occupational distributions since 1930.

Chinese Women Since World War II

The main change in circumstances for Chinese women is that they were allowed entry to the United States in large numbers for the first time after World War II. Many separated wives were able to join their spouses under the provisions of the Walter-McCarran Act of 1953, and whole family units were able to enter after passage of the liberalized 1965 immigration law (Li, 1977; U.S. Department of Justice, 1977). Since World War II female immigrants outnumbered males, and the sex ratio of the Chinese population now approaches equality, with the remaining imbalance existing only in the older age categories (U.S. Bureau of the Census, 1973). Women who have rejoined spouses or arrived with husbands are adapting to the post-war urban economy by entering the paid labor force. Handicapped by language, by family responsibilities, and gender and race discrimination in the skilled trades, both husbands and wives are employed in the secondary labor market—in low-wage service and competitive manufacturing sectors. The most typical constellation among immigrant families is a husband employed as a restaurant worker, store helper, or janitor and a wife employed as an operative in a small garment shop. The shops are located in, or close to, Chinatowns and typically are subcontracting firms run by Chinese. They often evade minimum wage laws by using an unofficial piece rate system (Nee and Nee, 1972).

An examination of the occupational distribution of Chinese-American women reveals a bimodal pattern. In 1970 (Table 7.2) Chinese women were concentrated in clerical (31.8%) and professional white collar work (19.4%), and in the operative category (22.5%). While the high proportion in white-collar fields indicates considerable success by second, third, and fourth generation women, generational mobility may be less than these figures suggest, since many professionals are actually recent immigrants of gentry origin rather than working-class Chinese-Americans who have moved up. Working-class Chinese women continue to be relegated to operative jobs in the garment trade. What Chinese women of all classes share is a higher than average rate of labor force participation (U.S. Bureau of the Census, 1973).

Post-war economic changes have undercut family enterprises such as laundries and small stores, so that working-class families today typically engage in dual wage earning. They encounter difficulties due to the long work hours of parents and crowded and run-down housing. Working mothers are responsible for not only the lion's share of domestic chores, but often raise their children almost single-handedly. Husbands are frequently employed in the restaurant trade, which requires them to be at work from 11 in the morning until 10 in the evening or even midnight. Thus they are rarely around while their children are awake. The women's own work hours are often prolonged because they leave work during the day to cook meals or pick up children. They make up the time by returning to the shop for evening work or by taking materials home to sew at night (Ikels and Shang, 1979). Their energy is entirely absorbed by paid employment and domestic responsibilities. The one ray of light is their hope for their children's future.

Mexican-American Women

The Chicano population is still characterized by continued migration back and forth between Mexico and the United States. In 1970, 16% of the resident population in the United States was foreign-born (Massey, 1982, p. 10). Not surprisingly, Chicanos remain concentrated in the Southwest, with 78% residing in California and Texas in 1979 (Pachon and Moore, 1981). Contrary to their image as rural people, four out of five (79%) resided in metropolitan areas. In line with the urban shift has been a sharp reduction in the percentage of men and women engaged in agriculture. The proportion of women employed as farm workers fell from 21.2% in 1930 to 2.4% by 1979 (Tables 7.1 and 7.3). Due to the

Table 7.2 Occupational Distribution of Black, Chinese-American, Mexican-American, and White Women in the United States, 1970

Occupation	Percentage Black	Percentage Chinese-American	Percentage Mexican-American	Percentage White[a]
Professional	11.3	19.4	6.4	16.6
Managerial	1.4	3.8	1.9	4.0
Sales	2.6	5.1	5.7	8.1
Clerical	20.7	31.8	25.9	37.0
Craft	1.4	1.2	2.3	1.8
Operative	16.5	22.5	25.8	13.7
Laborers (excluding farm)	1.5	0.9	1.8	0.9
Farming (including farm labor)	1.2	0.5	4.0	0.7
Service	25.5	12.8	20.6	15.3
Private household workers	17.8	2.0	5.5	1.9
TOTAL	99.9	100.0	99.9	100.0

SOURCES: U.S. Bureau of Census, *Subject Reports of the 1970 Census:* PC(2)-1B, *Negro Population, Table 7; PC(2)-1C, Persons of Spanish Origin,* Table 8; PC(2)-1F, *Japanese, Chinese, and Filipinos in the United States,* Table 22 (Washington, DC: Government Printing Office, 1973) and U.S. Bureau of the Census, Census of the Population: 1970, *Detailed Characteristics of the Population,* Final Report, PC(1)-D1, *U.S. Summary,* Table 226, (Washington, DC: Government Printing Office, 1973).
NOTE: a. Category comprised of all women minus black and Spanish origin.

mechanization of agriculture which caused a sharp decline in the total number of farm workers, however, Chicana women constituted a higher *proportion* of women in agricultural labor in 1979 than they did in 1930. For those still involved in migrant labor, conditions remain harsh, with extensive exploitation of children, despite child labor laws (Taylor, 1976).

The period from 1930 to the present saw a steady rise in the occupational status of Mexican-Americans. As with other racial ethnic groups the occupational dispersion of Chicanos is related to labor shortages during wars, especially World War II. In the post-war period, rising numbers of Chicanas found employment in clerical and sales jobs, though they still lagged behind white women, especially in sales. The lower rates in white-collar jobs were matched by over-representation in blue-collar and service occupations. Mexican-American women were concentrated in operative jobs, principally in garment factories, laundries, and food processing plants, which together accounted for 25.0% of their employment in 1979 (Table 7.3). These enterprises tended to be small competitive firms that paid minimum wages and were often seasonal. Another 23.4% of all employed Chicanas were in service jobs, including private household work.

Table 7.3 Occupational Distribution of Employed Black, Mexican-American, and White Women, 16 Years Old and Over, 1979

Occupation	Percentage Black[a]	Percentage Mexican-American	Percentage White
Professional	14.2	6.4	16.4
Managerial	3.4	3.5	6.8
Sales	3.1	5.1	7.4
Clerical	29.0	31.1	35.9
Crafts	1.2	1.8	1.9
Operatives	15.3	25.0	11.0
Laborer (excluding farm)	1.6	1.3	1.3
Farming (including farm labor)	0.8	2.4	1.3
Service (including private household)	31.5	23.4	18.1
TOTAL	100.1	100.0	100.1

SOURCE: U.S. Bureau of the Census, *Current Population Reports,* Series P-20, No. 354, *Persons of Spanish Origin in the United States: March 1979* (Washington, DC: Government Printing Office, 1980), Table 10. U.S. Bureau of Labor Statistics, *Employment and Earnings,* 27, No. 1 (1980), Table 22.
NOTE: a. Category consists of "black and other."

Mexican-American women have traditionally had among the lowest rates of labor force participation among racial ethnic women (Almquist and Weherle-Einhorn, 1978). However, in the 1970s Chicanas rapidly entered the labor market, so that by 1980 their rates were similar to that of whites, though lower than those for black and Asian-American women (Massey, 1982). The lower rates may be related to two other circumstances which usually depress employment: education and family size. Chicanas have the lowest education levels of the three groups and also have the largest number of children. These factors in turn mean that when Chicanas are in the labor force, they are at a great disadvantage. In 1976 nearly one-third (31.5%) of all employed Chicanas had eight years of education or less; comparable figures for blacks were 14.1% and for whites 7.6% (U.S. Department of Labor, 1977).

In short, though Mexican-American women have achieved greater employment parity with Anglo women, they continue to have lower educational levels and heavier family burdens. In addition, they encounter racial barriers to white-collar employment.

Black Women

Black women have also experienced shifts in employment since World War II. The postwar period saw a great decline in domestic service as a major category of women's work. Because black women were so concentrated in it they have shown the most dramatic decline. Whereas in 1940, three out of five (59.5%) employed black females were in domestic service, by 1960 that proportion had dropped to a little over a third (36.2%), and by 1980 to one out of fourteen (7.4%) (U.S. Census, 1933, 1973; Westcott, 1982). Partially replacing service in private households has been service employment in public establishments, particularly in food service and health care, where the number of low-level jobs has proliferated. These jobs accounted for 25.4% of black female employment in 1980, compared to 16.0% of white women (Westcott, 1982).

U.S. Census data (Table 7.3) show that black women are overrepresented in the operatives category, where 15.3% were employed in 1979, in contrast to 11.0% of whites. As in the past, there is a stratified labor market and a dual wage system. Baker and Levenson (1975a) examined the careers of black, Hispanic, and white graduates of a New York City vocational high school, and found that black and Hispanic women were disproportionately tracked into lower paying operative jobs in the garment industry, while better paying jobs outside the garment industry were reserved for white graduates. Years later the difference in pay and mobility was even greater as black and Hispanic women were progressively disadvantaged (Baker and Levenson, 1975b).

The last barrier to fall was white-collar employment. A dramatic increase in professional-technical, clerical, and sales employment took place after 1950. By 1979, the former accounted for 14.2% of black female employment, the latter two together for 32.1%. Differences remained, however, in that white-collar employment accounted for over two-thirds of white women's jobs, but less than half of black women's employment. In addition, within white-collar jobs, black women were concentrated in lower level jobs. For example, in 1980 black women constituted 10.8% of all clerical workers, but they made up over 15% of such lower level positions as file clerks, mail handlers, key punchers, and office machine operators, and less than 6% of more skilled positions as secretaries, bank tellers and bookkeepers (Glenn and Tolbert, 1985). In effect, though black women have experienced desegregation at the level of broad occupations, they have been resegregated at the finer level of detailed job categories.

Other measures also show continued disadvantage for black women. They have a 50% higher unemployment rate and somewhat lower earnings (U.S. Department of Labor, 1977). The largest gap is in terms of median family income, due to discrimination against black men. Even with the mother in the labor force, the median family income for black families with children under 18 years old was $14,461 in 1975 compared to $17,588 for similar white families (U.S. Department of Labor, 1977). Even though they could not raise family income to white levels by being employed, black women's wages made a bigger difference to overall family income. The gap between blacks and whites was even greater if the mother was not employed: the median for black families without mothers in the labor force was $8,912 compared to $14,796 for whites (U.S. Department of Labor, 1977). Regardless of income level, the economic fate of the black conjugal family rested on an economic partnership between men and women. Moreover, even among relatively affluent black families, the need to combat racism was a theme that infused daily life and absorbed the energy of parents in socializing their children (Willie, 1981). Women's role as nurturers required them to combat the daily assaults on their children's self-esteem and to be vigilant in protecting them from psychic injury.

Implications for Feminist Analysis

The history of racial ethnic women's work in the United States reveals their oppression not just as women, but also as members of colonized minorities. As members of colonized minorities, their experiences differed fundamentally from those used to construct Marxist-feminist theory. Thus, concepts within that framework require reformulation if it is to generate analyses that are inclusive of racial ethnic women. I will briefly examine three concepts in Marxist-feminist theory that need to be redefined to take into account the interaction of race and gender. These are the separation between private and public spheres, the primacy of gender conflict as a feature of the family, and the gender-based assignment of reproductive labor.

The growing separation of public and private spheres with industrialization was central to early Marxist-feminist analyses of women's oppression under capitalism. However, recent historical and comparative research has called into question the extent to which private and public constituted separate and bounded spheres for all classes and groups. Scholars note that in industrializing societies working class women engage in many income-earning activities, such as doing piecework at home, taking in boarders, or trading on the informal market, which cannot be easily categorized as private or public (Jensen, 1980). Moreover, industrial wage work and family life have been found to interact in complex ways, so that, for example, women's family roles may include and overlap with their roles as workers (Harevan, 1977).

The examination of racial ethnic women's work adds to the critiques growing out of this research.

The nature of the split, and the extent to which women are identified with the public sphere, seems to vary by class and ethnicity, and differences among groups in women's relationship to public and private spheres needs to be examined. Like many other working-class women, racial ethnic women were never out of public production. They were integrated into production in varying ways. Black women were involved in agriculture and waged domestic service from the time of slavery. Chinese-American women frequently engaged in unpaid labor in family enterprises, where there was little separation between public and private life. Mexican-American women were initially more confined to household-based labor than the other groups, but this labor included a great deal of actual production, since men's wages were insufficient to purchase the necessities of life. Thus, a definition of womanhood exclusively in terms of domesticity never applied to racial ethnic women, as it did not to many working-class white women.

Where racial ethnic women diverge from other working-class women is that, as members of colonized minorities, their definition as laborers in production took precedence over their domestic roles. Whereas the wife-mother roles of white working-class women were recognized and accorded respect by the larger society, the maternal and reproductive roles of racial ethnic women were ignored in favor of their roles as workers. The lack of consideration for their domestic functions is poignantly revealed in the testimony of black domestics cited earlier, who were expected to leave their children and home cares behind while devoting full time to the care of the white employer's home and children. Similarly, Chinese- and Mexican-American women and children were treated as units of labor, capable of toiling long hours without regard to their need for private life. This is not to say that racial ethnic women themselves did not see themselves in terms of their family identities, but that they were not so defined by the larger society, which was interested in them only as workers.

Another area of divergence is in the scope of what is included in the so-called private sphere. For racial ethnic women the domestic encompasses a broad range of kin and community relations beyond the nuclear family. Under conditions of economic insecurity, scarce resources, and cultural assault, the conjugal household was not self-sufficient. Racial and ethnic peoples have historically relied on a larger network of extended kin, including fictive relatives and clan associations, for goods and services. This means that women's reproductive work in the "private" sphere included contributions to this larger circle, within which women took care of each others' children, loaned each other goods, and helped nurse the sick. Beyond the kin network women's work extended to the ethnic community, with much effort being expended in support of the church, political organizing, and other activities on behalf of "the race" *(la raza)*. Women often are the core of community organizations, and their involvement often is spurred by a desire to defend their children, their families, and their ways of life (Ellesar, MacKenzie, and Tixier y Vigil, 1980; Gilkes, 1982; Yap, 1983). In short, race, as organized within a colonial labor system, interacted with gender (patriarchy) and class (capitalism) to determine the structure of private and public spheres and women's relationship to these spheres.

A second aspect of Marxist-feminist theory that requires reformulation in light of race is the concept of the family as a locus of gender conflict. The Marxist-feminist analysis of the family is a response to traditional approaches that treat the family as an entity with unitary interests; in particular, it challenges the functionalist view of the division of labor as complementary rather than exploitative. By focusing on inequality—the economic dependence of women and the inequitable division of labor—some Marxist-feminists see members of the family as divided in their interests, with conflict manifested in a struggle over resources and housework (e.g., Hartmann, 1981b; Thorne, 1982; for a contrasting view, see Humphries, 1977). In this view the conjugal family oppresses women; the liberation of women requires freeing them from familial authority and prescribed roles.

Examination of racial ethnic women's experiences draws attention to the other side of the coin—the family as a source of resistance to oppression from outside institutions.[3] The colonial labor system made it impossible for men of color to support their families with their labor alone and therefore ruled out economic dependence for women. The issue for racial ethnic women was not so much economic quality with husbands, but rather the adequacy of overall family income. Because racial ethnic men earned less, women's wages comprised a larger share of total family income in dual wage-earner families. In the case of family enterprises, common among Asian-Americans, family income depended on the labor of men and women equally. Thus, in both dual wage-earner and small business families, men and women were mutually dependent; dependence rarely ran in one direction.

As for the division of household labor, Marxist-feminist analysis sees it as benefiting men, who receive a greater share of services while contributing less labor. In the racial ethnic family, conflict over the division of labor is muted by the fact that institutions outside the family are hostile to it. The family is a bulwark against the atomizing effects of poverty and legal and political constraints. By transmitting folkways and language, socializing children into an alternative value system, and providing a base for self-identity and esteem, the family helps to maintain racial ethnic culture. Women do a great deal of the work of keeping the family together and teaching children survival skills. This work is experienced as a form of resistance to oppression rather than as a form of exploitation by men. In the colonial situation the common interest of family members in survival, the maintenance of family authority, and the continuation of cultural traditions are emphasized. This is not to say that there are no conflicts over the division of labor but struggles against outside forces take precedence over struggles within the family. Thus, the racial stratification system shapes the forms of intrafamilial and extrafamilial conflict, and determines the arenas in which struggle occurs.

A third concept in Marxist-feminist theory that would benefit from consideration of race oppression is the very useful notion of reproductive labor. Following an early brief formulation by Marx, Marxist-feminists identified two distinct forms of labor, production and reproduction (Sokoloff, 1980). Reproduction refers to activities that recreate the labor force: the physical and emotional maintenance of current workers, and the nurturing and socializing of future workers. In other words, people as well as things have to be produced. Although both men and women engage in production, women are still the ones who carry out most of the reproduction. In large part this is because much reproductive work remains at the household level, which is women's domain. In considering the situation of racial ethnic women, it is useful to recognize the existence of a racial as well as a sexual division of reproductive labor. Historically, racial ethnic women have been assigned distinct responsibilities for reproductive labor.

In the early industrial period racial ethnic and immigrant women were employed as household servants, thereby performing reproductive labor for white native families. The labor of black and immigrant servants made possible the woman "belle" ideal for white middle-class women. Even where white immigrant domestics were employed, the dirtiest and most arduous tasks—laundering and heavy cleaning—were often assigned to black servants. There was a three-way division of labor in the home, with white middle-class women at the top of the hierarchy, followed by white immigrants, with racial ethnics at the bottom. In the late industrial period, as capital took over more areas of life, reproductive activities also were increasingly taken out of the household and turned into paid services which yielded profits (Braverman, 1974). Today, such activities as caring for the elderly (old age homes), preparing food (restaurants and fast-food stands), and providing emotional support (counselling services) have been brought into the cash nexus. As this has happened, women have been incorporated into the labor force to perform these tasks for wages. Within this female-typed public reproduction work, however, there is further stratification by race. Racial ethnic women perform the more menial, less desirable tasks. They prepare and serve food, clean rooms and change bed pans, while white women, employed as semiprofessionals and white-collar workers, perform the more skilled and administrative tasks. The stratification is visible in hospitals, where whites predominate among registered nurses, while the majority of health care aides and housekeeping staff are blacks and latinas. Just as white women in tobacco manufacturing benefited by getting cleaner and more mechanized jobs by dint of the dirty preparation work done by black women, so white women professionals enjoy more desirable working conditions because racial ethnic women perform the less desirable service tasks. The better pay white women receive also allows them to purchase services and goods that ease their reproductive labor at home.

This point leads to a final consideration. It may be tempting to conclude that racial ethnic women differ from white women simply by the addition of a second axis of oppression, namely race. It would be a mistake, though, not to recognize the dialectical relation between white and racial ethnic women. Race, gender, and class interact in such a way that the histories of white and racial ethnic women are intertwined. Whether one considers the split between public and private spheres, conflict within the family, between the family and outside institutions, or productive and reproductive labor, the situation of white women has depended on the situation of women of color. White women have gained advantages from the exploitation of racial ethnic women, and the definition of white womanhood has to a large extent been cast in opposition to the definition of racial ethnic women (Palmer, 1983). Marxist-feminist theory and the internal colonialism model both recognize white men as the dominant exploiting group; however it is equally important to emphasize the involvement of white women in the exploitation of racial ethnic people and the ways in which racial ethnic men have benefited from the even greater exploitation of racial ethnic women.

Notes

1. The term racial ethnic designates groups that are simultaneously racial and ethnic minorities. It is used here to refer collectively to blacks, latinos, and Asian-Americans, groups that share a legacy of labor exploitation and special forms of oppression described in the body of this paper. It is offered as an alternative to more commonly used designations, namely, minority groups, people of color, and Third World minorities, each of which is problematic at some level.

2. Sokoloff (1980) points out that whereas earlier Marxist-feminists viewed gender oppression as a by-product of capitalism, what she calls "later" Marxist-feminists developed the concept of patriarchy as a separate system that predated capitalism and that interacts with class exploitation under capitalism.

3. This general line of argument may also apply to white working-class families. However, I would assert that there were crucial differences in the historical experiences of white working-class and racial ethnic families. The family system of the white working class was not subject to institutional attacks (such as forced separation) directed against black, Chicano, and Chinese families. Moreover, white working-class women were accorded some respect for their domestic roles.

References

Acosta-Belen, Edna. ed. 1979. *The Puerto Rican Woman*. New York: Praeger.

Almquist, Elizabeth M. 1979. *Minorities, Gender and Work*. Lexington, MA: D.C. Heath.

Almquist, Elizabeth M. and Juanita L. Weherle-Einhorn. 1978. "The Doubly Disadvantaged: Minority Women in the Labor Force." Pp. 63-88 in *Women Working*, edited by Ann H. Stromberg and Shirley Harkess. Palo Alto, CA: Mayfield.

Baca-Zinn, Maxine. 1982. Review Essay: Mexican American Women in the Social Sciences. *Signs* 8:259-272.

Baker, Sally Hillsman and Bernard Levenson. 1975a. Job Opportunities of Black and White Working-Class Women. *Social Problems* 22:510-532.

———. 1975b. *Earnings Prospects of Black and White Working Class Women*. Unpublished Paper.

Barrera, Mario. 1979. *Race and Class in the Southwest*. Notre Dame, IN: University of Notre Dame Press.

Barrera, Mario, Carlos Muñoz and Charles Ornelas. 1972. "The Barrio as an Internal Colony." In *Urban Affairs Annual Review* 6, edited by Harlan Hahn.

Blassingame, John. 1972. *The Slave Community*. New York: Oxford University Press.

Blauner, Robert. 1972. *Racial Oppression in America*. New York: Harper & Row.

Braverman, Harry. 1974. *Labor and Monopoly Capital*. New York: Monthly Review Press.

Brown, Carol. 1981. "Mothers, Fathers and Children: From Private to Public Patriarchy." Pp. 239-269 in *Women and Revolution: A Discussion of the Unhappy Marriage of Marxism and Feminism*, edited by Lydia Sargent. Boston: South End.

Brown, Jean Collier. 1938. *The Negro Woman Worker*. Women's Bureau Bulletin 165. U.S. Department of Labor. Washington, DC: Government Printing Office.

Byington, Margaret. 1974. *Homestead: The Households of a Milltown*. Pittsburgh, PA: University of Pittsburgh Press.

Camarillo, Albert. 1979. *Chicanos in a Changing Society.* Cambridge, MA: Harvard University Press.

Carmichael, Stokely and Charles V. Hamilton. 1967. *Black Power: The Politics of Liberation in America.* New York: Vintage.

Cheng, Lucie and Edna Bonacich. 1984. *Labor Immigration Under Capitalism: Asian Immigrant Workers in the United States Before World War II.* Berkeley, CA: University of California Press.

Clark, Kenneth. 1965. *Dark Ghetto.* New York: Harper & Row.

Coolidge, Mary. 1909. *Chinese Immigration.* New York: Henry Holt.

Davis, Angela Y. 1971. "Reflections on the Black Woman's Place in the Community of Slaves." *The Black Scholar* 2:3-15.

———. 1981. *Women, Race and Class.* New York: Random House.

Dill, Bonnie Thornton. 1979. "The Dialectics of Black Womanhood." *Signs* 4:543-555.

Easton, Barbara. 1976. Industrialization and Femininity: A Case Study of Nineteenth-Century New England. *Social Problems* 23:389-401.

Elesser, Nan, Kyle MacKenzie, and Yvonne Tixier y Vigil. 1980. *Las Mujeres: Conversations from a Hispanic Community.* Old Westbury, NY: The Feminist Press.

Fisher, Lloyd. 1953. *The Harvest Labor Market in California.* Cambridge, MA: Harvard University Press.

Fogel, William and Stanley Engerman. 1974. *Time on the Cross.* Boston: Little, Brown.

Foner, Philip S. and Ronald L. Lewis. 1981. *The Black Worker: A Documentary History From Colonial Times to the Present,* Vol. VI, *The Era of Post-War Prosperity and the Great Depression, 1920-1936.* Philadelphia: Temple University Press.

Frazier, E. Franklin. 1939. *The Negro Family in the United States.* Chicago: University of Chicago Press.

Garcia, Mario T. 1980. "The Chicana in American History: The Mexican Women of El Paso, 1880-1920—A Case Study." *Pacific Historical Review* 49:315-337.

———. 1981. *Desert Immigrants: The Mexicans of El Paso, 1880-1920.* New Haven: Yale University Press.

Genovese, Eugene. 1974. *Roll, Jordan, Roll.* New York: Pantheon.

Gilkes, Cheryl. 1982. "Successful Rebellious Professionals: The Black Woman's Professional Identity and Community Commitment." *Psychology of Women Quarterly* 6:289-311.

Glenn, Evelyn Nakano. 1983. "Split Household, Small Producer and Dual Wage Earner: An Analysis of Chinese American Family Strategies." *Journal of Marriage and the Family* 45:35-46.

Glenn, Evelyn Nakano and Charles M. Tolbert II. 1985. "Technology and Emerging Patterns of Stratification for Women of Color: Race and Gender Segregation of Computer Occupations." Revised version of a paper presented at the Women, Work and Technology Conference, University of Connecticut.

Goldman, Marion. 1981. *Goldiggers and Silverminers.* Ann Arbor: University of Michigan Press.

Gutman, Herbert G. 1975. "Persistent Myths About the Afro-American Family." *Journal of Interdisciplinary History* 6:181-210.

———. 1976. *The Black Family in Slavery and Freedom.* New York: Pantheon.

Harevan, Tamara. 1977. "Family Time and Industrial Time: Family and Work in a Planned Corporation Town, 1900-1924." In *Family and Kin in Urban Communities: 1900-1930.* New York: New Viewpoints.

Hartmann, Heidi. 1976. "Capitalism, Patriarchy and Job Segregation by Sex." *Signs* 1:137-169.

————. 1981a. The Unhappy Marriage of Marxism and Feminism: Towards a More Progressive Union. Pp. 1-41 in *Women and Revolution: A Discussion of the Unhappy Marriage of Marxism and Feminism,* edited by Lydia Sargent. Boston: South End.

————. 1981b. "The Family as a Locus for Gender, Class and Political Struggle: The Example of Housework." *Signs* 6(5):366-394.

Hirata, Lucie Cheng. 1979. "Free, Indentured and Enslaved: Chinese Prostitutes in Nineteenth Century America." *Signs* 5:3-29.

Hooks, Bell. 1981. *Ain't I a Woman: Black Women and Feminism.* Boston: South End.

Humphries, Jane. 1977. "Class Struggle and the Persistence of the Working Class Family." *Cambridge Journal of Economics* 1:241-258.

Ikels, Charlotte and Julia Shang. 1979. The Chinese in Greater Boston. Interim Report to the National Institute of Aging.

Jensen, Joan M. 1980. "Cloth, Butter and Boarders: Women's Household Production for the Market." *Review of Radical Political Economics* 12(2):14-24.

————. 1981. *With These Hands: Women Working on the Land.* Old Westbury, NY: Feminist Press.

Jones, Jacqueline. 1984. *Labor of Love, Labor of Sorrow: Black Women, Work and the Family from Slavery to the Present.* New York: Basic Books.

Katzman, David. 1978. *Seven Days a Week: Women and Domestic Service in Industrializing America.* New York: Oxford University Press.

Kessler-Harris, Alice. 1982. *Out to Work.* New York: Oxford University Press.

Kim, Elaine. 1983. *With Silk Wings: Asian American Women at Work.* San Francisco: Asian Women United of California.

Kingston, Maxine Hong. 1977. *The Woman Warrior.* New York: Vintage.

Lee, L. P., A. Lim, and H. K. Wong. 1969. *Report of the San Francisco Chinese Community Citizens' Survey and Fact Finding Committee* (Abridged Edition). San Francisco: Chinese Community Citizens' Survey and Fact Finding Committee.

Lerner, Gerda. 1969. "The Lady and the Mill Girl: Changes in the Status of Women in the Age of Jackson." *American Studies* 10:5-14.

————. 1973. *Black Women in White America: A Documentary History.* New York: Vintage.

Li, Peter S. 1977. "Fictive Kinship, Conjugal Ties and Kinship Claim Among Chinese Immigrants in the United States." *Journal of Comparative Family Studies* 8(1):47-64.

Ling, Pyan. 1912. "The Causes of Chinese Immigration." *Annals of the American Academy of Political and Social Sciences* 39:74-82.

Lyman, Stanford. 1968. "Marriage and Family Among Chinese Immigrants to America, 1850-1960." *Phylon* 29(4):321-330.

————. 1974. *Chinese Americans.* New York: Random House.

————. 1977. "Strangers in the City: The Chinese in the Urban Frontier." In *The Asian in North America.* Santa Barbara, CA: ABC Clio.

Massey, Douglas S. 1982. *The Demographic and Economic Position of Hispanics in the United States: 1980.* Report to the National Commission for Employment Policy. Philadelphia: Population Studies Center, University of Pennsylvania.

McLemore, Dale. 1973. "The Origins of Mexican American Subordination in Texas." *Social Science Quarterly* 53:656-670.

————. 1980. *Racial and Ethnic Relations in America.* Boston: Allyn & Bacon.

McWilliams, Carey. 1971. *Factories in the Field.* Santa Barbara, CA: Peregrine.

Melville, Margarita B. ed. 1980. *Twice a Minority: Mexican American Women.* St. Louis: C. V. Mosby.

Mirande, Alfredo and Evangelina Enriquez. 1979. *La Chicana: The Mexican American Woman.* Chicago: University of Chicago Press.

Mora, Magdelina and Adelaida R. Del Castillo. eds. 1980. *Mexican Women in the United States: Struggles Past and Present.* Los Angeles: Chicano Studies Publications.

Moore, Joan W. 1970. "Colonialism: The Case of Mexican Americans." *Social Problems* 17:463-472.

Moynihan, Daniel Patrick. 1965. "The Negro Family: The Case for National Action." Washington, DC: Government Printing Office. Prepared for the Office of Policy Planning and Research.

Nee, Victor and Brett deBary Nee. 1972. *Long Time Californ'.* New York: Pantheon Books.

Pachon, Harry P. and Joan W. Moore. 1981. "Mexican Americans." *Annals of the American Academy of Political and Social Science* 454:111-124.

Painter, Nell Irvin. 1976. *Exodusters: Black Migration to Kansas After the Reconstruction.* New York: W. W. Norton.

Palmer, Phyllis Marynick. 1983. "White Women/Black Women: The Dualism of Female Identity and Experience in the United States." *Feminist Studies* 9:151-170.

Pleck, Elizabeth H. 1979. "A Mother's Wages: Income Earning Among Married Italian and Black Women, 1896-1911." Pp. 367-392 in *A Heritage of Her Own,* edited by Nancy F. Cott and Elizabeth H. Pleck. New York: Touchstone Books.

Rodgers-Rose, La Frances. ed. 1980. *The Black Woman.* Beverly Hills, CA: Sage.

Saxton, Alexander. 1971. *The Indispensable Enemy: Labor and the Anti-Chinese Movement in California.* Berkeley: University of California Press.

Sokoloff, Natalie. 1980. *Between Money and Love.* New York: Praeger.

Sterling, Dorothy. 1979. *Black Foremothers: Three Lives.* Old Westbury, NY: The Feminist Press.

Taylor, Paul S. 1929. "Mexican Labor in the United States: Valley of the South Platte." *University of California Publications in Economics* 6(2):95-235.

———. 1937. "Migratory Farm Labor in the United States." *Monthly Labor Review* (March):537-549.

Taylor, Ronald. 1976. *Sweatshops in the Sun.* Boston: Beacon.

Thorne, Barrie. 1982. "Feminist Rethinking of the Family: An Overview." Pp. 1-24 in *Rethinking the Family: Some Feminist Questions,"* edited by Barrie Thorne and Marilyn Yalom. New York: Longman.

Tsuchida, Nobuya (ed.). 1982. *Asian and Pacific American Experiences: Women's Perspectives.* Minneapolis: Asian/Pacific American Learning Resource Center.

U.S. Bureau of the Census. 1933. *Fifteenth Census of the United States: 1930, Population, Volume V: General Report on Occupations* (Chapter 3, Color and Nativity of Gainful Workers). Washington, DC: Government Printing Office.

———. 1933. *Fifteenth Census of the United States: 1980. Population, Volume II: General Report, Statistics by Subject.* Washington, DC: Government Printing Office.

———. 1973. *Census of the Population: 1970.* Subject Reports, Final Report PC(2)1G. *Japanese, Chinese, and Filipinos in the United States.* Washington, DC: Government Printing Office.

U.S. Department of Justice. 1977. *Immigration and Naturalization Service Annual Report.* Washington, DC: U.S. Department of Justice.

U.S. Department of Labor. 1977. *U.S. Working Women: A Databook.* Bureau of Labor Statistics, Bulletin 1977. Washington, DC: Government Printing Office.

Weinbaum, Batya and Amy Bridges. 1979. "The Other Side of the Paycheck: Monopoly Capital and the Structure of Consumption." In *Capitalist Patriarchy and the Case for Socialist Feminism,* edited by Zillah R. Eisenstein. New York: Monthly Review Press.

Welter, Barbara. 1966. "The Cult of True Womanhood: 1820-1860." *American Quarterly* (Summer):151-174.

Westcott, Diane Nilsen. 1982. "Blacks in the 1970's: Did They Scale the Job Ladder?" *Monthly Labor Review* (June):29-32.

Willie, Charles. 1981. *A New Look at Black Families.* Bayview, NY: General Hall.

Wu, C. 1972. *"Chink" : A Documentary History of Anti-Chinese Prejudice in America.* New York: Meridian.

Yap, Stacey G. Y. 1983. *Gather Your Strength Sisters: The Careers of Chinese American Women Community Workers.* Unpublished doctoral dissertation, Boston University.

Afterword
Racial Ethnic Women's Labor: Factoring in Gender Stratification

RAE LESSER BLUMBERG

As a supplement to Evelyn Nakano Glenn's heuristic article, "Racial Ethnic Women's Labor: The Intersection of Race, Gender, and Class Oppression," I would like to factor in one additional dimension: gender *stratification.* Specifically, I would like to look at the gender division of labor and resources within the family/household for (a) Chinese-Americans, (b) Mexican-Americans, and (c) U.S. blacks, the three racial ethnic groups she analyzes. I will discuss them in that order, which, I suggest, also represents descending degrees of gender stratification for the racial ethnic groups in question.

In each case, I will first present the traditional division of labor and resources for the group and then present an overview of the group's structural history in the United States, and how this affected gender stratification, especially within the household. The central hypothesis of my gender stratification theory (Blumberg, 1984) is that women's control of economic resources relative to counterpart men is the single most important (though not the only) variable affecting women's relative equality. Therefore, for each racial ethnic group I will be looking at the extent to which women autonomously controlled income/economic resources, as well as at their labor. For the Chinese case, I also incorporate Glenn's article (1983), "Split Household, Small Producer and Dual Wage Earner: An Analysis of Chinese-American Family Strategies," where she does touch briefly on female autonomy.

Gender Division of Labor and Resources Among Chinese-Americans

The Chinese-Americans are the racial ethnic group with the highest traditional level of gender stratification. Glenn (1983) notes that most Chinese-Americans came from Guangdong Province in southern China, an irrigated rice growing area. It should be noted that irrigated rice is the most labor intensive farming system in the world. Except among the richer peasants, *everybody* works, from dawn to dusk. Therefore, in contrast to the millet-growing areas of the north where peasant women rarely worked in the fields and often had bound feet, these women were viewed as too necessary and valuable a source of labor to be thus crippled in the interests of patriarchy.

But hardworking as they were, the work of these women brought them little in the way of enhanced status. This was because they worked as *unpaid family labor;* they did *not* usually generate an income of their own. Another of my propositions—and supporting data—indicate that unless it generates independently-controlled resources, mere work is not enough to enhance one's stratification position. (For example, in the Acharya and Bennett studies of Nepal (1981, 1982, 1983) discussed in my "Income" article in this volume, women's unpaid work in family subsistence farming had no positive effect whatsoever on their input into household decision-making—and the amount of housework women did actually had a *negative* effect on their say in decision-making.) In addition, these hardworking women of the south still lived in one of the world's most patriarchal systems: a patrilineal, patrilocal society upholding a Confucian ideology emphasizing female subordination.

In sum, the traditional gender stratification position of Guangdong women was very low. Glenn describes three phases of the Chinese-American family. How did women's relative position within the family change in each phase?

Glenn calls the first phase of Chinese presence in the United States, from 1850-1920, the "split household family." During the years of open immigration, 1850-1882, half of the more than 300,000 Guangdong young men who came left wives behind. But the Chinese Exclusion

Act of 1882 precluded these women's migration. Instead, the husband would send remittances home to his patrilineal extended family, where his wife would initially have been a highly subordinate junior female. Although Glenn notes that the remittances were sent to the husband's male kin and the wife lacked formal authority, she argues that "most wives had informal influence and were consulted on major decisions" (1983, p. 39). I would speculate that the woman's influence was as an *agent* of her husband—on whom he might count to defend his interests against those of the patrilineal males receiving the money. (See Pahl, 1989 on the lower power of a woman exercising delegated managerial functions over household monies versus one who *controls* income.) Such a wife/agent, who did not have to subordinate herself to her husband in daily interaction, should have had more leverage than in the traditional Guangdong family, even though she lived under the immediate control of her husband's extended family.

Glenn terms the second phase, from the 1920s to the mid-1960s, "the small producer family." The Immigration Act of 1924 ended all Asian immigration, but by then a number of former laborers had accumulated enough capital to become merchants (mainly in small laundries, restaurants, and groceries). As merchants they legally could bring over wives and children from China—as free labor for the business. From the 1920s on, the number of families grew, especially after special acts in 1946 and 1953 facilitated entry of women and children. Husband, wife, and children worked long hours, often living above or behind the shop. The family pooled income via the "common pot." But unlike its counterpart in China, it was nuclear since, initially, there were no grandparents. Thus, according to Glenn, the wife had more autonomy than in Guangdong: not only was she an equal producer in the family economy (and in terms of Blumberg and Coleman's "micro-level discount factors" (1989), her husband really *needed* her contributions), she did not have to subordinate herself to in-laws.

The third phase, which Glenn terms "the dual wage earner family," began when the 1965 immigration law permitted the entry of over 20,000 Chinese per year. Most have been people of Guangdong background with some kin ties in the United States. They tend to arrive in nuclear families, with both husband and wife taking working-class, "secondary labor market" jobs in Chinatowns (e.g., he works as a waiter and she in a small garment shop). Glenn notes that the couple must pool their two low incomes to survive but that the wife's earnings comprise a greater share of family income—about half—in the United States than in Hong Kong, their port of departure. This should enhance her household power, according to my propositions in the Introduction to this volume. But her relative power might not be enhanced by much, because it is not clear just how much of her own or pooled income she actually controls/allocates—and, furthermore, one gets more power from allocating surplus income than mere poverty-level subsistence.

Interestingly, this most recent type of Chinese-American family is moving away from pooling all income into a "common pot"—Glenn writes that teens often gain financial independence from the family via part-time work. All in all, it also seems to be the least gender-stratified of the Chinese/Chinese-American families.

Division of Labor and Resources Among Mexican-Americans

Of the three racial ethnic groups Glenn analyzes, Mexican-American women historically have registered the lowest formal labor force participation. She cites Barrera (1979) who indicates that prior to the 1870s, Chicano families followed the "traditional division of labor," but notes that in rural areas, women's "housework" would have included tending gardens and caring for domestic animals. In terms of antecedents, it appears that an earlier, more sexually egalitarian tradition among the Indians began to be submerged by the Aztec conquest and then was inundated by the gender ideology of the conquering Spaniards (Silverblatt, 1980). The emergent *mestizo* population tended to follow the more patriarchal Spanish notion that "the woman is for the house." But although women were less likely to work in the fields than in Guangdong Province, the level of structural patriarchy otherwise seems much lower. Even in Mexico, women had property and inheritance rights and in many parts of the country, traded in the market at least partly on their own account. There was neither Confucianism nor patrilineage ancestor gods to further underline women's ideological subordination.

In the United States, from 1880-1930, economically active Chicanas often worked as part of a migrant family that followed the crops. Pay was by piece work but, according to anecdotal evidence (Covarrubias, 1978), was often paid to the male head. Under those circumstances, women may not have had as much leverage out of their earnings than if they received them directly. As Glenn notes, other Chicanas worked for the lowest wages in traditionally "female" jobs but the great majority were not part of the measured labor force.

Accordingly, despite the lower level of patriarchal traditions/ideology among the Chicanos, it is an open empirical question if the Chinese-American women of the "small producer" and "dual wage earner" phases actually exercised more household power than their nonearning or lower earning Chicana counterparts. To this day, Chicana women have the lowest labor force participation rates of the three groups, Glenn notes, adding that they have the fewest years of education and the most children—two factors which depress labor force activity. So, to the extent that Chicana women continue to be less likely to work and less likely to earn wages comparable to their menfolk (versus the Chinese-American and U.S. black cases), their gender stratification position must be considered lower than that of blacks and not necessarily above that of Chinese-Americans. To test this, one would compare Chinese-American and Mexican-American couples' patterns of household power, looking at both the degree of patriarchy in their racial ethnic group's ideology and the wage gap between spouses.

Gender Division of Labor and Resources Among Blacks

Most of the blacks who were brought to the New World in chains came from West African horticultural societies. As we know from the data on 376 horticultural societies in Murdock's *Ethnographic Atlas* (1967), in only about one fifth are men the primary labor force (see also Bryson, 1981). Other features which to this day remain quite prevalent in West African horticultural societies include general polygyny and unilineal kin groups, most frequently patrilineal-patrilocal ones. In addition, there is a common, long-standing tradition of a wife maintaining a completely separate purse vis-à-vis co-wives and a largely separate purse vis-à-vis her husband (e.g., Guyer 1988).

Furthermore, quantitative ethnographic data show that in those African horticultural societies where (a) women are important in farming, (b) polygyny is prevalent, and (c) the young couple resides with the groom's male kin, it is also highly likely that co-wives are housed separately (Blumberg with Garcia, 1977). Thus, traditionally, within a larger household compound, each woman and her children formed a subunit, with a separate dwelling and, often, some independent resources.

One controversial theory, most prominently set forth by Herskovitz (1937, 1941, 1943, 1958; Herskovitz and Francis, 1947; see also Bascom, 1941; Murdock and Wilson, 1972; Matthews and Lee, 1975) maintains that the high rates of economic activity and autonomy, as well as mother-child family forms, among contemporary U.S. black women represent "West African survivals." I suggest that it is useful to go back to earlier periods of black history for clues to the present "triple overlap" among gender stratification, family, and economy—but that one *also* must look to the extent that a previous structural/ideological pattern continues to "fit" with changed structural circumstances for the group in question. My argument is that "survivals" don't last long when structural conditions have shifted (Blumberg, 1978).

In contrast, I propose that the pattern of black women's high economic activity and autonomy persisted in the United States because it fit so well with the structural conditions in which blacks found themselves. First, slaveowners were quick to exploit black African women as *farmers,* which is hardly surprising considering their predominance in horticulture in most of their areas of origin.[1] Second, African women slaves' economic activities, whether as field hands (the lot of the great majority), house servants, laundresses, and/or breeders, were seen as their *own,* not part of family labor. These women might have lived with a mate but there was nothing to prevent the members of their household from being sold off separately. In fact, it appears that the only period when blacks frequently had a "common pot" family (Treas, this volume) was that of post-Civil War debt bondage sharecropping. Glenn (1985, p. 96) notes that sharecropper women were observed "to do double duty, a *man's share* in the field [even ploughing], and a woman's part at home." She also cites Hooks's (1981) argument:

> that landowners preferred sharecropping to hiring labor because black women were unwilling to be employed in the fields once slavery was abolished. With sharecropping women's labor could be exploited intensively, since women had to work hard alongside the men in order to pay off the ever-mounting debt. (p. 96)

In general, from 1870 on, Glenn documents that Afro-American women: (a) had higher rates of labor force participation than white women; and (b), due to the marginal and low wage employment of black men, brought in a larger share of household income even though they earned less than white women. In short, for most of their history in the United States, black women have earned and contributed a significant and *autonomous* income to their family/household coffers.

The propositions from my gender stratification theory suggest that black women's deep-rooted relative control of resources should translate to a fairly strong position of household power, even under poverty conditions. The relative weakness of patriarchal ideology among blacks should further insure that little of a black woman's economic leverage would be nibbled away by a negative "ideological discount rate." Little wonder, then, that Treas (see Table 8.1, this volume) found that black women and men were much more likely than their white counterparts to maintain separate bank accounts.

In sum, although I agree with Glenn that all three racial ethnic groups focused much energy on building the family as a bulwark against discrimination, I suggest that this did not preclude an "internal economy of the household" that has affected each group's level and configuration of gender stratification. Furthermore, I propose that their level of gender stratification is a dynamic, not static, force. As this Afterword suggests, it seems to vary in accordance with (a) the historical and structural shifts in the group's gender division of labor and resources, as well as (b) its traditional gender roles/ideology. Finally, as Glenn hints, these racial ethnic groups are differentiating internally by *class,* based on education, recency of immigration, and "economic niche." To the extent that these changing structural/class factors affect the gender division of labor and resources, we also can expect within-group variation in gender stratification.

Note

1. Glenn cites Hooks (1981) for the claim that "plantation owners often preferred women for the hardest field work because they were the more reliable workers" (Glenn, 1985, p. 95).

References

Acharya, Meena, and Lynn Bennett. 1981. *The Rural Women of Nepal: An Aggregate Analysis and Summary of Eight Village Studies,* Vol. 2. Part 9. Kathmandu, Nepal: Centre for Economic Development and Administration, Tribhuvan University.
———. 1982. "Women's Status in Nepal: A Summary of Findings and Implications." Washington, DC: Agency for International Development, Office of Women in Development. Mimeograph.
———. 1983. *Women and the Subsistence Sector: Economic Participation in Household Decision-Making in Nepal.* Working Paper Number 526 Washington, DC: World Bank.
Barrera, Mario. 1979. *Race and Class in the Southwest.* Notre Dame, IN: University of Notre Dame Press.
Bascom, W. R. 1941. "Acculturation Among the Bullah Negroes." *American Anthropologist* 43:43-50.
Blumberg, Rae Lesser. 1978. "The Political Economy of the Mother-Child Family Revisited." Pp. 526-575 in *Family and Kinship in Middle America and the Caribbean,* edited by Arnaud F. Marks and Rene A. Romer. Co-publication of the Institute of

Higher Studies in Curacao, Netherlands Antilles, and the Department of Caribbean Studies of the Royal Institute of Linguistics and Anthropology at Leiden, the Netherlands.

Blumberg, Rae Lesser. 1984. "A General Theory of Gender Stratification." Pp. 23-101 in *Sociological Theory 1984,* edited by Randall Collins. San Francisco: Jossey-Bass.

Blumberg, Rae Lesser, with Maria-Pilar Garcia. 1977. "The Political Economy of the Mother-Child Family: A Cross-Societal View." In *Beyond the Nuclear Family Model,* edited by Luis Lenero-Otero. London: Sage.

Blumberg, Rae Lesser, and Marion Tolbert Coleman. 1989. "A Theory-Guided Look at the Gender Balance of Power in the American Couple." *Journal of Family Issues* 10(2):225-250.

Bryson, Judith C. 1981. "Women and Agriculture in sub-Saharan Africa: Implications for Development (An Exploratory Study)." *The Journal of Development Studies,* 17(3):29-46.

Covarrubias, Juanita. 1978. Personal Communication.

Glenn, Evelyn Nakano. 1983. "Split Household, Small Producer and Dual Wage Earner: An Analysis of Chinese-American Family Strategies." *Journal of Marriage and the Family* (February):35-46.

———. 1985. "Racial Ethnic Women's Labor: The Intersection of Race, Gender, and Class Oppression." *Review of Radical Political Economics* 17(3):86-108.

Guyer, Jane. 1988. "Dynamic Approaches to Domestic Budgeting. Cases and Methods from Africa." In *A Home Divided: Women and Income in the Third World,* edited by Daisy Dwyer and Judith Bruce. Palo Alto, CA: Stanford University Press.

Herskovitz, Melville J. 1937. *Life in a Haitian Valley.* New York: A. A. Knopf.

———. 1941. *The Myth of the Negro Past.* New York: Harper.

———. 1943. "The Negro in Bahia, Brazil: A Problem in Method." *American Sociological Review* 8:394-404.

———. 1958. *The Myth of the Negro Past.* Boston: Beacon.

Herskovitz, Melville J. and F. Francis. 1947. *Trinidad Village.* New York: A. A. Knopf.

Hooks, Bell. 1981. *Ain't I a Woman: Black Women and Feminism.* Boston: South End.

Matthews, Lear and S. C. Lee. 1975. "Matrifocality Reconsidered: The Case of the Rural Afro-Guyanese Family." Pp. 513-525 in *Family and Kinship in Middle America and the Caribbean,* edited by Arnaud F. Marks and Rene A. Romer. Co-publication of the Institute of Higher Studies in Curacao, Netherlands Antilles, and the Department of Caribbean Studies of the Royal Institute of Linguistics and Anthropology at Leiden, the Netherlands.

Murdock, George P. 1967. "Ethnographic Atlas: A Summary." *Ethnology* 6:109-236.

Murdock, George P., and Suzanne F. Wilson. 1972. "Settlement Patterns and Community Organization: Cross-Cultural Codes 3." *Ethnology* 11:254-295.

Pahl, Jan. 1989. *Money and Marriage.* London: Macmillan.

Silverblatt, Irene. 1980. "Andean Women Under Spanish Rule." In *Women and Colonization: Anthropological Perspectives,* edited by Eleanor Leacock and Mona Etienne. New York: Praeger.

Part III

Contrasting Conceptualizations of the Household

8

The Common Pot or Separate Purses?
A Transaction Cost Interpretation

JUDITH TREAS

In some families, economic arrangements are characterized by the common pot. Members pool their resources into a joint fund that is then allocated to the consumption of various parties. In other families, financial management is characterized by separate purses. Individual family members hold at least some money and/or economic resources back. At the extreme, husbands, wives, and perhaps grown children share nothing, retaining complete ownership and control over their own income and assets.

One system recognizes individual property rights. The other merges individual economic interests into those of the collectivity. Separate purses assume that family members can disentangle their economic fates and fortunes. The common pot assumes that there is a single economic entity. Privatized or collectivized resources go to the basic identity of the family—as a corporate unit or as a collection of individuals. In economic formulations, this question is phrased in terms of whose preferences and utility function get maximized within the household (Folbre, 1986).

The choice between the common pot and separate purses—between collectivized and privatized accounting systems—obviously depends on many considerations, including the power relations between the generations (Thornton and Fricke, 1987) and the genders (Blumberg, 1988) as well as prevailing cultural ideologies (Zeliser, 1989). There is, however, a neglected dimension of institutional rationality to the organization of families and their finances. Whether families are collectivized or privatized is determined, in part, by transaction cost considerations.

In giving free reign to individual interests or subordinating them to the group, family members opt for alternative modes of organizing family exchanges. Individualistic, privatized family forms permit a market organization of family exchange, complete with bargaining according to economic principles of self-interest. Collectivized finances require that exchanges within the family be governed by social mechanisms—by norms (e.g., reciprocity, primogeniture), by values (e.g., altruism, filial piety), and by an authority structure (e.g., patriarchy). Families will tend to favor the organizational arrangement that governs exchanges most efficiently and expeditiously. That is, the common pot will have the edge over the separate purse when income pooling entails less coordination, fewer disputes, and easier monitoring of the myriad exchanges which make up family life.

Sometimes actors are very conscious of their choice to organize family life along privatized or collectivized lines. In the United States, where married couples practice everything from complete pooling to total separation of their money (Treas, forthcoming), some couples can clearly articulate how their financial practices minimize hassles and mesh with personal beliefs about individualism and commitment (Blumstein and Schwartz, 1983; Hertz, 1986; Smith and Reid, 1986). Their choice of common pot or separate purses may be a matter of trial and error, and arrangements that meet their needs at one point may be abandoned as the couple's circumstances change.

In other cultures, family members may not be called upon to choose explicitly between alternative ways of handling money and holding property. Rather the common pot (or the separate purse) is apt to be a normatively sanctioned family strategy. Given the circumstances in which most of the families find themselves, this particular arrangement works reasonably well to organize exchanges and to organize them without excessive transaction costs. Thus there is an element of rationality and efficiency in the economic organization of families; this is true both in societies where people make choices and in those in which there are no choices to make.

Common pot or separate purses, collectivized or privatized family forms, represent an important context in which the relative positions of men and women are worked out. By themselves, however, they do not determine whether gender relations will be egalitarian or not. In the early decades of this century, advice writers could vigorously debate whether the middle-class American housewife was more emancipated when she received an independent allowance from her husband or when she was granted free access to joint marital funds (Zeliser, 1989). To the extent that patriarchal authority systems dominate collectivized families with their common pots, they may disadvantage women in access to and control over resources. Of course, control is an elusive concept, because handling money is not necessarily the same as controlling it. When working-class British husbands turn over the management of household monies to wives, they demonstrate their ability to delegate the burdensome responsibility for making ends meet (Pahl, 1980). Although privatized families hold out the prospect of women controlling at least some resources, separate purses for men and women entail their own problems. A case in point is when Third-World women are expected to provide for the nutritional needs of children out of their own meager earnings (Blumberg, 1988).

This chapter elaborates on how transaction cost economies might be expected to influence the organization of family life and household finances. Drawing on insights from families and firms, we outline conditions that favor the common pot and those that encourage separate purses. This transaction cost approach has proven useful in understanding the financial practices of American couples today. To evaluate the generalizability of transaction cost logic, we consider Macfarlane's (1978, 1986) work which suggests that the individualistic relations within an earlier English society may be viewed as consistent with transaction cost expectations.

Conditions Affecting Family Organizational Economies

Family life may be thought of as an extraordinary complex of exchanges carried on between family members. Exchanges involve the give and take of goods and services under assumptions of reciprocity. Exchanges are not effected in a frictionless manner. They entail some transaction costs. The parties must come to agree on what is to be exchanged, how, and when. Under the rules of social exchange (Blau, 1964), payback terms may be left vague and open-ended, but this does not eliminate the need for some degree of negotiation and coordination. Arrangements must be made. Performance must be monitored. Obligations must be enforced. This regulation of exchanges involves costs in time, money, and energy. Transaction costs of family life are manifest in messages, negotiations, instructions, reminders, disputes, recriminations, and thanks.

Organizational arrangements that can minimize transaction costs are apt to be favored, as the "new institutional economics" (Williamson, 1975) has indicated with respect to commercial enterprises. Rather than resort to self-interested market principles of exchange, the collectivized family governs transactions through social mechanisms, including cultural norms, internalized values, and an authority structure. Under certain conditions, this highly personalized, social regulation of exchange is thought to deliver real transaction cost economies. These conditions include: (a) threatening environments (Pollack, 1985); (b) ambiguities in monitoring the performance of exchanges (Williamson, 1975; Ouchi, 1980); (c) continuity in social relationships (Williamson, 1975); and (d) fixed investments in specific individuals (Ben-Porath, 1980; Williamson, 1981). When these conditions are not present, market mechanisms are apt to organize exchanges more efficiently and expeditiously. In terms of family financial arrangements, the choice of common pot or the separate purses depends, in some measure, on factors influencing their relative transaction costs.

1. Threatening environments are generated by political instability, institutionalized expropriation, risky enterprises, and natural disasters. In a menacing world where the stakes are high, the trustworthiness of strangers is hard to ascertain. Family members, on the other hand, have undergone a long period of socialization and testing to ensure that they are reliable trading partners. They have imbibed an ethos of family loyalty. Being dependent on family approval, they are susceptible to its social controls. When the environment is, indeed, unpredictable, a commitment to a unified family viewpoint or "tradition" facilitates appropriate decision making in circumstances unanticipated by market contracts or bureaucratic rules (Ouchi, 1980, p. 139). Thus, in the face of threat, the social control of exchange within the collectivized family reduces transaction costs. First, social control discourages self-serving behavior with serious consequences for other family members. Second, it reduces the costs associated with assuring adequate performance. In contrast, individualistic, privatized organization allows for the distressing possibility of family defections in pursuit of individual gain; it also encourages the exploitation of external threats to exploit an advantage in bargaining with kin. Under threatening conditions, the privatized family demands more policing of kin and, therefore, is apt to be rejected, because it engenders higher transaction costs in regulating family exchange.

2. When the quality and quantity of what is exchanged is difficult to gauge, the collectivized family enjoys a transaction cost advantage. In the family, many exchanges involve this ambiguity. The fruits of joint production (e.g., parenting, play) are difficult to allocate to individuals. Love cannot be gauged directly, but only inferred indirectly from words and actions. Other instances of household production may

be regarded as either priceless (e.g., a mother's love) or impossible to commodify in dollars and cents (e.g., housework). When family members move beyond the household into school, workplace, and community, their performance becomes even harder to monitor. The more difficult it is to tell what one is getting in an exchange, the more important it is to be able to trust the intentions of one's trading partner. By emphasizing an internalized commitment to the interests of the corporate group, the collectivized family minimizes the need to monitor behavior, thus reducing transaction costs associated with family exchanges.

3. When relationships can be expected to be reasonably frequent and enduring, the social exchange mechanisms characteristic of the collectivized family can govern the dealings of its members very efficiently. There is ample opportunity to inculcate family values, cultivate dependence on kin, and demonstrate the effectiveness of family surveillance and controls. The continuous nature of exchanges offers an extended period of time over which to enjoy a return on start-up costs (e.g., negotiating agreements, training). Continuity also discourages sharp dealing, which can only lead to a tit-for-tat retribution in the long run. The uncertainty embodied in an extended time horizon is incompatible with the self-interested bargaining which the privatized family permits. Exchange relationships founded on trust are less vulnerable than contractual ones, because contracts can fail to anticipate contingencies and can permit the exploitation of short-term advantages at contract renewal. Thus continuity in relationships gives an edge to collectivized organization of families.

4. Investments in specific people lock individuals into exchange relationships. Because these investments can neither be readily liquidated nor transferred to other people, one's only prospect to recoup on the investment is within the context of the particular relationship. Indeed, the value of what is exchanged may depend on the identities of the transactors—as is amply illustrated in love relationships where shared histories deepen the emotional bonds. In other instances, the person-specific relationship may derive from the fact that practice makes perfect in satisfying one another's preferences and desires (Williamson, 1981). Sometimes cultural norms place special importance on particular persons (e.g., sons to perform certain religious ceremonies) so that individuals are not interchangeable. Where there are fixed, person-specific investments in family relationships, we would expect to find the collectivized family. Self-interested, hard bargaining with a family member is impossible when nobody else can supply the desired goods and services.

A Contemporary Example

As argued, many features of family life—common pot or separate purses, collectivized or individualized identities, social or market-like regulation of exchange—are determined by conditions affecting the relative transaction costs associated with each alternative. One arena in contemporary family life that mirrors the common pot/separate purse dilemma is the banking practices of American couples (Treas, forthcoming). Data on banking practices of approximately 14,000 married couples are available in the first wave of the 1984 panel of the nationally representative Survey of Income and Program Participation (SIPP) from the U.S. Bureau of the Census. For each bank account reported, respondents were asked whether the account was held jointly with a spouse. Although individual IRA and Keogh accounts were not included in the reporting, a wide variety of interest-bearing financial instruments were counted: passbook savings accounts in banks, savings and loans, and credit unions as well as money market accounts, savings certificates (e.g., CDs), and interest-earning checking accounts.

Nearly one quarter of couples said they had no interest-earning bank accounts. Among married couples reporting one or more accounts, two thirds said they kept all their funds in joint accounts. For the remaining one third, however, at least some money was said to be held back in a separate account. In fact, 17% of banking couples reported that all their accounts were separate accounts. Husbands were about as likely as wives to bank apart although wives were more likely to combine joint with separate accounts.

How a couple configures its bank accounts surely reflects many motivations. If an account is not in both partners' names, it may be because it is the household account of the family "bill-payer," because it is money parents have set aside on behalf of a child, or because it is an arrangement prompted by tax or legal considerations. Given the many likely influences on banking decisions, it is compelling to learn that the choice of joint or separate accounts adheres to a transaction cost logic. As we would hypothesize, the probability of having a separate account is greater when (a) the partners have low expectations for the continuity of the marriage, (b) their contributions to the union are easily measured, and (c) the spouses have no big, fixed investments in their marriage.

The determinants of banking practices are analyzed elsewhere within a multivariate framework (Treas, forthcoming). Table 8.1 presents simple odds ratios for several indicators tapping the conditions that imply a transaction cost advantage for separate purses. The figures

Table 8.1 Odds Ratios of Separate Bank Account(s) by Race: American Husbands and Wives in Couples with Bank Accounts, 1984

	Wives		Husbands	
	Nonblack	*Black*	*Nonblack*	*Black*
Previously divorced?				
yes	0.38	0.80	0.35	0.73
no	0.30	0.67	0.22	0.46
Previously widowed?				
yes	0.76	0.83	0.50	0.40
no	0.30	0.63	0.24	0.50
Wife works full time?				
yes	0.42	1.10	0.26	0.54
no	0.26	0.44	0.23	0.47
Husband employed?				
yes	0.31	0.72	0.25	0.53
no	0.29	0.51	0.20	0.36

represent the odds of having (as opposed to not having) a bank account in one's own name. The larger the odds ratio, the more likely one is to bank separately. Results are presented for black and nonblack husbands and wives in couples that report having one or more accounts.

Presumably, a personal experience with marital dissolution undermines confidence in the continuity of the current marriage and, hence, reduces the transaction cost advantages of a common pot and a joint bank account. The odds ratios clearly demonstrate this generalization holds for all groups except black husbands whose propensity to keep a separate account is not increased by widowhood.

When the spouses work outside the home, a paycheck offers an unambiguous lower boundary on each spouses' contributions to the marriage. The ease of metering marital contributions reduces the advantages of the common pot. Following Becker, Landes, and Michael (1977), the wife's full-time employment can also be interpreted as indicating lesser investment in the marriage itself. As seen in Table 8.1, when the wife works full time and the husband holds down a job, the spouses are more likely to maintain separate accounts. Black women with full-time jobs have a better than even chance of banking separately, as seen in an odds ratio exceeding 1. Both black husbands and black wives are strongly influenced to maintain separate accounts when the husband is employed.

As these data demonstrate, the banking practices of American couples are consistent with expectations derived from a transaction cost approach to the organization of family life. Another assessment of the usefulness of the transaction cost approach may be obtained by examining the fit between historical family patterns and social conditions.

English Individualism

Demonstrating that efficiency concerns transcend contemporary society, Macfarlane's (1978) provocative account of the origins of English individualism underscores many of the themes sounded by a transaction cost approach. The historical anthropologist challenges the conventional wisdom that England was transformed sometime after the fifteenth century from a collectivistic, peasant society to a society whose hallmark was individualism. Drawing on records dating as far back as the thirteenth century, he argues that England has all along been unique in its emphasis on private property and individualistic values.

Macfarlane's characterization of peasant society is central to his argument. In the rural societies which peasants inhabit, the self-sufficient farming family relies on its members to produce all the necessities of daily life. Most people live their entire lives in the same village with their interests subordinated to the needs of their family unit. They contribute their labor to the household, look to it for their livelihood, and accept its authority (e.g., as to whom to marry). Family members have inalienable claims to support, but land and other productive resources belong to the family, not the individual. Although men and women, parents and offspring, differ markedly in power, the patriarchal household head is largely a farm manager who has the fiduciary responsibility to secure the well-being of the corporate unit. While one can find fault with these generalities about peasant society (Homans, 1980), Macfarlane calls attention to a particular family form—one founded on the family's corporate ownership of property, the identification of individual interests with collective interests, the social regulation of exchange via norms, shared values, and an authority structure.

As described by Macfarlane (1978, 1986), England, during the period of 1250-1860, stands in sharp contrast to the collectivistic peasant tradition. Land belongs to individuals, not families. Landowners can (and often do) choose to sell it. They disinherit heirs. They also opt for nuclear families. Instead of marriages arranged by kin, they choose their own spouses on the basis of romantic attachment and rational calculation. They send youngsters forth to make their ways in the world as servants and apprentices. Children are not expected to send money home to a common pot tended by parents. Neither do parents routinely call on children for support in old age. If there is a collective "we" in individualistic English families, it is seen in the companionate husband-wife bond. Even here, however, wives maintain considerable independence—if not in comparison to contemporary Western societies, then at least in contrast to their historical counterparts and many traditional, non-Western examples. According to Macfarlane, women can own land, sue in court, support themselves, and spurn suitors their parents favor. In short, Macfarlane's England is a society founded on individuals and private property, not families and collective ownership. Indeed, pre-industrial English society already embodied the conditions that are thought to favor individualized, as opposed to collectivized, organization of family life.

First, England was an orderly society of established political and legal institutions. Since the state was strong enough to protect the rights of the people and discourage pillaging armies (Macfarlane, 1986, p. 104), there was less need for marital alliances to secure political influence and for broad kin networks to mount a call to arms. With its government and courts, England was hardly a threatening environment "where close kin are the only ones you can trust to guard the family land and the family honor against rapacious landlords and fellow villagers" (Macfarlane, 1986, p. 59). Given a lightly taxed and relatively affluent population (Macfarlane, 1986), neither bad harvest nor personal misfortune necessarily spelled catastrophe. In fact, a highly developed system of relief administered by the manor, the guild, the church, and later the state insured against risk—making life more secure and family less essential (Macfarlane, 1986, pp. 105-107). The stability and security afforded by English institutions reduced the threat posed by the environment.

Second, the money economy had thoroughly penetrated the countryside—as evidenced by the brisk market in land, the importance of wage labor, the money-lending and cash-cropping, and the specialized artisans and tradesmen who served the villages (Macfarlane, 1978, p. 68). Rather than produce exclusively for their own consumption, farmers sold crops and turned to the market to buy household goods, luxury items, and services (e.g., tailoring, butchering). A barter economy might have demanded a complicated series of swaps to dispose of, say, wheat and wind up with a fine linen garment. Widespread use of money, however, must have greatly reduced the transaction costs associated with market exchange. Indeed, the general affluence (which so impressed visitors from the Continent) and the cash economy no doubt encouraged the development of markets for what was once to be had only within the family. The main point is that money greased market transactions and offered one standard against which virtually any good or service could be evaluated.

Given the penetration by the cash economy, the collectivized family must have lost many advantages in organizing exchange. When goods could be weighed, graded, and assigned a cash value, there was less need to confine trades to the family in order to avoid getting cheated. When hired labor lived and worked with the family, their efforts could be as readily monitored as those of family members. (To be sure, family loyalties continued to offer reassurance of good performance, and men took wives, in part, because they were regarded as more trustworthy than servants [Macfarlane, 1986, p. 164]). The cash economy facilitated objective accounting of transactions. Rational calculation, standard units of measurement, and contractual setting of monetary value made it easier to monitor market exchanges and even to judge the worth of nonmarket contributions within the family. Thus the monetarized economy set the stage for individualistic organization of exchange even within families.

Third, village life could not have encouraged strong expectations of continuity in social relationships. Parish records suggest that many families died out or moved on over the course of several generations (Macfarlane, 1978, pp. 68-74). Active markets for land and labor ensured a high level of geographic mobility. A peculiar English practice called for boys and girls to bid an early farewell to the parental home in order to become servants, apprentices, or students elsewhere (Macfarlane, 1986, pp. 82-88). After years spent saving up for a farm or dowry, young working men and women might well settle in a community far removed from their parents. This residential (and economic) separation of generations continued into the parents' old age. The marital relationship was the most durable family tie, albeit one vulnerable to the higher death rates. Except perhaps among nobility, however, there is apparently no evidence of preference for kin intermarriage to maintain family ties and consolidate family resources (Macfarlane, 1986, pp. 245-251). Indeed, opportunities for rapid social mobility of individuals meant that social as well as geographical distance might separate kin. "Families did not move in a block, but shed some of their younger or less talented children. As a result, after several generations . . . grandchildren of the same person could be at extreme ends of the hierarchy of wealth" (Macfarlane, 1978, p. 69).

With the continuity of kin ties so compromised, the rationale for the collectivized family is undermined. When family relations are routinely disrupted, transactions among kin may be too infrequent, too episodic, or too uncertain to lend themselves to governance by nonmarket mechanisms of exchange. Norms, values, and an authority structure regulate exchanges very efficiently so long as exchange relations are frequent and long term. There is ample time to inculcate values stressing commitment to the family unit. Trustworthiness can be tested.

Opportunities for highly personalized family control are continuously presenting themselves. Outstanding obligations can work themselves out over the long haul instead of the short term. When social mobility, labor migration, and separate residence lower the frequency of kin exchanges, it may be more efficient to effect the transaction with self-interested bargaining, rather than to erect the complex social infrastructure of the collectivized family. The privatized family, which allows for the legitimate interests of individual family members, is favored under these circumstances.

In addition, the nature of English society discouraged exclusive trading relations based on fixed investments in specific kin. The relationship between husband and wife was one of affection and companionship, rather than pure necessity or convenience. This strong marital bond undoubtedly meant that affective investments were not focused exclusively on children. Neither, however, were marital affections seen as limited to a specific union. The speed and frequency with which widows and widowers remarried (Macfarlane, 1986, pp. 234-238) suggests that the joys of marriage were not confined to a particular relationship.

Even with respect to children, the English demonstrated altogether less concern with establishing exclusive intergenerational exchange relations. In Macfarlane's judgment, they showed less strong a desire for heirs (Macfarlane, 1986, p. 57), less biased a preference for sons (Macfarlane, 1986, pp. 53-54), less enthusiasm for adoption and fostering (Macfarlane, 1986, p. 62) than other Western and non-Western societies of the time. Despite the practice of primogeniture, resources were not concentrated on one heir. Efforts were made to provide some reasonable portion to other offspring as well (Macfarlane, 1986, p. 274). Younger daughters, launched when their parents were more economically established, might even fare better than their older sisters (Macfarlane, 1986, p. 264). Although the maintenance and education of offspring involved sunk costs, parents were not locked into relations with specific children since English Common Law permitted disinheritance. Given the strong marital bond, a relatively even-handed approach to children, and the constant opportunity to reallocate resources among kin, it would not appear that the English confronted big, irretrievable investments in specific family members; rather, they maintained a fluid and diversified portfolio of emotional attachments and financial commitments.

In dating English individualism back as far as 1200, Macfarlane argues that it could not have been caused by the Enlightenment, the Reformation, or the rise of capitalism. There was no Great Transformation, because English individualism was endemic to English society. A number of institutions—political, economic, legal, religious, and familial—came together to create conditions that favor the privatized and individualized family. The result was separate purses. This outcome was not inevitable; however, a collectivized solution to the organization of family exchange could have been sustained only at considerably higher transaction costs. While the accuracy of Macfarlane's characterization of English society will surely be debated for some time to come, the transaction cost implications are clear. If the English were, as Macfarlane (1978, p. 66) contends, "individualistic, rational and calculating human beings participating . . . fully in a market economy and a highly mobile society," these efficiency considerations could not have been lost on them.

Conclusion

The common pot and separate purses represent alternative ways of organizing the domestic economy of families. Whether income and assets are pooled or privatized goes to the heart of definitions of the family—as a corporate unit rightly subordinating the interests of its members to the good of the whole or as a collective of self-interested individuals. These two family forms entail different approaches to governing exchange. The individualistic, privatized family relies on bargaining according to market principles to organize exchanges within the family. The corporate family invokes a complex social infrastructure of norms, values, and authority to minimize the time, energy, and resources spent in orchestrating family give and take. Of course, the privatized and corporate family are merely ideal types; real families probably use aspects of both systems in organizing transactions, depending on what is being exchanged and by whom.

While recognizing that other factors may impinge on the choice of family form, this chapter emphasizes the efficiency considerations underpinning privatized or corporate family economies. Under some conditions, the corporate family requires less time and effort to regulate exchanges than does the privatized family. Given different circumstances, the contract and bargaining orientation of the privatized family would accomplish exchanges with lower transaction costs.

The banking practices of American couples conform to transaction cost expectations in that spouses maintain separate purses when their circumstances warrant it. As Macfarlane (1978, 1986) has argued persuasively, the English tradition has long emphasized families as collections of persons who, while often deeply caring and affectionate, maintained unique identities, individual interests, and separate property. Although this exceptional individualism set England apart, it was not unanticipated in the context of English society. An environment that posed few threats, a monetarized economy, low continuity of family ties, and a broad set of significant others set the stage for the English to see themselves as individuals first and family members second. These are conditions that give privatized families an edge over corporate families in terms of lower transaction costs associated with the organization of exchange.

As a means to understanding family life and the domestic economy, the transaction cost approach is attractive on several counts. It recognizes rational choices as a determinant of family form. It furnishes a conceptual scheme that leads to concrete predictions about the organization of families. It insists neither on kin consensus nor on individual self-interest in decision making within the family; whether a bargaining model is more appropriate than one that involves maximizing the head's utility function is a theoretical and empirical question.

References

Becker, Gary, Elisabeth M. Landes, and Robert T. Michael. 1977. "An Economic Analysis of Marital Instability." *Journal of Political Economy* 85:1141-1187.

Ben-Porath, Yoram. 1980. "The F-Connection: Families, Friends, and Firms and the Organization of Exchange." *Population and Development Review* 6:1-30.

Blau, Peter M. 1964. *Exchange and Power in Social Life.* New York: John Wiley.

Blumberg, Rae Lesser. 1988. "Income Under Female Versus Male Control: Hypotheses from a Theory of Gender Stratification and Data from the Third World." *Journal of Family Issues* 9:51-84.

Blumstein, Philip, and Pepper Schwartz. 1983. *American Couples.* New York: William Morrow.

Folbre, Nancy. 1986. "Cleaning House: New Perspectives on Households and Economic Development." *Journal of Development Economics* 22:5-40.

Hertz, Rosanna. 1986. *More Equal Than Others: Women and Men in Dual Career Marriages.* Berkeley: University of California Press.

Homans, George C. 1980. "Review of 'The Origins of English Individualism' by Alan Macfarlane." *Contemporary Sociology* 9:262-263.

Macfarlane, Alan. 1978. *The Origins of English Individualism: The Family, Property and Social Transition.* New York: Cambridge University Press.

———. 1986. *Marriage and Love in England: Modes of Reproduction 1300-1840.* Oxford: Basil Blackwell.

Manser, Marilyn and Murray Brown. 1980. "Marriage and Household Decision-Making: A Bargaining Analysis." *International Economic Review* 21:31-44.

Ouchi, William G. 1980. "Markets, Bureaucracies, and Clans." *Administrative Science Quarterly* 25:129-141.

Pahl, Jan. 1980. "Patterns of Money Management within Marriage." *Journal of Social Policy* 9:313-335.

Pollack, Robert A. 1985. "A Transaction Cost Approach to Families and Households." *Journal of Economic Literature* 23:581-608.

Smith, Audrey D. and William J. Reid. 1986. *Role-Sharing Marriage.* New York: Columbia University Press.

Thornton, Arland and Thomas E. Fricke. 1987. "Social Change and the Family: Comparative Perspectives from the West, China, and South Asia." *Sociological Forum* 2:747-749.

Treas, Judith. Forthcoming. "Money in the Bank: Transaction Costs and Privatized Marriage." *American Sociological Review.*

Williamson, Oliver. 1975. *Markets and Hierarchies.* New York: Free Press.

———. 1981. "The Economics of Organization: The Transaction Cost Approach." *American Journal of Sociology* 87:548-577.

Zeliser, Viviana. 1989. "The Social Meaning of Money: 'Special Monies.' " *American Journal of Sociology* 95(2):342-377.

9

Households as an Institution of the World-Economy

IMMANUEL WALLERSTEIN
JOAN SMITH

For the past 100 to 150 years, we have had a generally accepted image of the family and its historical evolution that has permeated our consciousness and served as part of the general conceptual apparatus with which we have viewed the world. This image had three main elements. First, the family was previously large and extended, but today (or in modern times) it has been getting smaller and more nuclear. Second, the family was previously engaged primarily in subsistence production but today it draws its income primarily from the wage-employment of adult (but nonaged) members. Third, the family was previously a structure virtually indistinguishable from economic activities but today it is a quite segregated or autonomous institutional sphere.

Challenges to the Conventional Image

Though still quite pervasive as a basic assumption in the world view of the majority, in the last 20 years or so the conventional image of the family has come under severe scholarly attack. There are at least four themes in that attack.

First, the conventional image of the family involves an evolutionary premise that all families everywhere are moving in a given direction, and that the degree to which they have moved thus is a measure of the

AUTHORS' NOTE: Copyright of this chapter is held by Immanuel Wallerstein and Joan Smith.

degree to which the society in which they are located may be thought of as advanced or modern. That is to say, this image of the family is an integral part of a developmentalist notion, which assumed that there exist multiple societies in the world, evolving in parallel directions, if at different paces, and that all are evolving furthermore in the direction of "progress" (Goode, 1963).

But developmentalism itself has come under severe challenge in recent years as a framework within which to interpret modern historical change. The logical and historical autonomy of the various societies presumably evolving in parallel fashions has been questioned. Rather, some have argued, all these so-called societies have in fact been or become part of an integrated historical system—that of the capitalist world-economy—which is arranged hierarchically in a self-reproducing system, and in which so-called core and peripheral zones perform very different roles and, hence, are structured quite differently. It would presumably follow from this that the patterns of the family (its composition, its modalities) might look systematically different in the different zones.

Second, the idea of the nuclear family as something historically progressive has been very much associated with the idea that the adult male was thereby liberated from the tutelage of his father and assumed independently his own responsibilities. This same adult came to be identified as the breadwinner because it was he who presumably sought wage work outside the household with which to support his family. This notion in turn became a basic element in our concepts of the world of work and the world of politics, peopled presumably ever more by these adult proletarian male individuals who faced employers and (sometimes) banded together politically. Along with this conceptualization of the male breadwinner has gone the concept of the (adult) female housewife (Parsons, 1955).

These concepts of "normal" family roles have of course also been under severe challenge—first of all by feminist scholarship and women's studies in general, which have contested the degree to which this kind of nuclear family (which of course has in fact existed, at least in some places at some times) can be considered to be "progressive" or "liberatory," in that the "liberation" of the adult male from his father was bought, if you will, at the expense of the increased subordination of the adult female to this same adult male, not to speak of the increased subordination of the aged father to his adult male son (Eisenstein, 1979).

In addition, quite apart from the political and moral conclusions which can be drawn about this kind of family structure, women's studies have raised basic questions about the assumptions the concepts have made about economic value and its creation. Specifically, we find ourselves in the midst of a long, still ongoing debate about how best to conceptualize the economic significance of housework and where it fits in the macroeconomy as well as in the budgetary realities of the household itself.

Third, since the 1970s there has been a growing literature on the so-called "second economy," variously referred to as "informal" or "underground" or "submerged." The image of the nuclear family implied a parallel image of a "nuclear economy," with equally clear boundaries and a specified, specialized role. This nuclear economy was in theory composed of legal, autonomous enterprises, each with its employer and employees, producing goods and services for the market within the framework established by state laws. This new literature has called attention to the multitudinous economic activities that occur outside this framework—evading legal restrictions or obligations (such as taxation, minimum wage laws, and forbidden production (Redclift and Mingione, 1985)).

Once again, the implications were double. It was not only that the model of economic production that underlay analysis was shown to be wrong, or at least inadequate to cover empirical reality, but also that the model of family income sources was correspondingly wrong. The adult male often had two employments, not one, and the second employment was frequently one in which the income was not wage-income. Similarly, both the unemployed adult male and the adult female housewife were frequently quite actively involved in this informal economy, and, therefore, the basic description of their occupation—unemployed, housewife—was wrong, or at least incomplete (Smith, 1984).

A fourth challenge to the traditional image has resulted from the enormous expansion of the so-called welfare state, particularly since World War II, and particularly in Western (or core) countries. These states have come to accept a wide series of obligation vis-à-vis citizens and/or national residents in general and additionally vis-à-vis specific categories of persons in particular, obligations which involve the periodic allocation of revenues to individuals on some specified criteria.

As the amounts have grown and the political encrustation has become deeper (despite continuing shrill opposition), it has become impossible to ignore the impact of such so-called "transfer payments" on income, and that in two respects. On the one hand, transfer payments have come to represent an even larger percentage of total income, indeed for some families the majority. And on the other hand, transfer payments are frequently conditional, and thus it becomes apparent that the "state" has thereby a very potent and quite obvious mechanism of affecting, even directing, the structure of the family (Donzelot, 1979).

And if all this were not enough, the careful reconstruction of family history that has become a major subfield of social history in the last 20 years has shown that factually the widespread image of the rise of the nuclear family does not bear the weight of careful archival inspection. The picture in empirical reality turns out to be extremely complex with no very simple trend-line, and one that varies considerably from region to region.

Reconceptualizing the Household as an Income-Pooling Entity

It seems, therefore, that there is much demand for a reconceptualization of the ways in which these presumably basic institutional spheres—the family, the workplace, the state—relate to each other in our modern world. We shall start with three rather simple empirical observations and argue that any conceptualization that does not encompass these three observations will be inadequate as an explanatory model.

Observation Number 1

Observation number 1 is that most individuals live on a daily basis within a *household,* which is what we call the entity responsible for our basic and continuing reproduction needs (food, shelter, clothing), and this household puts together a number of different kinds of income in order to provide for these reproduction needs. We make a distinction between households and families. The former refers to that grouping that assures some level of pooling income and sharing resources over time so as to reproduce the unit. Often the members of a household are biologically related and share a common residence, but sometimes they do not.

We can classify the multiple forms of income into five major varieties and observe that most households get some of their income in *each* of the five forms, at least if you measure their income not on a daily basis but on an annual or multiannual basis. These five forms are wages, market sales (or profit), rent, transfer, and subsistence (or direct labor input). None of these five categories is as straightforward and uncomplicated as we sometimes pretend.

Wages means the receipt of income (usually cash, but often partially in kind) from someone or some entity outside the household for work performed. The work is usually performed outside the household and hours of work are normally circumscribed (and legally constrained). We speak of someone being employed full-time when this person works a prescribed number of hours per week (these days, circa 35-45), 52 weeks a year (including vacation time, often legally prescribed). Someone is unemployed if, having been employed full-time, this person is no longer so employed but is seeking to resume being so employed. But, of course, we know that many persons receive wages for work that is part-time—in hours per week, in weeks per year (such as "seasonal" employment), in years per lifetime (such as "target" employment). And we know that sometimes this employment can involve work in the home, especially if the wages are based on piecework rather than on hourly compensation.

Market (or profit) income seems straightforward in the case of commodity sales. If someone in the household makes something and sells it in the local market, then the net income is clearly "profit" and the profit can be used (and normally is, in large part) for expenditure on immediate consumption, although some part of the net income may be used for "investment." Petty commerce is only a minor variant on petty manufacture in terms of its significance for providing household income. It is more difficult, however, to decide what is happening when services are being offered. If one babysits, or takes in washing, the income is often thought of as market income, similar to petty commodity production or marketing. If however one is a free-lance editor or computer programmer, the income is more often thought of as akin to wages. It may not be terribly important to resolve such a classificational problem.

Rental income seems to cover any income deriving from the remunerated use by someone outside the household of some entity to which we have (legal) property rights. We rent space in our own home to lodgers. We rent tools or facilities to neighbors. We deposit money in banks and draw interest therefrom. These days we also invest money in stocks and bonds and receive dividends. In theory, this last is a process of joining others to produce market income (and, therefore, a form of profit), but in practice it is a form of income much closer to that obtained by renting our property. It requires no work, only the forgoing of use. We can also rent our own persons. If one stands in a line for someone else, that is called selling a service. But suppose we substitute our presence for someone else's legal obligation (say, military service), as was once legal in many parts of the world, is this not more akin to rental (forgoing "normal" civilian life in return for an income)? And how is one to classify the newest of all commodifications, the income of the "substitute" uterine progenitor?

Transfers are receipts of income for which there is no immediate work-input counterpart. But of course the "immediacy" of the counterpart is difficult to circumscribe. If one receives state transfer income (old age insurance, unemployment benefits, work-injury compensation, welfare), it is certainly possible to argue that there have been significant counterparts at some prior point in time. To the extent that such transfers are based on "insurance" there have been cash inputs at previous times that required work-inputs to earn them. And even when the transfer payments require no prior insurance payments, it may be argued in many cases that they represent deferred compensation, collectively distributed, for previous work-inputs.

Private transfers are even more obscure in form. Most households receive irregular but predictable (and anticipated) private transfers of income (frequently denominated *gifts*). They receive these transfers from their "extended" families (e.g., on anniversaries, but often more importantly on the occasion of births, marriages, and deaths). They also receive such transfers from those superextended families we sometimes call *communities,* a category that overlaps but is not identical with another superextended group, our circle of friends. But are such transfers transfers? Are there not obligations of reciprocity, more or less faithfully observed? Perhaps these transfers should be thought of as ways of adjusting lifetime income to uneven curves of expenditure (for example, on the occasions of births, marriages, and deaths).

Finally, subsistence income is the most confusing category of all. Our use of the term derives from a model of a virtually nonexistent entity, the self-sufficient household that reproduces itself fully from what it produces and is thus truly autarkic. This autarkic model is largely a fantasy. However, it should not therefore be forgotten that virtually every household produces *some* of what it requires to reproduce itself, that is, produces some subsistence income.

The household may do this by hunting, gathering, or agriculture to obtain food for consumption. Obviously, this kind of household subsistence production is of diminishing significance, as the percentage of world labor-time (however remunerated) in such activities is on the decline. Household self-manufacture seems on the other hand as important a source of income as it ever was, even if the items thus produced are less likely to be the presumed basics (preserved foods, clothing, the house itself) and more likely to be the increasing number of do-it-yourself manufactures (in whole, or more often in part). And household subsistence services on the other hand seem to be actually increasing overall, rather than decreasing in labor-input. Households not only still for the most part prepare their own food, but they continue to maintain their shelter and clothing. Indeed, they probably spend far more time maintaining their shelter and clothing as the number of appliances available to be tools in this process increases. The tools do not seem to reduce the labor-input in terms of time—probably, the reverse—even if they usually make the labor-input require less muscle-power (Smith, 1987).

The mere listing of the multiple forms of income makes it very obvious that real income for real households is normally made up of all these components. The percentages vary (and are, as we shall see, difficult to compute), but two things at least seem clear. First, few households in the modern world, anywhere, can afford over a lifetime to ignore any of these sources of income. Second, wage-income, even for households that are thought of as fully dependent on it, remains only *one of five* components, and as a percentage probably rarely approaches, even today, a massive proportion of the total.

Observation Number 2

Observation number 2 is that there seem to exist rather dramatic differences in the real wage-levels of persons doing more or less identical work at more or less identical skill levels across world space and world time. That is to say, to put it in its most concise form, a skilled mason employed in construction activities receives considerably higher wages (however measured) in London than in New Delhi, and in London in the late twentieth century as compared to London in the early nineteenth century. This is such common knowledge that it is often not regarded as something that requires explanation.

Yet, on the face of it, this empirical reality flies in the face of almost all standard economic explanations for wage-levels. It should not be thus, and if it is thus momentarily, normal economic flows should end such anomalies over a relatively short space of time.[1] It is irrational in a capitalist world-economy that similar/identical activities should not be similarly compensated. In general, when explanations for such an anomaly are offered, they tend to be self-consciously noneconomic in character. The wage-differentials are said to be attributable to historic factors, or to cultural differences or to variations in political systems. Of course these are no explanations at all, but simply the listing of possible intermediate processes. One would want to know how these other constraints came into existence and when. This is all the more true when we observe both that particular wage differentials can and do change and that the pattern of wage differentials nonetheless persists.

Observation Number 3

Observation number 3 is that all the members of a household (or virtually all) produce *some* income for the household (on an annual basis probably, on a lifetime basis surely), and that the various sources of income are not to be *exclusively* identified with any particular members of the household. That is not to say, however, that there are not systematic patterns or correlations that vary with gender, age, class, or ethnic group.

Wages are identified with adult males. They are identified to the point that female wage work, child labor, employment of the aged or of retired workers constitute a phenomenon that is noticed and therefore is studied. Yet we know that wage work has never been exclusively the preserve of adult males. To be sure, the amount of wage-work by adult females, children, and the aged has varied considerably (although without as yet long trend lines) in what may be cyclical patterns. Still it is probably true to say that at most times and in most places the majority of wage-workers have been adult males and the majority (or at least a large plurality) of adult males have engaged in at least some wage-work during their lifetimes.

The earning of market income on the other hand is so flexible a procedure that it is hard to identify it consistently with gender or age roles. Worldwide and over time, men and women have engaged in it, even if some parts of the world seem to show cultural biases toward the higher participation (and the nonparticipation) of certain groups in market activities. One of the flexible features of market activities is that they are less tied to collective schedule-making than wage activities. It is therefore usually quite easy to do them for small amounts of time, facilitating their combination with other income-producing activities, and allowing them to be, so to speak, schedule fillers.

Many rental activities are collective household acts (at least in theory) and in addition require very little time. After all, what we mean by *rent* is income derived from a legal claim rather than from current activity. Of course the renter may be simultaneously purchasing services or commodities in addition to paying a rent, as when a lodger is served food or has clothes laundered. The rental of persons (which is not the most common of phenomena) may however be gender- and age-specific.

Transfers are also made in a sense to the collective household, but, not unlike other forms of income, they are usually made via an individual who is the legal recipient or the excuse for a transfer. The forms of transfers are many and the recipients, therefore, are in fact widely distributed across gender and age.

Finally there is subsistence income. Subsistence income shares with market income a considerable flexibility in the allocation (when and for how long a particular activity occurs) and shares with wage income an *imperfect* correlation with a particular age-gender role. We do identify subsistence income with the adult female, but that is for the same reasons we identify wage labor with the adult male. On the other hand, everyone—men and women, adults, children, and the aged—does some subsistence work, with variations according to time and place, with perhaps cyclical patterns, and with no long-term trend-line. But on the other hand, at most times and places the majority of the subsistence income has been produced by adult females, as this is what is implied by the concept "housewife," which has been a constant of the organizational pattern of the capitalist world-economy.

What then may we conclude from these observations? One thing surely: All members of the household (except infants and total invalids) are capable of obtaining income for the household by their labor inputs, and in most cases participate in income-securing activities. Another factor must, however, be stated more hesitantly: there are some patterns of gender-age correlation with income-procuring activities but it is far from perfect, and most persons engage in several different income-procuring activities—in a week, in a year, in a lifetime.

One last point should be made about income-pooling. What we are describing is how income comes *into* the household. This says nothing necessarily about how it is spent. Households may be structured in more or less authoritarian fashions. The income may be allocated unequally. Furthermore, the inflow of the income may be hypothetical. A particular member of the household, somehow earning cash income, may short-stop the process, by keeping part or all of the cash to spend. This is a "political" act. From the point of view of this analysis, this cash is still household income, because it in fact forms part of the pool that is redistributed. A member who shortstops income and spends it may not be allocated other income for the expenditures in question. In any case, the internal structure of households, and how power and goods are distributed internally, are not treated in this discussion.

The Household, the Workplace, and the State

How should we reconceptualize the interrelations between the household, the workplace, and the state? We suggest that we can make most sense of what is going on if we utilize a set of five orienting propositions, alerting us to what seem to be the processes at work.

1. The appropriate operational unit for analyzing the ways in which people fit into the labor force is not the individual but the household, defined for these purposes as the social unit that effectively over long periods of time enables individuals, of varying ages and of both sexes, to pool income coming from multiple sources in order to ensure their individual and collective reproduction and well-being. We shall call the multiple processes by which they pool income, allocate tasks, and make collective decisions *householding.*

The composition of the effective household becomes a central object for empirical research. We do not presume that all members of the household are necessarily kin, much less a nuclear family, although no doubt in most cases most members of a household are kin and probably close kin. Nor do we presume that a household is necessarily a group resident in the same house, or even in the same locality, although once again this is often the case. Households are defined as those who have de facto entered into long-term income-pooling arrangements. To be sure, this entails some set of mutual obligations, although no particular set is included in the definition.

This mode of defining the household is beset by all sorts of boundary problems. How long is long-term? How much pooling constitutes pooling? How many obligations constitutes an ongoing set of mutual obligations? As persons enter and leave households periodically (certainly by birth and death, and quite often for other reasons), over what sequence of time ought one to measure the pooling activities? We deliberately leave these issues without answers at the level of definition, making defining households both an object of study and not presuming that there is only one set of possible boundaries for a household.

2. There is a further reason for our vagueness about boundaries. The household as an income-pooling unit is not primordial in nature. It is an historically created institution, both as an institution in general and in its particular varieties. Of course it is not the only such historically created institution. Our holistic conception of the capitalist world-economy as an historical system leads us to consider all the institutions of this system as a collective mutual creation. The states and the interstate system, the enterprises, the classes, the nations and ethnic groups, the social movements, the sciences, the educational and health structures are all equally historically created in a single, interrelated process, which is a continuing one.

It follows that we must ask why any of these institutions has taken the form that it has, generically as a form and specifically in all its variations. None of this history is to be considered theoretically accidental, having no explanation other than it just happened to be that way for historical or cultural reasons.

In this case, the bounding of households is itself an historical process, which not only can but must be analyzed, as it is probably the key process in the functioning of householding and is what integrates this particular structure into the larger network of structures that constitute the capitalist world-economy. If bounding is key, then it behooves us to see what are the kinds of pressures to which the households are subject that lead them (or even force them) to modify their boundaries. We see three major kinds of pressures, which constitute our third, fourth, and fifth orienting propositions.

3. The capitalist world-economy operates through an axial division of labor that is hierarchical and involves commodity chains of production processes, some of which are more corelike and some of which are more peripheral. Any particular unit of production participates in one or multiple commodity chains. Furthermore, any particular unit of production competes with other units of production for its percentage of the total production for a specific point in the one or multiple commodity chains.

The number of competing units of production at particular nexuses of the commodity chain(s) is continually varying and can vary hypothetically from one to a very, very large number. This is the continuum of monopoly competition. It is quite clear that as the number of competing units in the world-economy as a whole goes down at any nexus toward one, the ability of the units of production located at this nexus to increase their net profit goes up, and as the number goes up toward some very large number, the ability to obtain net profit goes down. This is essentially the difference between being corelike and being peripheral.

It is further clear that the total net profit extracted at any nexus of a chain is related to the total net profit (or extracted surplus value) in the sum of all the nexuses. Thus, as one nexus becomes more or less profitable, it affects the level of profitability of other nexuses in the commodity chain or chains of which it is a part. That is to say, coreness or peripherality is a relation of one nexus to other nexuses. The nature of the actual economic activity is irrelevant, only the degree to which at any given point in time, participants (owners) at this nexus are in a more or less favorable position to obtain a larger or less large proportion of the total surplus value created in the commodity chain.

Commodity chains typically are very long with very many nexuses. Typically, too, the production units of a given nexus are located in a large number of political units, although the more corelike the nexus, the fewer the number of countries containing production units belonging to that nexus. And typically, it is difficult to go from one end of a commodity chain to the other without crossing frontiers (often many frontiers).

The modes of remunerating labor at different nexuses of the commodity chain are multiple. Two things are true: Most commodity chains will have various modes at different nexuses. Many nexuses will have more than one mode; that is, different production units on the same nexus may use different modes of remuneration.

Finally, it is clear that as the world-economy goes through its cyclical patterns of global expansion and global contraction, which reflect global ability to extract surplus value and, therefore, to accumulate capital, there will be pressures of varying intensities on the units of production to reduce costs. Global contraction will lead to squeezes that force units of production to find ways of reducing costs. One such way of course is to reduce the cost of labor. This may in turn lead to changes in the mode of remunerating labor.

Now what has all this to do with the structure of households? A very great deal. A household is a unit that pools income for purposes of reproduction. If the income it receives is reduced, it must either live on less income or find substitute income. Of course, there comes a point where it cannot survive on less income (or survive very long) and, therefore, the only alternative is to find substitute income.

The household with the least flexibility, as total income goes down, is the household most dependent on wage-income, since the ability to obtain wage-income (or a certain level of wage-income) is a function of the offer by someone outside the household of that wage-employment. A household can most readily affect its total income by investing its labor power in activities it can autonomously launch. It can do this most obviously in terms of subsistence income, and it can also try to do this in the securing of additional transfer-income, though this may be more difficult.

But the ability to secure nonwage forms of income is itself a function of the boundaries of the household. One that is too small (say, a truly nuclear family) may simply not have the hours available to generate the necessary income. On the other hand, a very extended household may have too much of a gap in income realistically to hope to overcome it. Such very extended households have however become relatively rare in the poorer strata of the world's households, which tend to vary from very small to medium in size. Ergo, typically, stagnations in the world-economy create pressures on small household structures to enlarge boundaries and to self-exploit more.

Seen from the perspective of the employer of wage-labor, it is preferable, other things being equal, to employ persons who are less rather than more dependent on wage-income (let us call such households *semiproletarian* households). A wage-worker in a semiproletarian household is more able to accept a low real wage since this worker may be able to assume that, via self-exploitation, other compensating forms of income will be available to him or her. The more proletarian (that is, wage-dependent) the *household,* the more the individual wage-worker is compelled to demand higher real wages (a so-called living wage). This is for example why we see, in times of stagnation in the world-economy, relocation of industries from one zone to another. They are moving primarily to reduce wage costs, and they can do this because of the household structures prevalent in the zone into which they are moving.

If this is so, then both the cyclical rhythms and the secular trends of the capitalist world-economy should affect the modal boundaries of household structures. The cyclical rhythms—the expansions and contractions of the world-economy—should lead to a shifting rhythm of modal household composition. Periods of expansion should see a shift in the direction of relatively greater wage-dependence and relatively narrower boundaries of inclusion, while periods of stagnation should see a shift in the reverse direction. Obviously, we are talking only of shifts and not sudden and complete transformation. And obviously too this will vary according to the degree to which particular subareas benefit from or are hurt by the global rhythms.

In addition, however, the world-economy has secular trends. The stagnation phases of the world-economy's rhythms are not symmetrical to its expansion phases. There results a certain "ratchet" effect, which leads to some long-term *slow* upward curves. The one that is most relevant here is the slow upward curve of worldwide proletarianization, which should find some reflection in a *slow* upward curve of the type of household structures most consonant with wage-dependence.

4. Thus far, the pressures on household boundaries of which we have been speaking seem to be nontangible, proceeding from obscure market forces to whose abstract consequences households feel it necessary to respond by altering their composition and perhaps their mode of functioning and internal decision-making. No doubt these obscure market forces are real and no doubt too households can perceive their effects and respond to them. There is a growing literature that suggests that households respond relatively rapidly to economic conditions, altering their composition and boundaries.

There are other forces which are more direct, more immediate, and more imperious. We tend to call such forces *political* and to locate them primarily in the state-machinery—or rather in the multiple levels and forms of state machinery—laws and policies that direct households about a large number of possibilities, and issues that determine their composition: possibilities and requirements of co-residence; financial and legal responsibilities; fiscal obligations, right to physical movement; constraints on the physical location of economic activities; rules concerning hours and remuneration of work; rules about market behavior; and eligibility for transfer income.

Indeed the list of matters about which the state legislates is extremely long, even in the more laissez-faire-oriented political regimes. Not only does the state legislate on a vast gamut of matters affecting the structure and composition of households, but it legislates constantly. That is, the rules are never set once and for all. They are regularly being revised.

The bases on which particular states decide to revise their rules are, to be sure, multiple. One major factor is the attempt of the state to maintain its own budgetary balance and the collectivity's economic survival (as reflected say in a "balance of payments") as this faces the changing realities of the world economy within which it operates. A state may decide it wishes to be the locale to which a large industry in another state may consider relocating because of world economic stagnation. It may then take concrete steps to ensure that the household structures of at least a portion of its citizenry are such, or become such, that the owners of the large industry will find a local market for wage-labor at wage-levels they find attractive.

Or a state may need to restore its budgetary balance which has been upset by some changes in the realities of the world-economy. It may then decide on major fiscal or social welfare reforms, which will affect the inflows and outflows of the state's treasury. Such changes may have a significant impact on budgetary calculations for particular groups of household structures, forcing them, in order to survive, to recompose the household.

Of course, the state may even be more direct. It may actually ordain household structures, by controlling the right to migrate (across frontiers, from rural to urban areas), or by decreeing certain legal obligations of kin to each other, or by making its own obligations to provide household income contingent on households being structured in specific ways, or by forbidding urban land to be used for agricultural purposes.

Thus, our fourth orienting proposition is that states always have policies about household composition and boundaries and, furthermore, that such policies are not simply givens, but are subject to change. States therefore constrain households. But conversely the state itself is the vector of political forces and households participate in these political forces that put pressure upon the state to move in specific directions.

5. Both the obscure market forces and the more visible state machineries appear to the household as something external to it, to which it has to respond in some way. But the realities of the world-system of which we are a part enter into the internal mental frameworks that we utilize to respond to these other apparently external forces.

Households think of themselves as belonging to communities, or multiple communities. If the boundaries of the community are derived from the obscure market forces, we call it a *class*. If the boundaries are derived from or related to existing or potential state structures, we call it a *nation*. In some sense, both class-consciousness and nationalism are conceived of as simultaneously subjective and objective realities. That is, we feel ourselves to be of a given class, of a given nature, but we also know that because they are defined in terms of external phenomena, membership is alterable. We can theoretically change our class affiliation or our national allegiance. Some people do (even if most do not). The possibility is nonetheless felt to be there, and by and large it is considered "legitimate" for a household to make a change should it wish to and/or should it be possible to do so. The "legitimacy" of such change is subject to certain constraints relating to the moment of change—it is frowned upon to shift membership at moments when the community is in crisis.

There is a third type of community affiliation which, in common conception, is thought simply to be there and which people claim is not somehow determined by external structures. We call this *ethnicity,* and by this we mean a collection of cultural norms, perhaps a common language, sometimes a religious affiliation, which mark us off from others *of the same class and nation.* It is furthermore believed that this community membership is not subject to change. That this is not in fact true does not diminish the importance of the widespread belief that it is true.

Our *ethnicity,* our *culture* (or *subculture*) is a crucial defining category for household structures—in two ways. Households are the prime socializing agency into the norms of ethnicity. We learn these norms as children within a household, and we are most immediately constrained to observe them—as adults or children—by others in the same household.

But what norms are they that we learn in a household and consider to be our culture or a good part of it? The norms relate to all areas of activity, but first of all and most importantly to the operation of the household itself. We are taught rules of legitimacy concerning sexual behavior. We are taught obligations (and their limits) of observing *non*market criteria in internal household transactions. We are taught norms about our sharing obligations, that is, with whom we ought to pool income that is juridically defined as owned by an individual.

We are also taught norms about how to relate to the work world and to the state. We are taught to be more (or less) industrious. We are taught to be oriented to upward mobility or to accepting our place. We are taught to be more submissive to the state (law-abiding) or more intransigent (individual independence or collective rebelliousness). We are taught to be more or less self-denying or self-indulgent. We are taught to define intercommunity obligations narrowly or broadly.

As one draws up the list of all the things that are involved in one's ethnicity, two things become obvious. It is a very broad list, impinging not merely upon the household structure but quite explicitly on how these structures should relate to economic and political institutions. Second, the list itself is constantly evolving. That is, the norms of a given ethnic group are themselves changing; indeed the very boundaries (and names) of the groups evolve. We see then that, far from being somehow just there, somehow more internal, ethnicity is simply a third modality by which the forces in the total historical system mold each other.

It consequently should come as no surprise to find a triple correlation which while not total, is strong: ethnicity, type of household structure, ways in which household members relate to the overall economy. We are very aware of this phenomenon in its most unpalatable form: discrimination in the work (or political) arena. But it operates as well, and more frequently, in subtler guises: by orienting households to greater or lesser wage-dependence, by legitimating (or not) certain kinds of market or subsistence involvement, by pressing toward or away from certain kinds of transfer payments.

A household normally has a single ethnicity. If, by marriage, there is a mixture, the intrusive element tends to convert, if not formally, at least de facto. If this does not happen, the household has survival problems. The household's ethnicity constitutes a set of rules that very largely ensures that it will operate in specific ways. If, because of changes in the world-economy, such modalities of action are no longer useful, ethnic groups find themselves under external pressure to evolve, that is, to change their norms, even to change their ethnic boundaries.

There is at this point one bugaboo to set aside. It may be said that our concept seems to diminish, underplay, or even eliminate the autonomous role of the household—the household as actor, and not as dependent variable. Not at all! The household is as autonomous as the state, the firm, the class, or indeed as any other actor. As autonomous or as little autonomous. All these so-called actors are part of one historical system; they compose it. They are determined by it, but they also determine it, in a process of constant interaction that is so imbricated that there is no prime mover. Had we set out to reconceptualize and analyze the state or the firm or the class it might have equally seemed, once the matter were laid out, that its autonomy as an actor had been denied. What is inherent in a holistic view of an historical system is that the actors are simultaneously produced by the system and produce (that is, constitute) the system. The whole issue of who is autonomous is a nonissue.

These then are our five orienting processes: the household as an income-pooling unit as our basic unit of analysis; the household as an entity whose boundaries and composition are subject to continuing change; the impact of the cycles and trends of the world-economy upon household structures; the role of the state-machinery in molding and remolding household structures; the role of ethnicity as a modality of socializing household members into particular economic roles, and the changeability of these norms. They add up to a concept of *household* and therefore of *householding* that serves as a basis of our analysis of empirical reality.

Note

1. According to most conventional accounts discrimination is impossible to maintain since "if all firms are profit-maximizers, then all will demand the services of the low-wage individuals, bidding their wages up until the wage differential is eliminated" (Stiglitz, 1973, p. 287).

References

Donzelot, Jacques. 1979. *The Policing of Families*. New York: Pantheon.
Eisenstein, Zillah R. 1979. *Capitalist Patriarchy and the Case of Socialist Feminism*. New York: Monthly Review Press.
Goode, William J. 1963. *World Revolution and Family Patterns*. New York: John Wiley.
Parsons, Talcott. 1955. *Family Socialization and Interaction Processes*. Glencoe, IL: Free Press.

Redclift, Nanneke and Enzo Mingione, eds. 1985. *Beyond Employment: Household, Gender, and Subsistence.* London: Basil Blackwell.

Smith, Joan. 1984. "The Paradox of Women's Employment: The Importance of Being Marginal." *Signs, X,* 291-310.

Smith, Joan. 1987. "Transforming Households: Working Class Women and Economic Crisis." *Social Problems, XXXIV,* 416-436.

Stiglitz, J. E. 1973. "Approaches to the Economics of Discrimination." *American Economic Review,* Papers and Proceedings of the 85th Annual meeting, *LXIII,* 280-298.

Part IV

Gender, Money, and Housework

10

The Division of Household Labor
Suggestions for Future Empirical Consideration and Theoretical Development

MARION TOLBERT COLEMAN

Since the early 1970s when Oakley (1974) asked London housewives if the husbands "helped" with a number of household chores, the literature on division of household labor has advanced on a number of different fronts. As reflected in the wording of Oakley's question on the "helpful" involvement of husbands in housework, her goal was not to question the assumption that housework was the wife's domain, but rather to argue that, in spite of its nonpaying status, housework was real work for women and, as such, worthy of legitimate sociological study. More recent scholars, weighing the impacts of the entrance of women into the labor force and the blurring of the lines between men's and women's work, have moved far beyond that early goal by focusing their attentions on the division of household labor between wives and husbands. As our knowledge of how much each spouse contributes to the care and maintenance of household and children has increased, our models for the understanding of that division of labor (or more accurately stated, the remarkable stability of that division) have likewise expanded. Not quite so well developed have been our inquiries as to precisely "who does what" or how our models that explain household division of labor can interface with larger theoretical frameworks.

The purpose of the present chapter is to address these latter two gaps in this literature; first, the issue of exactly how the work is divided,

AUTHOR'S NOTE: I would like to thank Rae Lesser Blumberg for her helpful comments on an earlier draft of this chapter.

if indeed some responsibility is taken by other persons, particularly by the husband. This specific missing piece of the picture, while interesting in its own right, also underscores the second gap: The factors underlying the division of household labor may actually be a more complex process than that for which existing explanatory models allow. Moreover, it may be of value to view division of housework as an outcome variable within a larger model of gender stratification rather than as an isolated dependent variable whose variation we are attempting to explain.

Current Thrust of the Literature

A survey of the most recent empirical work on division of household labor in U.S. families reveals that a large portion is directed at either *differences in time spent in* or *responsibility for* housework among various earner configuration households (Nichols and Metzen, 1982; Maret and Finlay, 1984; Yogev and Brett, 1985; Coverman and Sheley, 1986; Berardo, Shehan, and Leslie, 1987) or *determinants of time* spent by men in household activities (Model, 1981; Pleck and Staines, 1985; Barnett and Baruch, 1987).[1] As Warner (1986) observes, the most common data collection method for these studies is respondents' perceptions of relative responsibility. And while we have gained important new knowledge from these studies, there remains an untapped area related to the qualitative difference between the mere quantity of time spent in or responsibility for tasks (whatever they may be) and the actual nature of the work that must be done to complete a specific chore. As Robinson (1977) observed early on after analyzing the *Americans' Use of Time* data:

> Time-use data provided [a] unique but not definitive perspective on the current controversy over sex roles. First, simple time expenditure data do not reflect those subtle role demands that are involved in the performance of housework; that is the constant attention required throughout the day, week, or year; the continual changes and decisions about scheduling and priorities; the monotony and inevitability; and the unsettling combination of the hectic and the menial. (pp. 61-62)

The limited data we do have on actual labor performed by husbands underline his point that the nature of the specific tasks performed is a very important factor to be considered. Furthermore, typical time-use data are still not in as rigorous a form as would be needed to address this issue.

Thus a major reason for the lack of attention to *quality* of household activity may be the data themselves upon which researchers have been dependent. Very few data sets have the detail necessary to address this issue. Furthermore, much of the information we have about household division of labor comes from three major data sets. Although these vary in the detail of information collected on questions pertaining to housework and the method by which those data were collected, they share the common problem of being dated: In all three cases their most recent wave is over ten years old. These data sets are the *Americans' Use of Time* study, the Panel Study of Income Dynamics, and the National Longitudinal Surveys of Work Experience.

The *Americans' Use of Time* data is detailed since it is drawn from time diaries completed by respondents. However, Robinson (1977), who used the first wave of data collected in 1965-1966, reports most findings in terms of time differentials (although he does offer some discussion on the types of tasks husbands are most likely to take on). Coverman and Sheley (1986) compared the first and the second waves (the latter collected in 1975-1976), and their analysis differentiates only on the distinction of men's involvement in housework as opposed to child care.

The Panel Study of Income Dynamics was used most recently by Nichols and Metzen (1982) and Berardo, Shehan, and Leslie (1987). Nichols and Metzen used the 1968 through 1973 waves and Berardo used the 1976 wave. The data are quite limited, however: The survey asked respondents only to estimate the number of hours per week they spend on housework.

Finally, the National Longitudinal Surveys of Work Experience provide an even more limited picture: They asked women if they had sole, shared, or no responsibility for six general domestic tasks. Maret and Finlay (1984) used the 1976-1977 cohort file on mature women. While the time intervals covered by the three large-scale data sets do capture an important era of change in men's and women's roles, new data are needed to bring work in this area into the 1990s.

More recently, other researchers have been collecting their own data on housework. In general, the larger samples in this work have been less detailed and the in-depth studies have focused on a small number of cases. But even here, none have given detailed attention to what men do.

Among those researchers who collected their own data for studies in which housework was an important component of the overall model,

Huber and Spitze (1983) and Blumstein and Schwartz (1983) used a sole versus shared responsibility wording for 5 and 19 tasks, respectively. At the opposite end of the spectrum, Hood (1983) and Lein (1984) used multivisit, in-depth interviews. The benefit of this more detailed data collection is of course obvious. But the trade-off is the smaller number of cases on which data can be collected—Hood followed 16 families and Lein, 23.

Finally, the most detailed data set collected specifically on housework (collected in 1975 and reported most fully in Berk and Berk, 1979, and Berk, 1985) used the diary technique. Due to financial constraints, the fully elaborated technique was used only for wives, while husbands were asked to retrospectively account for their household involvement during two time blocks of a 24-hour period when they were most available for family or household work (a technique that Berk notes may be prone to overestimation by respondents). Although Berk's (1985) purpose was to study time, task, and responsibility allotments within a New Home Economics theoretical model, she does provide some preliminary data about what husbands say they do, but she does not make it a primary focus.

In sum, while researchers throughout the household division of labor literature have noted the importance of exploring who does which tasks, most have not specifically considered what husbands do in a well-developed or methodical fashion. The reasons for this omission include lack of detail in the data set being used and the fact that the researchers' primary interests are in another aspect of the question. At the same time, throughout the literature, there are some preliminary findings that, when brought together, provide an interesting picture of the housework involvement of husbands as well as underscoring the need for future investigation.

What Men Do: What We Know Thus Far

The remarkably unchanging, one-sided picture presented by the time data is appalling enough to those concerned about equitable division of household labor. And while a few studies indicate that some men, particularly those with higher education and young children, may be increasing their household and child-care involvement (Ross, Mirowsky, and Huber, 1983; Pleck, 1985; Yogev and Brett, 1985), most researchers still conclude, as Coverman and Sheley (1987) do, that men have not increased the amount of their participation, even in the face of the pressures caused by wives' increasing participation in the labor force. So what do men do in the small amount of time they devote to household labor?

The 1965-1966 time-use data used by Robinson (1977) revealed that the employed husbands in the sample spent the majority of their slightly more than eleven hours of housework per week in auxiliary household care and shopping.[2] The only two areas in which men spent comparable time to women were grocery shopping and house repairs. While the husbands of employed wives spent approximately half the time that their spouses did in child care, there was an important qualitative difference in this involvement as well. Fathers spent half of their time with the children in play while mothers spent only one tenth of theirs.

The 1975 data used by Berk and Berk (1979) showed that when housework was divided, it was done so along traditional sex-stereotyped lines. For instance, husbands' contributions in the morning hours primarily consisted of letting the pet out, emptying the trash, and putting the dishes in the sink. Moreover, the contributions of the husbands of nonemployed wives did not differ significantly from those of employed wives. As did Robinson, the Berks found that fathers' time spent in child care was spent in play, usually after dinner and while wives were engaged in the much less appealing task of doing the dishes. They also noted that husbands' involvement in unpleasant or traditionally female tasks (such as washing the dinner dishes) was not routine but rather appeared to be a periodic activity directly related to the unavailability of the wife (if she worked nights, for instance). In other words, they took on tasks when there was no one else to do them. Likewise, the husbands in Hood's (1983) study, "chose child care, cooking and shopping over housecleaning. Husbands tended to do what they liked doing or what absolutely had to be done in their wives' absence" (p. 179).

Besides their limited participation being in stereotypical activities, are there any other overarching characteristics of husbands' specific housework? Meissner (1977) found that the work that men prefer to take in households had at least one of the three following characteristics: (a) clearly defined boundaries as to what the job consisted of and when it was completed (such as mowing the lawn); (b) an element of discretion as to when the tasks could be done (as in repairs); and (c) greater leisure components (such as playing with the children). Lein (1984) similarly notes that husbands are most likely to relieve their wives of those tasks that are easiest and most rewarding. In child care, fathers are likely to choose socializing with their children. Tasks with more flexible schedules and those that stay finished longer are also more likely to be picked up by husbands.

These characteristics are extremely important to consider because they all have to do with the quality of the work, and, more specifically, its attractiveness. Oakley (1974) found that women's major complaints about housework were the monotony and the fragmentation of that work. In addition, most of the women who expressed dissatisfaction with housework also complained of loneliness. Thus existing evidence suggests that husbands take on tasks that are least likely to contain the characteristics about which wives most complained—leaving wives with the dirtiest of the dirty work. Lein (1984) remarks:

> Because the more flexible, longer-lasting chores are most likely to be assumed by men, women working in the home and on the job often find that, even as their husbands assume a greater share in the work of the home, the woman's share of the work becomes less pleasant, less flexible, and more frequently undone. Thus, fathers can be doing more without necessarily accomplishing a complementary improvement in mothers' lives. (p. xviii)

Unanswered Questions About Division of Household Labor

In-depth interviews with 72 couples on the specific division of housework were conducted by students enrolled in one of my undergraduate sociology courses over the 1985-1986 academic year. Their findings concur with these earlier observations. While these data are of course only suggestive, they raise some additional questions that further underscore the need for closer study of the qualitative aspects of household division of labor. If, as the evidence summarized above suggests, men who do housework take the jobs that are traditionally viewed as male and those that are considered the best jobs, will women actually choose to keep more than their fair share? Will they hesitate to cross over the division and mow the lawn or have the cars serviced if there is little ideological support for such a move and if there is no guarantee that they will not simply be adding more work to their load? Perhaps even more interesting to consider is the possibility that women keep virtually all the housework responsibility because, as Lein's comment suggests, otherwise, they are most likely to lose the most attractive, flexible, and social of the tasks and be left with the most monotonous, fragmented, and isolated chores.

The Berks' findings on father's involvement in after-dinner child care points up the need to delve further and ask what options in work are available at any one time, and who ends up with the most attractive task. Another subtle yet important difference that has yet to be studied in detail is the question of "responsibility for" versus "helping with." There is significant difference between knowing that someone will take on the responsibility for a task without being asked and having to make someone aware that the task needs doing and asking if he or she will do it. In the data collected by my students, several wives stated that they did a specific chore because it was just easier to do it themselves than to have to continually ask their husbands to do it. As an interesting sidenote, several also said they did the cooking or the laundry themselves because the few times the husband had done it, he had messed it up. Could husbands be engaging in a subtle form of domestic sabotage? Also, my students' data show that sharing of a task is an important aspect that needs to be considered. The most frequent chore husbands engaged in was grocery shopping, but it was not necessarily their responsibility. Rather, it had become an activity that the couple did together.

Finally, previous work (Berk and Shih, 1980) suggests that men and women do not always accurately estimate their time involvement in specific tasks. Men and women are likely to underestimate the time their spouses spend on sex-stereotyped chores, suggesting that neither may really know how much work is involved in the other's specific activities. Similarly, recent survey data (Harris and Gilbert, 1987) indicate that a much larger percentage of husbands than wives report sharing responsibility for what have traditionally been female tasks. My preliminary data also suggest that husbands define their involvement in the most egalitarian terms possible. For instance, one husband noted that he was responsible for making Sunday evening meals; the student interviewer footnoted her answer with the observation that his activity really consisted of picking up whatever take-out food he chose for that week. Another husband claimed he cooked his own dinners on evenings when his wife had meetings (supportive of the unavailability hypothesis), but his wife explained that she cooked his dinner and left it in the refrigerator with detailed instructions on how long to heat it. She also cleaned the dishes when she got home.

A Gender Stratification Framework

These unanswered questions show that, in spite of all we know about the division of household labor, there is still much that can be learned with a more detailed focus on quality of that division. However, such work, while substantively interesting in its own right, needs a theoretical base from which to emerge. During the 1970s and 1980s a number of frameworks have been offered in the attempt to explain wives' and husbands' relative contributions to household work. Huber and Spitze (1983) note four: time availability, relative power, sex-role attitudes, and taste for housework. Berk (1985) highlights the family power and the Marxist reproduction of labor power orientations as examples of "traditional frameworks" and uses the neoclassical New Home Economics. Finally Hiller (1984) summarizes six approaches: role differentiation, socialization-ideology, relative resources, time available, economic efficiency, and institutional independence.[3]

Each of these frameworks begins with household labor as the dependent variable and seeks then to build an explanatory framework. In doing so, each offers important insights into our understanding of the stability of such division in the face of enormous societal changes in women's roles. However, in spite of at least one attempt at bringing these disparate avenues of thought together (Hiller, 1984), the literature is still somewhat disjointed, and gaps remain. Moreover, Hiller's attempt at a more comprehensive model that focuses on the question of power dependence has as its dependent variable the ratio of husband's family work to wife's family work. In contrast, this chapter will suggest that our understanding can be enhanced by considering the question of household division of labor as an outcome variable within a larger theory of gender stratification, and exploration of the more detailed "niceness versus nastiness" quality of the tasks that are divided can perhaps attain the support that previous tests using a relative power model have not been able to consistently receive (Blood and Wolfe, 1960; Farkas, 1976; Huber and Spitze, 1983).

The theory of gender stratification presented is an adaptation of Blumberg's (1984) general theory of gender stratification to the U.S. marital dyad (see Blumberg and Coleman, 1989 for a detailed discussion of the model). While our model has roots in resource theory, its grounding in stratification theory enlarges it to consider a number of critical factors that early resource theory overlooked (such as the influence of culture; see Vanek, 1980).

In this model, we argue that a woman's overall economic power (operationalized as both the relative and absolute levels, and including the consideration of control over her income stream) within the marital dyad is affected by a number of "discount factors" at both the macro and micro levels that can enhance or diminish a woman's leverage in exercising her relative economic power. At the macro level, we suggest that the male-dominated hierarchy of the political economy, existing ideologies on gender, and birth cohort all affect the amount of power a woman can derive from her earnings. The micro-level discount factors exerting a similar but, in general, less powerful effect, include each partner's commitment to the relationship, attractiveness, and gender ideology as well as the husband's perception of need for the wife's income. This resultant "net economic power" is then available for women to gain leverage on a number of fronts within the couple relationship including fertility, economic, and domestic decisions; sexuality; and division of housework and child care.

Two final important intervening variables are (a) the stability versus the transitory nature of the economic balance and (b) class. We predict that there will be a different response in those cases in which the wife's economic power rapidly shifts in her favor (due to either an increase in her earnings or a decrease in his) as opposed to those in which the wife's relative power has been firmly established (consolidated) for a period of time. A husband who is suddenly confronted with what he considers an unfavorable shift in the couple's earnings ratio may perceive that change as a threat and attempt to counter his wife's power with his own.

Class is important to consider from the standpoints of both earnings and ideology. We know that, because of the limited range of earnings available to both males and females in unskilled or lower status jobs, the male/female earnings ratio among lower-class couples should be closer to parity than it is in middle-class and upper-middle-class couples where husbands quickly outdistance their wives in earning capacity. Moreover, higher-class couples are far more likely than their lower-class counterparts to get beyond a subsistence level of earnings to one of surplus. This subsistence versus surplus distinction will be particularly important on the question of the division of household labor (to be discussed in detail below). Finally, ideology also varies with class, with higher classes having been shown to hold more liberal and egalitarian ideals than lower classes (Mason and Bumpass, 1975; Mason, Czajka, and Arber, 1976).

While all these variables exert varying degrees of influence on the balance of power within the marital dyad, there are some general hypotheses that can be offered in the consideration of division of household labor within this model. I would predict that, *ceteris paribus:*

1. the greater a woman's net economic power, the more likely her husband will be involved in housework and child care;
2. the greater a woman's net economic power, the more likely her husband will see himself as "responsible" for tasks rather than "helping out"; and
3. the greater a woman's net economic power, the more equitable the division of the nice versus the nasty jobs between husband and wife.

While these three general relationships should hold, regardless of class, the process by which the ultimate responsibility for housework is determined within classes is actually a complex one involving the relationships summarized above between class and relative income and class and ideology. Furthermore, the two sets of relationships appear to predict opposite effects. The first, between class and relative income of spouses, would suggest greater household involvement of lower-class husbands and the second, between class and ideology, of middle- and upper-class husbands. Thus the three general hypotheses are not as straightforward or simplistic as they appear.

Let us consider lower-class couples first. Because, as suggested previously, the relative incomes of husbands and wives in these pairings are more likely to reach parity than in higher classes, I would expect these husbands to do more housework, to take more responsibility for such work, and to do more of the nasty tasks. On the other hand, these are the husbands who are both more likely to hold a traditional gender ideology and a traditional concept of division of household labor. Which factor will assert the strongest effect? Based on the general model, I would predict that relative income will not necessarily have a more powerful influence than ideology, but rather the third consideration, the presence of subsistence versus surplus income, will have an interaction effect with ideology. Specifically, husbands in lower-class families may find themselves unwilling participants in housework out of necessity. In such households where both spouses' incomes still provide only a subsistence-level income, men may be forced to take on housework and child care in spite of a traditional ideology that opposes such involvement. Some support for this prediction is offered in the Berks' study (1979), where they found that a major variable in husband's involvement was simply the wife's unavailability (most often due to shift work).

Furthermore, I would predict, that when such involvement takes place, it will be in the most desirable of the chores or, if it is indeed the dirty work, it will be only when there is no other person available to do it (as in the Berks' sample). And finally, when, out of necessity, the husband is forced to participate, I predict that he will do only the minimum amount to get the family's needs met until the wife is available to once again resume her appointed tasks. Thus he may fix dinner but it may be peanut butter sandwiches and canned soup—or he may get the children into bed on time but he may be tucking them into unmade beds.

For higher-class couples, there is a somewhat opposite but related set of relationships. Here, the inability of the wife to make much progress in closing the earnings gap between her and her husband would suggest that she would not have the power to be able to obtain much help from him. The more egalitarian ideology of higher classes, however, would predict an opposite effect. Again, the subsistence versus surplus consideration comes into play. For a couple that has surplus income, a third option becomes possible—he may make the decision to contract the work out so that he does not have to do it. In the event that such an option is not possible, or even to display his ideals of equality, the husband may take on a few of the more choice tasks so that his contribution can be seen and appreciated. His participation may actually be more symbolic or lip service to an ideal than a real commitment.

It is also important to remember that ideology exists at two levels in the model, the individual level and the societal level. Our gender stratification model suggests that the macro level exerts, in general, more influence than the micro level. A husband may voice an egalitarian viewpoint but actually be pulled more strongly by the more general sexist leanings of the macro level. Thus participation in a few high-profile, preferred chores may keep him in his wife's good graces when he is really not fully committed to a more liberal ideology.

Additionally, Lein (1984) found that the majority of couples in her sample who espoused an egalitarian ideology still allocated tasks in a sex-segregated fashion with wives taking on the housework because of their "expertise" and his higher salary. She concludes, "based on our sample, attitudes toward housework and the allocation of tasks do not appear to have a straightforward relationship to family ideology [whether it is viewed as an egalitarian or sex-segregated social system]. There may be considerable discrepancy between a family's professed ideology and its actual allocation of housework tasks" (p. 35). She also suggests that the practice of an egalitarian ideology may be difficult because the couple is breaking with the traditional model and the one they experienced as children, influences that can be defined as macro in origin. Lein does not take spouses' relative income into account, however, due to insufficient variation in her sample.

The solution to the housework situation in dual-earner, higher-class couples can become even more complex. For the growing number of young dual-professional couples where the earnings ratio may be near parity, the decision to contract this work out may reflect more of a stalemate on the issue rather than an opting out on the part of a husband who can afford it. In other words, her greater power afforded her by her high income gives her the right of refusal as well. Thus the goal for many affluent young couples is not to reach a more equitable division of labor but rather to get to the point where neither have to do the dirty work. In any event, the decision to contract out the housework to a third party must be carefully examined for this outcome may reflect a decision made by him to escape those duties, a statement by her that she refuses to bear the responsibility, or a joint decision reflecting the agreement that neither should have the burden.

And finally, an extremely interesting group to study will be those couples in which all three factors are present: surplus income, an equal or perhaps even greater than equal earnings ratio, and the stability of that income balance (i.e., cases in which the wife has consolidated her power). While this is still a small proportion of middle- and upper-middle-class couples, it is likely to be a group that will increase over the next few years as younger dual-career couples begin to reach the upper rungs of their professional ladders. We would expect these women to be in the most favorable position for exerting power and, in the division of housework, to have the most leverage in obtaining a favorable division of household labor.

Again, however, there may be some variation among these couples as well. Specifically, a subset of this group are those couples that are upwardly mobile, young ones in which the wife is earning more than the husband because she completed schooling prior to him. Here the student interviews also offer some suggestive data. Interviewers found that, even in this situation where the woman is working and earning the higher salary, men do not take on appreciably more housework. Indeed, his time at home, spent in study, is viewed as investment in the future and therefore assumes even more importance. Furthermore, even if her earnings have been high over a fairly long period of time, she may not be able to exert the power this consolidation would imply because the situation is viewed as a temporary situation that will be "corrected" once he completes schooling. While these couples certainly do not represent the total or even a majority of relationships with this earnings ratio, their reactions do suggest that other factors may be considered (or perhaps even seized upon) by husbands in unfavorable situations to keep the upper hand in the power balance.

In general, however, couples who have surplus income, where the woman makes as much or more than her mate, and this situation is stable (i.e., not viewed as a temporary condition), couples are "at the frontier." While they are still a relatively small group, they may well be an important bellwether group in two ways. First, they represent the clearest test of the hypotheses proposed above, and second, their answers to solving the dilemmas of housework and child care may have important policy implications for the future.

The extent to which these couples achieve partnership on the quality as well as quantity of housework and child care, opt for purchasing help, and even bypass part of the problem by curtailing fertility will be extremely important issues to unravel. To date, couples in which the wife wields economic power have not been the objects of systematic study. But because these couples are on the frontier of gender stratification and economic change, their arrangements and decisions may show us the future of women's double day, fertility trends, and the commercialization of housework and child care. In short, there are major macro-level consequences to how the micro-level burden of "reproductive labor" is distributed. A full exploration of the extent to which women's "net economic power" predicts these outcomes would seem to offer both social science and policy benefits.

In summary, the relationships among class, resources, and ideology are far from clear at this point, and their relative effects on the balance of power within couples, and more specifically as played out in the division of household labor, are far from being clearly defined. The purpose of this chapter, then, is twofold. First, it suggests that there is more to the question of household labor division than just who does what and for how long. While acknowledging that earlier researchers have recognized the need for more detail in the examination of housework, few have been able to really focus on the process by which the decision of who does what actually comes about. Some of the specific questions in need of future attention include:

1. what it is he does when the husband does it (particularly considering the nice versus nasty quality of the tasks);
2. whether he sees himself as being responsible for the task or merely helping out;
3. precisely when tasks are done (to address such particular factors as the availability of another person to do them, scheduling conflicts, and the urgency required);
4. options for participation in other tasks at the same time; and
5. whether or not the partner's definition of what he or she does is actually the work that is undertaken.

The second purpose of this chapter is to suggest that a general framework such as the Blumberg and Coleman model of gender stratification within marital dyads holds promise for the consideration of these more detailed issues and for the refinement of the resource theory perspective because it considers, at the same time, the complex added effects of gender role ideologies and presence of surplus versus only subsistence-level income. These are difficult questions that could well take a level of data gathering equal to or more complex than the Berks' massive time diary project. However, I believe that they are questions to which we must have answers if we are to fully understand the process by which couples have begun to divide up the tasks it takes to keep households running. We have made progress in changing our narrow-minded view that, not so long ago, substituted "women's work" for "housework." Yet I would venture to say that, in the decade and a half since Oakley's study, that change has only gone so far. If we were to interview her sample of wives today and again ask if their husbands ever changed the babies' diaper, we would probably get the same reaction from the two thirds of her wives who answered, "You're joking."

Notes

1. At this point in the discussion I am only interested in the substantive questions that recent empirical studies have attempted to address. An overview of the various theoretical frameworks that have guided much of this work appears below.

2. While Robinson refers to this 11.3 hours as a "paltry" contribution, it is still one of the highest estimates researchers offer for male participation. Part of the reason for the difference may be due to method of data collection, and specifically the fact that Robinson was categorizing all activity engaged in over a 24-hour period. Thus the tasks included under housework were likely to be more broadly defined. The time, however, is paltry when one notes that it was divided up between 3.5 hours of basic housekeeping, 4.2 on auxiliary tasks, 1.7 on child care (half of which was play), and the remainder on travel time.

3. Space precludes detailed elaboration of each of these frameworks, but it should be noted that some of these theories have received much more attention and development than others. There is a very large and well-developed literature on the Marxist/feminist reproduction of labor power. See Benston (1969) and Fee (1976) for classic discussions of this viewpoint and Hartmann (1981) for a more recent discussion. The resource theory literature has its roots in the classic Blood and Wolfe volume (1960) and was further developed by Farkas's (1976) and Scanzoni's (1978) work among others. Finally, the more recent focus on sex-role ideology as it relates to household division of labor is exemplified in the work by Berheide, Berk, and Berk (1976) and Perucci, Potter, and Rhoads (1978).

References

Barnett, Rosalind C. and Grace K. Baruch. 1987. "Determinants of Father's Participation in Family Work." *Journal of Marriage and the Family* 49:29-40.

Benston, Margaret. 1969. "The Political Economy of Women's Liberation." *Monthly Review* 21:13-27.

Berardo, Donna H., Constance L. Shehan, and Gerald R. Leslie. 1987. "Jobs, Careers, and Spouses' Time in Housework." *Journal of Marriage and the Family* 49:381-390.

Berheide, Catherine White, Sarah Fenstermaker Berk, and Richard Berk. 1976. *Pacific Sociological Review* 19:491-504.

Berk, Richard A. 1980. "The New Economics: An Agenda for Sociological Research." Pp. 113-148 in *Women and Household Labor,* edited by Sarah Fenstermaker Berk. Beverly Hills, CA: Sage.

—— and Sarah Fenstermaker Berk. 1979. *Labor and Leisure at Home.* Beverly Hills, CA: Sage.

Berk, Sarah Fenstermaker. 1985. *The Gender Factory.* New York: Plenum.

—— and Anthony Shih. 1980. "Contributions to Household Labor: Comparing Wives' and Husbands' Reports." Pp. 191-227 in *Women and Household Labor,* edited by Sarah Fenstermaker Berk. Beverly Hills, CA: Sage.

Blood, Robert O. and Donald M. Wolfe. 1960. *Husbands and Wives.* New York: Free Press.

Blumberg, Rae Lesser. 1984. "A General Theory of Gender Stratification." Pp. 23-101 in Sociological Theory 1984, edited by Randall Collins. San Francisco: Jossey-Bass.

—— and Marion Tolbert Coleman. 1989. "A Theoretical Look at the Gender Balance of Power in the American Couple." *Journal of Family Issues* 10:225-250.

Blumstein, Philip and Pepper Schwartz. 1983. *American Couples.* New York: William Morrow.

Coverman, Shelley and Joseph F. Sheley. 1986. "Men's Housework and Child-Care Time, 1965-1975." *Journal of Marriage and the Family* 48:413-422.

Farkas, George. 1976. "Education, Wage Rates, and the Division of Labor Between Husband and Wife." *Journal of Marriage and the Family* 38:473-484.

Fee, Terry. 1976. "Domestic Labor: An Analysis of Housework and Its Relation to the Production Process." *Review of Radical Political Economics* 8:1-8.

Harris, Louis and Gloria Gilbert. 1987. *The Phillip Morris Family Survey.* New York: Richard Weiner.

Hartmann, Heidi. 1981. "The Family as the Locus of Gender, Class, and Political Struggle: The Example of Housework." *Signs* 6:366-394.

Hiller, Dana V. 1984. Power Dependence and Division of Family Work. *Sex Roles* 10:1,003-1,019.

Hood, Jane C. 1983. *Becoming a Two-Job Family.* New York: Praeger.

Huber, Joan and Glenna Spitze. 1983. *Sex Stratification: Children, Housework, and Jobs.* New York: Academic Press.

Lein, Laura. 1984. *Families Without Villains.* Lexington, MA: Lexington Books.

Maret, Elizabeth and Barbara Finlay. 1984. "The Distribution of Household Labor Among Women in Dual-Earner Families." *Journal of Marriage and the Family* 46:357-64.

Mason, Karen O. and Larry L. Bumpass. 1975. "U.S. Women's Sex-Role Ideology." *American Journal of Sociology* 80:1,212-1,219.

Mason, Karen O., John L. Czajka, and Sara Arber. 1976. "Change in U.S. Women's Sex-Role Attitudes, 1964-1974." *American Sociological Review* 41:573-596.

Meissner, Martin. 1977. Sexual Division of Labor and Inequality: Labor and Leisure. In *Women in Canada,* edited by M. Stephenson. Toronto: Women's Educational Press.

Model, Suzanne. 1981. "Housework by Husbands." *Journal of Family Issues* 2:225-237.

Nichols, Sharon Y. and Edward J. Metzen. 1982. "Impact of Wife's Employment upon Husband's Housework." *Journal of Family Issues* 3:199-216.

Oakley, Anne. 1974. *The Sociology of Housework.* New York: Pantheon.

Perucci, Carolyn C., Harry R. Potter, and Deborah L. Rhoads. 1978. "Determinants of Male Family-Role Performance." *Psychology of Women Quarterly* 3:53-66.

Pleck, Joseph H. 1985. *Working Wives/Working Husbands.* Beverly Hills, CA: Sage.

Pleck, Joseph H. and Graham L. Staines. 1985. "Work Schedules and Family Life in Two-Earner Couples." *Journal of Family Issues* 6:61-82.

Robinson, John P. 1977. *How Americans Use Their Time*. New York: Praeger.

Ross, Catherine E., John Mirowsky, and Joan Huber. 1983. Dividing Work, Sharing Work, and In-Between: Marriage Patterns and Expression." *American Sociological Review* 48:809-823.

Scanzoni, John. 1978. *Sex Roles, Women's Work and Marital Conflict*. Lexington, MA: D.C. Heath.

Vanek, Joann. 1980. "Household Work, Wage Work, and Sexual Equality." Pp. 275-291 in *Women and Household Labor*, edited by Sarah Fenstermaker Berk. Beverly Hills, CA: Sage.

Warner, Rebecca L. 1986. "Alternative Strategies for Measuring Household Division of Labor." *Journal of Family Issues* 7:179-195.

Yogev, Sara and Heanne Brett. 1985. "Patterns of Work and Family Involvement Among Single- and Dual Earner Couples." *Journal of Applied Psychology* 70:754-768.

11

Money and Ideology
Their Impact on Power and the
Division of Household Labor

PHILIP BLUMSTEIN
PEPPER SCHWARTZ

The relationship between love and money was addressed by Engels (1884/1972) more than a century ago, but, curiously, his articulation of the impact of economics on relationships has been slow to influence the field of family research. In particular, a detailed discussion of how marriage is affected by differential access to, and authority over money has only in the past few years become a significant research area (e.g., Blumstein and Schwartz, 1983; Pahl, 1983; Blumberg and Coleman, 1989; Treas, forthcoming). If it were not for the long-standing concern with conjugal power, relative income might never have entered the list of variables treated in the family literature. Blood and Wolfe's (1960) pioneering work was the first major empirical research to consider money as a resource that might affect the balance of power between husbands and wives. Theirs was not an economic theory per se, but a theory of how each spouse might have a number of accumulated resources which would enhance power and influence in the marriage.

Resource theory, as originally proposed by Blood and Wolfe, was hotly debated for many years (e.g., Wilkening, 1968; Safilios-Rothschild, 1970). Critics argued that they had not taken into account cultural rules proscribing power for women that inhibited them from using their resources as effectively as men (Gillespie, 1971). Money,

AUTHORS' NOTE: The authors would like to thank Judith A. Howard and James C. McCann for advice on an earlier draft of this paper.

from this perspective, was not much of a resource for women because they generally have very little, and, when they have a substantial amount, they have been normatively inhibited from using it in a powerful way. By the time Blood and Wolfe's book was in its second decade, the general feeling among family sociologists was that their resource theory was inadequate for predicting conjugal power or other internal dynamics of the relationship. But even as resource theory per se has waned, research on money and its impact on marriage has received increased attention.

Since money in a capitalist society seems so patently associated with power, one can only believe that there was something about the cultural construction of western marriage that blinded social scientists until recently to the obvious importance of money in relationships. The ideology of companionate-partnership marriage made it difficult to look at the unseemly intrusion on the balance of power of variables that are supposed to have little to do with individual abilities and personalities. Even though we know that capitalism has a profound effect on culture and personality, it must have seemed too cold to imagine that money guides our deepest and most private relationships. Thus, except for Marxists and a few others guided by economic theories, the research community for many years uncritically accepted such concepts as *family income* without questioning how that income might actually be distributed. Recently, however, increasing empirical work has been addressed to the organization and distribution of family income (e.g., Pahl, 1983; Wilson, 1987; Blumberg, 1988). Our own initial analysis of 6,000 couples (Blumstein and Schwartz, 1983) indicates that the relationship between income and family dynamics is quite complex.

The inhibition to acknowledge the invasion of economic forces into something so "pure" and fine as love and marriage may also have reflected acceptance of the traditional division of labor in the family and its premise of "separate but equal" spheres of influence. We might have expected money to affect marital power when dowries were paid and lineages were maintained, but in modern America, where marriage is freely contracted and the couple is supposed to become a seamless entity, money was supposed to be a resource held in common, thereby giving neither party any advantage. To use an American sports metaphor, just because people are playing different positions on the team, does not mean a particular player is any less valuable—hence less powerful—than any other.

The impact of women's liberation philosophies and recent changes in women's labor force participation have caused scholars to question these assumptions. In an earlier work on couples (Blumstein and

Schwartz, 1983), we attempted to see how money might not only affect power in both institutionally approved and normatively variant relationships, but also have an impact on the division of labor in the household. We, like other researchers (Berk and Berk, 1979; Coverman, 1985), found that an equitable division of household labor was particularly resistant to the expected impact of women's participation in the labor force, and so we wanted to see exactly how work and money interacted to give women more or less influence in the home.

This paper attempts to refine our knowledge of how income, gender, power, and the division of labor interact in marriage. First, we wish to consider more than one way of measuring power. As others have said, there are different kinds of power and perhaps income affects each of them differently. Moreover, we wish to refine our knowledge of the circumstances under which a resource like money is active, and under which it is irrelevant. The power of money is not so easily discovered and we attempt to show in the analyses that follow that its impact on marriage is mediated by sex-role and marital ideologies, by the type of power struggle in progress, and by the kind of distribution system employed.

It is a truism to say that marriages are not all alike, but in the United States that simple statement is becoming truer by the day. As marriage and sex roles have become targets of sociopolitical critique, the variants on the traditional institution of marriage—both the bold and the inconspicuous—have proliferated, and many of these variants are ideologically guided. It is for this reason that we have considered ideological variations centrally in the data presented in this paper (see Blumberg and Coleman, 1989). Some sociologists would argue that talk is cheap (i.e., people may have ideological positions which they can easily express on such subjects as marriage and sex roles), but in reality those ideologies do not have any meaningful impact on behavior. For sociologists who hold this view, it is the material facts of life that are the true shapers of behavior and destiny. We enter this argument with the data of our study; we look at the undeniably material facts of income, and we look at ideology as well. As we sort through the findings, the data become the arbiters of the debate about the impact of ideology.

Method

The data for this paper are from a study that examined interpersonal relations in four types of couples: heterosexual married couples, unmarried heterosexual cohabiting couples, male homosexual couples, and lesbian couples (Blumstein and Schwartz, 1983). For the sake of reasonable brevity, this paper uses only the married sample ($N = 3656$).

Couples were sought for the study in a number of different ways, including the use of local and national broadcast and print media, solicitations in public gatherings (e.g., churches, synagogues, union meetings, PTA meetings), as well as some neighborhood canvassing. A lengthy questionnaire was completed independently by each partner in the couple. In general, the couples who returned questionnaires were predominately white and tended to be more educated than the nation as a whole. (See Blumstein and Schwartz, 1983, pp. 16-19 for a description of the recruitment process and pp. 593-602 for a statistical profile of the couples.)

Dependent Variables

In each of the two areas of couple life—housework and power—we have chosen several indicators for separate analyses. Our intention was to cover somewhat different facets of each area in order to provide a richer and more reliable picture.

Housework. We analyzed several housework measures. On the questionnaire, the variable *hours of housework* was measured with the question, "On the average, how many hours a week do you personally spend on household chores (including cooking, grocery shopping, laundry, etc.)?" Each spouse answered a separate questionnaire, yielding two individual level variables, *husband's housework* and *wife's housework*. The question was followed by nine response categories.[1]

Two additional housework items are couple-level measures based on the question, "Who does each of [the following] tasks more often, you or your partner?" The two items analyzed are *cooking the evening meal* and *doing the laundry*. These items were chosen because they represent two separate domains of traditional housekeeping, food preparation and cleaning, and unlike other potential items (e.g., cooking breakfast, vacuuming carpets) are performed in almost all couples' households.[2]

Relative power. Three measures of relative power have been included in separate analyses. The first, *decision-making power,* reflects the customary approach to power as control over decision making, and was worded, "In general, who has more say about important decisions affecting your relationship, you or your partner?" The other two items are responses to a general question, "Who is more likely to do each of the following things in your relationship, you or your partner?" The first of these items reflects the instrumental, directive connotation of the term power: "see oneself as running the show in our relationship" (*leadership power*). The other derives a reflection of relative power from its consequences: "give in to the other's wishes when one of us wants to do something the other does not want to do" (*conciliation power;* see Howard, Blumstein, and Schwartz, 1986).[3]

Independent Variables

Each spouse's income was measured in 1978-1979 dollars using 12 categories.[4] The mean income was $25,600 for all husbands and $8,300 for all wives. Among couples where both were employed full time, the comparable means were $23,700 and $14,900 (i.e., these women earned 63% as much as their husbands). We chose to use the two spouses' incomes as separate independent variables even though other analytic strategies were possible. The possibilities include the use of (a) a single spouse difference measure (adding as a control the couple mean income), (b) a single ratio measure of wife income to total couple income, or (c) the commonly used ratio of wife income to husband income. Our choice was largely motivated by the desire to be able to consider both husband effects and wife effects. However, the question lingers as to whether our choice affected the results. The first option of using couple difference and couple mean as two independent variables, it turns out, gives a simple transformation of the results using the technique we chose, but is less informative. Analyses were also performed using the ratio measures, and in no case was the substantive conclusions to be drawn from these analyses different from those discussed below.

Included in all regression equations were two additional variables ordinarily confounded with relative income, whose effects we wished to control: *relative age* and *relative educational level* within the couple. Both were measured in actual years. Because these relative measures are confounded with couple mean years of education and couple mean age, these two measures also were included in the equations.

Findings

Housework

All Married Couples

The effects of income on the housework of husbands and wives are shown in Table 11.1. The first two columns of Table 11.1, showing the regression coefficients in the total married sample, deserve particular attention, because this type of analysis—one based on a heterogeneous assortment of married couples—is typical of the approach often taken to the relationship between income and housework. The effects are strong and form an overall consistent pattern: both the husband's income and the wife's income are significant determinants of involvement in housework *for both spouses.* The man's income reduces his involvement and increases hers; similarly, her income frees her from housework and increases her husband's burden. This is true whether one considers hours of housework or the responsibility for particular tasks.

One might draw more precise conclusions from the unstandardized regression coefficients (*b*'s). For example, the slope for the regression of husband's hours of housework on husband's income is −0.707. This means that for each increment of $10,000 in a husband's income, his housework load diminishes by 0.707 hours (or approximately 42 minutes). The slope for the regression of *his wife's hours* on his income is +1.081, which means that as he gains each $10,000 in income, her housework increases by 1.081 hours (or approximately one hour and five minutes). Additionally, a $10,000 increment in a wife's income equates to an additional 36 minutes of housework for her husband (a slope of 0.604), but a reduction of four hours and 35 minutes for her (a slope of −4.583).

Further Analyses and Interpretations

We cannot, however, conclude our analysis with these simple findings based on the total sample of marriages, because they do not lead to a single clear interpretation. One of the possible lines of interpretation would focus on the capacity of income to buy the privilege of leisure, or at least freedom from household chores. Another might emphasize the ability of income to create power, which in turn affects the unequal distribution of housework. Before these interpretations can be accepted, however, we need to consider other principles which might account for the observed patterns. For example, on average, husbands and wives commit different amounts of time to the world of paid labor, and so the amount of time free to do housework is confounded with income.[5]

In order to consider this interpretation empirically, we calculated the same regression equations within a subset of couples, those in which both are employed full time (see the third and fourth columns in Table 11.1). Even though these couples represent a particularly modern form of Western marriage (and therefore give a biased view of that

Table 11.1 Regressions of Housework Measures on Husband's Income and Wife's Income[a]

	All Couples (N ≈ 3,600)		Dual-Earner Couples (N ≈ 1,200)	
	b	beta	b	beta
Husband's hours of housework				
Husband's income	−0.707	−0.182*	−0.356	−0.079*
Wife's income	0.604	0.098*	0.341	0.050
Wife's hours of housework				
Husband's income	1.081	0.115*	0.248	0.039
Wife's income	−4.583	−0.308*	−0.889	−0.092*
Relative contribution to cooking of evening meal[b]				
Husband's income	0.380	0.170*	0.060	0.021
Wife's income	−0.669	−0.189*	0.097	0.022
Relative contribution to laundry[b]				
Husband's income	0.543	0.218*	0.269	0.084*
Wife's income	−0.701	−0.177*	−0.089	−0.018

* $p < 0.05$.

NOTES: a. Unstandardized coefficients are multiplied by 10,000. All coefficients presented are net of couple mean age, age difference, mean education, and education difference. Among all couples, husband mean income is $25,600 (s.d. $15,300) and wife mean income is $8,300 (s.d. $9,600). Among dual-earner couples the husbands' mean is $23,700 (s.d. $13,100) and wives' mean is $14,900 (s.d. $8,600).

b. A *positive* coefficient indicates that the higher the income, the *less* the husband contributes to these activities relative to the wife.

institution), their heuristic value exceeds their representativeness because they allow us to begin to consider the effects of income on housework, net of participation in the paid labor force.[6]

Among these couples, as compared with the entire married sample, the relationship between income and housework is severely reduced. Support for the argument that income affects housework is greatly vitiated as one moves from the first two columns to the third and fourth columns in the table. While some of the relationships observed in the first set of regressions disappear altogether, there are some remaining coefficients which are worthy of discussion. For example, increases in the husband's income still reduced his own hours of housework, but much less than we might have concluded when looking at the entire sample. Similarly, increases in the wife's income reduced her labor, but much less than suggested by analysis of the total sample. It is important to note that in the dual-earner sample, a spouse's income does not affect the amount of housework of his or her partner. When we look at the two particular tasks, the relationships are especially weakened: Neither spouse's income affects the division of cooking responsibilities, while only husband's income has an impact on who does the laundry.

Let us consider the magnitudes of the unstandardized coefficients (b's), beginning with the effect of husband's income on husband's hours of housework, following a procedure similar to the one used earlier. On the basis of this coefficient (0.356) we infer that for every increase of $10,000 in his income, he performs 21 fewer minutes of housework. In contrast, an addition of $10,000 to the wife's income reduces her housework by about 51 minutes (−0.889). While we should not overlook the magnitude of this sex difference, we should also recall that these figures are much less striking than the ones derived from the entire sample.

The Part Played by Ideology

The dual-earner analyses can be used to support either of two arguments. On the one hand, we can emphasize the comparison to the full sample of marriages and argue that income effects are trivially small once both spouses are in the world of full-time paid employment. But the data also support the argument that even when labor force participation is factored out, a spouse's income does have a small, but noteworthy, impact on the housework performed by that person.

When we consider this second argument, however, we are left with a problem of interpretation. Two possibilities come to mind. The first is that the dual-earner couples are unique, not only in their pattern of labor force participation, but also because of an accompanying ideological departure from the patriarchal traditions of Western marriage. More precisely, they may have rejected the notion of *husband as good provider* (Bernard, 1981; Hood, 1986), and in rejecting the provider role, they reject the husband's unique responsibility for economically supporting other family members, as well as the implications of his responsibility for family organization. In other words, by questioning the husband's duty to provide, couples question whether his earning potential needs to be nurtured and enhanced by freeing him from housework. They may also be questioning the legitimacy of allowing him the privileged status implied by such freedom. Under this interpretation, it may be dual-earner couples' antiprovider ideology that induces a profound shift in consciousness, making them vigilant to what they may see as the deleterious influence of income, and which indeed shapes their household organization.

Table 11.2 Regressions of Housework Measures on Husband's Income and Wife's Income: Both Spouses Employed Full Time[a]

	Antiprovider Couples (N ≈ 370)		Male Provider Couples (N ≈ 240)	
	b	beta	b	beta
Husband's hours of housework				
Husband's income	−0.178	−0.038	−0.304	−0.077
Wife's income	−0.199	−0.029	0.183	0.027
Wife's hours of housework				
Husband's income	−0.073	−0.012	0.787	0.118
Wife's income	−0.500	−0.055	−2.212	−0.197*
Relative contribution to cooking of evening meal[b]				
Husband's income	0.026	0.008	0.093	0.036
Wife's income	0.001	0.000	−0.070	−0.016
Relative contribution to laundry[b]				
Husband's income	0.058	0.016	0.203	0.072
Wife's income	−0.083	−0.016	0.020	0.004

* $p < 0.05$.

NOTES: a. Unstandardized coefficients are multiplied by 10,000. The coefficients presented are net of couple mean age, age difference, mean education, and education difference. Among antiprovider couples, husband mean income is $22,000 (s.d. $12,300) and wife mean income is $15,400 (s.d. $8,300). Among male provider couples the husbands' mean is $25,100 (s.d. $13,600) and wives' mean is $13,200 (s.d. $8,100).

b. A *positive* coefficient indicates that the higher the income, the *less* the husband contributes to these activities relative to the wife.

We assessed this interpretation empirically by calculating the customary regression equations within two subsamples of the dual-earner couples: (a) those where both spouses endorse liberal antiprovider values and (b) those where both reject such liberal values.[7] The income effects from these regressions are shown in Table 11.2. The picture among the antiprovider couples, where none of the coefficients is significant, is unambiguous: *income has no relationship to housework, however measured.* The more traditional dual-earner couples, however, offer quite a different message. Among wives in couples who endorse the provider role, we continue to find a strong effect: their incomes reduce the amount of housework they do (2.21 hours per $10,000). At the same time, husbands' housework share seems impervious to income influences. On the basis of these data we may conclude that egalitarian antiprovider ideology plays a part in the reduced effect of income on housework which we observed among dual-earner couples.

Table 11.3 Regressions of Housework Measures on Husband's Income: Husband Breadwinner Couples ($N \approx 790$)[a]

	b	beta
Husband's hours of housework	−0.499	−0.156*
Wife's hours of housework	−0.453	−0.045
Relative contribution to cooking of evening meal[b]	0.109	0.088*
Relative contribution to laundry[b]	0.207	0.151*

* $p < 0.05$.

NOTES: a. Unstandardized coefficients are multiplied by 10,000. The coefficients presented are net of couple mean age, age difference, mean education, and education difference. Husband mean income is $30,600 (s.d. $15,400).
b. A *positive* coefficient indicates that the higher the income, the *less* the husband contributes to these activities relative to the wife.

Equity Considerations

This first interpretation focused on the fact that the composition of dual-earner couples includes a large number who have adopted a modern ideological approach to the marital institution. The second, and not incompatible, interpretation of the smallness of the income effects among dual-earner couples when contrasted to the effects in the entire married sample posits the operation of an implicit marital norm of equity, where time in the labor force is an alternative input to time spent in household chores. Under this formulation, income is not the operative force, but is simply a reflection of time in the labor force.

We can consider this interpretation empirically. Our approach here is not to focus on the dual-earner couples, but rather to inquire about the operation of a generalized marital equity norm. To do this we consider the traditional husband-breadwinner couples.[8] If there is an equity norm in these couples, then one would expect that if such wives were to move into the paid labor force, the organization of the household tasks would change. The logic behind the analyses performed on the husband-breadwinner couples is as follows: In these couples the wife is at home full time and has no earned income, and so there is no variation in either her income or in her labor force participation. Since we only look at couples where the husband is employed full time, there is also no variation in the husband's labor force participation. Under an equity formulation, where hours involved in various tasks are the operative inputs, we would have no reason to expect variation in husband's income to shape the division of household labor. This expectation is evaluated in Table 11.3.

The data show the expectation to be largely unfounded. The husband's income in these couples does not appear to affect his wife's hours of housework. Income does, on the other hand, clearly affect the husband's own contribution. Each increase of $10,000 relieves him of half an hour of housework (−0.499). We may also conclude that less time in both cooking and laundry is part of his reduced load.

Power and Privilege

It would appear, then, that for at least some marriages (traditional husband-breadwinner marriages), income has an impact on housework, above and beyond the labor force participation reflected by that income. These data cast doubt on a simple equity formulation based on time spent at work, but they are consistent with a power/privilege argument concerning husband's income and his involvement in household chores. It is possible to assess the power/privilege argument by adding measures of relative power as controls in the regression equations.[9] If power is the operating principle, the regression coefficients for husband's income should be reduced in these new equations.

The outcome of these analyses is not supportive of a power/privilege argument: If we look at the income effects for all four dependent variables, the change in slope is very small (varying between 0.15 and 0.32 standard errors), leading to the conclusion that the regression coefficients are virtually unchanged by the addition of the relative power measures. These analyses cast doubt on a simple power explanation of the income effects.[10]

Differences Between Spouses

We concluded above that income does not affect the household division of labor among dual-earner couples who ideologically oppose the husband-provider form of organization. One would expect that just as these couples have banished *income* as a determinant of their household labor, they might also have banished *biological sex,* itself, as a basis for their division of labor. This possibility is assessed by the data in Table 11.4.

Table 11.4 presents the mean levels of the housework measures for four samples. From left to right in the table, these are: (a) husband-breadwinner couples; (b) total married couples; (c) all dual-earner couples; and (d) the most extreme antiprovider couples.[11]

The means for husband's hours of housework show an interesting pattern. Husbands of employed wives do more housework than

Table 11.4 Means for Housework Measures

	Husband Breadwinner Couples	All Couples	Both Spouses Employed Full Time	
			All Couples	Antiprovider Couples
	(N ≈ 790)	(N ≈ 3600)	(N ≈ 1200)	(N ≈ 160)
Husband's hours of housework	5.28	6.57	7.33	8.40
Wife's hours of housework	32.64	21.34	13.87	12.01
Difference in hours of housework[a]	−27.26	−14.77	−6.54	−3.61
Relative contribution to cooking of evening meal[b]	6.60	5.17	4.09	3.38
Relative contribution to laundry[b]	6.79	5.20	4.01	2.67

NOTES: a. A negative score means the wife's hours exceed those of her husband.
b. A positive score means the wife's contribution exceeds that of her husband. The range is from −8 (husband does all) to +8 (wife does all), with zero meaning equal contribution.

husbands of homemakers, and antiprovider husbands do even more. And husbands of full-time homemakers do least. However, there is actually rather little variation among these groups.[12] Moreover, as we might expect (and others have found, e.g., Holmstrom, 1973), the wife's contribution decreases substantially as we move from left to right in the table: Employed wives do substantially less housework than full-time homemakers, and wives in sex-role liberal marriages do a bit less housework than typical employed wives.

The most striking findings are in the fourth column, where we locate the couples who have both dual employment and sex-role ideology conducive to equality in the household division of labor. Comparing the husbands' mean hours with the mean hours of their spouses shows a large and significant ($p < 0.05$) difference. Another way of saying this is that the couple difference mean (third row) is significantly greater than zero. Additionally, the two task item means are significantly different from zero ($p < 0.05$). These data forcefully show that *equality is far from being achieved in liberal dual-earner households* where the provider role is most forcefully rejected. Ideology, though perhaps potent, clearly has its limitations.

Table 11.5 Regressions of Power Measures on Husband's Income and Wife's Income[a]

	All Couples (N ≈ 3600)		Dual-Earner Couples (N ≈ 1200)	
	b	beta	b	beta
Decision-making power				
Husband's income	−0.152	−0.109*	−0.308	−0.205*
Wife's income	0.269	0.122*	0.336	0.147*
Leadership power				
Husband's Income	−0.243	−0.146*	−0.481	−0.253*
Wife's income	0.192	0.072*	0.379	0.131*
Conciliation power				
Husband's income	−0.043	−0.022	−0.104	−0.046
Wife's income	0.033	0.011	0.250	0.072*

* $p < 0.05$.

NOTE: a. Unstandardized coefficients are multiplied by 10,000. The coefficients presented are net of couple mean age, age difference, mean education, and education difference. A *positive* coefficient indicates that the higher the income, the *less* the husband's power relative to the wife's. Among all couples, husband mean income is $25,600 (s.d. $15,300) and wife mean income is $8,300 (s.d. $9,600). Among dual-earner couples the husbands' mean is $23,700 (s.d. $13,100) and wives' mean is $14,900 (s.d. $8,600).

Power

All Married Couples

Income effects on the relative power of spouses in the sample of all married couples are shown in Table 11.5. In the first two columns are the unstandardized and standardized regression coefficients for three dependent variables (decision-making power, leadership power, and conciliation power).[13] The greater the husband's income, the greater his decision-making and leadership power relative to his wife's. Likewise, the greater the wife's income, the greater her relative power on these two dimensions. Neither of these patterns obtains, however, for conciliation power, where the coefficients are very small. In sum, income affects the control over decision making and it affects patterns of leadership. It does not, however, have an observable effect on the third dependent variable, a measure of who wins when there is a conflict of interest, a measure which comes closest of the three to classical definitions of power (Weber, 1947; Blau, 1964).

The same distinction between *all couples* and *dual-earner couples* that was made in the housework analyses is found in Table 11.5. Here, however, the conclusions to be reached by moving from the regression coefficients on the left to those on the right are quite different. Whereas in the housework analyses (Table 11.1), the income effects observed in the total sample were substantially diminished in the dual-earner marriages, in the power analyses in Table 11.5, we see the reverse: the income effects are substantially *increased* in the dual-earner couples. In fact there is even a small but significant positive effect of the wife's income on conciliation power.

It is also worth noting that leadership power has a different relationship to husband's income than to wife's income. In order to offset the amount of leadership power gained for husbands by an increment of $10,000 in his income, wives need an increment of income of approximately $12,700 ($10,000 multiplied by .481/.379, the ratio of their unstandardized regression coefficients).[14] Given the sex-difference in mean income, it is appropriate to translate these figures into the number of hours it takes husbands and wives to "buy" equivalent leadership power. If we state the number of hours in terms of a ratio, then we find that these wives must, on average, work twice as many hours in paid employment (compared to their husbands) in order to acquire equivalent amounts of leadership power. By this same reasoning, we can consider the differences for conciliation power, (even though we are reluctant to make much of the husband's income coefficient). In this case, in order to counterbalance the conciliation power coming to a husband on the basis of an income increment of $10,000, his wife only needs an increment of approximately $4,200 ($10,000 multiplied by .104/.250, the ratio of the spouses' unstandardized regression coefficients). If we translate these figures into hours of paid employment, we see that wives, on average, must work 40 minutes as compared to their husband's 60 minutes, in order to achieve an equivalent increment in conciliation power.

Further Analyses and Interpretations

How might we account for the strong income effects in dual-earner couples? One possibility (following a line of argument similar to that used in the discussion of housework) is that some dual-earner couples take part in an ideological rebellion against traditional marital norms and understandings. The particular aspect of traditional family life we should investigate is the legitimacy of male authority. The man's traditional source of legitimate power has not derived from his income, or even directly from his ability to provide. Rather, it has emanated simply from his incumbency in the husband role. Following this reasoning, one

Table 11.6 Regressions of Power Measures on Husband's Income and Wife's Income: Both Spouses Employed Full Time[a]

	Antiauthority Couples (N ≈ 400)		Proauthority Couples (N ≈ 160)	
	b	beta	b	beta
Decision-making power				
Husband's income	−0.190	−0.168*	−0.547	−0.286*
Wife's income	0.287	0.157*	0.955	0.282*
Leadership power				
Husband's income	−0.260	−0.155*	−0.681	−0.295*
Wife's income	0.356	0.133	0.918	0.224*
Conciliation power				
Husband's income	−0.053	−0.025	−0.232	−0.099
Wife's income	−0.248	0.074	0.562	0.135

* $p < 0.05$.

NOTE: a. Unstandardized coefficients are multiplied by 10,000. The coefficients presented are net of couple mean age, age difference, mean education, and education difference. A *positive* coefficient indicates that the higher the income, the *less* the husband's power relative to the wife's. Among antiauthority couples, husband mean income is $22,900 (s.d. $13,500) and wife mean income is $15,700 (s.d. $8,400). Among proauthority couples the husbands' mean is $24,600 (s.d. $12,800) and wives' mean is $12,500 (s.d. $7,300).

should not be surprised if in traditional households the husband's power covaries only weakly with his income, or, for that matter, with his spouse's income. The operative source of power in these couples is traditional authority. In contrast, according to this line of reasoning, once couples have rejected male authority, they are thrown into a situation in which power derives more directly from the structure of the interpersonal relationships, not the least of which has to do with the distribution of valued resources. In this discussion the operative resources are the spouses' incomes.

We can examine this set of arguments empirically by repeating the regression analyses on subsets of the dual-earner couples chosen to reflect their ideological attachment to, or rejection of, husbandly authority.[15] In this analyses we expect to find stronger income effects within the antiauthority couples. The patterns of regression coefficients do not offer support for our argument (see Table 11.6). In fact, they are exactly the reverse of our expectations: for both decision-making power and leadership power, the income effects are significantly stronger in traditional proauthority couples than in the couples who reject husbands' authority.[16]

Based on these findings it is very difficult to sustain the notion that power in traditional couples derives so forcefully from male authority that resources such as income are irrelevant.[17] It is clear that no matter how much these couples legitimize the man's right to control, tradition and ideology do not stand in the way of a more resource-based power equation.

Our image of egalitarian marriages is also called into question by these data. Their lack of an institutionalized authority structure, we argued, would make them more vulnerable than traditional couples to the usual resource factors as determinants of relative power. Such is not the case, leaving us to speculate that their antiprovider ideology in some way tends to act as a brake on the unbridled effects of income. We might speculate that couples who accept the principle of patriarchal authority are oblivious to the political issue of conjugal power, while more egalitarian couples are both troubled by any power differences in their marriage, and are to some extent aware of how income (and other resources) may be an activating agent. In this interpretation, egalitarian couples' wariness of power differences extends to a conscious effort to subvert the usual equation linking resources with power.

Power and Dependency

The search for the source of the observed power differences in marriage has intrigued family researchers for decades. From Blood and Wolfe (1960) forward, the question of how resources enter into the picture has been a continuing basis for debate. But agreed (implicitly or explicitly) by virtually all participants in the debates has been an acceptance of *dependency* as the operating link between such resources as income, on the one hand, and conjugal power on the other. Seldom, however, have family researchers directly measured relative dependency between spouses, in order to evaluate how much this factor enters into the power formulation.

We have attempted to look at this question by introducing into the regression analyses measures of the spouses' relative dependency, in order to see how much their addition reduces the observed relationships between income and our measures of relative power.[18] The causal model being suggested is that as one's income increases relative to one's spouse, one's relative dependency decreases. As relative dependency decreases, one becomes more powerful (Emerson, 1962). In this model, dependency is an intervening variable between income and power.

The regression analyses are summarized in the third and fourth columns of Table 11.7. For both decision-making power and leadership

Table 11.7 Regressions of Power Measures on Husband's Income and Wife's Income, Incorporating Mediating Variables: Both Spouses Employed Full Time ($N \approx 1200$)[a]

Mediators	No Mediators		Dependency		Assertiveness	
	b	beta	b	beta	b	beta
Decision-making power						
Husband's income	−0.308	−0.205*	−0.233	−0.155*	−0.170	−0.113*
Wife's income	0.336	0.147*	0.251	0.110*	0.223	0.098*
Leadership power						
Husband's income	−0.481	−0.253*	−0.358	−0.188*	−0.275	−0.144*
Wife's income	0.379	0.131*	0.243	0.084*	0.207	0.071*
Conciliation power						
Husband's income	−0.104	−0.046	−0.113	−0.050	0.054	0.024
Wife's income	0.250	0.072*	0.264	0.076*	0.130	0.037

* $p < 0.05$.

NOTE: a. Unstandardized coefficients are multiplied by 10,000. The coefficients presented are net of couple mean age, age difference, mean education, and education difference. A *positive* coefficient indicates that the higher the income, the *less* the husband's power relative to the wife's.

power, the income effects of husbands and wives are substantially reduced by the addition of dependency to the regression equations. Even after controlling for dependency, however, the income coefficients still remain significant. For conciliation power, the substantial coefficient for the wife's income is left virtually unchanged by the addition of the dependency measures. On the basis of these analyses we conclude that dependency does intervene between income and decision-making power and between income and leadership power, but not between income and conciliation power. Additionally, dependency does not fully account for any of the observed relationships between income and power.

Income and Assertiveness

Another possible explanation for the observed link between income and power may be one of spuriousness. According to this approach, income accrues disproportionately to the spouse who has certain characteristics prized in the economic marketplace (i.e., ambition, talent, drive, aggressiveness, forcefulness, and so forth). Additionally, these are precisely the qualities that lead to that spouse's having greater power or leadership in his or her marriage. In this argument, income is spuriously related to power through the variable of assertiveness. We tested this hypothesis by introducing several relative assertiveness measures into the regression equations and observing any reductions in the income effects (see the last two columns in Table 11.7).[19]

The reduction in the income effects wrought by the inclusion of the assertiveness control variables is noteworthy. This is true for both spouses in the area of decision-making power and leadership power, and for wife's income in the realm of conciliation power. In the case of both decision making and leadership, however, the income effects net of assertiveness, while weakened, continue to be statistically significant.

On the basis of these analyses we conclude that for the three power variables, much, but not all, of the relationship between income and power reflects individual differences in personality between spouses. These individual differences in assertiveness, we would argue, are related in a complex dynamic way with the entire sex stratification system, a system in which beliefs about the qualities that men and women bring to their work are a crucial part. Nevertheless, whatever the source of these individual differences, they are conceptually distinct from money as a resource, and they must be considered when we make conclusions about the relationship between power and income.

Pooling

The substantial empirical literature relating income to spousal power within modern Western marriages has only recently begun to deal with what happens to the income after it has entered the household (exceptions are Pahl, 1983; Treas, forthcoming). Other literature (e.g., Blumberg, 1984, 1988), focusing on cross-cultural comparisons, has argued that wives' incomes only affect their power to the extent that they retain control over that income.

An evaluation of this hypothesis in the modern American case is difficult for a number of reasons. First, legal issues of community property to some extent define the situation for spouses. Second, community property, legally sanctioned or not, is institutionalized and richly sanctified in the ideology of American companionate marriage. Moreover, even when couples struggle to keep their assets separate, a number of complicating factors emerge. For example, certain purchases to which their incomes may be dedicated (e.g., home, automobile, children's education) require that at least part of both incomes be merged, and even though strict guidelines about how each spouse contributes to that merger may be enunciated, as a matter of practicality it is very difficult for either spouse to sustain the notion that the two funds are unmerged.

Finally, even when some middle-class wives do keep their earnings separate from their husbands' their money generally is earmarked for several special classes of purchases (i.e., family luxuries; personal luxuries; or replacement of the wife's services, through the employment of a housekeeper or babysitter). The wife "buys" her way out of her traditional duties; she is *not* given standing as a payer of basic debts and contributor to the elemental parts of the family's standard of living. More important, this symbolic division of the functions of breadwinner income versus wife income bolsters the institution of husband-provider. Because of this complex array of factors, we are inclined to be reluctant about making strong predictions about when and how the pooling or nonpooling of incomes affect the power those incomes bring.

We have attempted to test the pooling notion empirically. It is very difficult, given the foregoing discussion, to measure to what extent, and how, couples merge their incomes. We do, however, have an attitude measure regarding the desirability of pooling incomes.[20] As a first step in our consideration of pooling we added our pooling attitude measure into the regression analyses. For none of the three dependent variables did the unstandardized regression coefficient for the wife's pooling attitude exceed an absolute value of 0.05. Moreover, in none of the analyses did the wife's income coefficient drop by more than an absolute value of 0.01.[21]

This preliminary simple additive model is probably not a proper representation of Blumberg's conceptualization. Rather it might be preferable to consider income effects *within* couples who reject pooling, as compared with those who accept this form of economic organization. In order to assess the question posed in this manner, we replicated the original regression analyses separately in couples who favor the pooling of incomes and assets, and in couples who favor keeping money and property separate. Selected findings from these analyses are presented in Table 11.8.

The pattern of regression coefficients is quite striking, but not supportive of Blumberg's thesis. In the pooling marriages, where the wife's income ought to disappear into collective holdings and therefore not translate into power, female income does have significant effects on power.

Among couples who wish to keep money separate, Blumberg's thesis would lead to the conclusion that women's income would give them power. But the data in Table 11.8 show just the opposite. For none of the power measures is there a significant coefficient. If we may take the

Table 11.8 Regressions of Power Measures on Wife's Income: Both Spouses Employed Full Time, Varying by Attitudes toward Income Pooling[a]

	Propooling Couples (N ≈ 285)		Antipooling Couples (N ≈ 105)	
	b	beta	b	beta
Decision-making power	0.384	0.174*	0.209	0.106
Leadership power	0.609	0.243*	0.141	0.048
Conciliation power	0.390	0.128	0.258	0.081

* $p < 0.05$.

NOTE: a. Unstandardized coefficients are multiplied by 10,000. The coefficients presented are net of husband income couple mean age, age difference, mean education, and education difference. A *positive* coefficient indicates that the higher the income, the *less* the husband's power relative to the wife's. Among propooling couples, husband mean income is $25,400 (s.d. $13,000) and wife mean income is $15,500 (s.d. $10,400). Among antipooling couples the husbands' mean is $23,800 (s.d. $14,200) and wives' mean is $16,100 (s.d. $9,300).

perilous jump from pooling attitude to pooling behavior, we may conclude that wives' income does not bring them power when that income is kept separate from the joint household resources.

How can we account for this pattern of results? One possibility is that there may be multiple arrangements for wives to keep their money separate from that of their husbands. In one arrangement, as described earlier, a wife's income pays for luxuries (either her own or the family's) or for replacement of her services (housecleaning or childcare). In this situation her symbolic dependency on her husband as legitimate provider is unchallenged and consequently her income does not free her from the dependency of patriarchal marriage. In another arrangement, the wife keeps her income unmerged with that of her husband, but she accepts a substantial financial responsibility for the everyday maintenance of the household, and consequently her husband has ample opportunity to develop a significant fiscal dependency and thereby her income translates into power.

We can consider these two arrangements empirically by comparing two subcategories among couples who reject pooling. The first subcategory includes those who *reject the husband-provider idea,* and where we predict an income effect. The second subcategory of antipoolers includes couples who *accept the norm of the husband as provider,* and where we predict no effects of wife's income.[22] When the appropriate regression analyses are performed, the results bear moderate correspondence to these predictions. Among the first subcategory, couples who reject the legitimacy of husband as the provider (N ≈ 170), the regression coefficients for the three dependent variables are: decision-making power: $b = 0.298$ (*beta* = 0.189); leadership power: $b = 0.377$ (*beta* = 0.161); and conciliation power: $b = 0.386$ (*beta* = 0.139). The coefficient for decision making is statistically significant ($p < 0.05$), while the leadership coefficient does not quite achieve significance ($p < 0.09$), and the conciliation coefficient is not significant. Taken together, these findings suggest support for the hypothesis that keeping money separate gives power to wives in couples who reject the husband provider role (compare Blumberg, 1988).

Among the second subcategory, couples who *accept* the provider role ($N = 130$), the regression coefficients are, respectively, $b = 0.361$ (*beta* = .108); $b = -0.117$ (*beta* = -0.029); and $b = 0.019$ (*beta* = 0.005). None of these coefficients is significant and so these data do not allow us to conclude that income affects wives' power. From these analyses we may cautiously conclude that, for wives, keeping money separate does allow that money to give power, but *only* if that money has potential consequences, both symbolic and real, for the economic management of the household. Moreover, the mechanisms that support the institution of the provider husband rob women's income of the capacity to bring them power (compare Blumberg and Coleman, 1989).

Discussion

By looking at different kinds of marriages, we have been able to refine some observations on the interaction of gender, power, and housework. It is clear that the picture changes depending on whether one considers all married couples, or only dual-earner couples. This is true for a number of reasons, but the most important is that income is confounded with time available for housework. The advantage of concentrating on two-earner couples is that time available is held constant. The disadvantage, of course, is that our discussion must necessarily represent only one version of marriage, and not the most traditional one at that.

Looking at the findings for dual earners, we saw that income does affect who does more housework, but the effects are substantially weaker than we might have expected. A husband's high income releases him from housework, and a wife's high income allows her to do less, but in generalizing about the power of money, one has to note that *neither* spouse's income affects the *other's* housework. It does not appear to be the case that as one spouse does less (by virtue of an increase in income), the other makes up the difference. A high-earning partner may feel entitled to do less housework, and his or her partner may agree that a high earner should not have to be burdened with as many household duties (Blumstein and Schwartz, 1983). However, one spouse's liberation, we have learned, has nothing to do with an equalization of the division of labor. There seems to be no commonly held norm that automatically compels the partner of a high-earning spouse to contribute more. As a result, as more women enter the labor force and the income gap between the sexes declines, we might anticipate an overall decrease in the number of hours spent in household labor.[23]

Marital and sex-role ideologies play an important part in whatever relationship exists between income and housework. The male provider complex is so important that if a couple rejects it, then the spouses' incomes have no relationship to the division of labor in the household. However, if the male provider role is in force, women can reduce their housework by increasing their income. Perhaps their higher income gives them new freedoms because they have encroached on the privileges of the provider. While the primacy of ideology and its interaction with income seem to be a major explanation of the division of labor, the data do *not* support the idea that income affects power which, in turn, affects the distribution of housework. Power is apparently not the key explanatory variable.

On the other hand, one should not overinterpret our finding that those liberal couples who have rejected the provider role are less likely to let income differentials control the division of labor. While these couples may resist being controlled by the principles of the provider role, they do not institute a completely egalitarian household. The chores are not divided equally. Patriarchy is not dead.

There *is* a relationship between income and power, even if it does not account for variation in the division of household labor. Income does shape power when it is defined as control over decisions and when it is defined as who is the leader in the relationship. However, income's effects are much less clear when power is defined in terms of who wins and who yields when there is a conflict between the two spouses' desires. While this latter measure is least consistent with the way power has been operationalized in family research, it is most consistent with the way power has been conceptualized in sociology. What it may mean is that while income gives leadership it is not considered legitimate to exert power based on income in a partnership marriage. The ideology of modern marriage promotes give and take, allocates spheres of interest and primacy, and even has norms of considerate conciliation and retrenchment. The high earner may be able to invoke superiority on decisions because high income confers authority, but it is not legitimate in most marriages to have the leader—or even the "wiser person"—win all interspousal conflicts.

Interestingly, income's effects on power are stronger in dual-earner couples than in the entire sample. Trying to understand why, we considered the idea that in traditional one-earner couples patriarchy is the operative principle, and the distribution of power derives from male authority. This reasoning would suggest that there is no reason for income to matter. By way of contrast, we felt that in more modern marriages, where male authority is absent, market forces would take over and income would translate directly into power. This argument might seem convincing, but when we tested it with data, it was not supported. In fact, income affects power *more* in couples who support a male-authority ideology than in those who reject it.

What may be happening here is that traditional male-authority couples have affirmed a capitalistic ideology of service in exchange for support. Thus a husband who is a very good provider becomes more entrenched in and deserving of power, whereas a provider who fails to earn well is less legitimate and, therefore, less able to enforce demands or unilaterally make decisions. Ideology and income interact, granting greater power in traditional marriages to one spouse, but antiauthority ideology can greatly reduce or erase that advantage. We have been able to show that in those kinds of couples where money translates into power it is, in part, because differences in income create differences in dependency which shape the manifestation of power (see Blumberg and Coleman, 1989).

It also is important to consider individual characteristics as possible intervening variables. It is possible that income and power are both spuriously related to assertiveness, here conceived of as ambition, forcefulness, aggressiveness, and competence. Some agree that the kind of person who makes all that money is going to be dominant and that income is merely an expression of personality rather than the reason, in and of itself, for power in the relationship. Our data show that individual difference variables do influence power, but not entirely. Money still matters.

One final ideological element, orientation to private versus commingled resources, takes an important place in the power dynamics of married life. At first glance, our findings on pooling resources are not in accord with earlier cross-cultural work (Blumberg, 1988). Upon further specification, however, we discover greater convergence. We found that a wife's income only affects her power if she also rejects the idea of a male provider. In other words, if a wife keeps her money separate, her belief that her husband is the real provider undermines her independence and clout. Instead of creating a separate power base, she is merely excepting herself from what is probably the larger pool of money and just keeping a small amount of money for her own purposes. This "pin money" or household expense money, or money for luxuries, or even money used to run her whole life, is not part of the family's corporate monies and therefore she loses her right as a major "stockholder" to vote the "company's shares." Nonpooling can be a powerful tactic, but only if the nonpoolers have an ideology of corporate equality and partnership in the marriage.

Conclusion

We began this chapter with some speculations about why for many years scholars seemed so resistant to confronting the relationship between love and money. We focused on the cultural imagery that has infused American marriage, rich romantic imagery emphasizing the unity of the family, as though two spouses had but a single will, as though marriage were an ideal communist state, where incoming resources are unmarked, the immediate property of the collectivity.

It is impossible to get the historical distance necessary to judge whether this cultural imagery is alive and well, or whether it is dying without us being aware of its decline. We can, however, hypothesize some very real events that seem highly likely to modify, if not destroy, the romantic notions that make serious thought about love and money seem so repugnant. First, a legacy of women's liberation is a move on the part of many women to define themselves in terms of their relationship to the economy of paid employment, and there is no evidence that the economy is moving away from the use of dollars as a yardstick for measuring human worth and for defining human deserts.

More generally, the movement for women's liberation has raised the issue of justice for women in their relations with men. In particular, this can be translated into a question of the relationship between love and justice. Once justice is on the agenda, the question arises as to how a "just marriage" is to be defined. And in the defining process through which couples pass, it will be almost inevitable that the part played by resources enters the conversation.

Second, the "divorce revolution" has challenged the wisdom of subordinating individual welfare to the goals of the collectivity. It has become difficult to create the personal innocence necessary to render all income and property irretrievably collective. The battle between *ours, yours,* and *mine* becomes more salient in individual consciousnesses and more prominent in public discourse on intimacy. But the divorce revolution has spawned its own set of reactions, one of which is a longing for an imagined past. This breeds a desire to be able to submerge oneself into one's marriage in hopes of stabilizing its future. But this submergence has long been a major concomitant of women's oppression, and so this state of reaction does battle with the concerns about justice that seem unlikely to disappear.

Finally, the hegemony of a dominant version of marriage has disappeared, and each of the many new versions that have replaced it has its own accompanying body of ideological principles. *Ideology does make a difference.* And, as we have seen in this paper, those ideological principles focus on issues of resources, work, sharing, fairness, power, and authority. And, as we have also seen, these principles shape the actual connections between money and how couples live their lives.

Notes

1. The response categories were *none* (1); *five hours or less* (2); *six to ten hours* (3); *eleven to twenty hours* (4); *twenty-one to thirty hours* (5); *thirty-one to forty hours* (6); *forty-one to fifty hours* (7); *fifty-one to sixty hours* (8); and *more than sixty hours* (9). Responses were recoded to the midpoint of the category (for example, a response of between twenty-one and thirty hours per week was recoded to twenty-five hours.

2. These items were scored on a 9-point scale ranging from *I do this all the time* (1), through *We do this equally* (5), to *He[she] does this all the time* (9). In the regression analyses, responses by both partners were combined to create couple measures. We analyze cooking and laundry measures separately because factor analyses indicate that these two domains are independent.

3. All three power items were scored just like the cooking and laundry items, except that the conciliation item was reverse scored to give consistency. Additionally, for all three, individual responses were combined to construct couple measures.

4. These were: *no income* (1); *less than $2,500* (2); *$2,500 to $4,999* (3); *$5,000 to $7,499* (4); *$7,500 to $9,999* (5); *$10,000 to $12,499* (6); *$12,500 to $14,999* (7); *$15,000 to $19,999* (8); *$20,000 to $24,999* (9); *$25,000 to $29,999* (10); *$30,000 to $49,999* (11); and *$50,000 or more* (12). Again, as with hours of housework, the responses were recoded to the midpoint of the category.

5. For this paper we have assumed that hours of housework are what "remains" in a person's day after he or she has "contributed" time to employment. Although we have followed this assumption, there is also virtue in considering a reverse causal order, where time in paid employment is (negatively) "caused by" time spent in domestic activities. Some of the researchers who treat hours in household labor as the *independent* variable include Coverman (1983) and Shelton and Firestone (1989).

6. We have chosen to compare a dual-earner subsample to our overall married sample rather than simply introduce employment status variables as controls because we do not wish to assume that the relationships between income and various dependent variables are uniform across groups who have very different kinds of marriages.

7. Couples were treated as antiprovider when both spouses answered 1, 2, or 3 on a 9-point *strongly agree* to *strongly disagree* item: "The two partners [in a marriage] should

share the responsibility for earning a living for the household." They were treated as conservative if both answered 5, 6, 7, 8, or 9.

8. Husband-breadwinner couples were operationally defined as husbands who are employed full time and wives who respond to the employment question by choosing the alternative, "Taking care of the household is my full-time job."

9. The power items are the three described in the section titled "Methods."

10. One danger from drawing conclusions from the husband-breadwinner couples lies in whether the findings are a product of a traditional division of labor (where only the husband is employed) or whether they reflect what may be, in such couples, an ideological acceptance of patriarchal principles. To assess this question, we repeated the regression analyses of substantive interest, adding as controls measures of each spouse's attitudes toward the absolute legitimacy of the provider role. The purpose of these analyses was to see if the addition of these controls would reduce the effects of husband's income. The change in the coefficient for husband's hours was almost nonexistent, from -0.499 to -0.490. The change for cooking was from 0.109 to 0.077 (standard error of 0.052), and for laundry, from 0.207 to 0.154 (standard error of 0.057). These analyses suggest that ideology does not account for the husband's income effects.

11. For the comparisons in this table, antiprovider couples were chosen in a maximally extreme fashion, with both spouses endorsing 1 (*strongly agree*) on the relevant item.

12. Similar findings on the invariance of husbands' involvement in housework have been reported for example, by Clark, Nye, and Gecas (1978).

13. The zero-order correlations among the three power measures are as follows: decision making with leadership—$r = 0.592$; decision making with conciliation—$r = 0.306$; leadership with conciliation—$r = 0.359$.

14. This difference may be an example of what Blumberg and Coleman (1989) refer to in their discussion of discount factors.

15. We operationalized this variable with the attitude statement: "Even if the wife works the man should have major responsibility for the couple's financial plans." On this 9-point scale, couples were defined as antiauthority if both spouses chose 7, 8, or 9 at the *strongly disagree* end, and they were defined as proauthority if they both chose 1, 2, 3, or 4 at the *strongly agree* end. The same analyses were performed with a different ideology measure, "It is better if the man works to support the household and the woman takes care of the home," and the results were very similar.

16. For each dependent variable, statistical significance was inferred ($p < 0.05$) by comparing R^2 for two regression equations: (a) the usual regression equation based on all of the couples contained in Table 11.6, with the addition of a dummy variable representing the two couple subcategories, and (b) this latter equation with two interaction terms added for the dummy multiplied by each of the income measures.

17. Further support for this conclusion comes from an analysis of husband income effects within husband-breadwinner couples ($N \approx 790$). The regression coefficients for the three power dependent variables are: decision making: $b = -0.169$ (*beta* = -0.122, $p < 0.05$); leadership: $b = -0.373$ (*beta* = -0.277, $p < 0.05$); and conciliation: $b = -0.134$ (*beta* = -0.069, n.s.). These coefficients suggest that even in these most traditional of couples, husbands with greater income have greater power in decision making and in leadership.

18. A number of measures of relative dependency were developed. The first three specific measures were based on the question, "If something were to happen to your partner and you were forced to live without him[her], how difficult would it be for you to do each of the following?" The response format was a 9-point scale ranging from *extremely difficult* (1) to *not at all difficult* (9). The three relative dependency measures were the signed couple differences on the following items: *avoid loneliness, find another*

partner, and *maintain my present standard of living.* The fourth more global measure was worded: "If you and [your partner] . . . decide[d] to end your relationship, whose life would this disrupt more, yours or his[hers]?" The 9-point scale ranged from *mine much more* to *his[hers] much more.* For this item, the two spouses' responses were combined to create a couple measure. The last two measures were (a) differences between the partners' self-assessed self-sufficiency and (b) between the partners' ratings of each other's self-sufficiency. Even though there is considerable substantive redundancy in these several dependency items, it was felt that by including them all as simultaneous controls, we would maximize the impact of dependency as an independent variable.

19. A large number of partner difference scores were included among the assertiveness items. Five self-assessed items were: *aggressive, forceful, outgoing, ambitious,* and *accomplished in [one's] chosen field.* Five partner-rated items were identical. Again, there is substantial redundancy in these items, but we felt that by including them all, we would maximize the impact of assertiveness as a control variable.

20. The *agree-disagree* 9-point questionnaire item was worded, "The two partners should pool all their property and financial assets." An individual was considered to favor pooling if he or she answered 1, and to oppose pooling if she or he chose 5, 6, 7, 8, or 9.

21. The same analyses using husband's pooling attitudes showed similar disappointing results.

22. To avoid sample-size limitations, in these analyses we based subsample selection on only the wives' ideology measures.

23. We have not been able to discuss in this paper how much paid housework is beginning to replace that of wives and husbands who have high-paying jobs.

References

Berk, Richard A. and Sarah F. Berk. 1979. *Labor and Leisure at Home.* Beverly Hills, CA: Sage.

Bernard, Jessie. 1981. "The Rise and Fall of the Good Provider Role." *American Psychologist* 36(January):1-12.

Blau, Peter M. 1964. *Exchange and Power in Social Life.* New York: John Wiley.

Blood, Robert O., Jr. and Donald M. Wolfe. 1960. *Husbands and Wives: The Dynamics of Married Living.* New York: Free Press.

Blumberg, Rae Lesser. 1984. "A General Theory of Gender Stratification." Pp. 23-101 in *Sociological Theory 1984,* edited by Randall Collins. San Francisco: Jossey-Bass.

————. 1988. "Income Under Female Versus Male Control: Hypotheses from a Theory of Gender Stratification and Data from the Third World." *Journal of Family Issues* 9(March):51-84.

Blumberg, Rae Lesser and Marion Tolbert Coleman. 1989. "A Theoretical Look at the Gender Balance of Power in the American Couple." *Journal of Family Issues* 10: 225-250.

Blumstein, Philip and Pepper Schwartz. 1983. *American Couples: Money, Work, and Sex.* New York: William Morrow.

Clark, Roberta, F. Ivan Nye, and Viktor Gecas. 1978. "Husbands' Work Involvement and Marital Role Performance." *Journal of Marriage and the Family* 40(February):9-21.

Coverman, Shelley. 1983. "Gender, Domestic Labor Time, and Wage Inequality." *American Sociological Review* 48(October):623-637.

————. 1985. "Explaining Husbands' Participation in Domestic Labor." *Sociological Quarterly* 26(April):81-97.

Emerson, Richard M. 1962. "Power-Dependence Relations." *American Sociological Review* 27(February):31-41.

Engels, Friedrich. 1972. *The Origin of the Family, Private Property, and the State,* (A. West, Trans.). London: Lawrence & Wishart. (Original work published 1884)

Gillespie, Dair L. 1971. "Who Has the Power? The Marital Struggle." *Journal of Marriage and the Family* 33(August):445-458.

Holmstrom, Lynda L. 1972. *The Two-Career Family.* Cambridge, Mass.: Schenkman.

Hood, Jane C. 1986. "The Provider Role: Its Meaning and Measurement." *Journal of Marriage and the Family* 48(May):349-359.

Howard, Judith H., Philip Blumstein and Pepper Schwartz. 1986. "Sex, Power, and Influence Tactics in Intimate Relationships." *Journal of Personality and Social Psychology* 51(July):102-109.

Pahl, Jan. 1983. "The Allocation of Money and the Structuring of Inequality within Marriage." *The Sociological Review* 31(May):237-262.

Safilios-Rothschild, Constantina. 1970. "Study of Family Power Structure: 1960-69." *Journal of Marriage and the Family* 32 (November):539-552.

Shelton, Beth Anne and Juanita Firestone. 1989. "Household Labor Time and the Gender Gap in Earnings." *Gender & Society* 3(March):105-112.

Treas, Judith. Forthcoming. "Money in the Bank: Transaction Costs and Privatized Marriage." *American Sociological Review.*

Weber, Max. 1947. *The Theory of Social and Economic Organization.* New York: Oxford University Press.

Wilkening, E. A. 1968. "Toward a Further Refinement of the Resource Theory of Family Power." *Sociological Focus* 2:1-19.

Wilson, Gail. 1987. *Money in the Family: Financial Organisation and Women's Responsibilities.* Brookfield, VT: Averbury.

12

Gender Inequality
New Conceptual Terrain

SARAH FENSTERMAKER
CANDACE WEST
DON H. ZIMMERMAN

It is now a sociological truism that the manifestations of gender inequality in the family and in the economy are related. Countless studies (e.g., Blumberg, 1978, 1984; Amsden, 1980; Stacey, 1983; Beneria and Stimpson, 1987; Gates, 1987; Gerstel and Gross, 1987; Zavella, 1987; Stromberg and Harkess, 1988) demonstrate that while the "arrangement between the sexes" displays great variation across culture and time, it reveals unique stability in the connection between women's personal experience as wives and mothers, and women's social status as workers. We learn, for example, of the crippling constraint on women who, by virtue of their exclusion from adequately paid employment, are bound to an economic dependence on husband or father and, thus, to some form of servitude at home. With that familial and interpersonal expectation of servitude comes the institutional practices that further constrain the opportunities women can realize in employment. (For a review of work and family "linkages" see Chafetz, 1984; Blau and Ferber, 1985; Nieva, 1985; Hartmann, 1987.) And so the seesaw of gender inequality in its individual and institutional manifestations persists, even as historical period, particular cultural form, and social change foster variation in it.

AUTHORS' NOTE: This chapter is drawn in part from a paper by Sarah Fenstermaker presented at the annual meetings of the American Sociological Association, Washington, DC, 1985.

While the persistence and ubiquity of gender inequality has been well-documented, the mechanism by which related systems of inequality are maintained and intersect remains a mystery. As a result, social science has been able to empirically describe and explain gender inequality without adequately apprehending the common elements of its daily unfolding. More specifically, the lack of conceptual clarity surrounding the concept of gender—as distinct from sex—results in a failure to precisely articulate the relationship between forms of inequality as they are experienced, and to adequately anticipate change in them.

In this chapter, we draw on our earlier research on work and gender (Fenstermaker Berk, 1985a,b; West and Zimmerman, 1987) to set forth some assertions, not yet empirically tested, surrounding the concept of gender and how different forms of inequality intersect and complement each other. We argue that the conceptualization of gender as an interactional accomplishment affords a new and different understanding of the mechanism behind various manifestations of gender inequality. We suggest that members of society are motivated to "accomplish" gender along with whatever other social business they transact, and that institutions as well as individuals are held "gender accountable" in their daily dealings. Through this process, gender *stratification* becomes at once both an individual and institutional practice, providing an interactional "bridge" between different spheres of human activity. The result is what sociology has already so amply documented: the *outcomes* of gender inequality, revealed in the compelling connections between work and family as everyday, meaningful, "natural" facts of modern social life. (For a broad overview of these gender-related stratification "outcomes" see Marini, 1988.)

We first consider the current problematic status of gender as a sociological concept, and then recast the concept of gender as an interactional accomplishment. Using the example of women's labor market and household work, we argue that a reconceptualization of gender reveals the intersection between gender inequality at work and at home. With those examples set forth, our conclusion will suggest some potentially fruitful avenues of research on gender as a ubiquitous companion to all sorts of human interaction.

Traditional Conceptions

Gender as Individual Attribute

Increasingly, it is acknowledged that gender is a social construction, but a concept of gender that would allow for variation by setting, the actions of individuals, and prevailing institutional and cultural expectations has yet to be developed. Much of social science still relegates the study of gender to the effects of "sex," male or female, as an individual attribute or characteristic (for discussion, see Stacy and Thorne, 1985). Recently, Gerson (1986, p. 1) has pointed out that this conceptual dualism, where sex (male or female) and gender (masculine or feminine) are bifurcated effectively reduces gender back to sex, leaving little conceptual advance over earlier notions. Since there is no evidence to suggest an absolute or determinant relation between biological sex and the social meanings attributed to it, Gerson notes that we are "thereby artificially truncating the conceptual apparatus for observing and understanding the possible variation in gender relations" (1986, p. 1). Thus the goal of articulating variability in gender relations first requires a concept that itself resides in the dynamics of human interaction, and in the institutional structures that emerge from and are maintained by such interaction.

Gender as Role or Status

The conceptual waters are further muddied by the treatment of gender as a status, or role, that is, the social manifestation of maleness or femaleness in an uncharted configuration of social expectations. Traditionally, the notion of role has constituted a largely normative orientation that determined the ideal expectations and actions associated with those in various social locations (see also Lopata and Thorne, 1978; Thorne, 1980; Connell, 1987). Departing from that view, but providing no further precision, Goffman (1961, p. 93) defined role as "the typical response of individuals in a particular position." Thus the actual performance of a role turns on a specific social position, and a situated set of social actions. One problem with this view is that no concept of role can specify such actions a priori. The potential omnirelevance of gender in human affairs means that when paired with the concept of role, the result is like "the happy drunk" Connell describes (1983, p. 198): "the more it tries to take in, the more incoherent it becomes."

In the literature on women's work, social science has scarcely heeded the advice given 10 years ago by Feldberg and Glenn (1979) in their article on sociological approaches to women's work. They argued for systematic analysis of what they termed "gender stratification" on the job, with:

[examination of the] conditions which create and maintain gender differences and attitudes . . . [which] would enable us to sort out the impacts of formal organizational hierarchies and informal gender hierarchies, and the interaction between the two. (p. 78)

In the otherwise rich and revealing sociological project that followed, women's *work* was granted a prime place in the sociological agenda (e.g., Walshok, 1981; Oakley, 1974; Kahn-Hut, Daniels, and Colvard, 1982; Kaminer, 1984; Lorber, 1984; Sacks and Remy, 1984; Daniels, 1986), but the *relationship* between gender and work was not made empirically problematic.

Studies of women's employment as tokens have proved particularly valuable as they provided a chronicle of what it was to be different, visible, and often less powerful (e.g., Laws, 1975; Martin, 1980; Epstein, 1981; Adams, 1984; Yoder, 1984; Floge and Merrill, 1985; Zimmer, 1986) on the job. Yet such studies conceptualize gender as some combination of: (a) a role, (b) an individual attribute, that the token is motivated to alternately divert attention from, or draw attention to, and (c) a "master" status, that can inexplicably "intrude" into otherwise untainted interactions.[1] Indeed, to date, arguably the most influential scholarship on women's work (Kanter, 1977) rejects outright the unique role of gender in the experience of organizational tokens; instead, it is token status and not gender that determines women's experiences. Zimmer (1988) points out one crucial consequence of such a "gender-neutral" theory of women in organizations:

The major limitation of this approach is its failure to acknowledge the degree to which organizational structures and the interactions that take place within them are embedded in a much broader system of social and cultural inequality between the sexes. (p. 71)

The implicit presumption in such work is that one's gender could be *overcome* interactionally, eventually prove no longer noteworthy, nor require accommodation. And with that, the "real" business of the interaction might resume its central position. The fellows at work might well "forget" a coworker is a woman, much as they might "forget" one was born outside the United States or had a withered arm. In this sort of formulation, gender likely remains a feature of the individual rather than an accomplishment that emerges from interaction in a specific setting, and thus undermines any attempt to clearly articulate the various workings of gender *in situ*. Instead, an understanding of how gender unfolds in the course of other everyday activities must allow for the ways that social interaction can reflect and reiterate the gender inequality characteristic of society more generally. The concept should accommodate to authentic variability in its relevance to interaction, its meaning and salience to members, with content that could be endlessly and effortlessly adapted by participants to the situation at hand.

The next section will outline in detail the notion of gender as an accomplishment. As gender is achieved through ongoing interaction, the particular way in which it is accomplished in conjunction with other everyday activities (e.g., paid or unpaid work, recreation, and so forth) can only be determined as the interaction unfolds. Moreover, gender is not thought to be something that is "overcome," "gotten around," or otherwise risen above so that interaction can proceed unhampered. Instead, the accomplishment of gender is its own reward, and as a "natural" feature of daily life, its absence is more often notable than is its presence. And, from a theoretical point of view, gender is not a manipulable "variable" to safely ignore, hold constant, or examine as one's sociological sense dictates. Quite the contrary, to study some ongoing feature of social life—such as human work—is *necessarily* to explore gender in its unique and situated partnership with those activities.

Gender as Situated Accomplishment

Elsewhere (Fenstermaker Berk, 1985; West and Zimmerman, 1987), we argue that one's gender is not simply something one "is" but rather, it is something one does in interaction with others. To advance this claim, we stress the often overlooked but important distinctions among sex, sex category, and gender. We note that one's sex (female or male) is determined through the application of biological criteria that are established within a particular culture. These biological criteria may vary and even be in conflict with one another, however, categorization itself is compulsory. Assignment to a sex category is initially made on the basis of biological criteria, but more pertinently, everyday categorization is established and maintained by socially necessary displays of identification as a member of one category or the other. So, we note that while one's sex category "rests on" one's sex and can often serve as an emblem of it, one can sustain claims to categorical membership even if the presumed biological criteria are absent. Thus, preoperative transsexuals can "pass" as members of one or the other sex category (Garfinkel, 1967), and persons on the street can "recognize" a population of two and only two sexes from the dress and demeanor of those who inhabit the streets (Kessler and McKenna, 1978). We contend that gender is an accomplishment—"the activity of managing situated conduct in light of normative conceptions, attitudes and activities appropriate for one's sex category." (West and Zimmerman, 1987, p. 127) The key to our formulation of gender as an accomplishment is the notion of accountability; that is, the possibility of describing activities, states of affairs, and descriptions themselves in serious and consequential ways—for example, as "manly" or "womanly" behaviors.[2]

Now to the heart of the matter. Insofar as societal members know that their conduct is accountable, they will frame their actions in relation to how they might be construed by others in the contexts in which they occur. And insofar as sex category is omnirelevant to social life (Garfinkel, 1967, p. 118), it serves as an ever-available resource for the design and interpretation of social conduct. What this means is that an individual involved in virtually any course of action may be held accountable for her/his execution of that action *as a woman* or *a man*. One's membership in one or the other sex category can afford a means of legitimating or discrediting their other actions. What is more, virtually *any* pursuit can be evaluated in relation to its womanly or manly nature. For example, what will people think if Marcia becomes a police officer, fire fighter, or a Boy Scout troop leader? What will people think if John becomes a househusband or a preschool teacher's aide? To be a woman or a man and to engage in such extended and absorbing courses of action is to *do* gender, for involvement in them is accountable as *gendered activity.* And note, to do gender is not always to live up to normative conceptions of femininity or masculinity; it is to engage in action *at the risk of* being held accountable for it.

In this view, gender is not an invariant idealization of womanly and manly nature that is uniformly distributed in society. What is constant is the notion that women and men have different natures (Goffman, 1977) as derived from incumbency in one or the other sex category. And these different natures entail accountable differences. Just *how* different women and men are thought to be, and in what particular details, is subject to local and historical variation. Doing gender involves the management of conduct by sexually categorized human beings who are accountable to local conceptions of appropriately gendered conduct.

When gender is seen as an accomplishment, "an achieved property of situated conduct" (West and Zimmerman, 1987, p. 126), the focus of analysis shifts from the individual to the interactional and, finally, to the institutional level. We note of course, that in the most concrete sense, individuals are the ones who "do" gender. However the process of rendering something accountable is interactional in nature, with the idiom of accountability deriving from those institutional arenas in which social relationships are enacted. Hence, the accomplishment of gender must be seen as located in *social situations.* The task of "measuring up" to one's gender is faced again and again in different situations with respect to different particulars of conduct. The problem involved is to produce configurations of behavior which can be seen by others as normative gender behavior (Fenstermaker Berk, 1985, p. 203.)

What we have then is an essentially interactional, and ultimately institutional undertaking. From this perspective, gender is much more than an attribute embodied within the individual, or a vaguely defined set of role expectations. Here, gender becomes as theoretically central to understanding how situated human interaction contributes to the reproduction of social structure as is its practical importance to daily affairs, "both as an outcome of and a rationale for various social arrangements and as a means of legitimating one of the most fundamental divisions of society" (West and Zimmerman, 1987, p. 126).

The first implication of our formulation is that not only individuals but institutions are accountable to normative conceptions of gender. For example, Hochschild (1983, p. 175) observes that the job of airline flight attendant is something quite different for women than for men. She found that women flight attendants "are also a highly visible distillation of middle-class American notions of femininity," responsible for the "emotional labor" required to sustain market advantage and company profits. To the extent that the women involved in such labor are required to perform it as a function of their sex category, we can observe that in the course of the work, they are held accountable to notions of "essential" femininity. And likewise, for example, Hochschild notes that male flight attendants are more often charged with disciplinary tasks, such as remonstrating the "truly unruly" passenger or settling disputes among occupants of the flight cabin.

But beyond the issue of the flight attendants' individual accountability, we can observe that the airline industry is *itself* accountable to normative conceptions of gender. Advertisements that promise to "move our tails for you," those that invite the public to "catch our smile," and more recently, those that feature the "Singapore Girl—she's a great way to fly" cast the work of the *airlines* as the expression of essential femininity. Thus not only the flight attendant, but the airline presents itself and can be assessed in relation to gender.[3]

Second, even though sex category is potentially omnirelevant, the salience of gender cannot be determined apart from the context in which it is "done." Members of society inhabit many different social identities and these may be stressed or muted, according to the situation. Some occasions (e.g., organized sporting events, bachelor parties, baby showers) are expressly designed to provide for the routine display of behaviors that are normatively associated with one or the other sex category (Goffman, 1977). Other occasions (e.g., those involving the lifting of heavy objects or the changing of flat tires) seem conventionally expressive to begin with, their sheer typicality overwhelming the fact of their design. However, as Goffman (1977, p. 324) observes, heavy, dirty, and precarious concerns can be derived from *any* social situation, no matter how light, tidy, or safe these may seem in other contexts. Thus, the mother who, as a matter of course, may carry her 40-pound child into a grocery store, will find herself the recipient of offers from men who bag her groceries to "help" her carry a 10-pound bag to the car. In short, any social situation can be *made* to suffice for the accomplishment of gender, and it is in that making that gender is granted its salience in human conduct.

A third and related feature of this conceptual recasting is that the doing of gender does not require heterosocial groups. Indeed, as Gerson (1985) points out, the most exaggerated expressions of womanly and manly behaviors may be as readily observed in settings inhabited by members of a single sex category (e.g., Army boot camp, fraternity initiations), as they are in heterosocial contexts (e.g., a wedding reception). What heterosocial contexts do is highlight categorical difference in gender displays, and thus make the fact of gender accomplishment more noticeable. A Tupperware party, attended only by wives, can set the stage as well as a bridge game, attended by spouses. The point is that such situations "do not so much allow for the expression of natural differences as for the production of that difference itself" (Goffman, 1977, p. 324).

Fourth, doing gender is so fundamental to our ways of being and behaving in the company of others that it ought not be conceptualized as an intrusion or intervention in interaction. To be sure, its variable salience means that in some situations, its accomplishment will be more obvious than in others. For example, the entry of a member of one sex category (e.g., a woman) into a setting usually reserved for members of the other category (e.g., a military academy) may well elicit challenges to routinized ways of doing things. In response to such challenges, the celebration of the virtues of categorical solidarity can be lavish indeed. But in attending primarily to them, we run the risk of overlooking less ostentatious ones; for example, those that constitute membership in that setting in the first place (e.g., a men's club). Those activities may be no less constitutive of, for example, "essential" masculinity than the bonding that occurs in response to a woman's potential contamination of the setting through her presence in it.

Given this possibility, a final implication of our formulation is that in some situations, the accomplishment of gender may be the primary work that is being done. For example, Goffman (1977) notes that while size, strength, and age are generally normally distributed between members of two sex classes (females and males), selective pairing among heterosexual couples guarantees that boys and men will be clearly bigger, stronger, and older than the girls and women with whom they are paired. That such assortive mating practices are necessary or desirable in our society is, of course, debatable (especially on grounds of the differential in women's and men's mortality rates, and on the incidence of men's violence against women). What these practices ensure is that if situations arise in which greater size, strength, or age can be made relevant, boys and men will be the ones to display it, and girls and women to appreciate their display.

In short, the reformulation of gender as an achievement provides for an understanding of how the significance of our essential natures as women and men might vary, depending upon the setting, prevailing institutional and cultural expectations, and ultimately, on the actions of individuals. Below, we offer some examples of how gender works to maintain relations between various forms of inequality at work and at home.

Inequality at Home and Work: Old Wine, Hidden Additives

The distinctly American version of gender inequality finds the last 50 years marked by extraordinary change in the participation of women in public life (for discussion, see Blau and Ferber, 1985). Since the turn of the century the profile of the American women's work force has changed from a homogeneous one of primarily young, single, American-born white woman, to a work force virtually indistinguishable from the general population of women. This has meant change, of course, in not only who sought employment, but also for how long. Once only poor women sought employment after marriage; in the post-1950s period, mothers with older children joined the ranks. A generation ago, women who were mothers did not seek employment until their children reached school age. Today the pattern of labor force participation has become nearly a continuous one, in which women work from the time they initially enter the job market until retirement.

We find mass-media interpretations of this remarkable story everywhere; indeed we are inundated with this tale of white middle-class married women going to work: from television talk shows, where housewives and employed women are pitted against each other; to news programs that argue that everything from teenage pregnancy to increasing childhood obesity is linked to increased women's employment; to the countless magazine articles and self-help books on women *at* work, and what they have done (or can do) to the office environment.

The parallel concerns about managing the impossible work loads of employment and middle-class home life are no less telling in employed women's reluctant and somewhat shell-shocked admission that the "thirtysomething" husband appears little evolved from his "fifty-something" father, whose housework and child care were largely supplemental and severely constrained by concerns about what was appropriate "men's work." A model of social change is always presumed in which, subject to the demands of the marketplace, husbands' and wives' domestic labor was orchestrated in tandem; one might do a little more, and the other a little less, but it all "evened out" in the end.

After years of anticipating significant change in the division of household labor, social science is still searching for the "symmetrical family" heralded by Young and Wilmott (1973) nearly 20 years ago. In explaining the apportionment of work, researchers consistently find that work imperatives—the demands of the job, of children, of home— make a difference only to the household contributions of wives. Thus, while the presence of children and the nature of women's employment outside the home determine how much time wives devote to household labor, these factors do not significantly influence men's contributions to such labor (e.g., Bahr, 1974; Meissner, Humphreys, Meis, and Sheu, 1975; Farkas, 1976; Pleck, 1977; Berk and Berk, 1979; Fenstermaker Berk, 1985).

Although this is one of the most consistent findings in all of sociological research, it is tempting to fall back on our belief in transformative social change and simply ignore the data and their implications. Researchers either hopefully conclude that change is "on the way" (Fenstermaker Berk, 1985) as some small suggestions of it is overinterpreted, or worse, through a sort of sociological sleight of hand, eager observers conclude that change *has* arrived, and with it hope for the new egalitarian family (e.g., Pleck, 1985; Hertz, 1986).

A preoccupation with changes in the sheer participation of women in the labor force (and the presumed increased participation of men in household labor) neglects a more subtle but growing sense of disjuncture between what changes in women's labor force participation were expected to bring, and what sort of climate they have in fact wrought. In the case of the "dual linkages" between family and market work, the social change that has occurred has been described with little appreciation for the dynamics by which that social change stakes a claim in daily interaction, or becomes thwarted by traditional expectations and practices. But the dislocations we sense—both as social observers and as family members—between our expectations of change and the change we actually *experience,* may well be explained by this neglected dimension of gender inequality as it joins the worlds of labor market and private household. We suggest that our concept of gender can be employed to point toward the apparent but inexplicable resistance to the sorts of transformations expected in the "new" household, office, and factory.

Gender at Work

The social science literature on women and work is now blessed with numerous descriptions of women's lives on the job. Most are meticulously crafted accounts of the direct experience of women in all kinds of work, in various degrees of isolation from other women. Regardless of position, the *practice* of gender and its complex relation to the practice of work will support inequality on the job.

Howe (1977) offers a description of a waitress' least favorite customer—the "one man sitting alone." It is reminiscent of Hochschild's description of flight attendants, who were expected to bring gender accountability to bear on the work itself:

They often want you to entertain them. But I'm not there to keep them company if they're lonely . . . . The worst thing a customer can say to me when I'm pouring water with one hand, and putting bread on the table with the other, is "Honey why aren't you smiling?" (p. 113)

Far from the New York waitress, Fernandez-Kelly's (1983) compelling portrait of her field experience working at a sewing machine in a maquiladora, a plant on the Mexican side of the U.S.-Mexican border, suggests the intimate and "natural" relation between the subordination of the worker and the domination of women:

But this time my inquiry was less than welcome. Despite my over-shy approach to the personnel manager, his reaction was hostile. And then to me. "I told you already we do piecework here; if you do your job you get a wage, otherwise you don't. That's clear isn't it? What else do you want? You should be grateful! This plant is giving you a chance to work! What else do you want? Come back tomorrow and be punctual." (p. 115)

Fernandez-Kelly (1983) also reports on the early years of the maquiladora program:

> There were ingenieros [engineers] who insisted on having only the prettiest
> workers under their command. A sort of factory harem mentality had been at
> work. [Sandra] had known a man . . . who wanted as much female diversity
> as possible. He had a crew formed of women all of whom had—upon his own
> request—eyes and hair of a different color. Another one took pride in boasting
> that every woman in his line had borne him a child . . . . Sandra knew how
> to take care of herself, but she still thought it was better to have only female
> fellow workers. The factory was not a good place to meet men. (p. 129)

Accounts of women's work in the trades strike a similar chord,
regardless of the work, or the degree of tokenism represented at the job
site. From Walshok's (1981) study of female craft apprentices:

> I just kind of let them know it's my job and I didn't want guys hanging around
> waiting to help me do something. It was important to let them see I could
> handle the job. Sometimes you wish they would treat you a little more equal
> and not so helpless sometimes. (p. 217)

Another, similar reflection from two of Schroedel's (1985) respondents, a steel hauler and a shipscaler, respectively:

> But I found, like for me, you have to walk on a fence, you have to be willing
> to put up with a certain amount of teasing and carrying on, and joking. You
> can't just be straight-arrow rigid. You gotta be willing to be teased, to flirt
> back. You gotta be willing to just get along. (p. 11)

The shipscaler:

> In some ways, I still overlook a lot. I figure it's better than making a big deal
> out of it. You learn to be grateful to the men that are glad to have you there
> . . . . When a man found out I did my share and sometimes helped him on his
> job, he would begin to accept me and find another woman to be rude to.
> (p. 113)

Finally, a more subdued, but nevertheless recognizable reprise on the
gender accomplishment theme comes from women within the academy
(Aisenberg and Harrington, 1988):

> I am very aware of it now trying to chair the department, that people expect
> you to be an authority figure. They expect you to sort of stand above the rest.
> And there is a certain amount of that that comes with the role . . . . And yet

I think this is a style that I am not comfortable with . . . . I don't like competition that requires that in order for one person to win others have to lose . . . There are times that I think . . . that it would be better for me if I weren't so sensitive to losers. (p. 60)

The foregoing illustrates that when "gender-relevant" occasions transpire or are sought out at the work site, they are met by the structured status distinctions that surround all social relations; considerations of class, age, seniority, race and organizational station enter in. Yet these quotations suggest that insofar as the accomplishment of gender remains omnirelevant and ubiquitous, it provides a ready resource for the demonstration of inequality. Finally, these data suggest that the demands of gender do not *compete* for attention on the job; together they form one of the dimensions of the job that is daily enacted by participants.[4]

Gender at Home

Elsewhere (Fenstermaker Berk, 1985, pp. 203-204) we argue that the relatively uniform and lopsided patterns of household labor apportionment, while appearing irrational and unfair, nevertheless are elected by most households. The "rationality" of such a system, and an account for its unchanging quality is only made explicable through the conception of the household production process as comprised of two crucial components: the production of household goods and services, and the production of gender. In concert, and through their daily doing, the "natural" accomplishment of each is defined by the other, and the seeming asymmetry of who does what in the household assumes a status difficult to question or change. From this emerges the variety of individual members' adaptations to household arrangements and perceptions of choices made and contemplated. Thus child care (or laundry, or household repair, and so on) can become occasions for producing commodities (such as clean children, clean laundry, or new light switches), but it can also serve to reaffirm one's *gendered* relation to the work, and to the world.

The doing of housework provides the occasion for the accomplishment of work *and* the affirmation of the essential natures of women and men. Thus the seemingly irrational and inefficient organization of *work* becomes the meaningful achievement of *two* ends: work and gender. The wives quoted below (originally quoted in Fenstermaker Berk, 1985) accept the very tenuous ties of their husbands to household labor, suggesting that there is much more than work considerations in effect here:

> He doesn't do much. I get irritated at him at times. He's unaware that there are things for him to do . . . . He'd leave the paper on the couch, but now he picks it up. He does this for a month, forgets, and then I have to remind him.

And:

> He tries to be helpful. He tries. He's a brilliant and successful lawyer. It's incredible how he smiles after he sponges off the table and there are still crumbs all over. (p. 206)

The specific content of interactions around which work and gender are done "together" may vary, and the outcomes of gender inequality may look very different from one social location to another, but the contours of their *practice* are similar. Indeed, they are similar enough to conclude that the structural intersection of inequality as it is experienced in the family and in the economy is made possible by the mechanism of gender's interactional achievement.

There are thus countless occasions where gender becomes relevant to either who accomplishes the work, or the ways in which it is accomplished. And this is true regardless of the particular situations examined, the content of those interactions, the actors involved, or the extent to which other categorical-relevant concerns (i.e., race, class, age) are also introduced (see, for example, Cahill, 1986; Hurtado, 1989). Thus we are drawn back to the actual practice of gender inequality as it is experienced by women and men, and we suggest that it is at this level that economy and family combine to produce both change and continued inequities. Deep-seated, authentic social change will require a profoundly different organization of interactional practices around gender in *everyday* affairs. In conclusion, we suggest some ways in which such change may occur, and identify the empirical questions that are implied by our formulation.

Summary and Conclusions

Our aim in this chapter has been to respecify the concept of gender in order to better understand the mechanisms of inequality and subordination. We have proposed that gender be viewed, first, as an interactional accomplishment oriented to normative accountability. In this view, members design their conduct in anticipation of how others will construe (and evaluate) its gendered character. From this it follows that gender as a property of interaction will vary situationally. Women and men, then, *do* gender, but the work of gender is not an intrusion on otherwise neutral activity. Instead, it is a coextensive feature of everyday business, a seen but often unnoticed feature of the "natural" and "normal" social environment involving both work and play, and done in same sex and heterosocial groupings. As we have suggested above, a heterosexual context is not required for doing gender, and indeed, same-sex contexts may provide the most intense (and explicit) arenas for gender accomplishment. And although the production of gendered conduct may not be the primary *focus* of activity in these or other settings, it nevertheless is the nearly inevitable outcome.

It will be useful here to recall the discussion of household labor, and in particular the idea that work of a specific variety can produce not only the outcome or product targeted by that activity, but also gender. From this, it is a small step to the idea that a large range of activities, including occupational pursuits of all sorts, can be implicated in the production of gender. The workplace, after all, is a setting of activity and an arena of interaction. And, just as individuals hold themselves accountable to gender ideals, occupations also can hold themselves accountable to normative conceptions of gender.

The gendering of occupations is an institutional phenomenon, but it has intimate connections to the doing of gender in individual interaction. The socially evaluated properties of activities such as work may be appropriated as, and understood as, reflecting the innate characteristics of individuals. Such characteristics form the framework of accountability for evaluating the conduct exhibited in interaction. We might say (to put the case starkly) that, historically, it is men who go to war not so much because war demands the qualities and virtues commonly associated with manhood (warfare being quintessentially men's work); rather, in going to war, men appropriate the occasion and its resources to demonstrate and establish manliness.

The importance of such an understanding is underscored by the following reflections. First, while social scientists have tended to view gender as socially constructed, there is no satisfactory account available of the persistence of the fundamental notion that both women and men are differently constituted with respect to their behavioral and emotional potentials (whatever these might be in a given situation). Second, as we have argued, conduct in accord with one's "nature" appears to be treated as an accountable matter. As discussed previously (see also Fenstermaker Berk, 1985), the persistence both of an unequal distribution of household labor and the belief that the distribution of these tasks is fair and equitable, suggests that in doing housework both men and women also do gender.

In short, doing gender and doing work, while analytically separable, appear to be empirically intertwined. If we are to entertain the vision that one day inequality based on sex will be substantially overcome, we will need to understand the mechanisms by which it is sustained in institutional social arrangements. Those social arrangements daily provide for the reproduction of a framework of accountability that casts gender as an essential feature of the individual's very being. It is thus a potent force which in turn tends to ensure that even significantly altered social arrangements preserve the relevance of gender to conduct.

This is not a counsel of despair, but rather a recognition that finding the means to social change rests on a fuller understanding of how inequality is rooted in gender and understood as an accomplishment, and how interaction facilitates that accomplishment. That mechanism cannot be stipulated, it must be discovered.

Notes

1. This is reminiscent, of course, of the term "diffuse status characteristic" in the tradition of research on expectation states, and its treatment of sex and gender. (For discussion, see Webster and Driskell, 1985.)

2. We draw on Heritage's (1984, pp. 136-137) observation that members of society routinely produce descriptions that take notice of some activity (e.g., naming, characterizing, explaining, excusing, excoriating, or merely recognizing it) and locate it in a social framework (situating it in relation to other like and unlike activities). The fact that activities can be described in this way means that they may be undertaken with reference to their accountability, that is, how they might appear to be and are characterized by others.

3. More impressionistic examples abound in a culture steeped in images of individual determination and morbid nation-state competitiveness. We have, for instance, apparently survived the transition from a "cowboy" chief executive to a presidential "wimp" who later redeemed himself as a "tough guy" in Middle East showdowns.

4. Some caution on this issue is in order, however. An empirically adequate description of the accomplishment of gender at work should distinguish between those truly situated activities that participants orient to as part of their work, and *merely* situated activities that happen to occur in the workplace and involve participants who happen to be workers. Such distinctions would permit attention to the specifically gendered character of work, in contradistinction to the gendering of casual interaction as such. However, even as we call for such distinctions we fear the attendant distortions brought on by making gross categorical divisions between "work" and "nonwork" interactions.

References

Adams, J. 1984. "Women at West Point: A Three Year Perspective." *Sex Roles* 11:525-541.
Aisenberg, N. and M. Harrington. 1988. *Women of Academe: Outsiders in the Sacred Grove.* Amherst: University of Massachusetts Press.

Amsden, A. H., ed. 1980. *The Economics of Women & Work*. New York: St. Martin's.

Bahr, S. 1974. "Effects on Power and Division of Labor." In *Working Mothers*, edited by L. Hoffman and F. I. Nye. San Francisco: Jossey-Bass.

Beneria, L. and C. R. Stimpson, eds. 1987. *Women, Households, and the Economy*. New Brunswick, NJ: Rutgers University Press.

Berk, R. A. and S. F. Berk. 1979. *Labor and Leisure at Home: Content and Organization of the Household Day*. Beverly Hills, CA: Sage.

Blau, F. D. and M. A. Ferber. 1985. "Women in the Labor Market: The Last Twenty Years." In *Women and Work: An Annual Review, 1*, edited by L. Larwood, A. H. Stromberg, and B. A. Gutek. Beverly Hills, CA: Sage.

Blumberg, R. L. 1978. *Stratification: Socioeconomic and Sexual Inequality*. Dubuque, IA: William C. Brown.

Blumberg, R. L. 1984. "A General Theory of Gender Stratification. *Sociological Theory* 23-101.

Cahill, S. E. 1986. "Language Practices and Self Definition: The Case of Gender Identity Acquisition." *The Sociological Quarterly* 27:295-311.

Chafetz, J. S. 1984. *Sex and Advantage: A Comparative, Macro-Structural Theory of Sex Stratification*. Totowa, NJ: Rowman Allanheld.

Connell, R. W. 1983. *Which Way is Up? Essays on Sex, Class, and Culture*. London: Allen & Unwin.

Connell, R. W. 1987. *Gender and Power: Society, the Person and Sexual Politics*. Stanford: Stanford University Press.

Daniels, A. K. 1986. *Invisible Careers: Women Civic Leaders in the Volunteer World*. Chicago: University of Chicago Press.

Epstein, C. F. 1981. *Women in Law*. New York: Basic Books.

Farkas, G. 1976. "Education, Wage Rates, and the Division of Labor Between Husband and Wife." *Journal of Marriage and the Family* 38(3):473-483.

Feldberg, R. L. and E. N. Glenn. 1979. "Job Versus Gender Models in the Sociology of Work." *Social Problems* 25:524-538.

Fenstermaker Berk, S. 1985. *The Gender Factory: The Apportionment of Work in American Households*. New York: Plenum.

Fernandez-Kelly, M. P. 1983. *For We are Sold, I and My People; Women and Industry in Mexico's Frontier*. Albany: State University of New York Press.

Floge, L. and D. M. Merrill. 1985. "Tokenism reconsidered: Male Nurses and Female Physicians in a Hospital Setting." *Social Forces, 64:*925-947.

Frye, M. 1983. *The Politics of Reality*. Trumansberg, NY: The Crossing.

Garfinkel, H. 1967. *Studies in Ethnomethodology*. Englewood Cliffs, NJ: Prentice-Hall.

Gates, H. 1987. *Chinese Working-Class Lives: Getting By in Taiwan*. Ithaca, NY: Cornell University Press.

Gerson, J. M. 1986. "The Variability and Salience of Gender: Issues of Conceptualization and Measurement." Unpublished manuscript. Department of Sociology, Rutgers University.

Gerson, J. M. and K. Peiss. 1985. "Boundaries, Negotiation, Consciousness: Reconceptualizing Gender Relations." *Social Problems* 32:317-331.

Gerstel, N. and H. E. Gross, eds. 1987. *Families and Work*. Philadelphia: Temple University Press.

Goffman, E. 1961. *Encounters*. Indianapolis, IN: Bobbs-Merrill.

Goffman, E. 1977. "The Arrangement Between the Sexes." *Theory and Society* 4:301-331.

Goffman, E. 1979. *Gender Advertisements*. New York: Harper & Row.

Hartmann, H. I. 1987. "Changes in Women's Economic and Family Roles in Post-World War II United States." In *Women, Households and the Economy*, edited by L. Beneria and C. R. Stimpson. New Brunswick, NJ: Rutgers University Press.

Heritage, J. 1984. *Garfinkel and Ethnomethodology*. Cambridge: Polity.

Hertz, R. 1986. *More Equal Than Others: Women and Men in Dual-Career Marriages*. Berkeley: University of California Press.

Hochschild, A. R. 1983. *The Managed Heart: Commercialization of Human Feeling*. Berkeley: University of California Press.

Howe, L. K. 1977. *Pink Collar Workers: Inside the World of Women's Work*. New York: G. P. Putnam.

Hurtado, A. 1989. "Relating to Privilege: Seduction and Rejection in the Subordination of White Women and Women of Color." *Signs* 14:833-855.

Kahn-Hut, R., A. K. Daniels and R. Colvard, eds. 1982. *Women and Work*. New York: Oxford University Press.

Kaminer, W. 1984. *Women Volunteering: The Pleasure, Pain and Politics of Unpaid Work from 1830 to the Present*. Garden City, NY: Anchor Books.

Kanter, R. M. 1977. *Men and Women of the Corporation*. New York: Basic Books.

Kessler, S. J. and W. McKenna. 1978. *Gender: An Ethnomethodological Approach*. New York: John Wiley.

Laws, J. L. 1975. "The Psychology of Tokenism: An Analysis." *Sex Roles* 1:51-67.

Lopata, H. A. and B. Thorne. 1978. "On the Term 'Sex Roles'." *Signs* 3:718-721.

Lorber, J. 1984. *Women Physicians: Career, Status and Power*. New York: Tavistock.

Marini, M. M. 1988. "Sociology of Gender." In *The Future of Sociology*, edited by E. F. Borgatta and K. S. Cook. Newbury Park, CA: Sage.

Martin, S. 1980. *Breaking and Entering: Policewomen on Patrol*. Berkeley: University of California Press.

Meissner, M., E. W. Humphreys, S. M. Meis, and W. J. Sheu. 1975. "No Exit for Wives: Sexual Division of Labour and the Cumulation of Household Demands." *Canadian Review of Sociology and Anthropology* 12(4):424-439.

Nieva, V. F. 1985. Work and Family Linkages. In *Women and Work: An Annual Review, 1*, edited by L. Larwood, A. H. Stromberg, and B. A. Gutek. Beverly Hills, CA: Sage.

Oakley, Ann. 1974. *The Sociology of Housework*. New York: Pantheon.

Pleck, J. H. 1977. "The Work-Family Role System." *Social Problems* 24(5):417-427.

Pleck, J. H. 1985. *Working Wives/Working Husbands*. Beverly Hills, CA: Sage.

Rich, A. 1980. "Compulsory Heterosexuality and Lesbian Existence." *Signs* 5:631-660.

Sacks, K. B. and D. Remy, eds. 1984. *My Troubles are Going to Have Troubles with Me: Everyday Triumphs of Women Workers*. New Brunswick, NJ: Rutgers University Press.

Schroedel, J. R. 1985. *Alone in a Crowd: Women in the Trades Tell Their Stories*. Philadelphia: Temple University Press.

Stacey, J. 1983. *Patriarchy and Socialist Revolution in China*. Berkeley: University of California Press.

Stacey, J. and B. Thorne. 1985. "The Missing Feminist Revolution in Sociology." *Social Problems* 32:301-316.

Stromberg, A. H. and S. Harkess. 1988. *Women Working: Theories and Facts in Perspective*. Mountain View, CA: Mayfield.

Thorne, B. 1980. *Gender . . . How is it Best Conceptualized?* Unpublished manuscript. Michigan State University, Department of Sociology, East Lansing, MI.

Walshok, M. L. 1981. *Blue Collar Women: Pioneers on the Male Frontier*. Garden City: Anchor Books.

Webster, M., Jr. and J. E. Driskell, Jr. 1985. *Status, Rewards, and Influence: How Expectations Organize Behavior.* San Francisco: Jossey-Bass.

West, C. and D. H. Zimmerman 1987. "Doing Gender." *Gender & Society* 1(2):125-151.

Yoder, J. D. 1984. "An Academic Woman as a Token: A Case Study." *Journal of Social Issues* 41(4):61-72.

Young, M. and P. Wilmott. 1973. *The Symmetrical Family.* London: Routledge & Kegan Paul.

Zavella, P. 1987. *Women's Work and Chicano Families: Cannery Workers of the Santa Clara Valley.* Ithaca, NY: Cornell University Press.

Zimmer, L. 1986. *Women Guarding Men.* Chicago: University of Chicago Press.

Zimmer, L. 1988. "Tokenism and Women in the Workplace: The Limits of Gender-Neutral Theory." *Social Problems* 35:64-77.

About the Authors

Rae Lesser Blumberg is an Associate Professor of Sociology at the University of California, San Diego. Her research interests focus on theories of gender stratification and gender and development. Her publications include *Stratification: Socioeconomic and Sexual Inequality, Making the Case for the Gender Variable: Women and the Wealth and Well-Being of Nations,* and "A General Theory of Gender Stratification" in *Sociological Theory* (1984). She has conducted field research on development and/or gender in more than a dozen countries around the world, most recently in Ecuador, Nigeria, Guatemala, and the Dominican Republic.

Philip Blumstein is Professor of Sociology at the University of Washington. He is coauthor of *American Couples* (with Pepper Schwartz). He is currently working in the area of personal relationships. His interests include the study of marital roles and interpersonal processes.

Janet Saltzman Chafetz is Professor of Sociology at the University of Houston, where she has been since 1971. She completed her Ph.D. at the University of Texas, Austin, in 1969. During the past decade her work has reflected her dual interests in sociological theory and in gender stratification. In 1988 she published an overview of contemporary feminist theories in sociology (*Feminist Sociology*). Her 1984 book, *Sex and Advantage,* was a general theory explaining cross-cultural variation in the extent of gender stratification. Along with A. G. Dworkin, she has also published several papers and a book (*Female Revolt,* 1986) that attempt to explain why women's movements and antifeminist movements emerge and grow in specific times and places. Her latest publication is *Gender Equity: An Integrated Theory of Stability and Change* (1990).

Marion Tolbert Coleman is an Executive Associate at the Hogg Foundation for Mental Health and Adjunct Assistant Professor of Sociology at the University of Texas at Austin. She has coauthored theoretical work on the gender balance of power within couples with Rae Lesser Blumberg and coedited *Family Relations: A Reader* with Norval D. Glenn. Her most recent research is focused on the division of household labor within gay and lesbian couples.

Randall Collins is Professor of Sociology at the University of California, Riverside. His books include *Weberian Sociological Theory* (1986), *Theoretical Sociology* (1988), and *Sociology of Marriage and Family: Gender, Love and Property* (3rd edition coauthored with Scott Coltrane, 1990).

Sarah Fenstermaker is Professor of Sociology and Chair of the Women's Studies Program at the University of California, Santa Barbara. Her research has centered on gender inequality and women's work. She is the author of *The Gender Factory: The Apportionment of Work in American Households* (1985), and numerous articles on household labor and domestic violence. Her current research focuses on AIDS education in the public schools.

Evelyn Nakano Glenn is Professor of Women's Studies and Ethnic Studies at University of California, Berkeley. Her research focuses on women's work, especially concerning issues of technology and racial stratification. She has published widely on impacts of office automation on clerical work, racial ethnic women's employment, domestic service, and family. She is the author of *Issei, Nisei, Warbride: Three Generations of Japanese American Women in Domestic Service* (1986), and collaborated with the Women and Work Research Group in the volume *Hidden Aspects of Women's Work* (1987).

Joan Huber taught at Notre Dame and at Illinois, Urbana-Champaign. She is currently Dean of the College of Social and Behavioral Sciences at Ohio State. She was President of the American Sociological Association in 1989 and chairs the Committee on Women's Employment and Related Issues for the National Research Council. Her research interests are in gender stratification and her books include *Sex Stratification* (with Glenna Spitze) and *The Macro Micro Link*.

Cathy A. Rakowski holds a joint appointment in Women's Studies and Rural Sociology at the Ohio State University in Columbus. She lived in Venezuela from 1979 to 1986 where she engaged in research and worked as a consultant to various private, public, and international agencies, including the Corporacion Venezolana de Guayana, the national planning agency, and the United Nations Development Programme. In 1989, she initiated a longitudinal study of cultural and social change in eleven rural communities in a zone undergoing a regional development program in Venezuela.

Pepper Schwartz is Professor of Sociology and Adjunct Professor of Psychiatry and Behavioral Science at the University of Washington. She is coauthor of *American Couples* (with Philip Blumstein), and, most recently, coauthor and coeditor of *Gender and Intimate Relationships* (with Barbara Risman). Her research interests are in gender, family relations, and human sexuality.

Joan Smith is Professor of Sociology at the University of Vermont and Research Associate at the Fernand Braudel Center. She specializes in women's labor, both the waged and unwaged forms, and has published in such journals as *Feminist Studies* and *Signs*. She and her coauthor, Immanuel Wallerstein, are completing a book based on research carried out under the auspices of the Fernand Braudel Center on unwaged labor and labor force formation.

Judith Treas is Professor of Sociology and Chair of the Department of Sociology at the University of California, Irvine. Her current research extends her efforts to develop a transaction cost approach to family life by focusing on changing family relationships of the aged in less developed countries. With Keiko Nakao, she is engaged in a 25-year replication of American studies of occupational and ethnic prestige.

Immanuel Wallerstein is Distinguished Professor of Sociology and the Director of the Fernand Braudel Center for the Study of Economies, Historical Systems, and Civilizations at SUNY-Binghamton. He is the author of *Modern World-System* (in three volumes) and *Historical Capitalism,* as well as coeditor of *Households and the World-Economy.*

Candace West is Professor of Sociology at the University of California, Santa Cruz. Her research has focused on the relationship of gender to face-to-face interaction, especially conversation. She is the author of *Routine Complications: Troubles with Talk between Doctors and Patients,* "Doing Gender" (with Don H. Zimmerman), and "Conversational Shift Work: A Study of Topical Transitions between Women and Men" (with Angela Garcia). Her current work addresses the organization of "doctors' orders" in patients' visits to male and female physicians.

Diane L. Wolf is Assistant Professor of Sociology at the University of California, Davis. Her research has focused on the interactions among gender, households, labor, and structural change in Southeast and East Asia. Her book on the multiple interrelationships between female factory workers, their families, peasant agriculture, and industrialization in rural Java is forthcoming from the University of California Press.

Don H. Zimmerman is Professor of Sociology and Communication Studies at the University of California, Santa Barbara. His current research interests lie in conversation analysis with specific application to the study of emergency telecommunications. He is coeditor (with D. Boden) of *Talk and Social Structure* (in press). His recent publications include "Doing Gender" (with C. West), *Gender and Society* (1987), "Sequential and Institutional Contexts in Calls for Help" (with M. Whalen), *Social Psychology Quarterly* (1987), and "When Words Fail: A Single Case Analysis" (with J. Whalen and M. Whalen), *Social Problems* (1988).

NOTES